MW01125497

Hidden Cost of Freedom

Hidden Cost of Freedom

THE UNTOLD STORY OF THE CIA'S SECRET FUNDING SYSTEM, 1941–1962

Brad L. Fisher

Published by the University Press of Kansas (Lawrence, Kansas 66045), which was organized by the Kansas Board of Regents and is operated and funded by Emporia State University, Fort Hays State University, Kansas State University, Pittsburg State University, the University of Kansas, and Wichita State University.

Library of Congress Cataloging-in-Publication Data
Names: Fisher, Brad L., author.
Title: Hidden cost of freedom : the untold story of the CIA's secret funding system, 1941–1962 / Brad L. Fisher.
Other titles: Untold early history of the Central Intelligence Agency's clandestine funding system, 1941–1962
Description: Lawrence, Kansas : University Press of Kansas, [2024] | Includes bibliographical references and index.
Identifiers: LCCN 2024011356 (print) | LCCN 2024011357 (ebook) | ISBN 9780700637959 (cloth ; acid-free paper) | ISBN 9780700637966 (ebook)
Subjects: LCSH: Intelligence service—Finance—Law and legislation—United States. | United States. Central Intelligence Agency—History.
Classification: LCC JK468.I6 F57 2024 (print) | LCC JK468.I6 (ebook) | DDC 353.1/7244097309045—dc23/eng/20240928
LC record available at https://lccn.loc.gov/2024011356.
LC ebook record available at https://lccn.loc.gov/2024011357.

British Library Cataloguing-in-Publication Data is available.

Contents

Acknowledgments

It is with great pleasure that I can finally acknowledge and thank the people who significantly contributed to the research and publication of this book. I would first like to thank the late Larry McDonald, an archivist at the National Archives and Records Administration (NARA) in College Park, Maryland. I met Larry on my first trip to NARA amongst the finding aids on the second floor, where the textual records are pulled. After showing him a copy of the Dulles letter that inspired this book, and explaining my interest in the early CIA, he set me up with a cart containing all the declassified records for the Central Intelligence Group (which was already checked out, sitting idle on a cart in the back). On a subsequent visit, Larry took me upstairs to the third floor and introduced me to the CREST system. That was a game changer. I have been a high-end user of CREST for over twenty years. That said, it would be remiss not to thank the Central Intelligence Agency for establishing this invaluable source of historical information. I am deeply grateful to the Agency and could not have written this book without it.

After spending almost five years on the book's core narrative in complete isolation, and in desperate need of some scholarly feedback, I contacted the Georgetown University Book Lab in Washington, DC, in 2009, in hopes of commissioning a review of the manuscript. Carol Sargent, who headed the lab, coordinated a review with Dr. John Prados, a senior fellow at the National Security Archive at George Washington University. John's inspiring six-page review motivated the first major revisions of the book; he was also one of the reviewers for University Press of Kansas on the first round in 2022. Sadly, John passed away between the first and second review of the book, before I ever got to meet him, but I am eternally grateful to him for both of his critiques of my book and his many contributions to the study of US Intelligence.

After that first review, I spent the next ten years expanding the narrative to cover the decade after the passage of the CIA Act of 1949. By 2019, with the manuscript nearly ready for a publisher's review, I commissioned a second content review from Kevin Anderson Associates, an editing and writing services firm in New York. This time the manuscript was reviewed by Brunella Costagliola, an experienced editor and military history expert. We only spoke on the phone once for thirty minutes to discuss the book prior to her review. Brunella's in-depth review and insightful in-line comments convinced me that the book was nearly ready for publication. I then began what I anticipated would be the last series of revisions before submitting my proposal to agents and publishers. John and Brunella both encouraged me to add an epilogue that enunciated my own views on this subject. The epilogue was the last major addition to the book.

Joyce Harrison, the editor in chief at the University Press of Kansas (UPK), requested the manuscript for review on February 11, 2022. Joyce coordinated the review and the publication of the manuscript from beginning to end, and it has been a great pleasure working with her and UPK on this project. I am deeply appreciative of her support of my book and would also like to thank all the other great people I've worked with at UPK, especially the copy editor Janet Yoe, who helped me to put the finishing touches on the manuscript.

I also need to extend a special thanks to the other two eminent reviewers of my book. David Barrett, the political scientist and author of the groundbreaking book *The CIA and Congress*, was involved in the first and second reviews. David's thoughtful comments and detailed point-by-point review of the manuscript were instrumental in guiding my final revisions. I also received a powerful critique from the third anonymous reviewer of the book in the second round. This reviewer clearly got what this book is about and persuaded me to eliminate a few anecdotal "side streets," and to keep the narrative focused on the CIA's funding system. From an author's standpoint, it's comforting to know that your book was carefully read by experts in the field.

Lastly, I would like to thank some of my family members. My wife, Houra, "critically" reviewed my proposal and helped me to edit and organize it for agents and publishers. She was also with me when I discovered a copy of the "Dulles letter" in 2003 and has supported this project from the beginning. I would like to thank my Aunt Toots and my Aunt Joan, the daughters of E. Lyle Fisher, for their testimonies on their father and their overall support. I was vacationing with both of them in Costa Rica about ten years ago, when on our last night, my Aunt Joan unexpectedly handed me the original signed copy of the Dulles letter—which I then inconspicuously concealed in my suitcase before going through customs. Beth Fisher, my niece, worked with me on the cover design, and without knowing much about the CIA or my book, came up with a design idea that wonderfully captures what this book is about. Lastly, I would like to thank my parents who supported this project from the beginning and have eagerly awaited the book's publication. Over the years, I rarely discussed the book with my family, but my father, more than anyone else, pushed me to finally freeze the manuscript after nearly twenty years of work. I am dedicating this book to my father, Bob Fisher.

List of Abbreviations

BAPA	Budget and Procedures Act of 1950
CAT	Civil Air Transport
CIBTO	China-India-Burma Theater of Operations
CIA	Central Intelligence Agency
CIG	Central Intelligence Group
COI	Coordinator of Information
CREST	CIA Research Search Tool
DCI	Director of Central Intelligence
DDA	Deputy Director for Administration (CIA)
DDCI	Deputy Director of Central Intelligence
DDP	Deputy Director of Plans (CIA)
ECA	Economic Cooperation Administration
ETO	European Theater of Operations
FETO	Far East Theater of Operations
GAO	General Accounting Office
GSA	Government Services Administration
HASC	House Armed Services Committee
IG	Inspector General
IMINT	Imagery Intelligence
IIC	Interdepartmental Intelligence Committee
ISG	Intelligence Survey Group
ISO	Inspection and Security Office (CIA)
JCS	Joint Chiefs of Staff
MTO	Mediterranean Theater of Operations
NATO	North African Theater of Operations
NETO	Near East Theater of Operations
NIA	National Intelligence Authority
NRO	National Reconnaissance Office
NSC	National Security Council
OCB	Operations Coordinating Board
OGC	Office of General Council
ONI	Office of Naval Intelligence

OPC	Office of Policy Coordination (CIA)
OSO	Office of Special Operations (CIA)
OSS	Office of Strategic Services
PBCFIA	President's Board of Consultants on Foreign Intelligence Activities
PRC	Project Review Committee (CIA)
PSB	Psychological Strategy Board (US Intelligence Community)
PTO	Pacific Theater of Operations
SASC	Senate Armed Services Committee
SEAC	Southeast Asian Command
SFD	Special Funds Division (COI)
SFB	Special Funds Branch (OSS)
SI	Secret Intelligence (OSS)
SO	Special Operations (OSS)
SSU	Strategic Services Unit
TSS	Technical Services Staff (CIA)

Prologue

Edwin Lyle Fisher was my paternal grandfather. He died of heart failure at age fifty-five, several months before my third birthday. My grandfather remained an enigma to me until I was in my early forties. To this day, I have just one fleeting memory of him, standing alone in his backyard sometime shortly before he died. That nebulous image is, curiously, one of my earliest childhood memories. Still, I can barely remember even thinking about him as a child. I grew up thinking that my grandfather was a government accountant. As an adult I learned that he had actually been an attorney, not an accountant, and that, from 1946 to 1958, he had served as the solicitor general counsel of the General Accounting Office (GAO), a legislative agency responsible for overseeing the massive spending of the federal government.

At a family gathering in 2003, I told my Aunt Toots that I wanted to learn more about my long-deceased grandfather. She told me that she had found a box of family memorabilia in my grandparent's basement when my grandmother died in 1994, and she encouraged me to visit her anytime to explore its contents. On the first weekend in November that year, I drove to my aunt and uncle's scenic waterfront home at the mouth of the Chesapeake Bay, just past Solomon's Island. That weekend I learned just how little I knew about my grandfather.

As I relaxed in their living room on Sunday morning, drinking coffee and reading the morning newspaper, my aunt placed a large cardboard shipping box on the carpet in front of me. I spent the rest of that morning digging through old photographs, college report cards, newspaper clippings, speeches, personal letters, job applications from the 1930s, official correspondences from congressmen, and invitations to state dinners at the White House. The most surprising find, however, was a formal appreciation letter from Allen Dulles, the director of central intelligence (DCI), that had been presented to my grandfather on October 16, 1958, shortly after his retirement from the GAO.

Holding the letter in both hands, I glanced up at the agency's old letterhead and down at Dulles's sinuous signature at the bottom. I then read the first sentence: "Since you have recently retired at the end of a distinguished Government career, it is appropriate that we express to you our appreciation of the guidance, understanding and support you gave to this Agency throughout its growing years." The rest of the letter introduced me to a side of my grandfather's professional life that I'd never heard anything about:

CENTRAL INTELLIGENCE AGENCY
WASHINGTON 25, DC
Office of the Director
16 OCT 1958

Mr. Edwin Lyle Fisher
5122 Wessling Lane
Bethesda 14, Maryland

Dear Mr. Fisher
Since you have recently retired at the end of a distinguished Government career, it is appropriate that we express to you our appreciation of the guidance, understanding and support you gave to this Agency throughout its growing years.

Before the Agency was recognized by statute, it was only through techniques worked out with you that the Central Intelligence Group was able effectively to lay the foundations for the future Agency. Once formally established, the Agency was faced with a requirement for the authorities necessary to carry out its functions. Again your understanding of our responsibilities and the problem of undertaking them in the cold war era was a powerful influence in the passage of the Central Intelligence Agency Act of 1949. This act is now time tested, and our experience has shown that the wide authorities granted to this Agency are essential to its ability to perform effectively.

Many other times you have considered our problems, some of them perhaps unique in Government, and always we found your counsel constructive. It was therefore with great regret that we saw you leave the Government, but we extend our best wishes for a long career in the comparatively simple life of private industry.

Sincerely,
Allen Dulles
Director

I read this letter several more times over the next couple of weeks before I gave in to the growing urge to investigate the history alluded to in the second paragraph. Like any untold story on the CIA, I anticipated that some of the information might still be classified. Nevertheless, I was curious to learn whatever I could about this mysterious letter from the DCI. This personal research gradually snowballed into a much bigger story on the origin and early development of a clandestine system for funding the CIA. That story has taken me two decades to uncover and piece together.

The GAO seemed like the best place to start this investigation, and so I first sent an email to the organization's records department requesting information related to my grandfather's involvement with the "Central Intelligence Group" and the "Central Intelligence Agency Act of 1949":

Dear Sir or Madam,
My grandfather, Edwin Lyle Fisher, served as General Counsel to the GAO from 1946 to 1958. I am in the process of doing some historical research on his distinguished career in government and would like to acquire copies of some records pertaining to him. I am particularly interested in any available declassified GAO records relating to his involvement in the Central Intelligence Group (1946 to 1947), as well as his involvement in legislation relating to the Central Intelligence Agency Act of 1949. My grandfather died in 1962, when I was quite young, and so I never got to know him. I have begun to assemble a profile of him and his work from the letters, memos, pictures and other information that he left behind. I would appreciate any assistance that you can offer. Thanks.

Regards,
Brad Fisher

About a week later, somewhat to my surprise, I received a call at work from Jerry Cohen, an assistant general counsel at the GAO's Office of the General Counsel (OGC). He told me that my email had been forwarded to him, and he invited me downtown to GAO Headquarters for a visit and a formal introduction to the organization's general counsel, Anthony Gamboa. I enthusiastically accepted his invitation, which seemed to offer an opportunity to ask some questions about my grandfather's work with the CIA. Prior to my visit, Cohen placed me in email contact with the GAO's historian, Maarja Krusten, who coordinated my visit. On January 16, 2004, I took a DC Metro red line train downtown to Judiciary Square. From there, I walked a couple of blocks to the long, rectangular GAO building, which fit neatly between Fourth and Fifth Streets. I opted to bring the letter with me but decided on the trip downtown to reveal it only to the GAO historian and not to the lawyers at the OGC.

Jerry Cohen met me at the main security entrance and served as my escort during the first part of the visit, which started with a brief tour of the general counsel's office. Along one of the hallways hung a long line of life-size portraits of all the former general counsels, their eyes seemingly fixed on the people who walked past. As I stood looking up at my grandfather's giant portrait, I recalled that a much smaller version of the same picture had hung in the living room of my grandmother's Bethesda home. Cohen next escorted me into his neat, capacious office, where he explained matter-of-factly that he handled Freedom of Information Act requests. Looking me straight in the eye across his ornate desk, he politely asked why I was interested in this information. As I told him about my wish to learn more about my grandfather, the idea began to grow in me that there was more to this story. Because my grandfather had received the CIA appreciation letter six weeks after his official retirement, I suspected that it had never become a part of the GAO's institutional history. Cohen did not ask any more probing questions.

Maarja Krusten, more gregarious than Cohen, soon arrived to take over as my escort. When we were alone in her office, I handed her the letter to read but politely asked her not to make a copy of it.[1] We talked about the history of the agency until we were called back to the OGC, where I was introduced to Anthony Gamboa, his deputy, and the rest of his staff. An office administrator grabbed a Polaroid camera and snapped a couple of pictures: in one, Gamboa and I are standing together; in the other, I am standing alone in front of the giant portrait of my grandfather. During our fifteen-minute meeting, it became clear that neither Gamboa nor his deputy knew much about my grandfather.

I left that day without learning anything new about the letter's contents. I later requested additional documents from Krusten, but that request went unanswered. Some years ago, near the end of my research, I again requested several letters from the Records Department, this time providing specific B-File number references.[2] I already knew what was in them from other declassified CIA documents that discussed their contents. Although a GAO librarian said they were looking into my request, those documents were never provided and no explanation was offered—they never said they were being withheld, but, after a few back and forth correspondences, I heard no more from the librarian.

My first big break came when I learned that all the declassified CIA records were archived at the National Archives and Records Administration (NARA) in College Park, Maryland, just a few minutes from my home in Adelphi. Before long, I was visiting the archives during lunch breaks and after work, on an intermittent basis. Most of the declassified CIA records are stored in a digital archive known as the CIA Research Search Tool, or CREST. In 2000, CREST was made available in the third-floor library at NARA in College Park. Since then, the CIA has annually uploaded millions of once highly classified CIA documents into the database. In the early years, researchers could access the CREST system at one of five or so PCs placed around a long rectangular table in the middle of the library, inconspicuously surrounded by bookcases. At these computer terminals, users could search the voluminous CREST database by keyword, like "Lyle Fisher," or by the document's Electronic Standard Document Number (ESDN).[3]

Because the CIA supplied the paper free of charge, the only real obstacle for researchers was the availability of terminals.[4] This was less of a problem in the early years, when few people ventured up to the third floor to use CREST. Most scholarly research at the National Archives II facility took place one floor below, in the textual records section, where I also spent a great deal of time. Later, as more researchers learned about CREST, it became harder to find an open terminal. Nowadays, CREST documents can be accessed online from anywhere through the CIA's electronic library. Of course, it helps to know what you are looking for. CREST documents proved invaluable as I pieced together this previously untold story. Several of the key documents linking my grandfather to the CIA—the "family jewels" of my collection—were serendipitously declassified several years after I began this research.

My discovery of the "Dulles letter," as I now like to call it, started me down a long path that eventually circled back to the letter and why it was written. From CREST documents, I learned that Allen Dulles personally presented it to my grandfather at a private luncheon, held at the old CIA headquarters at 2430 E Street NW in Foggy Bottom. The event was attended by the DCI and a small group of the CIA's most senior administrative officials. I will return to this final meeting between Lyle Fisher and the CIA near the end of this story. By then, you will better understand why the Dulles letter was written.

PART ONE
BLACK BUDGETS AND PUBLIC ACCOUNTABILITY

1. The Problem of Funding a National Intelligence Service

Just as blood courses through a body and gives it life so money must flow within an intelligence network and give it impetus

—Robert Alcorn, OSS Chief of Special Funds, London, from 1943 to 1945

MONEY AND INTELLIGENCE

On August 7, 1946, senior officials from the Treasury Department, the GAO, and the Bureau of the Budget held a secret conference in Washington, DC, with top officials from the Central Intelligence Group (CIG), a relative newcomer to the US intelligence community. This rare gathering of the federal government's three most powerful financial controllers concerned an urgent matter of national importance: the establishment of a clandestine budget and accounting system for the CIG, the first peacetime intelligence service. This historically obscure conference ended with the creation of what was known as the "working fund." This extralegal funding system was used to secretly finance CIG's foreign intelligence operations and was instrumental in getting its administration up and running. More importantly, it paved the way for the statutory recognition of the Central Intelligence Agency in the following year.

When World War II ended in September 1945, the federal government began the arduous process of reverting to prewar statutes. Truman's emergency war powers were about to expire, and his administration faced daunting challenges, administrative and legal, in its effort to establish a national intelligence service. As the new agency began to take shape in the early postwar era, government planners pondered how to secretly fund covert foreign operations within the constitutional framework of the US treasury system.

The War Powers Act of 1941, passed in the immediate aftermath of the attack on Pearl Harbor, had transferred extraordinary emergency powers to the president. It authorized President Roosevelt to direct funds to secret intelligence operations "without regard to the provisions of law regulating the expenditure or accounting for funds of the United States."[1] Wartime spending of this kind exploited a new class of government funds known as unvouchered funds. The biggest spender of unvouchered funds during World War II was the Office of Strategic Services (OSS), a wartime intelligence service that carried out overseas operations under the Joint Chiefs of Staff (JCS). Inside the OSS, these funds became known as "special funds."

The OSS Special Funds Branch (SFB) was established to handle the byzantine financial administration of the clandestine services overseas. Between 1943 and 1945, this secret enterprise spun up a global network of special funds offices to disburse unvouchered funds to the OSS clandestine services operating in the war theaters. SFB agent cashiers requisitioned special funds from the chief disbursing officer at the Treasury Department and then secretly channeled this money to administrative hubs scattered across Europe, North Africa, and Asia, using secret government couriers and a network of domestic and foreign banks.

Special funds officers stationed abroad traded foreign currency in black markets, produced (and captured) counterfeit foreign currency for use in field operations, maintained a clandestine gold reserve overseas worth millions, kept thousands of foreign agents on the unvouchered payroll, and innovated new methods to covertly move Treasury funds between the United States and theater operations. By the end of the war, the SFB had established a worldwide administration to secretly disburse funds to the clandestine services abroad. Special funds proved vital to running a state-of-the-art intelligence service in wartime.

After the war, the termination of the OSS on September 20, 1945, was quickly followed by Truman's creation of the Central Intelligence Group on January 22, 1946. In a directive to the secretaries of the State, War, and Navy Departments, Truman established the CIG "under the direction of a Director of Central Intelligence" and placed the new organization under the authority of a senior-level intelligence board known as the National Intelligence Authority (NIA). Because the DCI was, legally, a coordinator, not a department head, he had no actual administrative powers. That turned out to be a major problem.

Truman's original vision for the CIG made sense on paper. The State, War, and Navy Departments would secretly channel funds to the CIG; in principle, this would enable the spy organization to operate overseas below the radar of Congress. This tripartite system, however, left the organization without congressional funding of its own and without independent statutory status. In the weeks leading up to the secret conference in Washington, DC, on August 7, the CIG had not yet established an operational footprint overseas.

The working fund was created by a consensus among the four participants at the conference. Under this extraordinary arrangement, the State, War, and Navy Departments were authorized to direct money from their budgets into a fund that would be under the control of the DCI, who, in turn, would act as a department head. Most importantly, though, the comptroller general of the United States, Lindsay Warren, delegated his certification authority to the DCI for the use of unvouchered funds on secret intelligence operations of a confidential nature. This extraordinary delegation of statutory authority had the effect of partitioning the fund into two mutually exclusive audit jurisdictions for overseeing the expenditure of vouchered (GAO) and unvouchered (CIG) funds. Notably, this special, quasi-legal agreement between the NIA, the GAO, the Treasury Department, and the CIG required the GAO and CIG to jointly audit the fund. From that point on the two agencies closely coordinated on fiduciary matters of mutual interest. Also important, the working fund facilitated the absorption of the SFB into CIG's administrative infrastructure in October 1946.

GAO support of the working fund was critical to the early development of a centralized intelligence function in the executive branch. In the meantime, the CIG sought statutory recognition from Congress. The GAO expected that Congress would establish a legal code for the use of unvouchered funds as part of CIA's founding charter. However, the secret enabling of a national intelligence service proved too controversial, and it was left out of the final draft of the National Security Act of 1947. Because special enabling failed to make it into the legislation, the Agency remained under the authority of the GAO-monitored working fund until the passage of the CIA Act of 1949.[2]

When the Agency began its operations on September 18, 1947, its general counsel, Lawrence Houston, worked to draft a legislative proposal to rectify the enabling problem. It took two years to shepherd CIA's enabling bill through Congress, following a major setback in 1948; but, on June 20, 1949, the so-called housekeeping bill became law. Although it would have long-term ramifications for the future of American intelligence, the national news media paid barely any attention to the bill before or after its passage.

The Central Intelligence Agency Act of 1949 provides the statutory foundation for the clandestine funding system of the CIA. Section 10b of the act authorized the DCI to spend government funds "without regard to the provisions of law and regulations relating to the expenditure of Government funds." And, for "objects of a confidential, extraordinary or emergency nature," the DCI—the spender of government funds—was granted the authority to certify the expenditure of those funds. The CIA act allowed the Agency to function as both a government agency and a private corporation, exploiting the legal and practical benefits of each to its operational advantage. Just as importantly, this statutory precedent fomented the emergence of a rich and powerful military-intelligence-industrial complex on a global scale, spawning whole new industries, which facilitated the flow of government funds between the public and private sectors.

THE INFORMAL CIA–GAO LIAISON

From 1946 to 1962, the GAO, the only legislative agency involved in the creation of the working fund, informally coordinated, first with the CIG (August 1946 to July 47) and then the CIA (July 1947 to July 1962), on its highly classified audit of the agency. In the interest of national security and public accountability, the audit brought together two most unlikely bedfellows—the first US spy agency and the government's top fiduciary watchdog. This historically obscure interagency liaison remained a vestige of the original working fund until 1962, when Joseph Campbell, the comptroller general, pulled the GAO out of the audit, following a failed three-year effort to modernize an audit system that had become no more than a rubber stamp.

Congress first learned about the working fund arrangement during the drafting of CIA's statutory charter in 1947. The controversial enabling matter was discussed, but the bill's paramount objective remained the unification of the armed services, a complicated matter in itself. Congress and Truman's drafting committee purposely left the special enabling of the CIA out of the bill; by default, it got deferred to a future legislative session. In the meantime, the armed services committees authorized the CIA to continue operating under the 1946 working fund arrangement.

Both the GAO and the CIA were disappointed with this outcome. The GAO was a government watchdog; from its standpoint, the working fund placed it in an awkward role because, for national security reasons, the comptroller general was obliged to delegate confidential funds authority to the DCI. The arrangement was inherently flawed. The comptroller general was effectively powerless to look behind the director's audit certifications on expenditures related to sensitive intelligence operations; but, as the top fiscal authority, the comptroller general was culpable for the fiduciary decisions made by the DCI. On the highly controversial matter of how to regulate and oversee the use of unvouchered funds, the GAO supported the transfer of fiduciary responsibility from the comptroller general to the DCI.

The CIA Act of 1949 was supposed to solve this statutory dilemma. However, serious questions were left unanswered: What was the extent of the DCI's confidential funds authority, and what, if any, limitations should be imposed on that authority? The first enabling bill for the CIA, proposed in 1948, failed to pass for reasons that will be explored later in the story. For now, it suffices to say that CIA insiders were especially concerned about the legal position of Lindsay Warren, the comptroller general, on both the use of unvouchered funds by an executive agency and the authority of the DCI to legally certify those kinds of expenditures. Warren's only known support for special CIA enabling legislation is found in a little-known letter he wrote to the budget director, James Webb, in the spring of 1948. Webb had requested Warren's endorsement on the evolving bill. In his formal response, Warren explained that "in an atomic age, where the act of an unfriendly power might, in a few short hours, destroy, or seriously damage the security, if not the existence of the nation itself, it becomes of vital importance to secure, in every practical way, intelligence affecting its security." His endorsement, which went against the GAO's cardinal audit principles, was centrally based on the extraordinary threat posed to the nation by nuclear weapons.

Lindsay Warren was arguably the only official in the federal government in 1949 who had enough political and fiduciary power to block the passage of the CIA Act of 1949. However, during the critical period when the statutory language was being finalized, Warren remained conspicuously detached from the legislative process, even though the bill, H.R. 2663, threatened to transfer the certification authority for unvouchered funds from the comptroller general to the DCI, the spender of those funds. His silence implicitly conveyed a neutral position toward Section 10b of the CIA Act of 1949; Warren's neutrality on Section 10b was part of a legal strategy that will be discussed in a later chapter.[3]

2. The General Accounting Office

THE US TREASURY SYSTEM

The comptroller general of the United States, the head of the GAO, is the nation's top accountant and also a principal legal authority in the treasury system. It would have been hard to exclude the GAO from discussion of a matter as sensitive as the expenditure of unvouchered funds overseas by a secret executive agency. The GAO was created under the Budget and Accounting Act of 1921 to be "independent of the executive departments." This signature act formally transferred the comptroller and audit functions from the Treasury Department to the GAO. These two functions were subsequently united under a single authority: the comptroller general of the United States. The Budget and Accounting Act, however, stopped short of establishing a new legislative agency. Only at the end of World War II did Congress pass the Reorganization Act of 1945, which declared the GAO to be "a part of the legislative branch of government." That act became law just one year prior to the secret conference of August 1946.

The GAO's statutory charter has evolved in response to the administrative needs of an ever-changing federal bureaucracy; it is a far different agency today than when it was created in 1921. Its origins and its institutional history, as mentioned above, are intertwined with the history of the US Treasury Department. When the First Congress convened on March 4, 1789, lawmakers faced three major institutional concerns: foreign affairs, national defense, and financial management. Congress first passed legislation creating the State and War Departments in the executive branch before it addressed the more controversial issue of the country's financial affairs. The battle lines between the legislative and executive branches formed around the delicate matter of financial management and the so-called power of the purse; and in this case, Congress showed more interest in the administrative details of the Treasury Department.

According to the first official GAO historian, Roger Trask: "Laws creating the War Department and the State Department were short and general, leaving specific organizational details for the executive branch to work out. Congress acted differently in the case of the Treasury Department; it passed a law intended to bind the department more closely to the legislative branch than to the executive branch." According to Trask, "There was extended debate on various features of the Treasury Act, and the result was a law full of details and specifics. The clear intention of Congress was to maintain control of the money."[1]

On September 2, 1789, the First US Congress passed the Treasury Act of 1789, creating the Treasury Department along with five statutory positions for the purpose of instituting fiscal control over the withdrawal and expenditure of public funds. The Treasury Act simply denoted Treasury as a "department," whereas the State and War Departments were explicitly referred to as "executive departments." The statutory positions named in the act were secretary, comptroller, auditor, treasurer, and register. The duties of each were defined without any reference to the president.[2]

The secretary of the treasury headed the department and was responsible for managing the federal government's financial affairs and reporting to Congress. The duties of the comptroller, the second most important position in the Treasury Department, were, according to the act:

> to superintend the adjustment and preservation of the public accounts; to examine all accounts settled by the Auditor, and certify the balances arising thereon to the Register; to countersign all warrants drawn by the Secretary of the Treasury, which shall be warranted by law; to report to the Secretary the official forms of all papers to be issued in the different offices for collecting the public revenue, and the manner and form of keeping and stating the accounts of the several persons employed therein. He shall moreover provide for the regular and punctual payment of all monies which may be collected, and shall direct prosecutions for all delinquencies of officers of the revenue, and for debts that are, or shall be due to the United States.

The comptroller settled all claims and demands for and against the United States and also served as the investigative arm of the Treasury Department with the power to investigate "delinquencies" and direct prosecutions to the Justice Department. The secretary and the comptroller were also required to countersign all Treasury warrants.[3] This legal procedure provided a verifiable check on the withdrawal of public funds at the initial transaction point at which money left the Treasury. Treasury warrants were the beginning of a paper trail that ended with a cache of vouchers and other materials that documented the expenditure of public funds by executive departments on congressionally approved budgetary items.

The auditor of the Treasury reviewed the records of the disbursing agents and certifying officers of the executive departments to assess accuracy and the purpose of the expenditures—to see that the expenditure of public funds was consistent with the intentions of Congress. The auditor's reports were then post-certified by the comptroller. The treasurer received, disbursed, and watched over the money deposited in the Treasury, while the register[4] maintained the financial records of the accounts.[5]

The delegates at the Constitutional Convention of 1787 were sharply divided over who should control the purse strings of the federal government: the legislative or executive branch. Should the power of the purse reside with the appropriator or the spender of the funds? The Federalists argued that the president—the only elected member of the executive branch—should be given the power to spend public funds at his discretion, based on bulk, nonspecific appropriations from Congress. Other delegates, such as James Madison and George Mason, insisted that the power of the purse rightly belonged to the elected representatives of the lawmaking body. In *The Federalist Papers,* Madison declared, "This power over the purse, may, in fact, be regarded as the most complete and effectual weapon with which any constitution can arm the immediate representatives of the people, for obtaining a redress of every grievance, and for carrying into effect every just and salutary measure." Madison saw the power of the purse as a constitutional constraint on the spending power of the executive branch.[6]

Article I of the US Constitution prescribes a legislative process for legally funding the federal government. This process ends with the passage of appropriation bills that bear the effect of law. Section 8 of Article I list the powers of Congress, whereas Section 9 lists the constraints on that power. The authority to withdraw money from the Treasury is not listed among the congressional powers, but rather in Section 9 among the constraints. Clause 7 states: "No money shall be drawn from the Treasury but in consequence of appropriations made by law; and a regular statement and account of receipts and expenditures of all public money shall be published from time to time."

Clause 7 can be logically decomposed into two distinct parts conjoined by a semicolon. This awkward concatenation occurred during the waning days of the Philadelphia Convention just before the US Constitution was frozen in time. The first statement limits congressional spending to appropriations approved by both chambers of Congress. The second part requires Congress to keep the citizenry informed about its spending. This statutory innovation in the US Constitution imposes a democratic constraint on the legislative power of the purse that had no precedent in the monarchical government systems of Europe.[7]

The early nineteenth-century legal scholar St. George Tucker argues in *Blackstone's Commentaries* that Clause 7 does indeed proclaim the right of the citizenry to know how the federal government is spending the wealth of the nation:

> All the expenses of government being paid by the people, it is the right of the people, not only, not to be taxed without their own consent, or that of their representatives freely chosen, but also to be actually consulted upon the disposal of the money which they have brought into the Treasury; it is therefore stipulated that no money shall be drawn from the Treasury, but in consequence of appropriations, previously made by law: and, that the people may have an opportunity of judging not only of the propriety of such appropriations, but of seeing whether their money has been actually expended only, in pursuance of the same; it is further provided, that a regular statement and account of the receipts and expenditures of all public money shall be published from time to time. These provisions form a salutary check, not only upon the extravagance, and profusion, in which the executive department might otherwise indulge itself, and its adherents and dependents; but also against any misappropriation, which a rapacious, ambitious, or otherwise unfaithful executive might be disposed to make.[8]

Tucker's reasoning can also be extended to include a constitutional prohibition against the secret appropriation of public money for government activities that Congress or the president decides the public is better off not knowing about. However, this interpretation appears to be in conflict with

Clause 3 of Section 5, which states, "Each House shall keep a journal of its proceedings, and from time to time publish the same, excepting such parts as may in their judgment require secrecy." Here, Congress imposed the same requirement on its official proceedings but went on to create an exception not found in Clause 7. It is unclear whether Clause 3 can be extended to cover appropriation law and the funding of the federal government. The phrase "from time to time" appears in both clauses; this incorporates a natural time lag into the legal definition, which loosely accounts for the time required to prepare reports and make them public. The phrase may also lend itself to a secondary interpretation that justifies a delay in the release of financial information due to its confidential nature, such as in cases of national security.[9]

THE BUDGET AND ACCOUNTING ACT OF 1921

The control of the purse does not end with the appropriation of funds. Congress has a legitimate constitutional interest in corroborating whether the money it appropriates to government is spent on congressionally authorized programs and operations. Otherwise, it would be like paying someone to do a job and then never checking to see whether the work was completed in a satisfactory manner or was even done at all (e.g., fraud). Congress, not the executive branch, is constitutionally responsible for publishing "a regular statement and account of receipts and expenditures of all public money." However, until 1921, all the financial reporting and internal controls in the US treasury system were carried out by the Treasury Department, whose top accounting officers worked for the president. Congress lacked the legal and administrative tools to compel financial oversight of the executive branch. Oversight of the treasury system in the early twentieth century relied on three institutional points of fiscal control: 1) the cosigning of Treasury warrants, 2) the disbursal of funds by the executive departments, and 3) the audit, certification, and final settlement of the expenditures made in accordance with the intent of Congress.

The wars of the nineteenth century placed additional stresses on the treasury system not normally encountered in peacetime. According to Trask,

> The Civil War, like the War of 1812, placed new demands and intolerable strains on the nation's accounting system. In order not to impede military operations, field officers received advances of funds, but routine accounting and subsequent settlement of accounts could not take place under these conditions. Settlements after the war ended were almost impossible—in many cases the necessary records were either never prepared or were lost or destroyed during the fighting.[10]

Funding demands in times of war often preempted the institutional checks and balances necessary to achieve high standards of public accountability. The enforcement of strict certification protocols during a war can result in administrative delays, precluding the military from receiving needed funds and supplies—but without these protocols, public accountability goes out the window.

Systemic financial stress was not limited to times of war. The gradual expansion of the federal bureaucracy also put pressure on the treasury system. Financial waste, duplication of effort, and the outright misuse of public funds by executive agencies worsened over time; and as the amount of the federal budget increased, so did the size of government and its administrative complexity. Two acts during the nineteenth century introduced accounting reforms to address festering problems within the treasury system. The first of these bills, passed in 1817, added a second comptroller and four additional auditors, with the intention of speeding up administrative processing. This reform, however, had the unintended effect of introducing nonuniform settlement procedures into the treasury system.[11]

A second more important piece of legislation known as the Dockery Act was enacted in 1894. Representative Alexander Dockery from Missouri chaired the joint congressional Dockery-Cockrell Commission, which consisted of three senators and three representatives. The Dockery Act replaced the second comptroller with an assistant comptroller and also added an additional auditor, bringing the total to six. Under this act, the comptroller was no longer required to routinely examine the auditor's settlements and was authorized to make an advance decision, called a preaudit, on the legality of a proposed payment, if requested by a disbursing officer or department head. These fiscal decisions were legally binding. Other parts of the bill improved the Treasury's audit control of both requisitions and expenditures.[12]

The budget system was also problematic and in need of reform. Every year, Congress had to figure out an annual budget for the upcoming year; this was a mind-boggling process that, into the early twentieth century, only loosely involved the executive branch. The Commission on Economy and Efficiency, appointed by President Taft in 1911, studied the matter and issued twenty-one reports. One of those reports recommended "the installation of a double entry bookkeeping system in the Treasury Department's Division." According to Trask,

> The Treasury Department accepted this recommendation, and Congress provided funding to implement it. By definition, "double entry bookkeeping" is debiting a transaction amount and crediting it to another. Under the new Treasury system, it meant keeping a detailed ledger of appropriations and expenditures. One author has observed: "The idea of the double-entry system had much to recommend it. It provided the means whereby the Secretary of the Treasury, the officer who advanced money to disbursing officers, could be kept informed of what happened to the moneys advanced. It was an automatic check on the auditors, whose decisions resulted in substantial sums being disbursed from the Treasury."

The commission made three major recommendations: development of a national budget system; consolidation of the Treasury auditing offices into a single organization, and installation of a uniform federal accounting system.[13]

Expenditure control was again a major problem during World War I; Trask noted that it "forced a vast expansion of administrative offices and resulted in major increases in federal spending, taxes and the public debt." The accountability problems blamed on the war years prompted Congress to institute deeper reforms. At the end of World War I, a House committee, headed by Representative James Good (R-Iowa), drafted legislation to reform the hopelessly broken system. The committee's first hearing was held in late September 1919. William Willoughby, director of the Institute for Government Research, is credited with drafting the legislation; he stated early in the hearings, "No organ that grants funds has fulfilled its obligation until it follows up and sees that the orders that it has given have been carried out." Good argued on the House floor that:

> At present Congress has no power or control over appropriations after they are once made. This control passes to the executive departments, and these departments practically audit their own expenditures, and the legality of expenditures by an executive department is passed upon by an official appointed, and who can be removed at any time, by the Executive. After appropriations are once made by Congress the control over expenditure of the money appropriated passes from Congress.

Representative Parrish (D-Wisconsin) lamented that "under the present system Congress makes appropriations and the money is turned over to the heads of the various departments of Government, and unless an expensive investigation is ordered Congress does not know whether the money was expended according to its wishes or not."[14]

On June 4, 1920, President Woodrow Wilson, with "the greatest regret," vetoed legislation to create a new oversight agency outside of the executive branch, based on constitutional objections. Although Wilson agreed with the goals of the bill, he argued that it was unconstitutional because it gave Congress the authority to remove the comptroller general and assistant comptroller general by "concurrent resolution of the House and Senate." He was not alone in his opinion that the duties of the comptroller were constitutionally rooted in the administration of the executive branch. Good persisted, though, and with the benefit of a newly elected Republican president and a Republican majority in the House and Senate, helped get the bill across the finish line. President Harding signed the Budget and Accounting Act of 1921 into law on June 10, shortly after taking office.[15]

This signature act created the US General Accounting Office and the Bureau of the Budget.[16] The establishment of the GAO redistributed the fiscal power of the Treasury by transferring the comptroller and auditor functions to the head of a new agency. The comptroller general of the United States[17] was first nominated by the president and then confirmed in the Senate for a fifteen-year term.[18] Although the GAO's charter was aligned with the interests of Congress, it was not declared to be a legislative agency in the original act. The Bureau of the Budget, headed by a budget director, functioned as an autonomous division of the Treasury

Department. The budget director reported directly to the president, not the Treasury Secretary. The Bureau of the Budget empowered the executive branch by centralizing control over the planning phase of the executive budget and the disbursement of funds to the various parts of the executive branch. In the decades to follow, the budget director emerged as one of the most powerful senior officials in the executive branch.

The GAO was created to manage and oversee the audit and accounting systems of the federal government. The Bureau of the Budget, in contrast, was created to coordinate the drafting of the president's budget proposal to Congress, and to manage the distribution of funding to the executive departments. Both agencies were expected to promote efficiency and accountability by eliminating waste and duplication of effort. Because the bill's enactment gave the executive and legislative branches powers that they previously did not have, it is hard to argue that it strongly favored one branch of government over the other. The act had its critics, but integrating the executive branch into the budgetary process was well within the language and spirit of the Constitution. In 1939, the Bureau of the Budget moved from the Treasury Department to the newly created Executive Office.[19]

President Harding nominated J. Raymond McCarl as the first comptroller general and Charles Dawes as the first budget director. Both of them were formerly lawyers and were influential members of the Republican Party. Congress intended for the comptroller general to serve as a quasi-judicial figure, whereas the budget director served at the pleasure of the president. The budget director could be removed at any time, but to remove the comptroller general would require an impeachment process. Over the first sixty years, twenty-five budget directors served the president, but there were only five comptroller generals during that time.[20]

Some critics of the GAO argued that the new system of oversight failed to distinguish between the independent functions of audit and settlement. These critics noted that GAO's auditing activities and methods of reporting were not well coordinated with the oversight activities of Congress. Lucius Wilmerding explains: "The accounts when audited were not submitted to Congress. They were declared before and passed by the accounting officers themselves, who were required by law not only to receive and examine but to 'settle and adjust' them." Wilmerding explains that the

GAO's establishment "did nothing to increase the retrospective control of Congress over expenditure" and "had the important effect of lulling Congress into a feeling of security." The GAO was still a young agency when Wilmerding published his critical analysis (1943), long before the passage of the Budget and Accounting Procedures Act of 1950.[21]

The new agency was, nevertheless, given real investigative powers. Section 312 of the Budget and Accounting Act states that "the comptroller general shall investigate, at the seat of government or elsewhere, all matters relating to the receipt, disbursement, and application of public funds," and that "he shall submit to Congress reports upon the adequacy and effectiveness of the administrative examination of accounts and claims in the respective departments and establishments upon the adequacy and effectiveness of departmental inspection of the offices and accounts of fiscal officers."

Section 313 of the law puts a little more muscle into the act, stating:

> All departments and establishments shall furnish to the Comptroller General such information regarding the powers, duties, activities, organization, financial transactions, and methods of business of their respective offices as he may from time to time require of them; and the Comptroller General, or any of his assistants or employees, when duly authorized by him, shall, for the purpose of securing such information, have access to and the right to examine any books, documents, papers, or records of any such department or establishment.

The GAO had the power to subpoena information from executive departments, but it had no enforcement powers in cases of fraud, extortion, and other financial crimes. When there was evidence of financial crime, the comptroller general had to turn that information over to the Justice Department for prosecution.[22]

EARLY YEARS OF THE GAO

Soon after assuming his role as the first comptroller general, John "Raymond" McCarl told Congress that the Budget and Accounting Act of 1921 "makes the General Accounting Office an independent establishment, entirely disconnected from all executive departments, and, as I conceive it, accountable to the Congress for what it does." Because the GAO was not a member of either branch, it had a confrontational role with both branches; indeed, McCarl himself was a controversial figure. In 1932, President Herbert Hoover issued an executive order that transferred the oversight duties of the GAO to the Bureau of the Budget. By then Hoover was a lame duck, having lost the election to Franklin Delano Roosevelt. No action was taken, and the executive order was allowed to expire. Once in office, FDR turned his attention to fixing the domestic economy. Hoover remained an outspoken critic of the GAO; years later, serving as chairman of the first Hoover Commission (1947–1949), he again urged Congress to return the authority of the comptroller to the Treasury Department.[23]

The GAO closely scrutinized the Roosevelt administration's New Deal spending during the Great Depression and thwarted "several of FDR's pet projects." McCarl, who had already served under three different presidents, felt the GAO should be impervious to "partisan politics," and under his leadership, the agency maintained a low bureaucratic profile. Trask explains: "During the New Deal period that began in 1933, McCarl avoided direct involvement in partisan politics. But his rulings against various Roosevelt administration spending proposals, and his expressed concern that Congress was not vigilant enough about regulating public spending, demonstrated his hostility to New Deal programs." McCarl portrayed FDR's signature achievement as an expensive series of "New Deal experiments." After he left office, he published a polemic against the New Deal in the *Saturday Evening Post,* titled "Government-Run-Everything." However, McCarl's strongest criticisms were directed at Congress. A strong advocate of reforming the system of disbursing Treasury funds to the executive department, McCarl favored a system that would place disbursing officers in an autonomous branch of the executive (e.g., Inspector General's Office).[24]

It took Roosevelt almost four years to nominate McCarl's successor. In 1939, with World War II on the horizon, Roosevelt finally nominated Fred H. Brown, a former senator from New Hampshire. Brown was confirmed unopposed in the Senate but resigned one year later due to illness. FDR next asked Lindsay Warren, the popular congressman from North Carolina, who had originally been his top choice. Warren had eschewed an interest in the position earlier, but, when Brown announced his resignation, he accepted the nomination and was unanimously confirmed in the Senate on the same day, August 1, 1940. He proved to be a strong leader of the GAO and was a key figure in the early development of a clandestine funding system for the CIG/CIA in the postwar era.

PART TWO
SECRET INTELLIGENCE FUNDING IN WARTIME

3. The Office of Strategic Services

CENTRAL INTELLIGENCE

Years before the National Security Act of 1947 established the CIA, a clandestine financial administration was developed to manage foreign intelligence operations abroad during World War II. The nation's first intelligence service, the Coordinator of Information (COI), was created in 1941, and a special division was established to disburse unvouchered funds to the clandestine services. The COI was soon supplanted by the OSS, which, once activated overseas, functioned as a wartime intelligence service under the JCS. The OSS conducted a broad range of intelligence activities during World War II.

The COI's small special funds division was transformed into the Special Funds Branch (SFB), just prior to the activation of the OSS overseas. By war's end, the SFB had a worldwide network of special funds offices for secretly disbursing unvouchered funds to the OSS clandestine services. The war years provided the perfect cover for the long-term development of this administrative infrastructure. When the war ended, the SFB was preserved in the War Department and then was absorbed into the CIG shortly after the August 1946 conference.

Prior to World War II, each executive department had to consider the importance of intelligence relative to its own budget and operations. With the sudden rise of Hitler's Germany and a spike in foreign spy activity within the United States, political attitudes in Washington started changing. In 1938 alone, the Federal Bureau of Investigation (FBI) handled 634 foreign counterespionage cases, compared to an average of 35 in previous years.

In response to this alarming trend, President Roosevelt took action to improve interdepartmental information sharing. He sent a confidential message to the secretaries of State, War, Navy, Treasury, and Commerce, the US attorney general, and the postmaster general on June 26, 1939, directing them to form an intelligence board, the Interdepartmental Intelligence Committee (IIC), whose members included the heads of the FBI, the Office of Naval Intelligence, and the Military Intelligence Division of the army. This non-statutory government "board" mediated the exchange of information circulated among agencies on intelligence matters of mutual interest. It was not an agency, however, because it was not created by statute and had no earmarked funding from Congress. The IIC also lacked a centralized authoritative structure and an integrated financial system for funding joint operations.[1]

THE COORDINATOR OF INFORMATION

As Great Britain was fighting for its survival against Germany in the Battle of Britain, President Roosevelt issued an executive order on July 11, 1941, naming William J. Donovan as the coordinator of information. This new senior position in the administration was unprecedented, and came across to some people as the appointment of an intelligence czar in the Executive Office. Bill Donovan, ambitious, principled, and daring, was one of the few advocates for the creation of a national intelligence service in the lead-up to the United States' entry into the war. His long career spanned war, business, and politics. After World War I, "Wild Bill" Donovan returned from Europe a decorated army colonel. The nickname, which his troops had given him for his intrepid military exploits in combat, followed him for the rest of his life.

Donovan worked relentlessly in everything he did. In the early 1920s, as a young attorney, he managed to run a private practice in Buffalo while he also served as a US attorney at the Justice Department in Washington. As it happened, while he headed the Crime Division of the Justice Department, he was briefly J. Edgar Hoover's boss. Donovan was well acquainted with Franklin Roosevelt; the two were former classmates at Columbia Law School and by the early war years had become fierce interparty rivals in both state and national politics.[2]

Prior to his appointment on July 11, there existed no organization for Donovan to head. FDR's order left him with the formidable task of starting up the nation's first national intelligence service on what was supposed to be a shoestring budget. The *New York Times* broke the news two days earlier, noting that the COI was "without precedent in the government's operations." Roosevelt empowered Donovan "to collect and analyze all information and data, which may bear upon national security; to correlate such information and data, and to make such information and data available to the President and to such departments and officials of the Government as the President may determine." With the intention of improving coordination among intergovernmental intelligence units—units that had practically no history of coordination—the order further stated that "several other departments and agencies of the government shall make available to the Coordinator of Information all and any such information and data relating to national security."

In addition, the COI was authorized "to carry out, when requested by the President, such supplementary activities as may facilitate the securing of information important for national security not now available to the Government." Purposely vague, this statement was considered sensitive enough that the White House "left it out of its public release" because, according to Roosevelt's advisors, it "was not clear to many" and would "lead to much questioning." Although FDR's directive prudently stopped short of declaring Donovan to be the head of US intelligence, its immediate effect was to sow seeds of dissent inside the military. In an attempt to appease the military, Roosevelt's July 11 order stated: "Nothing in the duties and responsibilities of the Coordinator of Information shall in any way interfere with or impair the duties and responsibilities of the regular military and naval advisers of the President as Commander in Chief of the Army and Navy." The assurance, however, did little to placate military commanders, such as Major General George Strong, the head of G-2, or the head of the FBI, J. Edgar Hoover, who saw Donovan as a territorial threat.[3]

Donovan received an office in the State, War, and Navy Building, next to the White House, within earshot of the budget director. As part of the Executive Office, he had more access to the commander-in-chief and the nation's top budget man than did any of Roosevelt's top military advisors. The intelligence chiefs of the Office of Naval Intelligence (ONI), the army G-2, and the FBI voiced concern that Donovan would use his new authorities and proximity to the president to centralize the command and control of US intelligence. To be fair, there is no evidence that Donovan ever sought to undermine the military's authority. He understood that if the COI was to operate effectively in the war theaters, it would require high-level military support and coordination.

Imposing no explicit budgetary limitations on the size of the COI[4] or the scope of its mission, Roosevelt offered only this guideline: the COI budget should remain "within the limits of such funds as may be allocated to the Coordinator of Information by the President." Donovan was authorized to "employ necessary personnel and make provision for the necessary supplies, facilities and services." From his sanctuary inside the Executive Office, Donovan and his close advisors prepared a budget for the upcoming fiscal year, with the future of the organization in mind.

In his first allocation letter, on July 25, FDR transferred $350,000 from the president's emergency fund to the COI, to help pay for the accumulating organizational expenses. That same day, the president signed another allocation letter that transferred $100,000 to a special account at the Library of Congress for building an administrative system for the collection and analysis of intelligence. Donovan told the budget director, Harold Smith, that $100,000 was not nearly enough and asked for the authority to transfer another $75,000 to the fund set up at the Library of Congress; the request was approved. The official history of the COI's Procedures and Budget Branch notes that this transfer "caused considerable trouble and confusion later on" at the budget bureau and the Library of Congress.[5]

This seed money financed the COI during July and August, before there existed a COI budget office. The first budget proposal completed at the end of the summer caught the budget bureau completely off guard. According to Thomas Troy,

> When Donovan asked the Budget Bureau on July 3, to assign him someone who would assist on budget, organization, space, and other general administrative matters, it had no reason to expect any unusual problems. It, like the public, had been led to expect that the new organization would be a relatively small staff which would simply digest and present to the President in brief and orderly fashion the "scattered reports" which FDR often found "hopelessly confusing." The truth was that Donovan, impatiently readying for war, was an empire builder.[6]

Atherton Richards, one of Donovan's earliest recruits, "was given the authority . . . to develop a preliminary budget." According to Troy,

Richards, the wealthy president of the Hawaiian Pineapple Company, "had none too clear an idea of what to do or how to proceed." By September, the COI's original budget estimate of $1,454,700 had ballooned to $10 million. Donovan then requested a large injection of funding from the budget bureau to jump-start his organization, including an allotment of unvouchered funds for special training in the collection of intelligence and special operations. From the start, Donovan had envisioned the COI's activation in the war theaters.[7]

The FBI, the ONI, and G-2 fought to prevent the COI from encroaching on their jurisdictional territory. Military insiders—aware of Donovan and FDR's intentions—foresaw the winds of change several months before FDR's directive of July 11. On April 8, Brigadier General Sherman Miles, the assistant chief of staff to Major General Strong, head of G-2, "worriedly wrote" the chief of staff, General George Marshall: "In great confidence O.N.I. tells me that there is considerable reason to believe that there is a movement on foot, fostered by Col. Donovan, to establish a super agency controlling all intelligence." Donovan's military critics, who resisted the future expansion of the organization behind the scenes, only posed a serious threat to his plans during the first year.[8]

EARLY DEVELOPMENT OF A CLANDESTINE FINANCIAL ADMINISTRATION

By September 1941, Donovan had a senior team of officers. Cecil W. Barnes headed the business office and Dr. A. Rex Johnson served as the chief of the Budget and Planning Office. When Thomas G. Early, one of Donovan's senior administrators, left for England, Johnson, as acting executive director, subdivided the office into separate sections: budget, and planning and procedures. The budget section handled the "budgetary operations of the COI," which included the "analysis and development of estimates and justifications." The planning and procedures section was responsible for "planning and developing organizational structure, preparing administrative procedures, and producing all directives such as General Orders, Special Orders, etc."[9]

It seems unlikely that Donovan's intelligence organization could have grown so rapidly without a dependable source of unvouchered funds. On September 3, the COI received his first installment of unvouchered funds, which FDR authorized in a signed allocation letter. With one stroke of his pen, the president transferred $100,000 to the COI from the president's emergency fund. FDR's allocation letter stated that the money could be used at the discretion of the COI "for purposes, which, in the opinion of the said Coordinator of Information, are of such a confidential nature as may not in the public interest be itemized."[10]

Atherton Richards, special assistant to Donovan, oversaw the early development of an administration for handling unvouchered funds and made decisions "in all matters pertaining to the use of Special Funds." Johnson and Richards soon met to iron out "methods of control . . . in connection with the expenditure of Special Funds" and submitted a budget proposal to the budget bureau on November 7. The COI budget proposal asked for $10,560,000; a quarter of this amount was earmarked for special funds. With a budget, a staff, and a source of unvouchered funds, Donovan, Richards, Early, Barnes, and Johnson met to discuss the administration and allocation of what were now being called special funds. Donovan, Early, and Johnson decided that $1,500,000 would be directed to special operations (SO) and $1,000,000 to secret intelligence (SI).[11]

For administrative purposes, special funds for SO and SI were called K (SO) and L (SI) funds and were disbursed to the clandestine services by a small staff in the office of the COI. These nondescript designations were soon changed to the less arbitrary SA/G (K) and SA/B (L). The letters G and B corresponded to the person heading the division: M. Preston Goodfellow and David K. Bruce. According to the official history, the Budget and Planning Office "protested vigorously at the designation of these activities . . . realizing that such titles would only exist so long as the incumbent individuals remained in their respective capacities." The new names were adopted anyway but were later changed to SO and SI. There was no chief of special funds at this very early juncture; Richards oversaw the office until the creation of the Special Funds Division in January 1942.[12]

Under the First War Powers Act, the president could make regulations, spend money, and reorganize the executive branch as he saw fit without going to Congress; however, Section 1 declared that "no redistribution of functions shall provide for the transfer, consolidation, or abolition of the whole or any part of the General Accounting Office or of all or any part of its functions." The GAO was then still an autonomous agency, not a statutory member of either the legislative or executive branches. It was, therefore, considered to be outside of the president's jurisdiction. On the same day that the president signed the war powers act into law, Comptroller General Lindsay Warren signed Accounts and Procedures Letter No. 3428, which authorized the COI's use of unvouchered funds under the president's emergency fund. This policy statement established a new special expenditure category for unvouchered funds. The audit and final certification of this special class of funding was handled internally by the COI under a special arrangement with the Treasury Department that apportioned public funds into vouchered and unvouchered spending categories. It was these categories that determined the official standards of recordkeeping, accounting protocols, and audit control.[13]

The handling of unvouchered funds favored anonymity and security over public accountability. No one in the government knew how this new class of funds should be accounted for operationally. The clandestine divisions required a highly specialized financial system for the disbursal and audit of unvouchered funds. Such a system was created to transfer these funds from the US Treasury to field agents through a complicated web of accounts that exploited the anonymity of the private banking system. For security reasons, only a few people in the organization could know the identity of the spender or the purpose of the expenditure. Unvouchered funds, for which no voucher[14] was submitted to the General Accounting Office, were supposed to be used only "in instances where the use of vouchered funds would divulge information prejudicial to the public interest, and where the services or materials necessary could not be purchased with vouchered funds or acquired from the military, naval or other government services for security reasons."[15]

On January 19, 1942, shortly after the attack on Pearl Harbor, Donovan established the Special Funds Division (SFD) in the COI to manage the disbursement, recordkeeping, and audit of unvouchered funds. At this point, the unvouchered funds disbursed by the SFD to the clandestine services were used mainly to support the activation of domestic training facilities.

William "Lane" Rehm, a fifty-year-old retired investment banker from

Connecticut, was recruited to head the new division. In his memoirs, former OSS agent Donald Downes says that David Bruce, the head of OSS SI, and Averell Harriman, a powerful American businessman with strong political ties to Washington, "recommended [Rehm] because earlier in his life he had been called upon to handle large sums of money when what was needed was incorruptible integrity and a lasting contempt for money, and those who worship it."

Downes, who socialized with Rehm and his wife, describes his friend as looking "like Cotton Mather." According to Downes,

> In the twenties the Harriman's noticed a small, brilliant, shoe-string financial journal published by Lane Rehm. At their invitation he began a career in investment banking. But Lane Rehm wanted to be a painter. So in his forties he quit banking cold—having saved almost enough money to keep one of his Wall Street colleagues in whisky and golf balls. He and his wife Louise, bought a farm near Kent, Connecticut, and Lane, between chopping wood and shoveling snow, began to paint seriously. Big salaries couldn't lure him back. But when he was called to Washington with the country at war, he willingly put aside his paint, his shovel and his axe.

He had "hard, blue eyes, impossible to look into while telling a lie. A straight, closed mouth, with almost no lips. The stern face of a puritan until he smiles, and when he smiles, he couldn't look less like a puritan—for he is gay, and jolly and civilized—three most *unpuritan* vices."[16]

Rehm built a secret financial system for the handling of unvouchered funds from the ground up, with virtually no institutional experience to draw on. In the Special Funds Branch History,[17] Rehm explains:

> The accounting system I started followed instructions received from the Treasury Department. The books represented a simple set of accounts, designed, I believe, for unvouchered money, recording each procedure from the initiation of a voucher to the cashing of a Treasury check allowing for expenditures, or an expense account, and advances to subordinate agent-cashiers. For security, I opened two other books in which were entered all transactions with "agents." Totals from the "agent" journal were transferred to the main set of books which made possible a record without

> divulging the names of the agents. For security, pseudonyms for agents were used for some time, until this procedure became too complicated.

The two other books he refers to in the branch history were known as the "secret journal and ledger." Rehm recalls, "From the beginning, it was understood by everyone that S.I. was to be a 'secret' organization, and according to the way older governments had developed intelligence, 'secrecy' was all important."[18]

Rehm was the top COI/OSS agent cashier for special funds. He recalls, "My appointment as Agent Cashier was arranged by Cecil Barnes, then Chief, Budget and Finance. . . . The Treasury approved my appointment, and upon receiving my first check, opened a personal account with the Riggs National Bank." To protect the security of the intelligence system, this money was transferred directly into personal accounts set up in his name. This arrangement was overseen by G. F. Allen, the Treasury Department's chief disbursing officer, who cosigned the three-party agreements among the bank, the agent cashier, and the Treasury Department.[19]

In a letter to Allen dated March 25, 1942, Rehm wrote: "Yesterday I opened an account with the Bankers Trust Company of New York City. I want to have it recorded that the money I have deposited does not belong to me. . . . I would appreciate it if you would sign your name at the lower left-hand corner of the letter and return it to me so that I can send it to the Bank." During his first several months, Rehm set up these special accounts at some of America's top financial institutions, including the Riggs National Bank and American Security Trust in Washington, the Wilmington Trust Company in Wilmington, Wells Fargo in San Francisco, Bankers Trust, and Chase National Bank in New York City.[20]

As late as May 1942, there were a total of twenty-one SO personnel serving abroad, including six technicians. Bradley Smith writes in *Shadow Warriors*:

> The majority of early S.I. postings abroad were to United States embassies and consulates in the neutral countries of Europe, Africa, and the Middle East and to the American diplomatic mission in Vichy France. A few intelligence missions using traveling scholars and businessmen were tried, and there was much consideration and experimentation with other ways to dis-

> guise agents, especially in places like Bern and Cairo, but placing S.I. men within State Department overseas missions continued to be the standard form of cover.[21]

In February 1942, Donovan established an undercover COI office at 630 Fifth Avenue in Manhattan to handle "secret intelligence matters" for SI. The top secret New York office closely coordinated with British Intelligence, the London office, and the COI special training facilities. Rehm coordinated with the New York office and spent his first several months on the job shuffling between New York and Washington. With SI agents stationed at US embassies abroad, Rehm used secure State Department channels to transfer confidential funds overseas. Special funds for SI and SO were also used for "cover corporations," the "payment of salaries of certain personnel not openly employed by COI," and the funding of "training programs for undercover agents and special ops."[22]

While Donovan worked to build a global intelligence service capable of carrying out a wide range of activities, his adversaries sought to undermine his longer-term ambition of building a centralized intelligence service. In addition to their concern that Donovan was encroaching on their jurisdictional territory, the military judged internal security to be subpar and susceptible to enemy penetration. According to Troy, Major General Strong (G-2) and Admiral Harry D. Train (ONI) considered Donovan to be "dabbling in a military preserve or proposing operations upon which they frowned" and saw him as "an inexperienced interloper whose schemes were a threat to security, efficiency, and military success." Until FDR ordered the transfer of the COI from the Executive Office to the JCS, the future of Donovan's vision hung in the balance.[23]

THE OSS MAKEOVER AND THE ACTIVATION OF THE CLANDESTINE SERVICES

In less than a year, Donovan built up a multifaceted intelligence organization from scratch. Incorporating the COI into the JCS organizational power structure was initially unthinkable; but, once the nation was at war, some top military leaders suggested that the COI's maturing assets could be exploited overseas in the war theaters. This idea began as a whisper but soon gained powerful supporters inside the JCS, namely, Lieutenant General Bedell Smith, the secretary of the Joint Chief of Staff. Smith "worried about 'the dangerous possibilities to security and plans' if COI were not under the JCS control." Incorporation of the COI into the US military complex promised to give military leaders more control over Donovan and his growing empire. It also accommodated Donovan's future aspirations, for the COI needed the support of the military to operate in the war zones.[24]

President Roosevelt created the OSS on June 13, 1942, by military order. The COI, which resided inside the Executive Office, was transferred to the OSS and was placed under the jurisdiction of the Joint Chiefs of Staff. Donovan was, on the whole, pleased with this new arrangement; he was still the head of the organization, with a new title "Director of Strategic Services." Some at the time, including FDR, had thought that the COI might be liquidated once under command and control of the JCS, but that never happened.[25]

By September 1942, the OSS was preparing for the formal activation of the SI and SO divisions, meaning that special funds would soon be disbursed in far greater amounts. In October 1942, the SFD was reorganized as the SFB; and, on November 17, Donovan sent an official letter to G. F. Allen, the chief disbursing officer at the Treasury Department, designating his top agent cashiers with certification authority for special funds. Letters of certification, worded identically other than citing a specific individual's name, required the agent cashier to take an oath:

> I certify that expenditures were actually made in the amount on this voucher according to reports in this office and that it would be prejudicial to the public interest to disclose the names of recipients, the dates and names of the places in which the expenditures were made. The expenditures were made incident to collecting and analyzing confidential information and data bearing upon the national security of the United States. It was impractical to obtain receipts for payment made without revealing identity and jeopardizing the success of the activity.

Special funds, therefore, were not subject to public scrutiny and were "accounted for solely on the certificate of the Director of the Office of Strategic Services." Donovan was both an intelligence czar and the comptroller of special funds: the buck stopped with him.[26]

The OSS was officially activated by the JCS on December 23, 1942, with the issuance of JCS 155/4/D. This historic directive charged the OSS with the "planning, development, coordination, and execution of the military program for psychological warfare." JCS 155/4/D was the first in a series of directives (JCS 155 series) to define the functions of the OSS in the war theaters. The JCS 155 series gave Donovan the green light to begin building an international intelligence network financed with unvouchered funds. Over the next three years, OSS field missions were established in strategic cities throughout Europe, Northern Africa, the Middle East, Asia Minor, China, India, and Burma.[27]

The COI could never have expanded so rapidly in size and scope if it had been incorporated into the military from the beginning. The OSS was saved from dismemberment by the development of an administrative infrastructure under the COI for overseeing the disbursal, recordkeeping, and audit of unvouchered funds.

4. The OSS Special Funds Branch

SPECIAL FUNDS

Plans for the partial militarization of the OSS had been in the works for months. According to the US War Report, "In the summer of 1942 the new position of OSS under the JCS, made it apparent that the agency would be subject to considerable expansion. It was obvious that the establishment of military theaters of operation overseas would require OSS, as an auxiliary of the armed forces, to establish large bases for intelligence, guerilla, and special operations." The new JCS directive cleared the way for Donovan to start building an extensive network of operational bases and sub-bases across Europe, North Africa, and Asia.[1]

In preparation for the OSS to conduct intelligence activities in the war theaters, the financial administration was separated into two branches: Budget and Finance and Special Funds. The Budget and Finance Branch had two offices. The Budget Office was subdivided into compartmentalized sections for vouchered and unvouchered funds. The Finance Office exclusively managed OSS vouchered funds, while also providing administrative cover for the SFB. The SFB handled all the special funds directed to the clandestine services operating overseas.

In January 1943, the SFB moved its staff offices in downtown Washington from the first to the second floor of the secretive Temporary "Q" Building in the Foggy Bottom neighborhood. Later that year, the whole office moved again, this time to the South Building in the OSS headquarters complex located at 2430 E Street NW, near the Lincoln Memorial. Budget and Finance also moved its main office from the dilapidated Building 14 in Foggy Bottom to the North Building of the OSS headquarters complex. The North and South Buildings flanked Donovan's headquarters at 2430 E Street, which from 1947 to 1962 also served as CIA's headquarters. The compartmentalization of the budget and accounting system into vouchered and unvouchered funds generated two sets of accounting records, one accountable to the GAO and one certified by the OSS strategic director alone.[2]

SFB chief Lane Rehm had remained busy in the previous year setting up a secret financial pipeline between the Federal Reserve and a network of US banks. In the Special Funds Branch History, Rehm says: "Everything that was done at the beginning was considered and initiated with 'secrecy' and 'security' in mind." The financial system for unvouchered funds was designed to hide the disbursal of special funds directed to OSS field operations. The OSS War Report states that special (or unvouchered) funds "were necessary to the maintenance of cover, whether of a corporation, a training installation, a recruiting office or an agent or group of agents in enemy or enemy-occupied territory. Unvouchered funds therefore constituted the modus operandi of the most secret operations in which OSS engage."[3]

After the war, Robert Alcorn, who headed the SFB Office in London from 1943 to 1945, published two memoirs that offered readers a rare glimpse inside the bizarre world of special funds. In one, published in the early 1960s, Alcorn talks candidly about the importance of unvouchered funds to the OSS:

> Under the authority granted the OSS the secret funds were an outright grant and were subject to no accounting of any kind. This was an obvious security measure. In the first few months of its existence, OSS funds came from the president's emergency fund, and they were doled out by the President as they were needed with no questions asked. Then as the OSS grew and flourished, a separate budget was established. The funds made available to the organization under the proper appropriation were labeled "unvouchered." That was the key word, for it meant that no other agency had any authority whatsoever to demand an accounting for the expenditure of the monies involved. It was assurance that no scrutiny would ever be made of how these funds were spent. It was most vital to the success of the operations of OSS for, like tracing a river to its source, the flow of secret money could divulge the whole vast network of OSS.

He further recalls that "as the organization grew and its operations became more complex and intertwined a full scale international secret banking system developed within the OSS. From Washington the lines reached out around the world until we were able to finance operations by code cable between such vastly separated areas as Chungking and London or

Lisbon and Calcutta." The CIA inherited this secret banking system from the SFB in 1947. The SFB, therefore, serves as the starting point for any investigation into the origins and early establishment of CIA's clandestine financial system.[4]

According to Alcorn: "Millions in cash in dozens of foreign currencies passed through the Special Funds officer's hands for the implementation of the expanding espionage and sabotage missions. As far as the Government was concerned [the money] could have been thrown in the air. . . . Currency inventories, gold inventories, jewels and the like, they were all there in a top-secret file for our own enlightenment—and protection." Alcorn insists that the "Special Funds Branch could show at a glance where the bulk of the money was being spent," but declassified SFB records more accurately suggest that the handling of special funds was rife with accountability problems from the onset. Because this system was not subject to GAO audits like the rest of the federal government, the legal notion of accountability with respect to secret OSS operations rested solely with the special funds officers responsible for the unvouchered accounts.[5]

Secretly moving funds around the war theaters was a dangerous business, and complex operational planning was required to protect the security of the funds and the identity of the agent. The SFB London War Diary explains, "Whereas money is the very core of a successful intelligence chain it may also prove to be the most dangerous single element whereby that chain may be rendered valueless and sterile." The OSS War Report further divulges:

> In order to protect the secret agents who would use the moneys, Special Funds endeavored to avoid repetition of successful operations, and not to rely upon any single pipeline for the movement of funds longer than absolutely necessary. Once an initial supply of funds had been successfully placed at the disposal of an agent, means were studied to keep the agent currently supplied through multiple operations. For example, at one time money was channeled into a country through seven distinct types of operations.[6]

The special funds officer represented the operational link between the agent and the money and was known as the "control." According to Alcorn,

> The agent, the man in whom the organization has invested so much in terms of training and equipment, in terms of confidence, is the focus of everything. . . . He has an opposite number, a control, who is just as vital to the success of a mission as is the agent himself. . . . There must be a close personal bond between an agent and his control, an unwavering confidence mutually felt and expressed, and a twenty-four-hours-a-day, seven-days-a-week loyalty and availability. Without this, there is nothing.[7]

Supplying funds to undercover officers in the war theaters was a risky game of cat and mouse, and every possible precaution was taken to prevent currency notes used in intelligence operations from being traced back to the US government. The OSS War Report says that the SFB "devised and put into effect intricate procedures by which the procurement and disbursement of unvouchered funds, both in the United States and abroad, were camouflaged so that the money's connection to the OSS was not revealed through the various transactions."[8]

COMMAND AND CONTROL IN WASHINGTON

The SFB field offices overseas disbursed unvouchered funds to the clandestine services operating in the war theaters. These funds were first requisitioned from the Treasury Department's chief disbursing officer by Colonel Rehm's agent cashiers in Washington. SFB agent cashiers then used the private banking system to secretly channel special funds from the United States into bank accounts overseas that belonged to the special funds station chief. Colonel Rehm faced the daunting task of building an administration that could disburse millions of dollars to OSS missions scattered worldwide and that could also, in the end, render accountability for that money. Reflecting on the SFB after the war, Rehm lamented, "For each new step the organization took it seemed that we could never handle the financial and accounting details as we would have wished."

Rehm established a management structure that centralized the control of special funds in Washington. Three main divisions—Accounting, Cashier, and Foreign Exchange—were established to manage and control the flow of special funds to OSS operations. What began in January 1942 as a small office, consisting of Rehm and four assistants, quickly grew into a global enterprise, which at its peak employed over 170 men and women stationed all over the world.[9]

Edgar M. Lucas headed the Accounts Division and was in charge of the bookkeeping and auditing of special funds. He was a seasoned security analyst and business consultant prior to the war, and he ran the division into the early postwar era. In 1939, Lucas and a small group of investors had purchased the Citizens Gas Company in Salisbury, Maryland; Lucas served as the director and treasurer of the company. He describes his prewar background to Rehm in a letter found in his personnel file: "I was responsible for all accounting, bookkeeping and financial transactions of the company."

When Lucas joined the OSS on September 17, 1942, he inherited the single-entry accounting system that Rehm had started in the early months of the SFD; payments were still being recorded in Rehm's "secret journal and ledger." That accounting system proved inadequate for tracking the millions of dollars suddenly being disbursed to operations abroad following the activation of the OSS. In deference to Rehm, Lucas described the system as "an excellent attempt at maintaining security but from a practical point of view soon became absolutely unworkable, as the number of agents increased and as domestic personnel began to take on the role of agents."[10]

Lucas abandoned the secret books and ledger in June 1943 in favor of a new system that organized agent accounts by approved projects. He recounted that the posting of agent accounts for a given project was "carried directly to the agent's ledger pages from the agent cashier disbursing records." These early reforms, however, were hardly enough; remarkably, it was not until the following year that the Accounts Division and its foreign stations switched from single-entry to a more standard double-entry accounting system.[11]

The Cashiers Division was managed by the top SFB agent cashiers, whose offices were on the third floor of the South Building with Rehm and the other senior personnel. Agent cashiers were certified and bonded by the chief disbursing officer of the Treasury Department and had the authority to secretly requisition and disburse Treasury funds to OSS intelligence activities. Senior SFB agent cashiers, like Rehm, disguised the money's association to the US government by depositing the special funds requisitioned from the Treasury into personal accounts.[12]

Doug M. Dimond joined the Cashiers Division in November 1942 and ran the special funds operations for the OSS special and morale operations branches. Dimond was the only agent cashier that handled both the disbursing and accounting duties for the clandestine projects under his control. Charles J. Lennihan Jr. handled the secret intelligence accounts and joined the SFB shortly after the activation of the OSS. His top deputy, R. G. White, joined the OSS about the same time. White eventually took over Lennihan's duties due to a serious but undisclosed medical condition.[13] Rehm diligently lured an investment guru named Robert H. I. Goddard to the SFB. Goddard agreed to join the OSS shortly after Rehm and Lennihan visited him at his lavish home in Newport, Rhode Island, in early February 1943. When Goddard arrived in Washington, Rehm named him assistant to the director and soon upgraded his title to deputy chief of special funds.[14]

Emerson Bigelow headed the Foreign Exchange Division. His role was to coordinate the buying and selling of foreign currencies and gold stocks to meet OSS operational demands. The SFB history states that Bigelow "spent approximately twenty years between World War I and World War II in foreign exchange activities, a part of this time in South America." Bigelow was responsible for the transfer of "secret United States funds abroad which were necessary to maintain OSS intelligence and other special operations." He also provided "for certain extra foreign balances in certain areas in such a manner as not to so far as possible, disclose the fact that the United States Government had sizeable cash deposits in these areas." Bigelow received substantial support from his top assistant, Alice Sweeney, who arrived at the OSS from the Department of Interior in October 1942. Sweeney eventually took charge of "Bigelow's Agent Cashier bank account, having charge of receipts and disbursements, initiating and preparing necessary requisitions for reimbursement of funds, and maintaining ledgers required by the U.S. Treasury in connection therewithin."[15]

The top SFB paymasters in Washington were bonded for amounts up to $200,000 in the beginning; the amount was increased to $500,000 in January 1943 to meet the rapidly growing operational demands of the clandestine services. In mid-June 1943, after the SFB's first foreign office was opened in London, Bigelow's bond was raised to $1,500,000.[16]

OSS field operations depended on a flow of special funds into the war theaters in a variety of different currencies. The insatiable need for operational cash on hand led to the stockpiling of foreign currency in a multitude of currencies. Although banks and open exchange markets were considered preferable, special funds officers overseas, nonetheless, "engaged in world-wide black-market operations." This was because some foreign currencies were too scarce or costly to purchase on open markets. Black markets, of course, were also more discreet.[17]

The SFB gold reserve provided another important source of currency for the SFB. The Foreign Exchange Division amassed gold "for purposes vital to the war effort and in connection with certain operations for which other forms of payment would be inadequate." The availability of hard currencies, such as gold, protected the OSS against the depreciation of the volatile paper currencies circulating in the war-torn regions of Europe and Asia. Recipients were also more likely to hold onto this precious commodity until after the war, effectively removing it from circulation, unlike paper currencies, which continued to circulate and were easier to trace. Gold was purchased from sources all over the world "with full cooperation of the Treasury and in compliance with Federal regulations." In keeping with federal regulations, Bigelow on several occasions purchased gold outside the United States and then "transported it to foreign offices where it could be held with no violation of US regulations." At its peak, the OSS gold stock was estimated to be worth almost $2,000,000—about $30,000,000 in today's dollars. The Monetary Branch of the Foreign Exchange Division kept detailed records on all currencies "sent to and between foreign offices" and tracked exchange rates for gold and all foreign currencies used in OSS operations.[18]

The SFB also participated in the counterfeiting of currency. It was a dirty little secret, but the United States, Great Britain, Germany, and Japan all participated in counterfeiting operations, and Bigelow had the authority to use these forgeries in secret operations. These funds, known as slush funds, were kept in separate repositories but were accounted for like ordinary funds.[19]

Rehm and his senior staff controlled the SFB's funding operations from Washington, but strategically important regional offices in New York and San Francisco also played an important role in the funding system. Regional offices functioned as conduits for the transfer of special funds to OSS operations in Europe and Asia. The New York office was created under the COI in February 1942. As an inconspicuous satellite office, it handled the administration and funding for the SI Branch. Later, under the OSS, the office played a critical role in the transfer of special funds to SFB outposts in Europe and North Africa. On March 30, 1943, Rehm appointed E. K. Merrill to manage special funds operations at the highly secretive New York office at 630 Fifth Avenue.

Merrill describes what his position entailed in the SFB history:

> The duties of this office have, of course, been mainly those of carrying out the New York end of financial transactions for Special Funds Office, Washington, and attending to the payment of Special Funds required to meet payments of payrolls, consultants' fees, and certain projects incident to the operations of the OSS New York office. The former included the procurement of foreign currencies and credits through banks, business corporations and individuals, in accordance with instructions from Special Funds, Washington. In addition to acting as agent cashier for the direct expenditures of money, there have been—from time to time—certain projects established which required their own bank accounts, for which funds were advanced from my agent cashier account to the accounts of a subordinate agent cashier or others directly in charge of such projects.[20]

In November 1942, in preparation for the activation of the OSS, the SFB established a top secret training facility in Towson called Area E, Maryland, where SFB personnel received two weeks of special training in the handling of special funds. During the first year, special funds were primarily routed between New York and London; by mid-1944, the ebb and flow of unvouchered funds had changed, and larger amounts were being channeled to the OSS war activities in Southeast Asia. The establishment of bases in the Far East Theater of Operations (FETO) forced the SFB to spin up an administrative infrastructure to support those funding operations in Asia. In September 1944, the SFB established its first West Coast office at 406 Montgomery Street in San Francisco, headed by

Lt. William Macintosh. The West Coast office financed the training of OSS officers at Catalina Island off the southern coast of California, and also their deployment overseas.[21]

Between 1943 and 1945, SFB offices and more remote substations popped up across Europe, North Africa, the Middle East, Southeast Asia, and China. According to the War Report, "Special Funds carried on its own financial operations, had an extensive network of field representatives, and maintained an organization in Washington through which centralized control was exerted over field transactions." Coordination between Washington and the foreign field offices was "vital in the case of Special Funds, as its world-wide financial activities were interrelated, and a given action in one area could influence simultaneous or subsequent actions in other regions."[22]

SPECIAL FUNDS IN THE WAR AGAINST GERMANY

In December 1941, the COI dispatched a "group of about 4 or 5 individuals" to London under State Department cover. These were "the first persons to appear on the Special Funds payroll of the London Mission." They were sent to London "for the purpose of recruiting, training, and dispatching agents to the field for operations." The London mission was a small outfit until the activation of the OSS. From then on, it served as the European Theater of Operations (ETO) headquarters for the OSS. The OSS established an office in London at 72 Grosvenor Street, near Hyde Park. According to the SFB London War Diary, under the COI "each of the individuals sent from Washington for assignment to London would be given a fund for the accomplishment of his mission to be accounted for directly to the Chief of Special Funds [Rehm] in Washington." In some cases, Rehm disbursed unvouchered funds directly to COI officers in Washington before their departure. Once officers were overseas, Rehm used secure state and military couriers to "pouch" funds to London. The activation of the OSS in 1943 rendered this relatively simple arrangement completely inadequate from the standpoint of accountability. The OSS was expanding so fast at this point that it sometimes had to borrow money from the US Army to fund its operations.[23]

The role of foreign banks grew as the OSS and its financial operations expanded abroad. Trusted foreign banks operating in neutral countries afforded secure depositories for large OSS reserves of currency. German intelligence monitored cash flows through the banks of Europe and North Africa, looking for large currency transfers. Paid informants and German agents posing as bank employees kept the Germans informed about money transfers and suspect accounts. It was not always operationally safe to transfer money around Europe using banks. Riskier methods of delivering funds, such as airdrops, sometimes offered the only option for supplying special funds to OSS agents in enemy territory.[24]

The SFB established its first overseas office in London on June 1, 1943, at 71 Grosvenor Street, next door to the OSS headquarters. After a brief search, Rehm appointed Robert Alcorn to head the London office. Alcorn was the first SFB officer dispatched overseas to manage the distribution of special funds to field operations in ETO. Most special funds officers stationed overseas were selected for their strong employment history in business, finance, or accounting. Alcorn, in contrast, had virtually no prior experience in financial administration before joining the COI in January 1942. He, nonetheless, was well-educated and well-traveled. Alcorn graduated from Dartmouth in 1931 and did graduate work at Cambridge University in England. A document from his interview notes that he had "traveled and visited in most of the countries of Europe, the Mediterranean and Northern Africa, parts of South America and most of the United States." Accordingly, he was "fairly" fluent in French and could "read Italian fairly fluently." He applied for a position at the COI and underwent a series of interviews that included one with Donovan, where it serendipitously came up that Donovan and his father had once worked on a legal case.

Robert Alcorn was initially assigned as a senior interviewer in the COI Personnel Division, where he became better acquainted with Donovan. In October 1942, Alcorn was transferred to the South Building to serve as executive officer to the chief of the Research and Analysis Branch, William Langer. Walking the halls of the South Building, he eventually crossed paths with Rehm, who just happened to be looking for the right person to run the special funds office in London.[25]

Once selected for special funds work, Alcorn received crash training at Area E before he departed for London. After having been with the organization for just over a year, he now headed the critically important special funds office in London. In his memoir, Alcorn unabashedly admits to having "found balancing his own checkbook a monumental challenge"; still, he recalls that Donovan told him not to worry about his lack of accounting experience, for there would be other people around him to work the numbers. In London, he reported to the OSS base commander, David Bruce. Alcorn, who started with the rank of army captain, finished the war a highly decorated lieutenant colonel.[26]

Alcorn managed and oversaw the disbursement and control of unvouchered funds. His personnel file provides a comprehensive list of his responsibilities and duties:

> It is the responsibility of this officer to coordinate all foreign currency requirements with respect to operations of the other branches in the organization, to provide special currencies for agent operations behind enemy lines, and to maintain proper contacts with other field offices of OSS in order to facilitate the proper flow of currency requirements between OSS ETOUSA and other theaters, to co-ordinate all OSS requirements for the British, French, and other Allied services with respect to joint operations. It is the responsibility of this officer to control expenditures under approved budgets for all projects of a secret nature, to give financial advice in the planning of projects. It is the further responsibility of this officer to maintain proper records concerning all monies under his control, to provide proper analysis of all expenditures, Fund Offices, audit and combine the reports of such offices.

The London office centralized the control of special funds in ETO, which allowed Washington to better monitor the flow of special funds from the United States to OSS operations in Europe. After Alcorn's arrival, all special funds accounts at London banks were transferred into his name. Alcorn says, "All of the agents and saboteurs run by the OSS in the European theater of operations, from the Baltic to the Mediterranean, were handled from London."[27]

Banks in London remained operational and offered financial services to its clients throughout the war. Alcorn recalls that "London offered practically the only war zone where any semblance of routine banking could be followed. Everywhere else we were on a strictly cash basis. But in London we were able to establish bank accounts and use checks for some of the items that did not involve security to a dangerous degree." Only a few top bank officials—the bank president and vice president—ever knew of the secret arrangement between the bank and the special funds officers that owned the accounts. To tellers and other midlevel bank officials, men like Alcorn simply appeared as important bank customers in a shell-shocked city still bustling with financial activity. Alcorn writes, "I've often wondered what some of London's more conservative bankers thought a young American officer was doing in a war area with hundreds of thousands of dollars in extremely active checking accounts. And yet they were seeing only the thinnest edge of the coin."[28]

Shortly after Alcorn arrived in London, the second SFB officer was dispatched overseas: Edward Fay was sent as a "special representative" of the SFB to assume control of the OSS gold reserve in Gibraltar. This 6.5-square-kilometer piece of real estate, fondly known as "The Rock," had been a British territory since the early part of the eighteenth century. Overlooking the strait of Gibraltar, this promontory at the opening to the Mediterranean Sea was known as the northern pillar of Hercules in ancient times. Gibraltar, due to its strategic importance, was heavily fortified in 1940 and placed under British military control. Its entire population of thirty thousand people was forced to evacuate when, in November 1942, General Eisenhower, commander-in-chief of the Allied Forces in North Africa, set up his headquarters on The Rock in the lead-up to the invasion of North Africa, code-named Operation TORCH.

Fay was classified as a civilian when he left the United States; but, for "cover purposes," he was commissioned as an army second lieutenant after his arrival. This caused confusion. He was considered a civilian from the OSS standpoint, but the army viewed him as a military officer. Soon after arriving in Gibraltar, Fay "was ordered to active duty." Rehm spent the next several months unsuccessfully trying to have Fay transferred back to the OSS. The army finally released him in July 1943, only after a routine medical examination revealed that he had a glass eye, a medical disability that rendered him unfit for military service. The SFB branch history reports that Fay "acted as the guardian and custodian of the large gold reserve held on The Rock," and "flew thousands of Louis d'Ors [French gold coins] to Cairo and to Algiers" for use in secret OSS operations while stationed in Gibraltar. In October 1943, Fay moved his base of operations to England, where he had direct access to London financial markets and could more easily blend into the civilian population.[29]

OSS operational headquarters were set up to support three major theaters in the war against Germany: ETO, the North African Theater of Operations (NATO), and the Near East Theater of Operations (NETO). In addition to offices around OSS operational bases, forward SFB missions were also spun up to better control the disbursement of special funds to a rapidly growing list of OSS projects. These were spread out over a large geographical area, some deep in enemy territory. The North African Theater, which formed after the Allied invasion of North Africa, included Sardinia, Corsica, and Sicily.

Major John Williams, the third person to join the SFB after Rehm, established an administrative headquarters in Algiers in April 1943. Once that was up and running, Williams got reassigned to British intelligence in West Africa as a special OSS liaison officer. His top assistant, Second Lieutenant David C. Crocket, took over for him as the chief of special funds in Algiers. Crocket majored in modern European history at Harvard and was fluent in French. Before joining the OSS, he was the executive director of a Boston short-wave radio station that received secret financing from MI-6. To support OSS funding operations, he set up a confidential personal account at the Bank of France, through which operational funds were disbursed to the clandestine services in fourteen different currencies.[30]

At times, "huge sums of money" had to be transported "under hazardous conditions" in and around combat areas. Crocket's duties required extensive travel, often at great personal risk. Once, his plane "got into difficulties flying at nine-thousand feet, in mountainous territory"; he bailed out and parachuted to safety just before the plane crashed into the mountains. Crocket also "procured seventy-four million French francs for use in pre-D-Day intelligence services." Nearer to the end of the war, Crocket made all the financial and logistical arrangements for the secret surrender talks known as Operation Sunrise.[31]

Theater boundaries were redrawn after the Allied victory in the Battle of Normandy, and Southern Europe became the epicenter of Allied military operations. Afterward, the OSS NATO headquarters was moved from Algiers to Caserta, Italy, where it became the Mediterranean Theater of Operations (MTO). Over the next year, the SFB expanded its financial operations throughout the MTO using forward missions staffed with fully certified special funds officers. The SFB also established roots in NETO, which covered the Middle East, Turkey, and parts of Eastern Europe. The main SFB office in Cairo handled financial operations for SI, counterintelligence, and OSS Research and Analysis activities in Syria, Lebanon, Palestine, Transjordan, Iraq, Saudi Arabia, Iran, Afghanistan, and Turkey. It also disbursed funds to special, secret, and morale operations in Greece, Albania, and Yugoslavia. Lt. Holt Green[32] departed Washington in May 1943 to head this office, but like Williams, he moved on to a more senior position after a few months. Thomas Bland replaced Green as the chief of special funds on January 1, 1944.[33]

When the OSS recruited him, Los Angeles native Thomas "Barney" Bland was managing projects in the Middle East for Douglas Aircraft. He had started with Douglas as an accountant in 1939, and within four years was managing foreign projects. He spent over a year on a project in Abadan, Iran, and had just started working on a new project in Eritrea when he joined the SFB. A corporate manager in his mid-thirties, Bland took over the Cairo office from an army lieutenant, but, unlike Alcorn and Crocket, he was never assigned military rank. Instead, his corporate profile around the Middle East served as a cover for his role in the OSS. The OSS had to request a deferment of Bland's eligibility status from his local draft board during the war, noting that he was involved in secret government activities critical to the war effort.[34]

Bland opened a personal account at Barclays Bank in Cairo on December 31, 1943. A copy of the confidential three-party agreement with the bank states, "The writer desires to open an account with you acting in the capacity of Special Assistant to the Director of the Office of Strategic Services. Such account will be in the writer's individual name but none of the funds at any time in this account will be his property and such funds shall at all times be subject to withdrawal as herein provided." This agreement was signed by the SFB theater chief, Barclays, and the Treasury Department. The Treasury Department, the true owner of the funds, could withdraw the money at any time. By mid-1944, the Cairo office was reporting expenditures of around $75,000 per month and had a total cash reserve of over $1.5 million.[35]

After D-Day, Cairo, and NETO in general, were of lesser importance, and SFB made some key personnel changes. In fall 1944, Rehm recalled Bland to Washington for a more important assignment, and Bland's deputy, Nick Steichen, took over as head of the Cairo office. Bland's accounts were transferred into Steichen's name on December 12. Steichen ran special funds operations out of Cairo into the postwar era and was still heading the office when the Central Intelligence Group was formed in January 1946.[36]

The SFB offices overseas represented nodal points in a funding network that moved large amounts of money throughout Europe and North Africa. Emerson Bigelow candidly discussed the movement of special funds in the SFB history; he explains, "Without an understanding of the importance of the secrecy of capital movement, the problems facing the Special Funds Branch and their progressively successful solutions cannot be fully appreciated." Special financial methods were used to obtain needed currencies and to transfer large sums of money among the SFB offices in each theater. Bigelow says, "It became necessary therefore for us to set up a system whereby our Algiers Office, for example, might call upon our Lisbon office for the purchase of let us say, Italian Lira, not locally obtainable in Algiers."[37]

SFB's Lisbon office, opened in October 1943, exclusively worked to procure and transfer foreign currencies to other regional SFB offices. Under State Department cover, Gardener B. MacPherson arrived to head the Lisbon office and oversee the purchase and sale of foreign currencies in the Lisbon exchange markets. These financial operations were complex. For example, to avoid using American currency in Europe, Portuguese escudos and Spanish pesetas were secretly purchased in Buenos Aires, using Argentine currency. The escudos and pesetas were then transferred to Lisbon for the purchase of other currencies. MacPherson faced the problem of having to acquire a multitude of foreign currencies, some of which were hard to come by in open markets.[38]

Bigelow notes, "Our problem involved (a) the quiet circumvention of the regulations of each country without arousing the suspicions of the banks, which we knew were under orders to inform their respective governments, and (b) to do this if possible, without having the enemy learn about it." As Bigelow reports, "In most countries all banks within the country were required to report to the government any sizeable or unusual bank transactions, particularly cable transfers of money from outside of the country and more particularly when done for the benefit of a resident alien." In some cases, money disbursed to field agents "passed through a chain of no less than seven bank accounts or individual's hands, all for the sake of preserving the secrecy of the operation." On this point, the branch history writes, "There was at this time, no precedent to follow and no universally accepted practices to adopt. . . . Moving sizeable sums of money within and without a country under masked operations is never simple." German intelligence engaged in large-scale operations designed to trace the movement of currency, using financial methods that included "marking money, recording serial numbers, and the issuance of special notes." The SFB, in turn, collected its own financial counterintelligence during the war years. A German banker from Berlin was one of SFB's most valuable foreign agents; throughout the war, he provided vital information on German plots to trace currency to the Allies without discovery.[39]

New SFB missions were set up in Stockholm and Madrid at the end of 1943. Politically neutral, Stockholm, like Switzerland, attracted spies from all over the world. The first OSS officer was sent to Sweden in the fall of 1942, and seventy-five SI officers worked to gather information on the Germans. Iver Olsen arrived in Sweden in December 1943 to head the SFB office in Stockholm "under Treasury cover."[40]

The OSS Madrid office was opened during the fall of 1943. Although Spain, under dictator General Franco, was neutral, it gave material support to the Nazis. The Allies sought information about German intentions on the Iberian Peninsula and, at its southern tip, the English territory of Gibraltar. Some fifty OSS officers in Madrid were working under State Department cover, posing as "petroleum attachés in the American oil mission building near the embassy," when James McMillan arrived, likewise under State Department cover, in January 1944 to head special funds operations there. In addition to active support of intelligence operations in Spain, the Madrid office secretly moved currency from Portugal through Spain to SFB funding centers like Algiers, Caserta, and Cairo.[41]

The OSS was a hybrid organization consisting of military and civilian personnel. The government status of the special funds officer varied by the individual. Most of them, such as Alcorn and Crocket, were fully commissioned military officers. Other SFB officers, like MacPherson, McMillan, and Olsen, with roles in the civilian sector, were sent to Europe under official cover from the Treasury and State Departments. SFB chiefs wore many hats. Their duties brought them into contact with a diverse array of officials that included bankers, military officers, diplomats, Treasury officials, and OSS field commanders. Alcorn and the other SFB chiefs were cleared at the highest level and worked directly with the heads of the OSS operational units to determine how much money was needed for each specific project. They also had the power to delegate disbursing authority in smaller amounts to subagent cashiers in the SFB. Alcorn was the highest bonded SFB officer stationed overseas. His bond, which was initially set at $100,000 in 1943, was increased to $500,000 the following year.[42]

Switzerland, like Lisbon, was a major banking center for Central Europe and was strategically situated at the war's financial epicenter. The Swiss capital was crawling with spies from all over the world. Allen Dulles, known as Agent 110, arrived in Bern in November 1942 under State Department cover to head the SI office in Switzerland, just before the Germans closed the Swiss border with France. The OSS Swiss mission produced some of the most highly valued intelligence on the Germans; after D-Day, it served as a key financial center for OSS operations.[43]

A memorandum from Donovan to FDR, dated May 27, 1942, related that a qualified financial representative from the Treasury Department, Charles Dyar, had been found to control the Swiss special funds accounts. Dyar was "picked out of a group of three men who had undergone training in codes and intelligence procedures at the COI's training center." Dyar, previously a financial officer of the Treasury, was fluent in German, French, and Dutch. Donovan told the president, "We have finally worked out with the State Department the appointment of a representative of this organization to proceed to Bern as 'Financial Attaché.' The representative is a man of almost a life-time experience in an analogous type of work. He will head up our service there." In June 1942, Dyar started his work as a Treasury Department attaché and assumed responsibility for disbursing special funds to Dulles and other OSS agents in Switzerland. He became known as Agent 227.[44]

Prior to the liberation of France, when the Swiss banking system was "virtually cut off from contact with other areas," Alcorn and Crocket directed special funds into Switzerland using clandestine methods. By early 1944, the Swiss mission had five officers, twelve cipher and translation clerks, and over a hundred foreign agents and paid informants. After the French–Swiss border reopened in 1944, OSS sought out better inroads to Swiss exchange markets. After Rehm and Lucas invested considerable effort and time to obtain financial reports from 227, they became frustrated and concerned about the state of his accounts. The Swiss mission had spent a little over $2 million dollars (SFr 8,944,724) since Dyar's arrival.

After he was recalled to the United States in 1944, Rehm dispatched an SFB auditor to Bern to review 227's accounts. Rehm informed Dyar of this in a letter:

> When 110 [i.e., Dulles] was recently in Washington, he was most cordial to our suggestion of an examination of the accounts which you maintain. Inasmuch as you have been unable to forward any reports, it appears that this is a good time for an official of this branch to make an examination and audit of your accounts and submit detailed reports to us in our established form. He will not only go over the past accounts, but he will also set up your books and records so they will conform to the accounting procedures used by all foreign offices.[45]

Thomas Bland returned to Washington in December 1944 to receive additional training at Area E. He was then given confidential instructions and dispatched to Bern to replace Dyar as Agent 1062. While in Washington he sent his former deputy, Nick Steichen, a brief cable saying that "I will probably be here for another three weeks or a month after which time will be going out again to join 110. Under this new set-up, I will be known as 1062 or Banker." Steichen's reply to the cable leaves no doubt as to the identity of the sender: "Your letter dated on 13 February 1945 arrived and it was rather surprising to hear from a number. However, your particular signature—the initial 'B'—was easily identified." Barney Bland arrived in Bern under State Department cover on March 27, 1945, together with

William Peratino, Agent 1006, the SFB field auditor for ETO. Peratino audited 227's accounts back to 1942.[46]

Agent 1062's top priority was to convert 227's accounts to double-entry accounting, the system to which all SFB offices around the world were switching. The tricky assignment required 1062 to reconcile the expense, payroll, and currency accounts with the new system. It was not an easy task because 227's accounts were not in good shape, and they included irreconcilable suspense items. A letter from Agent 1062 to Colonel Rehm (Agent 128) gives an update on the state of things: "I know that you fully appreciate that the tie-up in the records will require a little doing but I trust that my method of accomplishing the task will not cause you any confusion—if so, call on me and I'll be able to clarify the difficulties." Swiss financial operations were spread out, making it practically impossible to closely examine the accounts in other major cities:

> As you can see from this report we have offices all over the country—Lugano, Basel, Zurich, Geneva—and individuals operating at large, so it is no small matter to keep track of the operation on paper. And of course rigid control is out of the question unless I have time to travel. . . . The best that I can do is put on a little pressure here and there without pressing it far enough to hinder the operations as they exist for their main purpose of obtaining information, etc.[47]

The surrender and the end of the war was near by now and Barney Bland was helping Rehm to certify and close OSS special funds accounts in Switzerland.

SPECIAL FUNDS IN THE WAR AGAINST JAPAN

Donovan eagerly pursued a role for the OSS in the Far East and Pacific Theaters but faced an uphill battle in both. General Douglas MacArthur, who relied on his own intelligence network in the southwest Pacific Theater of Operations (PTO), saw no need for OSS involvement in his military operations. The SFB set up a makeshift office in Honolulu in anticipation of working with Admiral Chester W. Nimitz, but, without an official liaison, there was not much for the SFB chief, Commander R. Davis Halliwell, to do. Honolulu was the last scheduled stop on Colonel Rehm's world tour of SFB operations in September 1944. He despairingly noted in his trip report, "Upon reaching Honolulu I expected to find Comdr. Halliwell[48] starting his work with Admiral Chester W. Nimitz but the opposite was true. Halliwell had acquired satisfactory office space and set up for operations as planned. But all activities in this theater had been stopped and as a result Comdr. Halliwell was waiting for the situation to clear up." The Honolulu office never amounted to much and was shut down before the war ended.[49]

The Far East Theater of Operations posed a different set of political barriers, but in Southeast Asia Donovan managed to get his foot in the door. FETO spanned a large swath of Asia that included parts of China, Burma, India, Ceylon, Indochina, Thailand, Malaysia, and Singapore. Various parties weighed in on what role, if any, the OSS would play in the region. Generalissimo Chiang Kai-shek, commander of the Chinese National Revolutionary Army, and General Joseph Stillwell, the commander of US forces, strongly opposed activation of the OSS in China; the British opposed the establishment of OSS bases in India, concerned that the Americans would stir up anti-imperialistic sentiment. The prospects were not great, but there was a strategic interest in reclaiming the Burma Road from the Japanese. This was a major supply route, which linked the cities of Chungking, Kunming, and Lashio across harsh terrain, and it was under the watchful eye of the Japanese. Although strategically important to the war effort, it was a messy job that no one else wanted.[50]

OSS Detachment 101 was the first SO unit dispatched to Asia. It departed for China on May 29, 1942, after several months of training under the leadership of Captain Carl Eifler. En route to China, Stillwell diverted Detachment 101, first to New Delhi, and then to the northeastern Indian state of Assam, where in October 1942, a more permanent base camp was established on a tea plantation in Nazira. Detachment 101 was tasked with sabotaging Japanese military operations along the Burma Road. The first SO men parachuted into Burma on February 7, 1943, just over a month after the activation of the OSS. For the next two years, Detachment 101 carried out paramilitary operations against the Japanese in the tropical jungles of northern and central Burma.[51]

No special funds officers were dispatched to FETO until the arrival of Major George Gorin on September 1, 1943. Gorin lived in a tent encampment at Nazira. Upon his arrival, he established bank accounts at Lloyds Bank and the Imperial Bank of India in Calcutta; the latter had a regional branch in Dibrugarh, a short drive from Nazira. Gorin's duties included "obtaining cash from the Treasury fifty miles away, the answering of all correspondence, maintaining pay records of several hundred agents and employees, the initiation of allotment for such agents, making payments to them, and taking care of various financial matters on their account, the keeping of accounting records, and the preparation of Detachment and Washington reports"[52]

Calcutta was a strategic financial center in eastern India. All the money transmitted to Gorin from Washington first passed through the banks of Calcutta. In addition to its active foreign exchange markets, Calcutta banks offered the SFB a full range of financial services. The Indian banking system furnished a relatively secure means for moving OSS funds around the country. Dibrugarh, for example, was almost a thousand miles from Calcutta. The British, like the Germans, closely watched the movement of American money through the banks of India. Special funds, nevertheless, could be securely transferred between Calcutta and Dibrugarh without tipping off Japanese intelligence.[53]

Before Gorin arrived, one of Eifler's men, Major Robert Aitken, had maintained the accounts of Detachment 101. Recounting his early experience, Gorin reported that "in the early days of Detachment 101 operations in Burma, explicit and direct instructions were given by the Commanding Officer to field groups that no books of accounts were to be kept on monies sent in for use in field operations—and that such monies were to be written off the books." It was Eifler who insisted that all operational advances be reported as a bulk expense when received, which made it virtually impossible for Gorin and other SFB auditors to settle and certify Detachment 101's accounts at the war's end.[54]

Gorin was the only trained special funds officers living on-site, and he had to use non-bonded personnel from Detachment 101 to disburse money to the various training centers and forward bases around the region. This impossible situation was slow to change. For the first three months, Gorin was the only certified special funds officer in the region.

His first subagent cashier did not arrive in Nazira until May 1944, almost nine months after his arrival; what is even more stunning is that he had no full-time bookkeeper until January 1945. Rehm visited the Nazira base camp during his 1944 world tour of SFB operations. His report noted that the detachment had over five thousand foreign agents on its unvouchered payroll, with plans of increasing that number to ten thousand.[55]

To further improve the control of special funds, Gorin sent SFB subagent cashiers trained to disburse funds to forward bases at Bhamo, Myitkyina, and Akyab in Burma. Of course, it took time to find the right people, train them, and station them at remote SFB field offices. The disbursement of special funds to Detachment 101 reached its peak of about $200,000 per month at the end of 1944. Gorin reflected in one report that "while some Special Funds difficulties were due to lack of personnel, many were the result of the peculiar nature of the Detachment and its geographical set-up." At times, official procedures were simply ignored, for the "forward movement of operations could not be impeded merely for lack of approving signature." The SFB, as will be shown, never fully reconciled Detachment 101's disbursements with its expenditures for the period before Gorin arrived. Dimond's accounting records for 1943 show that Colonel Eifler approved the expenditures of over a half million dollars, for which there existed no financial records. Eifler later insisted on "complete clearance and relief from responsibility" and adamantly refused to sign a certification accepting responsibility for the expenditures of Detachment 101.[56]

The focus of the war effort was shifting from ETO to fighting the Japanese in FETO and PTO. Donovan had been trying to gain a foothold in China since the early days of the COI, without much success.[57] The breakthrough came when the United States and the Chinese Nationalists formed an alliance on April 15, 1943, known as the Sino-American Cooperative Organization. Though it took time, it was agreed that OSS could have a new regional base in Kunming, an important financial center strategically located where the Burma Road crosses from Burma into China. Special funds officers in the new SFB office in Kunming adapted quite well to the black market system, where Indian rupees and Dutch guilders could be exchanged for Chinese National (CN) dollars at bargain prices.

Once the OSS had a strong footing in FETO, Chungking, China,[58] emerged as another important financial center, alongside Calcutta, for transmitting special funds to the SFB. The city had served as the provisional capital of the Republic of China under Chiang Kai-shek since 1938. After the attack on Pearl Harbor, the city became strategically important in support of military and civilian operations. Chungking was protected from all directions by mountains, giving the city natural protection against would-be invaders. However, its remote location in central China made travel there by any means both difficult and expensive, which affected the financial operations of the SFB. Joseph Leete, SFB chief in New Delhi, candidly told Rehm in the summer of 1944, shortly after his arrival, "At this time the growing conviction came over me that Chungking, although the provisional capital of Free China, was as far as our business is concerned way out in the sticks. It is difficult of access, and is definitely not the center of military operations, or an advantageous place in which to conduct financial operations."[59]

In support of special funds operations, the Treasury Department sent a financial attaché, C. E. Evans, to Chungking, a major entry point for the unvouchered Treasury funds being disbursed in FETO. Although the first OSS outpost in Chungking opened at about the same time as the London office, it did not disburse special funds in large amounts until the OSS began ramping up its operations in FETO.

During the summer of 1943, the Southeast Asian Command (SEAC), a British–American alliance under Admiral Lord Louis Mountbatten of the British Navy, further expanded the operational presence of Allied forces across a large region that spanned India, lower Burma, Ceylon, Siam (Thailand), Malaya, and Sumatra. SEAC headquarters started out in New Delhi but was soon moved to Kandy in Ceylon. In March 1944, a major reorganization divided FETO into sub-theaters: the China-India-Burma Theater of Operations (CIBTO) and SEAC. Administrative control was divided among the main OSS detachments: Detachments 101 (Nazira and Calcutta), 202 (Chungking and Kunming), and 303 (New Delhi) in CIBTO, and Detachment 404 (Kandy) in SEAC.

Until SEAC was established, Major Gorin was the only SFB officer in the entire FETO. Then Rehm began sending special funds officers overseas, laying the groundwork for an SFB funding system in the Far East. Joseph Leete headed special funds operations in CIBTO, and Joseph Croll was sent to Kandy to head special funds operations for SEAC. Leete's headquarters started out in Calcutta (Detachment 303) but soon moved to Delhi.

Croll's new life in Kandy was a world apart from his time working as a full partner in the Wall Street brokerage firm Asiel & Company. Although OSS had originally trained him for SO work, the rapid expansion of special funds operations in the Far East Theater created an increased need for highly qualified officers with strong financial backgrounds. Croll arrived in Kandy in early March 1944 with a bond of $100,000. Like Gorin, he assumed control over accounts previously managed by OSS officers who lacked formal training in special funds. In Kandy, three special funds officers and a secretary shared a small room with just two chairs and a filing cabinet; crowded conditions "made any conversation a hindrance to everyone else." They had no adding machine of their own and, at the end of each month, would borrow one from the army office seven miles away. In his trip report on SFB's global operations, Rehm wrote: "As always happens when OSS builds up an organization, unless a Special Funds Officer is at work at the beginning, records are not all that they should be. But Capt. Croll with his two assistants were reconstructing records as best they could." As Rehm lamented, "To deal with figures in such surroundings does not make for accuracy or clean records." Because Detachment 404 was also disbursing money to OSS projects without clearly specifying which branch was responsible for spending the money (e.g., SI, SO, X-2, Communications, R&A, etc.), this made "the accounting extremely difficult to break down into branch expenditures." Accounting for secret expenditures was, as a result, being "done on an arbitrary basis," according to Rehm.[60]

Joseph Leete received the usual special funds training at Area E and then met with Dimond, Lennihan, and G. F. Allen of the Treasury Department for a secret briefing before leaving the United States. Leete, a forty-six-year-old naval attaché in Cairo, had recently been promoted to the rank of commander. He looked like a good fit on paper, but soon after he arrived in Calcutta, Dimond severely reprimanded him for some questionable financial decisions. Leete defended his actions and, in a letter to Rehm, awkwardly explained, "The financial transactions between Washington and me have been equally confusing to me. I believe the misunderstandings have their origin largely in the lack of a complete understanding of the situation from Calcutta all the way to Chunking before I left Washington. At that time, believe it or not, I did not know how much money was budgeted for 101 or for 202; nor did I have a true picture of how this money was transmitted or received." Here, he is alluding to his meeting with Dimond, Lennihan, and G. F. Allen prior to his departure. Goddard's scathing reply to Leete started: "We regret the confusion in your mind regarding the Projects for 101 and 202. Doug Dimond's recollection is that the monthly budgets and method of transmitting funds, etc., were all gone over in detail with you." In the margin, Leete scribbled in pencil, "*No!*" Goddard proceeded to quote a letter from the Treasury Department: "We confirm cable sent you at the wish of the Treasury to return the second $100,000 in Treasury checks obtained from Mr. Evans, as follows: 'TREASURY DEPARTMENT REQUESTS THAT YOU IMMEDIATELY DEPOSIT WITH EVANS, CHUNGKING, ANY UNCASHED TREASURY CHECKS WHICH MAY STILL BE IN YOUR POSSESSION.'"[61]

Either Leete was not told everything, or he did not fully understand his instructions from Washington. It seems he lacked the experience and communication skills to manage the complex financial operations in the Far East Theater, seventy-five hundred miles away from Washington. Rehm later wrote Gorin that he "was not at all satisfied that Joe Leete was or could do the job I expected of him"; in his permanent OSS record, he wrote: "Subject was not equipped as a Special Funds Officer but I was desperate for someone at the time. Comdr. Leete had handled money in Cairo so I thought that he might adapt himself to my requirements."[62]

Ensign Gunner Mykland was the SFB chief in Kunming; he handled financial operations for Detachment 202 and closely coordinated his financial activities with New Delhi. Mykland adapted well to the chaotic war atmosphere in the Far East, and his unique abilities did not go unnoticed. Thomas Coughlin, the OSS base commander in CIBTO, was so impressed by Mykland's performance in the field that he took him from the SFB to serve as his executive officer. Mykland was still running the Kunming office when Rehm visited the region in September 1944, but by then, his top assistant, Corporal Charles N. Davis, was in the process of being trained as his replacement. Davis went on to enjoy a long career in special funds with the CIA.

Rehm was astonished by the loose security he observed in Kunming, noting in his trip report: "Due to the problem of getting things over the 'hump' Mykland has no safe. Even though he has substantial amounts of CN$ on hand most of the time the only depository he can use is a wooden file. This, of course is shocking but under the circumstances there is nothing else that can be done." The SFB's heavy reliance on black exchange markets worldwide required the development of nonstandard accounting rules. These markets were secretive and completely unregulated, but, as with ordinary markets, money was made and lost in the exchanges. Mykland, a savvy trader of currency, found that black markets offered the most favorable rates and also had the advantage of concealing large financial transactions from Chinese security forces. To compare rates, Rehm arranged for Evans—the Treasury Department attaché in Chungking—to provide a record of his official transactions to compare with Mykland's, "this being the only reliable way to measure Mykland's purchases."[63]

Slush funds (i.e., counterfeit currency) also circulated in the war theaters and were in high demand in Southeast Asia. SFB chiefs kept slush funds separate from real currency, in different safes; otherwise, this money was accounted for like real money. Bigelow gave SFB chiefs, such as Gorin, the green light to use slush funds in operations whenever it was considered effective in meeting operational objectives. Bigelow wrote Gorin, "The whole matter of a United States Government Agency obtaining these reproductions and using them is a 'most secret' one, not only insofar as today's records are concerned but also so far as tomorrow's records may be concerned." In another letter to Joseph Croll, Bigelow writes:

> I have received acknowledgment of receipt by Major Gorin of a shipment from here of 5000—10 rupee notes—slush. In reply to a request by us of Major Gorin for samples, he has returned some samples of "slush notes." He then goes on to say that these notes are believed to be genuine. For clarity's sake, would you please let us know promptly what you people in the Far East Theater mean when you refer to "slush." For your information, we have been using the term slush when we have referred to American or British made reproductions of Japanese Government notes and have not referred to the Japanese made notes. There are three kinds of currencies apparently in Burma and NEI—namely—a) Burma rupee notes made by the Indian

Government, b) Burma rupee notes made by the Japanese Government and used by the Japanese military and c) American or British reproductions of (b). Please tell me which one is slush.[64]

After returning to Washington, Rehm appointed Captain Emmett "Eck" Echols to replace Leete as the CBI's special funds theater chief. Echols was privately recommended by his friend David Crocket, the SFB chief in Algiers and Caserta. Crocket introduced Rehm and Echols during Rehm's global tour of SFB financial operations. Echols then was serving as an assistant services officer for OSS Company A in Algiers. In mid-December 1944, Echols received special funds training at Area E in Maryland and also got detailed instructions from Washington. He was promoted to major before his arrival in Kandy to take over financial operations for Detachment 404. Emmett Echols deserves special mention here because for fifteen years he ran special funds operations for the CIA, and during that time he helped to pioneer the development of CIA's clandestine financial system.[65]

Echols majored in history at Yale University and received an MBA from Harvard Business School. Then, back in his hometown of Milwaukee, he worked for the British accounting firm Peat Marwick Mitchell & Co. and started a family with his wife, Janet. As a senior accountant in the firm, Echols prepared tax returns and supervised audits for a living—not the kind of work that normally conjures up images of spying, sabotage operations, and black markets. By the time he met Rehm, Echols had a solid financial background and had proven himself in the field. Crocket provided Rehm with a three-page letter of recommendation that remains in Echols's personnel file. Another anonymous recommendation describes Echols as "one of the most outstanding officers I have known. Professionally he is well qualified. He has shown initiative, intelligence and, above all, results to a marked degree. . . . His work compares favorably with many Lt. Colonels, which rank his predecessor held. In his field he has few equals." Echols turned out to be a whiz kid at managing the clandestine finances of the OSS in a war zone.[66]

Just before Echols arrived to take over for Leete, Washington administratively separated Calcutta from Detachment 101 to form Detachment 505. This reconfiguration in the SFB network severed the close financial link between Calcutta (Detachment 505) and Nazira (Detachment 101), for by then 101 was in the process of being liquidated. As Echols explained in a letter to Donovan in Washington, "Detachment 505, owing to its strategic location, has been established as the central funding agency for both the India-Burma and China Theaters." CIBTO was also split up into two sub-theaters: China and India-Burma. The India-Burma and SEAC sub-theaters were subsequently united to form a single theater that was headquartered in Kandy, Ceylon. Echols, in turn, replaced both Leete and Croll. Charles Davis, the head of special funds in Kunming, remained in charge of special funds operations in the China theater.[67]

Echols was given a rather sizable staff of eight special funds officers, twelve enlisted men, and three stenographers. As the theater chief, Echols immediately had to deal with some serious problems of accountability. SFB accounts at the different detachments were finding significant financial discrepancies that were linked to inter- and intra-theater transfers, which Echols defined as the "transfer of funds, expenses, and advances from one Detachment to another." For example, say that Detachment 202 purchased supplies for Detachment 101. The expense incurred often remained on the books of Detachment 202, instead of being transferred back to Detachment 101. This systemic problem deeply concerned Washington and would later complicate the task of reconciling the individual accounts for each detachment. Echols told Lucas in a letter to Washington that some "transfers [were] picked up twice and some never picked up either because the transfer notice was never received or when received was not clearly stated and it was impossible to tell whether the transfer should be picked up or was merely for information." Reforms introduced by Echols made the system of accounting for transfers more transparent to Rehm's senior staff back in Washington.[68]

Echols also had to deal with the liquidation of Detachment 101 and the certification of the final audit. Gorin was eager to head home but could not leave his post until Washington signed off on the audit. Until August 1943, the accounts of Detachment 101 remained under Eifler's control. Gorin took control of the records upon his arrival. According to Gorin, "In connection with this closing of the books and the final audit of 101 Special Funds accounts, there are several matters which should be mentioned now. First, the books (vouchers and cash books) for the period during which Major Aitken handled Special Funds here were surrendered last August [1944] by me to Comdr. Leete in Calcutta." Washington refused to accept Detachment 101's accounting due to a $400,000 discrepancy. On that matter, Echols told Gorin, "Irrespective of the reasons, two problems result. Reports to Washington which they can reconcile must be rendered. In addition the errors, by us or Washington, resulting in a discrepancy of over $400,000 must be corrected." Of course, most of the discrepancy was attributed to the accounting prior to Gorin's arrival, but the gist of it was that the SFB still had to reconcile the books. In plain truth, when expenditures could not be reconciled with disbursement records, they had to be certified retroactively in bulk amounts as a means of quietly closing the books. In November 1944, Dimond disbursed special funds to Detachment 101, Detachment 202, and SEAC in the amounts of $200,000, $100,000, and $100,000, respectively, to retroactively account for inconsistencies in the books. By the end of the war, Washington had little choice. The blanket certification of "suspense items" offered a convenient way of settling bad unexplained accounts. Echols's impressive handling of both the transfer problem and the convoluted audit of Detachment 101 caught the attention of Rehm and others back in Washington. He was a top recruit at the end of the war.[69]

ACCOUNTABILITY LOOPHOLES

The use of special funds in war theaters overseas was a stress on SFB's evolving accounting system following the activation of the OSS. On September 1, 1943, G. F. Allen, the Treasury Department's chief disbursing officer, sent a formal letter to Robert G. White, a top agent cashier in the South Building, acknowledging the phenomenal growth in special funds operations:

> The tremendous growth in the volume of business handled in the accounts of agent cashiers in recent months and in the amount of public funds outstanding in the hands of such agents, has prompted this office to request the cooperation of all concerned to the extent of keeping the volume of payments handled by agent cashiers within reasonable bounds, preventing

needless withdrawal of funds from the Treasury and recuing agent cashier balances where considered excessive.

With the activation of the OSS, unvouchered funds began flowing overseas in response to the demands of the clandestine services. No one considered the repercussions of transferring American dollars overseas in large amounts, which were then converted to foreign currency and stockpiled for use in field operations.[70]

The Treasury Department, the GAO, and the SFB introduced reforms during the last eighteen months of the war to address problems with the accounting of unvouchered funds. At the root of the problem was the initial requisition of Treasury funds. At this key transaction point, special funds disappeared into the secret personal accounts of bonded SFB agent cashiers. In January 1944, the Treasury Department opened foreign offices in London and Chungking to disburse special funds directly to the SFB station chiefs. This improved the Treasury Department's control over the special funds and allowed theater chiefs such as Alcorn and Echols to requisition money directly from Treasury attachés stationed overseas.

Rehm wrote Alcorn that the new system "will make it unnecessary to transfer through the Bankers Trust Company or any other commercial bank. You will act as Approving Officer." This change partly eliminated the need for large overseas transfers by SFB agent cashiers in Washington and New York; more importantly, the new control measure created an alternative path for securely channeling money to the OSS. This measure by no means eliminated the need for people like Dimond and Bigelow; its enduring effect was to increase the financial capacity of the system. The bonds on the agent cashiers in Washington were not lowered, but, in fact, were increased. Moreover, SFB agent cashiers were withdrawing large lump sums and then immediately charging the entire amount to expenditures before they disbursed the funds. G. F. Allen severely censured the SFB for this practice in several memos to Rehm and his senior paymasters.[71]

There was legitimate confusion inside the SFB over how to properly account for the purchase of foreign currencies. On May 30, 1944, Rehm and Lennihan met with G. A. Allen and E. J. Brennan, Allen's deputy, to discuss whether or not the exchange of currency could be legally considered a commodity for accounting purposes. Did the purchase of foreign currency using government funds constitute an expense at the time of the purchase? All agreed that foreign currency transactions represented a legitimate expense, but from a legal standpoint, the comptroller general of the United States, Lindsay Warren, had the final say.

On June 1, two days later, Colonel Rehm and James Donovan, the OSS general counsel, met with Warren and GAO's general counsel, J. C. McFarland, to discuss this. No one in the OSS knew for sure how Warren would view the matter. Donovan afterward noted in a memo to Edward Buxton, the acting OSS director, that they went into the meeting prepared for the worst: "If we found that [Warren] refused to advise us even informally on the subject, we then might have to turn to the Attorney General." They were relieved to find that the two GAO officials largely agreed with the prevailing view inside the SFB that the exchange of currency constituted an expense. However, the GAO officials also "declared that the Agent-Cashier who conducts the various day-to-day transactions in foreign exchange should keep a profit-and-loss account in which these transactions should be noted." The OSS was advised to account for a loss as an "operating expense" and to account for profits as a "miscellaneous receipt," which later would be returned to the Treasury.[72]

Bill Donovan was overseas when the meeting took place, but promptly sent a letter to Warren upon his return, graciously thanking him for his advice:

> Dear Mr. Warren,
>
> I returned from France yesterday and have been informed of the conference on 1 June 1944 in your office, at which you and your General Counsel discussed with our General Counsel and Chief, Special Funds Branch, several matters relating to foreign currencies purchased out our Special Funds. In other instances, in the past my staff have called to my attention the helpful assistance which your office has given us in certain of the difficult accounting problems confronting this agency.
>
> Since I am keenly aware of my responsibility with respect to our funds, I want you to know that I appreciate your experienced aid in this matter. You may rest assured that the advice of you and Mr. McFarland, on the problems discussed at the recent conference will be followed by this agency in all respects.

Donovan referred to matters involving the "purchase" of foreign currencies using special funds. This same issue resurfaced shortly after the establishment of the working fund for the CIG in 1946.[73]

It was the responsibility of the SFB chief and the OSS base commander to authorize the disbursement of special funds for use in field operations. Decisions about the use of special funds were often made in the field without any clear regulations or policy guidelines to follow, which placed all the responsibility on the shoulders of the SFB chiefs. The OSS Legal Division, the forerunner to the OGC, played an important advisory role in the use of special funds. One primary duty of lawyers dispatched to foreign field offices was to render opinions that addressed the legal ambiguities associated with the use of special funds. The War Report notes that the Legal Division "gave constant attention to problems of the Special Funds Branch, advising and assisting in the determination of financial procedures with respect to unvouchered funds in order to insure proper and accurate accounting for expenditures." In early 1944, A. William Asmuth Jr., from the Legal Division, "was given a desk in Special Funds Branch," and Captain John S. Warner served as his top assistant. Warner later served as the deputy general counsel to Lawrence Houston at the CIA.[74]

In May 1944, another major reorganization of the OSS moved the SFB higher in the organizational chart. As the War Report recounts, "It became evident that Special Funds represented such a highly specialized function, so closely connected with the operations of the principal branches which it served, that independent status was required." The financial administration of special funds was also being integrated into the operational infrastructure of the clandestine services. Now the SFB was moved out of the Services Directorate and elevated to a position directly under the Office of the Strategic Director. At this important juncture, Donovan formally delegated his certification authority to Rehm: "The Special Funds Branch shall be responsible to the director for the custody, use of and accounting for Special Funds." This transfer of authority is proclaimed in the preamble of the official branch history, which is aptly referred to as the "Special Funds Bible."[75]

The OSS routinely used unvouchered funds for SI and SO missions, but as the war neared its end, SFB chiefs were under pressure to use vouchered funds whenever possible. Working with the GAO and the Treasury Department, Congress created a new wartime category of vouchered funds under the National War Agency Appropriation Act on June 28, 1944. Like unvouchered funds, vouchered funds in this category could be spent "without regard to the provisions of law and regulation relating to the expenditure of Government funds or the employment of persons in Government service."[76] However, unlike unvouchered funds, these funds remained under the GAO's jurisdiction. In contrast with special funds, these accounts were audited by the GAO; the office could ask questions about how the money was used, that is, it could look behind the certificate.[77]

By late spring 1944, all SFB foreign offices were instructed by the Accounting Division to switch over to a double-entry accounting system. The new standards required that expenditures, transfers, and conversions be reported monthly in dollar amounts. Financial reports were supposed to contain a balanced account for each foreign currency in dollar units, but that did not always happen. After these reforms went into effect, Lucas severely criticized the accounting practices of the foreign offices in a letter to Alcorn:

> It has recently come to the attention of [the] Special Funds Office that in some of the theaters the Special Funds Officers have failed to maintain any coordinated system between accounting entries in the various ledgers and the basic documents, such as receipts for money, authorizations, expense accounts, etc. The result has been that the files of some of the field offices contain a mass of receipts, often in foreign languages, with no means of associating them with the entries which have been made in the ledgers.[78]

With the end of the war in sight, Rehm and Lucas realized that the SFB would soon have to demonstrate accountability for the money that had passed through its hands. In early 1945, Rehm created an autonomous field auditing division to carry out independent site audits of all the SFB offices around the world. He appointed William Peratino, an experienced special funds officer, as SFB's top field auditor in ETO. Peratino led the effort to audit the books of Agent 227 in Switzerland and conducted the final audit of Crocket's accounts at the Mediterranean Theater headquarters in Caserta. Second Lieutenant Frederick Richards was the top field auditor in FETO. Richards first audited the books in Kunming, Detachment 202, and then traveled to Nazira for the final settlement and certification of Detachment 101's books.[79]

The accountability problems of the OSS remained in-house, for the most part. However, one extremely damaging report was eventually seen by President Harry Truman, shortly after he took the oath of office following the death of FDR. This highly classified investigation of the OSS was conducted by Richard Park, an intelligence officer in G-2 who worked under Major General Strong—Donovan's nemesis. According to Park, in a secret meeting with the president on November 27, 1944, Roosevelt directed him to personally carry out a global investigation of the OSS—an action that Strong would have been strongly in favor of. The investigation led to what is known as the Park Report, but the actual story behind this investigation remains murky at best.

The Park Report details an alleged investigation of OSS's global operations; it focuses on the use of special funds. Because the report offers little insight into the inner workings of the SFB, it is somewhat suspect. Park concluded that:

> If the O.S.S. is investigated after the war it may easily prove to have been relatively the most expensive and wasteful agency of the government. With a $57,000,000 budget, $37,000,000 of which may be expended without provision of law governing use of public funds for material and personnel, the possibilities of waste are apparent. . . . It is believed the organization would have a difficult time justifying the expenditure of extremely large sums of money by results accomplished.

Perceived lack of security in the OSS was a popular criticism of the agency leveled by Donovan's detractors. Park minced no words, stating in his official report, "The security of the O.S.S. which should be above question is poor, both here and abroad." He concludes: "If the O.S.S. is permitted to continue with its present organization, it may do further serious harm to citizens, business interests, and national interests of the United States." Although Truman never mentioned the Park Report in any of his later writing, he wasted little time in terminating the OSS when the war ended. He also kept Donovan out of the postwar planning for a future peacetime intelligence service.[80]

By the war's end, few people in the US government knew of the SFB's financial operations or its geographical extent. The few who understood the importance of unvouchered funds in the intelligence arena believed that the future success of any peacetime intelligence service depended on preserving the SFB and its global administration.

5. The Central Intelligence Group

SPECIAL FUNDS AND THE STRATEGIC SERVICES UNIT

On September 20, 1945, Truman issued Executive Order 9621, which liquidated the OSS and divided its most valuable assets between the State and War Departments. The War Department bounty included 9,028 OSS employees (of a total of 10,390). On that same day, Truman fired Bill Donovan in a personal letter that began, "My Dear General Donovan"; in another letter, he instructed Secretary of State James Byrnes to "take the lead in developing a comprehensive and coordinated foreign intelligence program with all Federal agencies concerned with that type of activity."[1]

The Strategic Services Unit (SSU) was formed in the War Department from the remnants of the OSS clandestine services and its financial administration, namely, special funds. It was formally activated on September 29, 1945, for the purpose of continuing the ongoing postwar intelligence operations of the OSS in Europe. Basically a scaled-down version of the OSS, the SSU was supposed to have a brief existence. OSS Asian operations were mostly liquidated at the end of the war; a modest infrastructure was left to support the continued flow of unvouchered funds into Europe. Robert Alcorn remained in Europe after the war and was instrumental in establishing major funding centers in London, Paris, and Berlin, with the Paris Office serving as the headquarters.[2]

There was no easy way to separate the administration of vouchered and unvouchered funds. Both were essential to running the OSS, but sharp reductions in funding forced organizational changes during the summer of 1945. On June 30, the SFB (unvouchered) and the Finance (vouchered) Branch were reunited within the Services Directorate in a reconstituted Finance Branch that included subdivisions for special funds and fiscal.[3] Lane Rehm headed the new branch and oversaw the administration of both vouchered and unvouchered funds. Doug Dimond, the agent cashier for SO, headed the special funds division. Special funds provided financial support for postwar intelligence operations in Europe. Another highly recruited financial officer, Kenneth Woodring, headed the fiscal division. Woodring served as COI's assistant chief of the Budget and Finance Division under Cecil Barnes, and later headed the (former) OSS Finance Branch. He went on to have a long career high up in the CIA's financial administration.[4]

With SSU's activation, its general council had to field legal questions related to the use of unvouchered funds in a postwar operational environment. The most pressing question was whether Donovan's confidential funds authority as strategic director could be transferred to the secretary of war by the president under Executive Order 9621. In response to these pointed questions, the OGC concluded: "It is the opinion of this office that Executive Order No. 9621 legally transfers to the secretary of war the authority granted . . . to the Director of the Office of Strategic Services to account for objects of a confidential nature solely on the certificate of the Director and that such a certificate would be a sufficient voucher for the amount therein certified." This legal opinion effectively authorized the secretary of war to continue disbursing special funds on his certificate in support of the SSU's overseas operations.[5]

Rehm, Dimond, and Lucas wanted no part of a future intelligence service and tendered their resignations, requesting to be discharged at the earliest possible time. Bigelow agreed to stay on after he was promised a raise. All of these key figures remained with the SSU for a few additional months to ensure continuity. Lucas's replacement, Sergeant Vernon Turner, also wanted to leave but lacked enough military credit for a discharge. Rehm expanded the Accounts Division at the end of the war, adding a subdivision to conduct site audits overseas. Turner headed that subdivision and oversaw the audit of special funds offices around the world.

The departure of key SFB officials opened the door for other special funds officers to move up inside a new and growing bureaucracy. Many found the work challenging and exciting; it gave them the opportunity to see the world in an adventurous government job that bore tremendous fiduciary power. The SSU recruited the cream of the crop from the remaining SFB officers, and many went on to serve the country during the Cold War. Emmett Echols, the star SFB prospect from Kandy, wrote to his friend and former SFB colleague Bob Barker in March 1947: "As you see by the newspapers the world is still a very interesting place and your guess is as good as mine to the future. I must admit the idea of being overseas where things are happening is very appealing."[6]

Robert Alcorn, next in line to inherit Rehm's fiefdom, also expressed a desire to return to his former life. Like Rehm, he agreed to serve a few months longer until an adequate replacement was found. Alcorn returned to Washington in November 1945 for additional training; in early January, he initially replaced Dimond as chief of Special Funds. Just before Alcorn took over for Rehm, the budget office joined the Finance Branch and was renamed the Budget and Finance Branch. Alcorn replaced Rehm as chief a few days before the creation of the CIG on January 22.

Alcorn sent a letter to Lois Frauenheim, the special funds chief in Austria, shortly before he resigned his position in May. Written just three months before the secret August 1946 conference, it provides intriguing insight into the makeup of special funds and gives an organizational outline of operations in Washington and worldwide. He starts off talking about Washington: "The shop is more streamlined than ever and is well salted with personnel who have had field experience. Eck will take over with such support as Emmerson Bigelow, Robey Read, Charlie Davis, Verne Turner, Mrs. Hall, Mrs. Jones, and Mrs. Welborn, to mention a few. And in the wings vacationing, but alerted, are Barney Bland, Nick Steichen, Charlie Ratchford, and Armand Poyant, so we are well cushioned." Next, he divulged the personnel heading the remaining special funds offices in Europe and Asia: "By now Jim MacMillan is in London, Doris Werntz is in Paris, and of course Fred Richards is in Bern, Frank Mangeng in Germany (with Miss A'Lousie Charles on the way to him), Ralph Roberts in Stockholm, Gardner MacPherson in Lisbon and Madrid, Bill Bryant in Cairo.[7] And, with Singapore and Calcutta closed out, Barker is replacing Julian in Shanghai. In short, we are fairly well covered. . . . I therefore feel that I can now bow out of the picture and head for the Connecticut hills."[8]

Edward R. Saunders, chief of the Budget Division, replaced Alcorn as head of the Budget and Finance Branch.[9] Saunders stands out as arguably the most significant holdover from the OSS. He came from the Federal Deposit Insurance Corporation (FDIC) in the fall of 1943 to serve as the chief of the OSS Budget Division in the Budget and Finance Branch, where he helped to restore order to a "sorely depleted staff." In 1950, DCI Bedell Smith named Saunders as the first comptroller of the CIA, a position he served in for over ten years. This appointment stabilized the financial administration at the chief level. Below Saunders, Emmett Echols ran the special funds division, which now consisted of "twenty-five to thirty-five persons." David Odgan headed the Fiscal Division, with "thirty-five to forty-five persons," and Kenneth Woodring ran the Budget Division, with "ten to fifteen persons." All of these men played important roles in the future development of CIA's clandestine funding system.[10]

THE FIRST PEACETIME INTELLIGENCE SERVICE

On January 22, 1946, President Truman sent his historic letter to the Secretaries of the State (James Byrnes), War (Robert Patterson), and Navy (James Forrestal) Departments, directing them to form a supreme intelligence board called the "National Intelligence Authority" (NIA). The board would have four voting members: the Secretaries of State, War, and Navy and a personal representative of the president. Truman's letter further stated, "Within the limits of available appropriations, you shall each from time to time assign persons and facilities from your respective Departments, which persons shall collectively form a Central Intelligence Group, under the direction of a Director of Central Intelligence, assist the National Intelligence Authority." Truman named Fleet Admiral William D. Leahy to be his personal representative on the NIA.[11]

The NIA was tasked with the planning, development, coordination, and oversight of the US intelligence agenda. The DCI, a new member of the US national security establishment, was designated to serve as a coordinator between the NIA and CIG; the DCI was also a nonvoting member of the board. Truman's selection of Rear Admiral Sidney Souers, deputy director of the ONI, to serve as the first DCI was a move that surely helped to appease Forrestal, secretary of the navy, who had acquired little from the breakup of the OSS. Souers never coveted his new title and agreed to serve only until a more suitable candidate could be found.[12]

Building a functioning spy organization from scratch required money, people, and office space. It was agreed that the State, War, and Navy Departments would secretly channel funds to the CIG in a 1–2–1 tripartite arrangement, in which the War Department contributed twice as much as the others. It was thought that the president's goals for the CIG could be better accomplished by keeping Congress out of the funding process, but this idea proved shortsighted.[13]

The CIG was a far cry from the national intelligence service that Donovan once envisioned. Its material assets, personnel, and finances depended on funds received from its three powerful financiers. And the DCI, a nonvoting member of the board, had no real power to influence the decision-making of the NIA, nor was he CIG's department head in a statutory sense. This posed a dilemma: the DCI was a coordinator with no real authority over the group. Thomas Troy wonderfully captures this conundrum in his administrative history: "[Truman's letter] created a headless body and bodyless head! It created a 'Central Intelligence Group' to work 'under the direction of a Director of Central Intelligence.' The CIG was not 'headed' by the DCI; nor was the DCI the 'head' of the CIG. CIG worked 'under [his] direction.'" According to Troy, the DCI "directed the work of the people who were assigned to him, but they were not his people to hire, train, assign reassign, direct, supervise, retire, or fire; they were simply on loan to him."

Troy states that Souers "served others' ideas, had several bosses, had neither money nor people of his own, and literally had no 'house,' or organization, of his own in which to be master." Truman selected Hoyt Vandenberg to replace Souers in June. The CIG was still not up and running at that point.[14]

BUDGET AND ACCOUNTING WOES

The NIA had to build a national intelligence service from scratch, using money, people, and office space from its respective departments. It issued its first two directives on February 8. NIA Directive No. 1 placed the CIG under the NIA's authority and established a rudimentary charter for the organization. NIA Directive No. 2 provided the blueprint for CIG's organization and functions, which consisted of an Administrative Section, a Central Planning Staff, a Central Reports Staff, and a Central Intelligence Services. The Central Planning and Report staffs, which were started under Souers, still had no authorization when he stepped down. The CIG started out with a staff of 165—sixty-one assigned to Central Reports, forty to Central Planning, and sixty-four to the Administrative Section. Office space was found in the "New War Department Building" at Virginia Avenue and Twenty-First Street.[15]

On April 2, 1946, the NIA issued a directive that prepared for the liquidation of the SSU. NIA Directive No. 4 stated: "The national interest demands that the complete liquidation of SSU shall not be accomplished until it is determined which of its functions and activities are required for the permanent Federal foreign intelligence program, and should therefore be transferred to the Central Intelligence Group or other agencies in order that its useful assets may not be lost." The CIG was being set up to absorb the SSU's administrative infrastructure.

It was the breakup of the OSS all over again, except that the CIG was not yet ready to absorb the SSU's operational assets. The NIA directive placed no timetable on the transition. In the meantime, it allowed the SSU, via the Finance Division, to provide off-the-books funding to the CIG: "During the period of liquidation, the SSU should be administered and operated so as to service, to the extent practical, the intelligence agencies subject to our coordination. The Director of Central Intelligence shall issue the necessary directives required to accomplish this mission." In addition to serving as a liaison between the NIA and the CIG, the DCI also served as a liaison between the SSU and the CIG. The SSU, having inherited the OSS's assets and agenda at the end of the war, seamlessly continued to conduct postwar operations in Europe.[16]

After serving just four months, Souers stepped down and passed the torch to Hoyt Vandenberg, another insider in the nascent intelligence community. Souers's departure from the intelligence business was short-lived, however. A year later, he was named executive secretary of the National Security Council, and, from September 1947 to January 1950, he served as a direct liaison between the NSC and the CIA—ironically, with duties very similar to those he had performed as DCI.

The NIA selected Lieutenant General Hoyt S. Vandenberg, the assistant chief of staff for G-2, from among the leaders of the burgeoning intelligence community. This selection was in most respects a popular choice. Probably his most important attribute, from the NIA standpoint, was that he was the nephew of Arthur Vandenberg, the powerful Republican senator from Michigan. It can also be argued that, behind the scenes, his appointment finally ended the long-standing feud that had started between Donovan and Major General George Strong. The forty-seven-year-old Vandenberg was consumed with personal ambition, and he was well positioned to leave a mark on the future of American intelligence.[17]

Lawrence Houston, the former OSS legal counsel, transferred from the SSU to serve as Souers's chief counsel soon after the creation of the CIG. By now, Houston realized that the DCI had no statutory power and, consequently, could not run CIG's administration like a department head. At the root of all this lay the festering problem of how to secretly fund the agency in the longer term using unvouchered funds. In Souers's final report to the NIA before he stepped down, he concluded: "The National Intelligence Authority and the Central Intelligence Group should obtain enabling legislation and an independent budget as soon as possible, either as part of a new national defense organization or as a separate agency, in order that (1) urgently needed central intelligence operations may be effectively and efficiently conducted by the Central Intelligence Group, and (2) the National Intelligence Authority and the Central Intelligence Group will have the necessary authority and standing to develop, support, coordinate and direct an adequate Federal intelligence program for the national security." The problem of funding was compounded by the DCI's lack of authority over CIG's day-to-day operations.[18]

Vandenberg had little time to ease into his new job. On June 13, just three days after he had been sworn in, the new DCI received an alarming memo from Lawrence Houston admonishing him about the great challenges ahead. Houston bluntly explained that in trying to enforce his administrative authority over the CIG he would be walking a legal tight rope, for the DCI had no real power or authority to do anything. Even so, he still bore legal responsibility for the group's actions. It was a classic catch-22. Houston candidly told him that the DCI was "purely a coordination function with no substance or authority to act on its own responsibility in other than an advisory and directing capacity." Houston further informed him that he had no legal authority "(A) To take personnel actions; (B) To certify payrolls and vouchers, (C) To authorize travel; (D) To procure supplies directly for itself, or enter into contracts." The real problem, though, was "that CIG has no power to expend Government funds." Although the secretary of war could give the DCI discretionary authority to spend unvouchered funds, "the certification of the voucher would have to be done by the Secretary."[19]

If this was not enough to give Vandenberg pause for thought, Houston went on to explain that under the Independent Offices Appropriations Act of 1945, the CIG could only receive funding for one year. Houston's memo ended on this despondent note: "After 22 January 1947, [State, War, and Navy] could not even furnish unvouchered funds to the Director, . . . and it would be questionable whether the Departments could furnish personnel and supplies paid for out of vouchered funds." In an interview with author John Ranelagh many years later, Houston recalled: "We went to the books and found there was a statute which said there could not be an organization set up in the executive branch for more than one year without statutory background. There was no statutory background at all."[20]

Vandenberg then took the issue to the NIA; in response, Directive No. 5 was issued on July 8. Titled "Functions of the Director of Central Intelligence," it more explicitly spelled out the DCI's functions in the day-to-day operations. Still, this was far from an act of Congress. Under this NIA directive, the DCI's duties were defined around three broad areas of intelligence: 1) correlation and evaluation of intelligence relating to national security, and dissemination of intelligence reports within the government; 2) planning the activities of the US intelligence community related to national security; and 3) performance of "such services of common concern as the National Intelligence Authority determines can be more efficiently accomplished centrally." However, it was not at all clear that the NIA had the legal authority to name the DCI as CIG's chief administrator.[21]

Vandenberg next established the Office of Research and Evaluation and the Office of Special Operations (OSO). Research and Evaluation handled the correlation, collation, evaluation, and reporting of intelligence estimates, whereas special operations remained the core of the clandestine services. OSO was officially activated on July 11, the fifth anniversary of Donovan's appointment as COI. The Office of Research and Evaluation started operations on July 22; soon afterward, its name was changed to the Office of Research and Estimates, which better conveyed its role as a provider of intelligence estimates to decision-makers.[22]

On July 17, at the fourth meeting of the NIA, Vandenberg argued in favor of seeking statutory recognition for the CIG, which in turn would provide the DCI with confidential funds authority and a congressional source of funding. He argued that "he must have his own funds and be able to hire people." He asserted that "an adequate and capable staff" was urgently needed to carry out the functions of the CIG and that it was "extremely difficult administratively to procure the necessary personnel under the present arrangement."

In a challenge to Vandenberg's assessment, Secretary of State Byrnes said that it was his "understanding that the N.I.A. was intentionally established as it is to avoid the necessity for an independent budget." Robert Patterson, the secretary of war, agreed in general with Byrnes's assessment, but added that the rapidly growing national intelligence system was "designed to conceal, for security reasons, the amount of money being spent on central intelligence"; he further emphasized that "it would be difficult to explain to Congress the need for intelligence funds without jeopardizing security." Presenting a different view, Admiral Leahy suggested that the budgetary woes of the CIG should have been anticipated because "it was always understood that C.I.G. eventually would broaden its scope." Leahy suggested it was now time for the NIA to "attempt to get its own appropriations," but he felt these appropriations "should be small, since the three departments should continue to furnish the bulk of the necessary funds." He advocated continuing the status quo, mainly because of the need for secrecy, for he was "convinced that C.I.G. must have funds for which it does not have to account in detail." Leahy, of course, was alluding here to unvouchered funds.

To counter the NIA's arguments, Vandenberg simply did the administrative math: "Each personnel action must be handled at present by 100 people in each department. This means that knowledge of C.I.G. personnel is exposed to 300 people in the three departments." He argued that handling personnel actions within CIG itself would improve security and that a tripartite funding system required "defending three separate appropriations acts before the Senate and the House of Representatives." Vandenberg proposed unifying the budget under one entity, which he claimed would better conceal the CIG and its operations. Leahy argued against moving too quickly: "With regard to a bill to obtain an independent budget and status for N.I.A., the President considers it inadvisable to attempt to present such a bill before Congress. The President feels that there is not enough time for the N.I.A. to give this question sufficient study." It was left to Vandenberg to point out that the NIA and the CIG were not the same bureaucratic entity. He reminded the principals that "C.I.G. is not an agency authorized to disburse funds. Therefore, even with funds from the departments, it would require disbursing and authenticating officers, plus the necessary accounting organization in C.I.G. He felt that this was requiring four fiscal operations where one should suffice."[23]

The bottom line was that "without money there could be no personnel actions," and none of the solutions proposed by the principal members removed "the difficulty of obtaining funds from the Departments." Vandenberg pointed out that only $178,000 of the $300,000 requested from the NIA had been made available to the CIG. He wanted his own budget because the "C.I.G. could never be certain of receiving the funds which it requested and defended unless they were appropriated directly to C.I.G." And, as Houston had cautioned earlier, he "needed money, the authority to spend it, and the authority to hire and fire."[24]

Vandenberg won the day, and, by the end of the meeting, Secretary Byrnes agreed to discuss CIG's funding problems with the budget director and "report back to the Authority." He, in turn, set up meetings with the budget bureau, the Treasury Department, and the GAO to discuss possible solutions to the CIG's funding problems. He reported to the NIA in a July 30 memo: "The Bureau of the Budget and the Treasury Department have definitely indicated a willingness to cooperate, and the General Accounting Office has promised to give the matter sympathetic consideration." Treasury and the GAO both agreed that a formal request should be made and that it would "be considered expeditiously."[25]

With these assurances, Vandenberg drafted a letter to Treasury Secretary John Snyder and Comptroller General Lindsay Warren for the NIA members to sign. The letter asked the Treasury Department and the GAO for assistance in setting up a special working fund for the CIG, citing Truman's January 22 directive as the underlying authority: "The National Intelligence Authority has, through a series of directives to the Director of Central Intelligence, established over-all policies for foreign intelligence activities related to the national security, and has directed that the Central Intelligence Group engage in certain centralized intelligence activities that are of common interest to the Departments herein concerned." This letter candidly admitted that the "threefold method of supply has become so cumbersome as to impair seriously the administration of the Central Intelligence Group and is becoming an important threat to the security of its operations." The NIA was looking to the government's two most powerful financial controllers for help, an action they originally had hoped to avoid.[26]

Warren, tellingly, did not send a formal replay. A handwritten note by E. Lyle Fisher appears at the bottom of the NIA letter, noting: "This matter was discussed personally with the Comptroller General, the details and procedures were explained to him, and he authorized establishing the working fund as requested." From this point on, the GAO kept the discussions informal and worked through back channels. The first meeting was set for August 7. At this historical juncture, Lyle Fisher, the acting general counsel, was just beginning his long-term involvement in the development of a clandestine budget and accounting system for the CIA.[27]

PART THREE
SECRET INTELLIGENCE FUNDING IN PEACETIME

6. Public Oversight of the Atomic Bomb

THE GAO AND THE ATOMIC ENERGY ACT OF 1946

The atomic bombs dropped on the Japanese cities of Hiroshima and Nagasaki awakened the world to the destructive potential of a nuclear war. The possibility that enemy powers could use nuclear weapons against the United States engendered a compelling rationale for the use of unvouchered funds in peacetime. In the early postwar era, the newly formed Senate Special Committee on Atomic Energy drafted historic legislation aimed at transferring control of the US nuclear weapons program from the military to the civilian government. The Atomic Energy Act of 1946 created, among other things, a five-member civilian board known as the Atomic Energy Commission (AEC).

On April 4, 1946, Comptroller General Lindsay Warren, Assistant Comptroller General Frank L. Yates, and acting General Counsel E. Lyle Fisher appeared before the special committee chaired by Senator Brien McMahon (D-Connecticut). Committee member Senator Harry Byrd had learned during an informal discussion with his old friend Lindsay Warren that Warren was completely in the dark about an obscure provision in the bill on confidential expenditures that transferred the audit and certification powers of the comptroller general to the AEC. The passage of this bill would have stripped Warren and the GAO of the authority to audit the AEC's disbursals and expenditures in matters related to the development of nuclear weapons.

Section 10 of the bill authorized the AEC commissioners to spend money on anything "which the Commission shall determine and certify to have been necessary to carry out the provisions of [the] act." From Warren's standpoint, the most objectionable aspect of the provision was that it gave the AEC absolute control over the funds appropriated to it by Congress. Furthermore, it did not assign certification authority to a single person, such as the committee chairman, leaving no single person on the AEC individually accountable for the financial decisions of the committee. Warren repeatedly attacked the provision during his testimony, on the grounds that individual accountability was an essential part of the treasury system.[1]

Warren stated that he was "unalterably opposed" to the provision, pointing out that, with the exception of Byrd, no one had consulted him about the objectionable language:

> It is not necessary for me to remind you that the General Accounting Office as well as the comptroller general is an agent of the Congress. We are entirely disassociated from the executive branch of the Government, and that view was reaffirmed by the Congress with passage of the recent reorganization bill which provided that the comptroller general of the United States and the General Accounting Office are a part of the legislative branch of the Government. Therefore, except for the friendly interest of Members of Congress who believe in responsible fiscal accountability, naturally we would have no way in the General Accounting Office to know of provisions such as this. The General Accounting Office in my opinion is the last great bulwark in this Nation for the protection of the taxpayers against unbridled and illegal expenditures of appropriated funds. . . . An analysis of [the provision] will show you and will convince you that it is a mockery and a fraud.[2]

Senator Byrd asked Warren the first question: "It was stated to the committee by one of the associates of the committee that these provisions have been agreed to by the assistant general counsel of the Comptroller General's Office. Is this correct?" Warren replied, "Senator, that is absolutely incorrect. He is here today. Mr. Fisher is acting general counsel. Mr. Ellis is one of my administrative assistants. They are two of the ablest men that we have in the General Accounting Office. They have my full confidence, and they tell me that never, directly or indirectly, did they agree to any such provision as this, which is contrary to the entire policy of our Office."[3]

Warren proceeded to argue that if the bill passed it would eliminate a critically important check on the spending of the executive branch. He contended that it would be negligent for Congress to give the spender of public funds the statutory authority to secretly certify their own expenditures: "The difference lies between an examination by those who spend the money and one by an independent agency looking over it which is not responsible under the executive branch of the Government but is responsible to the Congress itself."[4]

There was also fear that the provision on unvouchered spending would be a slippery slope that would be seized upon by other executive departments in the national security establishment. Assistant Comptroller General Frank Yates told the committee, "It is the effective result of the audit by the General Accounting Office which flows from the knowledge on the part of the spending officers that the General Accounting Office can disallow credit or withhold funds. Now, if you will write in the law that the very spending agency, the Commission itself, can by a stroke of the pen remove any disallowance of credit or withholding of funds, then all responsible officers for funds know that the Commission under which they are operating can save their own skins, and your effective deterrent is gone."[5]

One of the committee members asked Warren whether there was some other language that he would approve of to which he responded:

> Notwithstanding the provisions of any other law governing the expenditure of public funds, the General Accounting Office in the settlement of the accounts pertaining to the operations of the Commission may allow credit for any expenditure shown to have been necessary to carry out the provision of this Act. Now that leaves the law just as it is, but puts the discretion in the comptroller general rather than in the Commission, because then Congress has a target to shoot at if there is anything wrong. You would never find anything, you would never hear anything, about the Commission handling these. But if I should do anything wrong, then I am subject to removal or impeachment, and you have got it centered in one person—not that I want that authority. Instead of leaving that discretion in the Commission, under this language you would leave it in me.[6]

Warren was distinguishing here between individual and group accountability. With the former, a person is held legally accountable for a government action, and that person can be impeached or even prosecuted "if there is anything wrong." In the US system of financial management, the disbursing agents, certifying officers, and, ultimately, the comptroller general are individually accountable for the financial transactions of the US government. In contrast, the provision in question would leave legal accountability for a government action evenly and diffusely distributed among the small group of individuals that formed the AEC—all short-term political appointees. Public policy decisions in general tend to be group-oriented decisions. Congressional legislation, for example, clearly falls into the category of group accountability because the whole Congress ultimately bears responsibility for the adverse social effects of bad bills and pork barrel spending appropriations that benefit a few at the expense of the citizenry as a whole.[7]

The Special Congressional Committee on Atomic Energy removed Section 10 from the AEC Charter, after "the War Department advised that it was not interested in the blanket exception" for the AEC. The Atomic Energy Act of 1946 was signed into law by President Truman on August 1, 1946, the week before the August 7 meeting. Declassified CIA records reveal that Lawrence Houston schooled himself on the AEC case prior to drafting special enabling legislation for the CIA. Houston's April 22 memo, with subject header "GAO and Unvouchered Funds," states, "Mr. Warren's testimony will not be printed for some time but Captain West promised to . . . send us copies when they came through." Houston appears to have been acutely interested in acquiring insight into Warren's strong views on unvouchered funds.[8]

THE GAO AND THE MANHATTAN PROJECT

Warren, intent on getting his point across, dramatically declared at a key moment in his testimony: "I may surprise the committee when I tell you that we were in on the atomic secret from the very beginning." He went on to say:

> I have had no conversation with General Groves in several months. I will say, however, that he has personally thanked me and other officials of the General Accounting Office several times for our fine cooperation and I understand that in a public speech here in Washington, before a group of scientists, he expressed high commendation of the work of the General Accounting Office. . . . I would suggest if you have any doubt as to this coop-

> eration that you might ask General Groves, because I will say this for him: From the very beginning he has insisted upon a full audit and a full accountability to the General Accounting Office. Now, if that went on in war, if we passed upon $2,000,000,000 of these expenditures in war, I cannot see the argument as to why they should not be audited in peace.

The GAO had audited the most highly classified project in the history of the United States without Congress knowing about it.[9]

Leslie Groves also testified at the hearing and told the committee, "I always had the very strong personal feeling that it was a very desirable thing, because it gives the United States the protection it needs and it also removes from the officer who is responsible, a tremendous responsibility. It would be a very bad thing . . . to remove these accounts [of AEC] from the control of the Comptroller General." General Groves alluded to Warren's testimony in his 1963 memoir on the Manhattan Project, *Now It Can Be Told*: "In view of the unusual procedures by which we obtained funds and that we had to follow in spending these large sums of public money, I derived particular satisfaction from the testimony that the Comptroller General of the United States gave before the Senate's Special Committee on Atomic Energy."[10]

Warren and Groves met for the first time soon after Enrico Fermi's historic experiment on a squash court at the University of Chicago on December 2, 1942, in what proved to be the first controlled nuclear reaction. With this successful demonstration, the US government began planning for the construction of facilities to manufacture enriched uranium and plutonium, the main ingredients for an atomic bomb. The plants were costly to build and were kept secret from the American public. Only a few companies had the size, expertise, and industrial know-how to take on such a huge and costly project.

In April 1943, Secretary of War Henry Stimson sent Warren drafts of two contracts with DuPont, noting, according to Trask, "their extreme secrecy and requesting that knowledge of the existence and provisions of the contracts be limited to Warren and whoever reviewed them in GAO." When they met, Groves gave Warren a copy of the letter that Vannevar Bush, director of the Office of Scientific Research, had sent to Roosevelt, asking the president "to approve a special project (the atomic bomb work) and to authorize the chief of engineers to enter into contracts necessary to carry on the project." Wanting a single lead contractor, Groves secretly solicited the DuPont Company in late October 1942. He offered the company a negotiated contract that promised to cover all DuPont's costs of production—most of which were not well quantified at this stage of the bomb's development—in addition to a guaranteed profit. It was more than a carrot on a stick; Groves was prepared to pay DuPont whatever it demanded.[11]

A single representative from DuPont observed Fermi's experiment, which likely helped gain the company's willing participation. DuPont's risk-averse executives, however, remained skeptical about the project's viability and the potential liability involved. They were, after all, being asked to develop the production facilities for the most destructive weapon that the world had ever known. The stakes were incredibly high.[12]

After initially rejecting Grove's offer, DuPont finally agreed to take on the project, on three conditions: no profit, no patent rights, and absolute indemnification from any liability. In addition, DuPont insisted on getting Warren's preapproval of its contract with the government. Groves, with little choice, called Warren and arranged a meeting to discuss the project.[13]

Groves recalls in his memoir that one of Warren's "principal assistants, who was called in to handle its details, opposed the idea very strongly, pointing out that it was contrary to all existing procedures, that it would open the door to similar requests in the future and thus would completely upset the orderly conduct of business in the office, which theretofore had consisted exclusively of passing upon the legality of payments for work already accomplished." Warren chose to support the project, declaring, "I promised General Groves to do it and I see every reason why we should and none why we should not." Roger Trask mentions in a footnote that the identity of the principal assistant had never been established.[14]

On September 27, 1944, Warren met with Under Secretary of War Robert Patterson and two military generals at the GAO, where he "learned more about the nature of the military project GAO had been auditing." Trask writes that "it is unlikely that the auditors conducting the audit knew the reasons for the disbursements." Warren was told at the September meeting that the project had "reached the point that its secrecy can no longer be safely guarded if disbursements in connection with the program must be made in the usual way." The War Department looked to Warren to authorize Groves to "spend funds while keeping records that were to be made available for an audit directed by the comptroller general." Warren approved the plan, which dispensed with the usual audit procedures to ensure secrecy and expedite the availability of funds.[15]

The Manhattan Project's funding was hidden in the War Department's massive budget—with the GAO's tacit knowledge. Groves explains, "In justifying our requests for these funds, we were handicapped not only by the very size of the project and its many uncertainties, which made it impossible to budget in advance, but by the overriding need for secrecy, in the spending as well as in the getting [of the funds]." When a financial officer at Manhattan Engineer District "questioned a rather sizeable MED voucher that passed over his desk for payment," his superior told him, "You will forget that you know anything about it. Just forget that you spoke to me about it. Just pay all MED bills and discuss the matter with no one."[16]

On February 18, 1944, seventeen months after the project commenced, Henry Stimson, the secretary of war, General Marshall, the chairman of the Joint Chiefs of Staff, and Dr. Vannevar Bush met confidentially with Sam Rayburn (D-Texas), the Speaker of the House, John McCormack, the House majority leader, and Joseph Martin (R-Massachusetts), the House minority leader, to discuss the financing of the project.[17] Another meeting took place later that month with top leaders of the Senate. Groves remarks in his memoir, "The Congressmen indicated their approval without reservation. They said that, while the amount of money needed was large, they were in full agreement the expenditures were justified, and that they would do everything possible to have the necessary funds included in the coming Appropriations Bill" for fiscal year 1945.[18]

A legislative system was devised on the fly to satisfy the special requirements of the Manhattan Engineer District. Groves writes that "it was agreed at this time that Rayburn would be given advanced notice of how our requests for appropriations would be inserted in the bill." Rayburn would then "pass this information to McCormack and Martin, and the three of them would then tell a few members of the Appropriations Committee that they had gone into the subject with Secretary Stimson and General Marshall and that these items should not be questioned. The other members of Congress would be given only the most general reasons for the need to accord special handling to our requests for funds." This ad hoc arrangement marks the beginning of a special legislative system for funding secret government projects.[19]

7. Original Sin

During its first six months of existence, the CIG survived on seed money siphoned from the massive budgets of the State, War, and Navy Departments. This tripartite funding system kept the spy organization under the radar of Congress during its infancy, but it created other problems that threatened the CIG's future viability. As the former deputy chief of the CIA historical staff, Michael Warner, explains: "Congress initially paid scant attention to the new Central Intelligence Group. Indeed, CIG had been established with no appropriations and authority of its own precisely to keep it beneath Congressional scrutiny." The CIG faced legal and bureaucratic obstacles from the beginning, all related in some way to the use of unvouchered funds.[1]

One problem was that the position of DCI was ambiguous—not an administrative head, the DCI functioned as a coordinator between the NIA and the CIG. Additionally, the CIG was an interdepartmental organization; it was not a congressionally funded agency with a statutory charter. The DCI was in a no-win position. He lacked the legal authority to run the CIG's day-to-day operations; and, if he did head the organization, he would be accountable to three powerful bosses. His hands were tied.[2]

By the summer of 1946, the CIG was a mere shell of the organization President Truman had originally envisioned. Critically understaffed and with virtually no operational infrastructure of its own, the CIG was barely able to function. The plan from the beginning was for the CIG to eventually absorb the SSU, but as of July 1946, the merger of these two spy services—one operational (SSU) and one not (CIG)—still appeared to be a long way off. A declassified CIA document recounts:

> Although the services and facilities of SSU were utilized by CIG, it was administered as a separate entity. It was soon recognized by the CIG that to accomplish the desired objectives in connection with the coordination of intelligence for national security purposes, it would be necessary to provide for unified central operations on an augmented basis, and to gain direct control over the personnel, facilities, and funds required to accomplish centralized intelligence functions.[3]

In the July 30 letter to Secretary of the Treasury John Snyder and Comptroller General Lindsay Warren, the NIA proposed the creation of a clandestine funding system to conceal the source of CIG's money (Treasury, War, State, and Navy Departments), where it was going (domestic and foreign banks), and what it was being used for (e.g., espionage, covert action, training, and research and development). The NIA also wanted the Treasury secretary and the comptroller general to recognize the DCI as the de facto administrative head of the CIG. Most importantly, the comptroller general was asked to delegate confidential funds authority to the DCI for the expenditure of unvouchered funds. The DCI would then be authorized to certify and audit the unvouchered funds applied to secret intelligence operations. It was not a totally off-the-wall request. President Roosevelt had delegated this authority to the strategic director of the OSS during World War II.[4]

The NIA had reason to anticipate the support of the Treasury secretary and the budget director because both served under the president. However, the GAO had recently been declared a legislative agency by statute and was now under the authority of Congress. Also, Warren's endorsement of the proposal was far from certain. After meeting with Vandenberg following the July 17 meeting of the NIA, GAO representatives "promised to give the matter sympathetic consideration." Just a few months earlier, Warren had strongly denounced a bill before the Senate Special Committee on Atomic Energy that would transfer confidential funds authority to the Atomic Energy Commission. Now, Warren was being asked to empower the DCI with the same boundless authority that he had repeatedly characterized as a "fraud and a joke" in his earlier testimony. There was one important difference in this case: the NIA was requesting that Warren delegate certification and audit powers for unvouchered funds to the DCI; he was not being asked to formally relinquish those powers. Also, the DCI would be individually accountable to Warren on matters pertaining to the certification of unvouchered funds.[5]

On August 7, a highly classified conference, with senior representatives from the CIG, the Treasury Department, GAO, and the Bureau of the Budget, took place at an undocumented location in Washington, DC. The top CIG administrator, Walter Ford, informed DCI Vandenberg later that day: "The establishment of subject fund requires considerable administrative detail in order that moneys made available may be used by the C.I.G. without reference to contributing departments." At several follow-up meetings, the complex legal and administrative details of the working fund arrangement were ironed out.[6]

On August 9, CIG, Treasury, and GAO representatives met "to clear legal language in the delegations from the Secretary of War to the DCI and to establish channels for the transmission of vouchers, personal actions and similar paper." At the meeting, they approved "an administrative system to account for both vouchered and unvouchered funds." On August 12, CIG representatives met with officials from the War Department and the Bureau of the Budget "to secure signatures for the following types of delegation: personal actions, certification of vouchers, contracting authority, agent cashiers, etc." The CIG Budgetary Advisory Committee met on the following day to approve the 1947 budget for the CIG.[7]

In the meantime, between August 7 and 12, senior officials from the CIG and the GAO worked together behind the scenes to set up the special budget and accounting system for CIG's administration, which consisted of both vouchered and unvouchered funds. The history of this divisive legal issue is chronicled in a multipage memorandum for the record produced by the CIA's OGC. According to the memo, "there was some doubt in GAO on the legality of the proposed delegation to the Director." In the July 30 letter, the NIA proposed the establishment of "a special working fund under Section 601 of the Economy Act of 1932." This Depression era act authorized the Treasury secretary to set up "special working funds as may be necessary." Special working funds were encouraged as a means of improving financial coordination among government agencies on matters involving the purchase of goods and services for national defense work. The congressional intent in this case was to save the government money by improving procurement efficiency in the military. It had nothing to do with authorizing the use of unvouchered funds for off-the-books government intelligence services.[8]

The GAO rejected this interpretation of the act but agreed to support the creation of the working fund under two recent military appropriation acts. The CIA memo references "an unsigned draft letter" prepared by the GAO on August 12 for Warren to sign. The letter refers to "a working fund arrangement under a different authority." Both acts authorized the use of discretionary funds by the department head for sensitive military activities. The Military Appropriation Act of 1947, for example, provided exemptions "for all emergencies and extraordinary expenses arising in the War Department . . . , but impossible to be anticipated or classified." In this case, "payments from this appropriation may, in the discretion of the Secretary of War, be made on his certificate that the expenditures were necessary for confidential military purposes." The GAO's counterproposal reconciled the impasse with the NIA, but there remained the vexing legal matter of how to empower the DCI as the head of the CIG without a statutory mandate.[9]

The CIA memo points to a handwritten note initialed "E.L.F."[10] on the unsigned draft letter, stating:

> I called [name blacked out] of Central Intelligence Group about this and advised him that the proposed delegation of authority was extremely doubtful as to some matters but that it did not lack color of authority and that under the circumstances, considering the nature of the Agency, this Office probably would go along with the delegation with the understanding the entire matter would be made the subject of specific legislation at the first reasonable opportunity.

The GAO was walking a fine line as it weighed in on the proper balance between government accountability and national security.

GAO and NIA representatives met on August 14 to "discuss disbursing and auditing procedures," which were specially customized "to ensure security with respect to the confidential operations of the Central Intelligence Group." E. Lyle Fisher, the GAO's acting general counsel, presented the GAO's proposal and led the assiduous effort to devise an auditing system acceptable to Warren, the NIA, and the CIG. Thomas Troy[11] alludes to the meeting, noting that "CIG had received some temporary assistance on its administrative and financial problems when, working with the Bureau of the Budget, the Treasury, and the Comptroller General—especially the latter's General Counsel, Lyle Fisher—it persuaded the NIA to establish a 'working fund' for its use."[12]

The GAO proposed a dualistic administrative model with two independent budget and accounting systems for handling vouchered and unvouchered funds. It was analogous to the administration of the OSS.

The working fund was to be jointly audited by the GAO and the CIG. The comptroller would have audit jurisdiction over the vouchered accounts, whereas the DCI would be delegated audit authority for CIG's unvouchered accounts. In deference to the CIG's security requirements, the GAO agreed to conduct quarterly audits of vouchered funds on-site, using a small number of GAO auditors cleared through the CIG's security office. These auditors maintained permanent offices at the CIG and, later, at the CIA. It was a special arrangement, indeed, that forced the GAO to perform an unconventional role in government that was without historical precedent. GAO audits at that time were still carried out at the organization's central headquarters in Washington, DC.[13]

On August 15, CIG executive[14] Walter Ford sent a letter to Lindsay Warren informing him of the consensus reached at the conference with his general counsel:

> Under the site audit procedure outlined . . . it would be preferable to have special auditors designated by the General Accounting Office and approved by CIG from a security viewpoint to make periodic audits of the original and basic documents located physically in the CIG files. It is recommended that these audits be made at the end of each quarter since current audits will not only alleviate certain administrative difficulties but will enable us to immediately recognize security problems which may develop. CIG will provide space and safes for the original vouchers and accompanying basic documents for the use of the General Accounting Office auditors and examiners. If this proposal is acceptable, it would be necessary for several individuals or teams to be provided by the General Accounting Office, namely, one individual as a contract examiner, possibly two each for the audit of commercial vouchers and civilian travel, and an additional team for the purpose of auditing pay rolls.[15]

Over a decade later, Houston recounted Fisher's involvement in the August 1946 meetings in a letter to the DCI, "Mr. Fisher arranged for the special audit system for those Agency expenditures reviewed by the General Accounting Office so that the audit is conducted within our walls by specified, cleared auditors. These funds are, therefore, hardly less secure than our confidential funds, and the audit is maintained almost on a current basis which is an invaluable aid in the event of exceptions."[16]

In a memo dated August 21, Vandenberg informed the NIA that the "special working fund" had been established, and in a letter to Vandenberg on August 28, Warren approved the working fund arrangement, stating that "the procedure proposed provides that all disbursements will be made through the account of the Chief Disbursing Officer, Treasury Department, and that all original documents will be retained by the Central Intelligence Group for current audit by the General Accounting Office."[17]

On September 5, the NIA sent Warren a formal letter signed by all four principals, authorizing the DCI to serve as both the head of the CIG and the comptroller of unvouchered funds:

> In order to comply with the Presidential Directive of 22 January 1946 that the Director of Central Intelligence perform such services of common concern as the National Intelligence Authority determines can be more effectively accomplished centrally, we now on behalf of the Departments we represent, and in our capacity as member of the National Intelligence Authority, authorize the Director, subject to policies established by the National Intelligence Authority, to control, supervise, and administer the working fund with full powers in respect thereto as would otherwise have been exercised by us over the funds contributed to the working fund by our respective Departments, including the powers and authority granted by the Military Appropriation Act, 1947, and the Naval Appropriation Act, 1947, approved July 8, 1946, pertaining to certificates of expenditures and determinations of propriety of expenditures.[18]

The establishment of the working fund now cleared the way for CIG's absorption of the SSU. An administrative order issued on August 21 states: "All employees will give only the Central Intelligence Group as a reference regardless of if they are a member of the CIG or SSU. The name Strategic Services Unit will not be used." A declassified top secret document chronicling the administrative history of the CIA's financial operations reports:

> Almost simultaneous with the delegations of authority of 5 September 1946, the SSU personnel and facilities began to be transferred to the CIG. Theoretically, the transfer of all the personnel, functions, and facilities of SSU were supposed to be completed as of 20 October 1946. Actually, the account-

ing and reporting requirements for SSU obligations and funds continued, and it was the summer of 1947 before a clear-cut separation of SSU and CIG accounts and obligations was effected.[19]

Excerpts from John Magruder, the SSU director, in a letter dated September 6:

> All SSU overseas establishments will be liquidated effective close of business 19 October 1946. . . . The use of vouchered funds overseas will be discontinued and all salaries and expenses incurred after 19 October will be paid from "Special Funds." . . . All obligations incurred on or after 20 October must be for and on behalf of CIG. SSU vouchered obligations incurred prior to that date must be paid from SSU funds by 31 October 1946. . . . As of COB 19 October new and separate CIG financial books will be opened.[20]

In a letter dated September 12, Vandenberg informed Secretary of State James Byrnes that the SSU would be officially terminated on October 19. Emmett Echols, the head of the SSU Special Funds Division, subsequently pouched a secret memo to the special funds chiefs in London, Paris, Lisbon, Madrid, Stockholm, Bern, Heidelberg, Vienna, Rome, Cairo, and Shanghai, providing instructions for the formal transfer of the SFD to the CIG: "New Accounting procedures have been prepared and will be forwarded to you at the earliest possible date."[21]

On September 26, Vandenberg followed up Echols's memo with an official letter to Emmett Brennan, the new chief disbursing officer in the Treasury Department, designating Emerson Bigelow, Emmett Echols, and Thomas Bland as agent cashiers. They were bonded by the Treasury Department "to carry advances up to the amount of $200,000" and to disburse funds to CIG-controlled accounts in the United States and abroad. By now, all three of these SFB veterans were deeply involved in the administration of special funds for the CIG.[22]

The financial administration of unvouchered funds was a fluid situation, and in the beginning the CIG and the GAO closely coordinated on fiduciary matters of mutual interest. On the covert side, unresolved legal questions remained relating to the disbursement of funds to the clandestine services outside of the United States. On November 12, Houston met with Lyle Fisher at the GAO OGC to obtain the GAO's legal opinion on two specific questions related to the CIG's global financial operations. Houston's deputy, John Warner, the CIG special funds chief, Emmett Echols, and the assistant chief of the GAO's Audit Division, "Mr. Johnson" participated in the meeting. Houston documented this meeting in a seven-page declassified top secret memo to Vandenberg. According to the memo, the CIG and GAO met "to discuss certain basic problems concerning the treatment and handling of Special Funds overseas with proper officials of the General Accounting Office."

Houston explained to the DCI that "in each case the procedure or theory practiced by Special Funds is contrary to normal Government regulations, but in both cases, it was felt by representatives of CIG that these practices and theories were necessary to operation and justifiable in view of the special circumstances and the controls exercised by Special Funds." Houston then added: "It was felt that it would be inadvisable to request a written opinion from GAO or even a firm oral approval; the most it was planned to achieve was, by explaining what Special Funds proposed to do and how they proposed to do it, to put the office on record that it had kept the interested Government office informed, and so to forestall any criticism of bad faith or negligence in possible future investigations or special situations."[23]

Both questions involved the secret transfer of special funds from the US Treasury to CIG's growing list of administrative hubs overseas. The first concerned "the practice of considering foreign currencies purchased by Special Funds as 'commodities' to the same extent as other property used for operational purposes." The OSS brought this problem to the attention of Lindsay Warren in 1944 with respect to the buying and selling of foreign currencies. The purchase of a rental property, a plane ticket, a hotel room, or a government vehicle all constituted expenses that involved the purchase of a real commodity and that required the payment of government funds for that commodity. American dollars were first converted into foreign currencies before they could be used to purchase goods and services overseas. The CIG sought to treat the purchase of foreign currency with American dollars the same as the purchase of a more tangible commodity.[24]

Elaborating further, Houston explained that

these foreign currencies are obtained in various and often devious manners, and, that while full accountability is kept of the eventual expenditure of the foreign currencies, for practical purposes it is desirable to consider the American dollars used in the purchase as expended. This permits stockpiling of required foreign currencies in all parts of the world against projected operations. Such stockpiling is necessary to service world-wide secret intelligence operations, the successful performance of which requires long range planning and preparation.

From a government standpoint, the conversion of American dollars into a foreign currency—aside from the cost incurred in the exchange—was not a real expenditure of public funds on goods or services and could not simply be written off as a purchase.[25]

Houston argued that an intelligence service functioned differently from other agencies working overseas: "In ordinary exchange transactions, the foreign currencies would be 'money' as much as the dollars with which they are bought, but once purchased and committed to future clandestine operations, they lose their exchangeability and become, in effect, commodities which are carried over for expenditure beyond the fiscal year as are other commodities, and not credited back to the old appropriation and charged to the new, as dollars would be." The practical problem of properly accounting for fiscal year carryovers was of secondary importance as far as the CIG was concerned. The need for secrecy was the real problem. As a security measure, they wanted to conceal the money trail from the US Treasury as soon as the money left the country, which was considered a matter of national security. Treating foreign currency as a commodity offered the most practical means of hiding the actual spending on covert operations because it disassociated the foreign currency from the original American dollars used to purchase it.[26]

Fisher expressed his opinion that the question of good or bad faith was the real crux of the matter:

> Mr. Fisher stated that, while he had not given the matter much thought, he would have assumed that CIG would have to stock-pile currencies for its confidential operations, as it was obviously a necessary move. He concurred that the question of bad faith was the important point, stating that if CIG put in reports of a million dollars a month for purchase of foreign currencies

> throughout the year and then in June, at the end of the fiscal year, reported ten million, they would immediately question the last report on the grounds of bad faith. Mr. Houston referring to Mr. Echols for confirmation, assured Mr. Fisher that CIG would so maintain its foreign exchange activities that it could at all times show that the currencies purchased were for reasonably foreseeable expense of projected operations. It was Mr. Fisher's informal opinion that such a showing would be satisfactory in case of general investigation, or complaint on individual items, and that within such bounds of good faith it would be proper to consider as expended all dollars exchanged for foreign currencies.[27]

Echols, of course, claimed here that CIG's procedures accounted for the expenditure of unvouchered funds overseas; however, as far as the GAO was concerned, these funds disappeared into a black hole.

The second question discussed at the meeting "had to do with the treatment of dollar advances sent overseas either for expenditure as dollars or for later conversion into foreign currency." This matter more specifically related to the $200,000 bonds issued to each of the CIG's three agent cashiers. Houston explained, "When the agent-cashier sends dollars overseas, in strict theory he is making advances to be accounted for later. If they are treated merely as advances, he may not request reimbursement from the Treasury until he has completed the accountings, unless the Treasury were willing to allow each agent-cashier to carry huge outstanding advances far in excess of his bond." The CIG again sought to treat "overseas dollar advances, for the purpose of replenishment to agent-cashiers only, as actual expenditures." As in the previous case of foreign currency exchanges, the CIG proposed treating the transfer of funds to its overseas hubs as actual expenditures. This way the agent cashier would be in a position to requisition additional funds from the US Treasury against their bond, which in effect, increased the potential cash flow to foreign operations.[28]

When asked by Fisher how this matter had been handled in the past, Houston candidly told him that "the procedure outlined above had, in fact, been used." Unvouchered funds were still being treated the same way, based on wartime protocols. Paraphrasing the GAO's position, Houston wrote:

> In view of this, Mr. Fisher said he would advise that CIG continue to use this practice until such time as GAO, for one reason or another, might request that the practice cease; he turned to Mr. Johnson who said that that would be his advice also. He did not state that GAO would, of its own volition, request CIG to change its practice in this matter, but said it was always possible that investigation or some special incident might compel them to require different handling.

At the end of his memo to Vandenberg, Houston explained:

> No official ruling or opinion was obtained, and the attitude of Mr. Johnson and Mr. Fisher, while extremely friendly, showed that official rulings might well be averse to the needs of CIG. . . . Mr. Fisher said he was sure further efforts would be made to investigate past intelligence confidential expenditures, but implied that the pressure would come from Congress and not his office. He stated, as was well known, that Mr. Warren, the Comptroller General, was opposed to the use of confidential funds and they would be increasingly hard to obtain.[29]

On December 18, in a follow-up memo to Walter Ford, Houston restated his concerns about the November meeting with the GAO officials. He urged Ford to brief Vandenberg on his fiduciary responsibilities as the comptroller of unvouchered funds:

> We feel that while there is no immediate necessity, this is a subject which the Director should, at his convenience, study sufficiently to be aware of the essential problems involved; they are fundamental to the handling of Special Funds and consequently are his eventual responsibility. In case of investigation they might well be the focal point of criticism, although in our opinion the techniques and methods used are quite justifiable, and if properly explained there would be an adequate answer to any such criticism. We believe that these points would not be brought out in a special or superficial investigation, but only in the event of a full-fledged survey of the past fiscal operations.[30]

The GAO played a major role in the original establishment of the working fund. According to the CIA's first historian, Arthur Darling: "It was clear to everyone that the Group could not have been in operation at all without the cooperation of the comptroller general and the General Accounting Office." The working fund, though far from a permanent solution to the CIG's funding woes, paved the way for the creation of the CIA in the following year and for the passage of the Central Intelligence Agency Act of 1949, two years later.

8. The Protagonist, the Enabler, and the Antagonist

CAST OF CHARACTERS

The CIA's worldwide funding system came into existence following activation of the OSS in Europe in January 1943. The SFB established the administrative foundation for disbursing unvouchered funds to the clandestine services, and between 1943 and 1945 the handling of unvouchered funds continued to evolve into the early postwar era. Many top OSS officers, never named in any history books on the CIA, transitioned from the OSS to high-level administrative positions in the future intelligence agency. Eck Echols and Edward Saunders, for example, were key figures in the long-term development of CIA's clandestine financial administration. But there were many others as well.

At the August 1946 conference, the CIG and the GAO established a secretive liaison, formed around the joint audit of the fledgling spy organization. This interagency liaison was never formalized, even under the CIA Act of 1949. The only point of contact consisted of meetings and phone calls between the two general counsels: Lawrence R. Houston and E. Lyle Fisher. In a 1958 memo to Allen Dulles, Houston writes that "all our major dealings with that office were through him [Fisher]."[1] Nevertheless, the fact that these meetings did take place can be reconstructed from other declassified CIA memos that document what was discussed and who was there, albeit with redactions—especially concerning who was there.

Lyle Fisher, Lawrence Houston, and Allen Dulles played important but entirely different roles in the long-term development of a clandestine financial system for the CIA. Although Dulles did not attend the 1946 conference, his impact on that development was felt long before he became DCI in 1953. It is perhaps fitting, then, that the only time these three men were in the same room together was at the retirement lunch for Lyle Fisher on October 16, 1958.

THE PROTAGONIST: E. LYLE FISHER, GAO GENERAL COUNSEL (1946–1958)

Lindsay Warren appointed Edwin "Lyle" Fisher[2] to succeed John McFarland as the acting GAO general counsel several months before the August 1946 conference. From 1946 to 1958, Fisher served as the GAO's primary contact to the CIG/CIA. Although his personal background and legal philosophy are not widely known, the latter can be reconstructed based on the testimony he gave before Congress on numerous occasions, the speeches he made over his career to diverse audiences, and the informal rulings he gave to the CIA in confidence.

Lyle's father, Frederick Fisher, immigrated to the United States from London around 1880 at the age of sixteen. According to family tradition, he raced horses in the midwestern circuit and met his future wife, Catherine Welsh, one afternoon at the track in Ottumwa, Iowa. They married on June 5, 1897, after Fred agreed to give up horse racing and settle down in Ottumwa. The couple had ten children but not much money. Their fifth, Lyle, was born on February 26, 1907. Eva, the first, was born in 1901, followed by Ted (1902), Ernie (1904), and Harry (1906). Harry was born with significant health complications and died in 1931; he made it to twenty-five, though, outliving all the medical prognostications. Lyle, the next in line, was followed by Margaret (1909), Ralph (1911), Herbert (1912), Don (1913), and Floyd (1920).

Lyle grew up in a small white house in Ottumwa with no running water. After he was named general counsel, he was interviewed by a reporter from the *Washington Times-Herald.* Part of the 1948 article focused on Lyle's childhood:

> You can't keep work on his desk. He is still the same Bullet Fisher he was in high-school athletics—quick and energetic. He is a streamlined operator and he is general counsel for the general accounting office. . . . He was born in Iowa, one of 10 kids, and had a rough childhood. He remembers still the time they cut a little bare elm tree (Iowa has no evergreens) and wrapped its branches with colored rags to make it a Christmas tree, "No presents, of course." He went to school and worked—and went to school and worked—and finally came to Washington as a stenographer.[3]

His personal life coalesced around school, church, family chores, and a night job. He was the first child in his family to receive a high school diploma and spent two years after high school at the Iowa Success School, a "commercial college." There he learned speed typing and stenography, valuable administrative skills for anyone looking for a government job at that time. His future wife, Dorothy Henderson, also attended the Iowa Success School, and the two met on a blind date. Dorothy was born and raised in Eldon, Iowa. They were married in 1931 and settled into an apartment in the District of Columbia. Their first child, Robert (Bob), was born on January 9, 1935.

In 1928, on the cusp of the Great Depression, Lyle Fisher moved to Washington, DC, in search of a stable government job. First, he served as the personal secretary for the chairman of the American Battle Monument Commission, General John J. Pershing, who, at the time, was the highest-ranking military officer in the history of the United States. Over the next few years, Lyle worked several jobs while taking night classes at National University. He earned a law degree from National University in 1933 and began his career at the GAO in April 1936, just a few months before the first comptroller general, J. Raymond McCarl, completed his inaugural fifteen-year term. The Great Depression ruined many promising Wall Street careers, but for some, like Lyle Fisher, who had nothing to begin with, those uncertain years offered an unparalleled window of opportunity.

At the GAO, he started as a claims examiner in the Miscellaneous Section of the Claims Division. From there, he inconspicuously climbed the ladder of the GAO's growing bureaucracy through a series of promotions. He was briefly in the Contracts Section of the Claims Division, before he transferred to the Claims Review Examining Section. During that time, Lyle earned the respect of his supervisors and colleagues for his speed and efficiency. A 1948 biographical sketch in the agency's in-house newspaper, the *Watchdog*, describes Fisher's early years: "After joining the General Accounting Office, his progress within the Claims Division was marked with an unusual degree of rapidity. In fact, his work was outstanding both in accuracy and speed—particularly the latter—and just recently one of his former supervisors remarked that 'it was difficult to keep work on his desk!'"[4]

In 1938, while Fisher was on a temporary assignment at the Office of the General Counsel (OGC), General Counsel John McFarland asked him to stay on as a senior attorney. The year proved to be a pivotal one for Lyle. Dorothy gave birth to their second child, Joan, and his father, Frederick, passed away. His new OGC position opened an auspicious path for rapid advancement in the legal department. Under McFarland, he quickly moved up the chain of command, first to principal attorney and then, on May 1, 1942, to assistant general counsel. He was the deputy general counsel when McFarland announced his retirement.

An essay Dorothy wrote in 1959 intimates that he worked on the classified GAO review and audit of the DuPont contracts:

> The pressure of my husband, Lyle's work had been enormous. Every conceivable legal problem arose between Government and Industry with the expansion of our war machine and he was in a "The buck stops here" Government position. Most of this work was top secret but most secret of all had been his work identified as "The Manhattan Project," later known as the "Atomic Energy Commission." His office hours were spent mostly in conferences and deskwork done at home until far into the night.[5]

Although the specific nature of his involvement is unknown, he likely reviewed DuPont's contract with the federal government.

Lyle's position in the government spared him from the draft, but that reprieve only increased his sense of guilt over not serving in the war. His younger brothers Don and Floyd fought in the war and died in 1944, just two months apart, in separate plane crashes. On the war years, Dorothy writes:

> The DC area had seemed like a magnet that drew brothers, nieces, nephews, and cousins, coming and going into Navy, Army and Air Force. While we joked about our "Canteen" operation, it wasn't funny when the rationing coupons were low, the lines long, and the moral support and hospitality we so wanted to extend, was so difficult to manage. . . . Instead of the children having a happy, carefree childhood, they too were involved in the confusion and tension of the influx of company, grief for their uncles, wartime activities of gathering newspapers for recycling, helping plant and harvesting our Victory garden, year-work, etc.

In 1946, after McFarland announced his plans to retire, Lindsay Warren appointed Lyle Fisher as the acting general counsel and, on September 1, 1947, formally named him general counsel. When the war ended, the GAO was embroiled in a major investigation involving the settlement of the government's war contracts. These audits uncovered numerous cases of fraud and misuse of government funds during the war. Warren put most of the blame for this debacle on the government's preference for negotiated contracts. In a negotiated contract, the government agreed to cover all a company's costs of production in addition to a guaranteed fixed profit that was independent of the total cost. On top of that, the terms of the contract were hidden behind a wall of secrecy. Some companies fraudulently increased their profits by overbilling the government for their actual expenses.[6]

A week after his appointment as general counsel, Fisher testified before a House investigating subcommittee on the corruption surrounding the final certification and closure of the government's war contracts. He blamed the misuse of public funds on the War Contract Termination Act of 1944 and further lambasted the bill for precluding the GAO from conducting a creditable audit of government contracts. The *Washington Post* reported the next day:

> E. L. Fisher, chief counsel for the General Accounting Office, said that the war contract termination act of 1944, provisions of the tax laws, and certain other legislation which prevented a GAO audit before settlement of war contract claims undoubtedly would cost the taxpayers millions of dollars. Fisher admitted that a change in legislation now would be like locking the stable door after all, but the tail of the horse had gone through, but he said, it would prevent misuses of public funds in the future. The matter, Fisher declared, had been thoroughly threshed out at the time. Congress passed the legislation in question, but experience showed that Congress had made a mistake in surrendering the right watchdog of the Treasury, to scrutinize war contract settlements before they were made.[7]

At about this time, the OGC reviewed an early draft of the Armed Services Procurement Act of 1947, which established the government's rules for military procurements. The GAO rejected the legislation at first, arguing that the bill gave the military too much freedom to engage in negotiated contracts without a clear justification based on need. Years later, Lyle talked anecdotally about the early legislative history of the act in one of his many speeches:

> At the time the Armed Services Procurement Act of 1947 was passed, I was General Counsel of the General Accounting Office. The Bureau of the Budget asked us to report on the first draft of the bill. We thought certain provisions of the bill would have given the military departments too much freedom of action and we made an adverse report. This report was referred to by the proponents of the bill as "the kiss of death." Nevertheless, there followed a series of discussions on the bill with Department of Defense Officials. . . . The provisions of the bill to which objection had been made were modified to the satisfaction of the General Accounting Office. We then made a more favorable report and the bill was enacted into law in February 1948. I had the pleasure of being invited to the White House to witness President Truman sign the measure, at which time it was hailed as a fine and important step forward.[8]

Coat and tie were standard attire for male employees working behind desks in the late 1940s. Though most GAO employees ate lunch in the cafeteria, they sat at tables with other people of similar government rank and title. According to Lyle's two sisters, he never fully acclimated to the formality and decorum that went along with his high government status.[9] The biographical article in the *Washington Times-Herald* alluded to this, noting that "he . . . wears a hat so rarely that the other day when he went to attend a White House bill-signing he had to stop on the way and buy a hat and didn't know his size."[10]

Lyle maintained a good rapport with his legal staff: he was a hard worker and also friendly and down-to-earth, as noted in the fiftieth anniversary issue of the *GAO Review* (1971):

> Mr. Fisher won the loyalty and admiration of the employees in the General Accounting Office by his ability, powers of arbitration and a capacity for hard work—plus a sense of humor and a sociable personality—and certainly his rise in the Office may be attributed to his perseverance in many difficult tasks and his fidelity to the trusts imposed in him. . . . Although Mr. Fisher was frequently referred to as "Judge Fisher" when he testified on the Hill, he

> was not an austere administrator. He will be remembered by the attorneys for his frequent visits to all the sections and offices under his jurisdiction. Even after he became General Counsel he continued as an active member of the General Counsel bowling team. The attorney-trainee recruitment program which Mr. Fisher established in 1954 was one of his favorite projects and he maintained personal supervision over it until his retirement.[11]

In the summer of 1946, the impromptu August conference on the working fund forced Lyle to abruptly cancel his summer vacation plans. Lyle and Dorothy had not been back home since the start of the war and had planned a road trip to Iowa in August with their three young children to visit their two families. On August 14, after presenting the GAO's proposal to the NIA, Lyle informed both families that something had come up and they would not be able to make the trip. At the outset, no one attending the conference knew how long it would run, but a consensus on the working fund was reached in the following week. On the evening of August 21—the same day that Vandenberg informed the NIA that the working fund had been established—Lyle told the family at dinner that he had cleared his schedule and the trip was back on. They hastily packed the car the next day and left for Iowa on August 23. They returned on Labor Day weekend, a week later.

On the return trip, the family had to stop at a gas station in Indiana after one of their tires blew out. While they sat waiting for the tire to be fixed, Dorothy noticed that her oldest son, Bob,[12] seemed to be "extremely languid and content to doze." When queried, Bob "complained of arm pain, which he said felt like electric shocks." The family checked into a hotel in Indiana. Dorothy recalls in her 1959 essay: "Between lightning striking too close for comfort and Bob crying out like a wounded animal, around 4:00 a.m., I aroused Lyle for a conference. I knew Bob had the classic symptoms of Polio and I suggested we start for home and get medical attention rather than possibly being quarantined in Indiana." At a hospital in Washington, a spinal tap confirmed the family's worst fear. Following the August 7 conference, Lyle had driven halfway across the country for a family reunion, riding an emotional high. Suddenly, he faced a new reality: his eldest son had polio and, early on, no one knew the long-term prognosis.

THE ENABLER: LAWRENCE HOUSTON, CIA GENERAL COUNSEL (1947–1973)

Lawrence Houston was a key figure in the drafting of the National Security Act of 1947 and the CIA Act of 1949. CIA scholars would be hard pressed to find a figure more central to the development of the Agency than Houston. In retirement, he gave only a few interviews on the record; most of them were about CIA matters, not his personal life. He was born in St. Louis, Missouri, on January 4, 1913,[13] and his father, David F. Houston, was chancellor of Washington University. Soon after Lawrence's birth, President Woodrow Wilson selected David Houston as his secretary of agriculture. In 1920 the president nominated him as Treasury secretary, and he served in that position until the end of Wilson's term. In his youth, Larry Houston spent his summers sailing around Cape Cod and Oyster Bay. He graduated from Harvard University in 1935 and received his law degree from the University of Virginia in 1939. Houston volunteered for the army in 1943 but was turned down for active service because of his poor vision. Eventually the army drafted him and "sent [him] to basic finance school at Fort Benjamin Harrison" in Lawrence, Indiana. Houston was assigned to the Justice Advocate General (JAG) Corps, in part because it granted waivers on the eyesight requirement. In July 1944, Houston became one of the first JAG attorneys to join the OSS. He was sent to London on September 29, 1944, to receive additional training.[14]

From April to September 1945, he served as the general counsel to the OSS base in Cairo. There he worked closely with the chief of special funds, Nick Steichen, "advising and assisting in the determination of financial procedures with respect to unvouchered funds in order to insure proper and accurate accounting for expenditures." His superior officers were greatly impressed with his abilities. One of them remarked in his personnel record: "Outstanding officer. Well balanced, intelligent and very objective" and "Has been of tremendous value to NETO and the OSS generally in helping settle claims and evolving fiduciary policies." In Europe, Houston mastered the legal side of special funds. He returned to the United States, in early November 1945, to serve as the SSU chief counsel in Washington. With the creation of the CIG on January 22, 1946, DCI Souers selected Houston to serve as his general counsel.[15]

Lawrence Houston witnessed the establishment of the Agency from the very beginning and served as its general counsel longer than the next eight general counsels combined. He knew more about the family jewels and the clandestine funding of the CIA than anyone. During his long tenure, he handled every legal matter of importance affecting the CIA, often with few historical precedents to guide him.[16]

THE ANTAGONIST: ALLEN DULLES, DIRECTOR OF CENTRAL INTELLIGENCE (1953–1961)

Allen Dulles headed the CIA from 1953 to 1961, longer than the combined tenure of his four predecessors. He was also, notably, the first civilian to run the Agency. Dulles, more than his predecessors, exploited ambiguities in the CIA Act of 1949 that further empowered the position of DCI. Born on April 7, 1893, in remote Watertown, New York, near Lake Ontario, Dulles had one brother and three sisters. John Foster, the oldest child in the family, was born in 1888. Three sisters, Margaret, Eleanor, and Nataline, were born in 1890, 1895, and 1898, respectively. Eleanor, like her two younger brothers, had a long and distinguished career in the federal government. Much less is known about Allen's other two sisters. The Dulles brothers were well schooled and enjoyed all the comforts of an aristocratic upbringing. Their father, Allen M. Dulles, was a third-generation Presbyterian minister; their mother, Edith Foster Dulles, was the daughter of John W. Foster. Foster served as the secretary of state for Benjamin Harrison, and his uncle Robert Lansing later served as the secretary of state for Woodrow Wilson.

John Foster, Allen's maternal grandfather, grew up in Indiana; he fought for the North in the Civil War and retired with the rank of general. After the war, Foster had a successful law practice and demonstrated an affinity for politics. Along with assignments as a foreign diplomat, Foster earned prominence as an international relations lawyer. As chairman of the Indiana Republican Party during the 1872 presidential race, he ardently campaigned for Ulysses S. Grant. Grant won and nominated Foster as his minister plenipotentiary to Mexico. In 1881, soon after President James Garfield took office, he was mortally wounded by an assassin who fired two shots at him from close range. While Garfield lay incapacitated, Vice President Chester Arthur took over the duties of president and recalled Foster to the United States. Two years later, President Arthur appointed Foster as the minister plenipotentiary to Spain.

In 1892, John Foster succeeded James Blaine as President Benjamin Harrison's secretary of state. Blaine, one of the most influential American statesmen in the post–Civil War era, suffered from chronic kidney disease, and poor health forced him to resign near the end of Harrison's first term. Foster served for only eight months. Arguably, his most distinguished foreign policy initiative was his support of the rebellion and coup d'état against the Hawaiian monarchy of Queen Liliuokalani. After the overthrow of the queen's government, the Harrison administration, just before its term ended, quickly signed a treaty that annexed Hawaii to the United States. Foster later wrote, "The native inhabitants had proved themselves incapable of maintaining a respectable and responsible government." Cleveland defeated Harrison in the next election, and, once in office, publicly denounced the treaty; the Senate, in turn, failed to ratify it. It should be noted that Foster introduced a new system of assigning military attachés to embassies and legations, although the formulation of this initiative more than likely started under Blaine.[17]

The paternal side of the Dulles family was deeply involved in the Presbyterian Church during the Second Great Awakening, which swept across the United States during the first half of the nineteenth century, and religion played a central role in Allen's upbringing. Stephen Kinzer wrote, in his book *The Dulles Brothers,* "Religiosity permeated the Dulles household. Morning rituals were only part of their piety. Each Sunday the boys attended three church services, carrying pencil and paper so they could take notes on their father's sermons. Afterwards the family would discuss and analyze them." Even as religion infused the Dulles brothers with a strong sense of purpose, their career paths appear to have been influenced more by their mother's side of the family, which was rooted in the foreign affairs of the United States. Allen was born a couple of months after John Foster retired from public life. Foster spent time with both grandsons as they were growing up; when they were older, he took them under his wing and introduced them to political elites around Washington.[18]

Allen and John Foster both attended Princeton University—founded by Presbyterians—and both graduated with academic distinction, although John Foster was the better student. Both also received law degrees from George Washington University. Elder brother John Foster went straight from college to law school and then to the prestigious Wall Street law firm of Sullivan and Cromwell, where he became a full partner. Allen was a devotee of the party scene and dated many women at Princeton; he was indecisive about his future. On the day he graduated in 1914, he eagerly accepted a teaching fellowship at a missionary school in India. This impulsive decision to travel abroad allowed him to defer major career decisions that he was not yet prepared to make. He later recalled in his book *The Craft of Intelligence*, "After graduating from college a few months before the outbreak of World War I in 1914, sharing ignorance about the dramatic events that lay ahead, I worked my way around the world, teaching school in India and then China, and traveling widely in the Far East." On June 28, 1914, Allen sat sipping tea with a friend at a French café in Paris, oblivious to the shouts of newsboys announcing the assassination of Archduke Ferdinand of Austria.[19]

He returned home during the summer of 1915, where he began to think seriously about his future. Never short on ambition, Allen looked to his politically connected grandfather, John Foster, and his "Uncle Bert," President Wilson's secretary of state, for guidance and inspiration. The two sides of the family pulled him in opposite directions, but Allen readily accepted an entry level position in the Foreign Services, with private aspirations to become secretary of state himself. Allen's missionary work gave him the opportunity to see the world, but he had no deep interest in dedicating his life to the church.

Allen was assigned to the US Austrian Embassy in Vienna and arrived there on July 7, 1916. While he performed the tedious litany of consular duties required of a third secretary at the US Embassy in Vienna, he also schooled himself on the basic tools and methods of the intelligence trade. Foreign service officers serving abroad were trained in all the latest cryptological methods of sending and receiving sensitive State Department messages between the embassy and Washington. Years later, looking back on the experience, he writes, "I was, in fact, an intelligence officer rather than a diplomat."[20]

The United States declared war on Germany on April 6, 1917, the day before Allen's twenty-fourth birthday. The embassy in Vienna was evacuated, and its entire staff was moved across the border to the US Legation in Bern, Switzerland. In Bern, Allen collected and analyzed political intelligence for the State Department's Division of Information. According to two of his biographers, Allen just barely missed out on a major intelligence coup on Easter Sunday, the morning that his train from Vienna arrived in Bern. A call came through the US Legation from an unknown Russian émigré, who was urgently asking to meet with someone from the diplomatic staff. No one was around, so Allen, the new arrival, was asked to come down to the legation to take the call. He reluctantly agreed; but, having already made other plans, he budgeted little time for the matter, which seemed to him innocuous and not requiring immediate attention. He politely told the caller he could not meet with him that day but would be happy to meet with him on the following day. The mysterious voice on the other end of the line told him that Monday would be too late, before hanging up. The unknown caller, according to his biographers, was Vladimir Lenin, the leader of the Bolsheviks, who boarded a train on Monday for Russia after speaking briefly with a young Allen Dulles. Allen kicked himself for years for blowing his chance to meet with Lenin, but years later he turned it into a great story for young CIA case officers.[21]

At the end of World War I, both Allen and his brother John Foster attended the historic 1919 Paris Peace Conference at Versailles. President Wilson appointed John Foster Dulles as legal counsel of the US delegation in Paris. Allen was assigned to the American Commission to Negotiate Peace and was involved in drawing the boundaries for the nation of Czechoslovakia. He also supervised American field agents in Paris, as part of his involvement in the collection of political intelligence. In Paris, he crossed paths with Ralph Van Deman, the major in charge of the War Department's Military Intelligence Division (MID), and he likely also encountered Herbert Yardley, the head of the Black Chamber, who was residing in Paris for the conference.[22]

Allen met Martha "Clover" Todd during this period, and the two were married in October 1920. They raised three children: Clover Todd (1922), Joan (1923), and Allen (1930). It was a dysfunctional marriage; for most of her adult life, Clover suffered from depression that was likely exacerbated by Allen's relentless pursuit of mistresses. Shortly after the wedding, Allen was assigned to the US Embassy in Constantinople. The young couple lived in a two-story apartment that overlooked the Bosporus. From this perch, Allen witnessed the expansion of the Soviet Union into neighboring Georgia. When Allen was promoted to head of the Near Eastern Division of the State Department in 1922, the couple, with their first child on the way, returned to Washington. Over the next four years, Allen shuffled back and forth between Washington and the Middle East, promoting American oil interests and the development of the early oil industry.[23]

By this point in his career, Allen realized that moving up through the ranks of a giant bureaucracy like the State Department was slow, monotonous, and unpredictable. Although he enjoyed the overseas work, his life as a diplomat was complicated by marriage and children. He found life in Washington to be mundane and tedious. He completed his law degree by taking night courses at George Washington University, and in 1926, left his promising career path in the Foreign Services to accept a much more lucrative position at the law firm of Sullivan and Cromwell, where his brother John Foster was a full partner. Allen was also named full partner in 1930—though not before failing his first board exam.

Sullivan and Cromwell specialized in international finance; it was one of the most powerful law firms on Wall Street, with a long list of powerful clients on both sides of the Atlantic. On this point, Peter Grose, one of Dulles's biographers, writes:

> To call the Sullivan and Cromwell of the 1920s a law firm is to miss the point. The partnership of lawyers at 49 Wall Street constituted a strategic nexus of international finance, the operating core of a web of relationships that constituted power, carefully crafted to accrue and endure across sovereign borders. Whether in railroads, chemicals, nitrates from Chile, or sugar from Cuba, the mammoth trusts and cartels found their way to profits—with more than a little help from their friends the lawyers.[24]

Allen never achieved the same level of success in the firm as his older brother, but the work provided for a comfortable and luxurious lifestyle. On frequent travels overseas, he socialized with the rich and powerful, while living the life of a bachelor. A longtime member of the Council on Foreign Relations (CFR), Allen published many articles in the late 1920s and the 1930s for the organization's prestigious journal *Foreign Affairs*.

In 1932, Norman Davis, a friend and former mentor at the State Department, asked Dulles to attend the Geneva Disarmament Conference with him. Davis had served as under secretary of state under President Wilson when Dulles was still in the State Department. Soon after FDR won his first presidential election, he met with Davis and Dulles at the White House to discuss the upcoming talks. The pair then crossed the Atlantic aboard the SS *Manhattan.* This was shortly after Adolf Hitler was elected chancellor of Germany, and, on this trip, the two met with Hitler—coincidentally on Allen's fortieth birthday (they had met with Mussolini the previous year). Unlike the stories he would tell about the time he almost met Lenin, Dulles never talked about this meeting. In a footnote, Peter Grose says that, when he mentioned the meeting during an interview with Richard Helms, a longtime OSS and CIA colleague, Helms was surprised and said he had never heard the story before.[25]

Allen Dulles and Bill Donovan both grew up in the state of New York, were prominent Wall Street lawyers, and were active members of the New York Republican Party. Donovan recruited Dulles for COI undercover work in the early months of 1942, shortly after the attack on Pearl Harbor. Using his position at Sullivan and Cromwell as cover for his intelligence work, Allen maintained two offices, one at 49 Wall Street and one at 630 Fifth Avenue, next door to William Stephenson, the famous British spymaster. Soon after the establishment of the OSS, Donovan dispatched Dulles to Bern, Switzerland, to serve as the OSS SI station chief. Switzerland was strategically important because of its neutral political status, its proximity to Germany and Italy, and its central role in the banking industry of Europe. Dulles knew the city well from his previous assignment there with the State Department. On November 2, 1942, Allen Dulles departed the United States and crossed from German-occupied France into Switzerland on the day before the border was closed; it was not reopened until after the liberation of France in 1944. He was in good company. Spies from all over the world came to Bern, looking for revealing nuggets of information that could prove useful to the war effort.[26]

When the war ended, Allen Dulles returned to his former life with Sullivan and Cromwell. He still maintained all his political connections from his many years with the State Department; and, from 1946 and 1950, he served as president of the Council on Foreign Relations. In the postwar years, the legend of Allen Dulles started to take shape. He returned as one of the most prominent intelligence experts in the nation, next to Bill Donovan, but without the baggage that brought about the demise of the OSS and Bill Donovan. Congress and the National Security Council were soliciting his opinions on the intelligence business long before he joined the Agency. Before he officially joined the CIA in 1950, Dulles influenced its early development within the shadows of the US government.

9. Legalizing the Working Fund

SECRET ENABLING AND THE CIA CHARTER

With the creation of the working fund, the arduous process began to establish a system for disbursing unvouchered funds to foreign operations all over the world as part of the future agency's permanent charter. The CIG could not have functioned without it. The working fund compartmentalized the highly classified audit of the CIA into two audit jurisdictions for certifying vouchered (GAO) and unvouchered (CIA) funds. Just as importantly, it facilitated the CIG's absorption of the SSU's financial administration. However, the working fund was a quasi-legal arrangement; it did not receive the blessing of Congress in 1946.

Thomas Troy says that the enabling of the agency was "much talked about" during the hearings on the National Security Act. From the CIA standpoint, enabling was a critical issue; however, Lawrence Houston's best efforts to have enabling language included in the Agency's founding charter failed to make an impact on the drafting committee. A memo from George Elsey to Clark Clifford, the special counsel to the president, expressed frustration with CIG's persistence:

> C.I.G. is up to its old tricks again. It has submitted "informally" the draft of a proposed bill to be submitted to Congress very similar to the two previous drafts which Vandenberg has sent to you in recent months and which you filed without further action. . . . I suggested [to the Budget Bureau] that CIG be informed that there was no necessity for such [enabling] legislation. . . . The Budget [Bureau] concurs in that position and will inform C.I.G. that it is inappropriate to propose legislation at this time in view of the President's support of the Unification Bill.

Charles Murphy, the principal drafter of the bill, insisted "that all but the barest mention of the CIA would be omitted from the proposed legislation." Murphy, according to Troy, "thought the material submitted by CIG was too controversial and might hinder the passage of the merger legislation." The National Security Act of 1947 passed on July 26, 1947, without the inclusion of any special enabling.[1]

The bill was massive, containing three titles and twenty-seven sections; shoe-horned into Section 102 was the CIA charter. Section 101 established the NSC. The act also liquidated the CIG and NIA. By then, the two armed services committees knew about the existence of the working fund and were content to leave it in place for the time being. Both agencies were disappointed with the outcome. As with the previous arrangement, the comptroller general delegated certification authority to the DCI. The working fund was expanded to include a separate account for the NSC; those funds were "made available to the NSC in the same manner as funds made available to the CIA."

CIA ENABLING LEGISLATION

The third DCI Admiral Roscoe Hillenkoetter submitted CIA's first legislative proposal on special enabling to the chairmen of the House and Senate Armed Services Committees in early February 1948. After a few iterations in the House and Senate, a Senate bill known as S. 2688 emerged from the closed-door hearings. This bill had just seven provisions, but several of them were without precedent in the US statutory code. Section 7b of S. 2688 was of most concern to the GAO because it transferred certification authority for unvouchered funds from the comptroller general to the NSC. Its language was similar to that used in the provision that Warren had vociferously repudiated in his 1946 testimony before the Senate Special Committee on Atomic Energy; that provision had sought to transfer his certification authority to the AEC—a small group of political appointees.

On March 3, 1948, Budget Director James Webb sent a draft of the new bill to Comptroller General Lindsay Warren, requesting his review and endorsement. Warren disliked Section 7, to put it mildly. But like it or not, the new era of confidential funds and black budgets had arrived. Under the advice of his legal counsel, Warren endorsed the bill in his reply to Webb, but he qualified his endorsement by expressing his misgivings on the record. Other than his testimony in 1946, this letter was Warren's only official statement on the transfer of audit authority from the comptroller general to someone else. Warren told Webb,

> While sections 3, 6, and 7 of the proposed enactment provide for granting much wider authority than I would ordinarily recommend for Government agencies generally, the purposes sought to be obtained by the establishment of the Central Intelligence Agency are believed to be of such paramount importance as to justify the extraordinary measures proposed therein. The importance of obtaining, correlating, and disseminating to proper agencies of the Government intelligence relating to national security under present international conditions cannot be overlooked. In an atomic age, where the act of an unfriendly power might, in a few short hours, destroy, or seriously damage the security, if not the existence of the nation itself, it becomes of vital importance to secure, in every practical way, intelligence affecting its security. The necessity for secrecy in such matters is apparent and the Congress apparently recognized this fully in that it provided in section 102(3) 3 of Public Law 253, that the Director of Central Intelligence shall be responsible for protecting intelligence sources and methods from unauthorized disclosure.[2]

The AEC could have made similar arguments. What was different in this case? The NSC, after all, comprised a group of cabinet members. Considering his previous testimony, why did he choose in this case to approve such language? There is one important difference between the CIA proposal and the 1946 bill on Atomic Energy: the chairman of the NSC was the president. NSC directives, therefore, carried the weight of an executive order. It should be emphasized here that the budget bureau obtained Warren's approval for Section 7 before the statutory language was finalized.

Both armed services committees held hearings on CIA's enabling legislation in tightly controlled closed-door sessions. Hillenkoetter testified before the House Armed Services Committee (HASC) on April 8, 1948. Houston consulted with the committee's general counsel prior to his testimony and wanted to know which questions were of greatest interest to the committee. He was told the committee was most interested in the answers to four questions. Houston carefully explained how to answer each one in a three-page memo that he gave to Hillenkoetter on the day of his testimony. First, the committee wanted a clearer understanding of how the CIA had previously been able to function without the special authorization contained in the proposed legislation. Houston's response to this question recounted the early history of the working fund and the GAO's quasi-legal role in the system:

> Only through the splendid cooperation of the Comptroller General's Office and the other departments and agencies concerned were interim procedures devised for proper administration of these funds. Even with such cooperation, continual problems of administration were encountered, and operations were hampered by restrictions on the use of funds. It was partly due to the Agency's needs and partly due to the suggestion of the Comptroller General's office that this legislation was drafted to provide a proper legal basis for administration of the Agency's functions.

Second, the committee wanted to know which features of the bill had no precedent in existing law. Houston cited Sections 6 and 7. Section 6a authorized CIA's use of hidden accounts to conceal the transfer of funds to foreign operations without regard to the provisions of law. Section 6 promised to legalize what, until then, had only been a quasi-legal practice. Section 6f exempted the CIA from having to disclose the organization, functions, names, official titles, salaries, or numbers of persons it employed; this allowed the agency to conceal the names of most of the people it employed, other than the director and the other top CIA officials. Section 7a and 7b permitted the Agency to spend all its appropriations without regard to the provisions of law. CIA's vouchered funds were essentially identical to the special class of vouchered funds that Congress had approved during the war, which also allowed for the expenditure of GAO-audited funds without regard to law.[3]

The last two questions on Houston's list were more specifically directed at the DCI's confidential funds authority as stated in Section 7b—the section of greatest interest to the GAO. The committee wanted to know how the CIA proposed to obtain appropriations without disclosing the amount and their source. Houston emphasized that "setting forth the purposes for which sums made available to the Agency may be expended has a novel feature in that it will, in effect, be permanent appropriations language for the Agency." The OSS and the CIG had acquired these authorities, but they were never permanent in a statutory sense. In the case of the OSS, they were covered by special authorities delegated to the president under the War Powers Act of 1941. Houston explained to Hillenkoetter: "We believe that the past system of earmarking certain funds in regular appropriations for subsequent transfer to the CIG Working Fund has prevented disclosure of the amount and source of funds available to the Agency." The proposed law promised to further simplify CIA's special funding system by transferring absolute control over the agency's unvouchered funds to the executive branch.[4]

Lastly, the committee wanted to know about the safeguards and controls in place for the handling of unvouchered funds. On this matter, Houston described how the working fund operated:

> All vouchered expenditures are audited within CIA by representatives of the General Accounting Office especially detailed for that purpose. For unvouchered expenditures, the Director has appointed Special Funds' officers as his personal representatives for their administration. Recognizing, however, that he has the sole ultimate responsibility for the propriety of unvouchered expenditures, he has laid down detailed rules and regulations outlining the purposes for expenditure and the controls and approvals which will apply. He has appointed Certifying Officers who are responsible for auditing all unvouchered expenditures to see that they come within these regulations. If there is doubt as to compliance with regulations, the Certifying Officer may refer any question to the Office of the General Counsel for review and recommendation to the Director. Any exceptions or unusual circumstances require personal action by the Director. As a further safeguard, the Director has appointed an Executive for Inspection and Security with a staff of auditors and fiscal experts, who make periodic general inspections of all books and accounts and such special investigations as the Director may require.[5]

The committee apparently accepted Warren's letter to Webb as a formal endorsement; only from the DCI did they hear directly why the CIA needed Section 7. Hillenkoetter opined in his testimony that the bill had the strong support of the comptroller general, which he corroborated by selectively quoting parts of Warren's letter:

> We have been advised by the Bureau of the Budget that there would be no objection to our presenting this legislation for the consideration of the Congress. It has been strongly endorsed by the Comptroller General, the Honorable Lindsay C. Warren, to the Director of the Bureau of the Budget in a letter dated 12 March. In taking cognizance of the "much wider authority" granted under this bill than the comptroller general would "ordinarily recommend for Government agencies generally," he stated that "the purposes sought to be obtained by the establishment of the Central Intelligence Agency are believed to be of such paramount importance as to justify the extraordinary measures proposed therein."

Warren would never have called his letter to Webb a strong endorsement of the bill. Although there is no doubt that he wanted to extricate the GAO from its unconventional legal administration of the working fund and that he looked to Congress to weigh in and issue statutory guidance on the use of unvouchered funds, he was uncomfortable with language that promised to transfer unlimited fiscal authority to the executive branch.[6]

Hillenkoetter suggested that the provisions in the proposed act were left out of the bill because those details would have made the bill excessively complex:

> It was felt that to place so much detail into an overall unification bill would unnecessarily burden the latter. As a matter of fact, it was generally agreed that this present type of detailed legislation had no place in the broad terms of the unification act which was seeking to establish a general structure rather than to outline detailed procedures. Therefore, it was decided to omit from the unification bill the administrative provisions for the Central Intelligence Agency.

The record shows that Houston did everything in his power to have these details included in Section 102. It was, in fact, the drafting committee and Congress, not the CIA, that decided to defer enabling to a future session. Hillenkoetter, for his part, made it sound like this was all part of the plan from beginning: "It was agreed that passage of the unification bill would be followed by detailed enabling legislation for the Agency and these facts were brought out in hearings in both the House and Senate."[7]

The language of Section 7b underwent two significant modifications before it was brought to a vote in the Senate. Both involved the recipient of confidential funds authority. The version of the bill that Warren approved transferred certification authority from the comptroller general to the NSC. This scenario made little sense, for it would have established a system similar to what existed under the CIG before the creation of the working fund. In that tripartite system, the senior members of the NIA served as controllers of the CIG's funding. The budget bureau and the CIA met with the Senate Armed Services Committee (SASC) to discuss Section 7b, and it was decided to transfer certification authority for unvouchered funds to the budget director, instead of the NSC. This change made sense from an administrative standpoint because the budget director asserted fiscal control over the CIA and NSC budgets. Having the budget director serve as the comptroller of unvouchered funds would have been more appealing to Warren. This change was a win-win. In good faith, Houston kept the GAO in the loop by privately informing Lyle Fisher. A CIA memorandum for the record reports, "This was informally cleared with Mr. Fisher, General Counsel to the Comptroller General, and submitted to the House and Senate Committees accordingly." This subtle tweak to the language in Section 7b was not the last one, however.[8]

One more change was made to Section 7b just before the final draft of the bill was brought to a vote in the Senate. According to Houston, the SASC decided in closed session that the certification authority should reside with the DCI, not the budget director. The reasons for this change are not entirely clear. The most likely argument was that the director was the person legally responsible for sources and methods and that, therefore, the fiscal power should reside with the DCI. Houston always insisted that the SASC, not the CIA, requested this change. But one thing is sure: it was made without first consulting with the GAO. This time Houston did not inform the GAO of the eleventh-hour change, in good faith, as he did when the first modification was made after Warren's endorsement. This oversight appears to have been a political calculation on his part. The version of Section 7b brought before the Senate placed confidential funds authority in the hands of the DCI, the spender of unvouchered funds. In a twist of fate, however, the bill failed to pass in the House, which left

Houston with a lot of explaining to do when it came time to gain approval from the GAO for the same provision in 1949.[9]

THE BOGOTÁ RIOTS

By all accounts, S. 2688 should have passed because the bill had the unanimous support of both armed services committees. Yet, this signature piece of national security legislation would die in Congress for reasons that are inseparably linked with the Bogotá Riots of 1948 and the sequence of political events that followed. The riots occurred ten days after the start of the Ninth International Conference of American Republics, which brought together representatives from nations throughout Latin America to promote democracy and economic development. Senior diplomats from countries throughout North, Central, and South America arrived in Bogotá, Colombia. The United States sent an eighty-member delegation that included Secretary of State George Marshall, Secretary of Commerce Averell Harriman, World Bank President John McCloy, and the president of the Import-Export Bank.

The conference, which began peacefully on March 30, was thrown into a frenzy a week into the proceedings by the brutal murder of Jorge Gaitán. Gaitán, the charismatic leader of Colombia's Liberal Party, was a well-known political figure. His brazen killing, which occurred in broad daylight, triggered riots all over the city, during which over two thousand civilians were killed. Mobs broke into the conference headquarters and ransacked the facility. The *Washington Post* reported, "Violent rioting broke out in Bogotá, splattering the city with blood shortly after noon today. . . . There was complete anarchy. Police and troops were firing in the streets. It was a flaming, full-fledged revolt, a wild uncontrolled bloodbath." The conference attendees retreated to the safety of their hotels, where they remained sequestered until the restoration of peace five days later. The conference reconvened a week later and on April 30, ended jubilantly with the ratification of the charter of the Organization of American States (OAS).[10]

No one from the US delegation was injured during the riots, but preliminary reports revealed that, prior to the start of the conference, the CIA had received multiple warnings of a potential disturbance. Arthur Darling, the CIA's first historian, described the affair, "From the beginning of the year warnings had been coming into the Central Intelligence Agency that a campaign of anti-imperialism would be aimed at the United States." It was suspected "that there might be an attempt by Liberals to overturn the Conservative Government in Colombia, and that Communists were interested in the plans for demonstrating against the United States during the conference." Just one week before the conference convened, a more specific secret dispatch was received, "saying that 'Communist-inspired agitators' would attempt to 'humiliate' the secretary of state upon his arrival 'by manifestations and possible personal molestation.'"[11]

According to Darling, "Politicians who aspired to be President found Harry S. Truman responsible, not for the assassination of Jorge Gaitán, to be sure, but for failure to know about it in advance." Many people immediately suspected that the killing was politically motivated. Only later was it learned that Gaitán was not killed for political reasons. The killer turned out to be an anonymous person with no political connections. Gaitán had defended the man accused of murdering the killer's uncle.

The first reports to reach the national media pointed the finger squarely at the CIA and the DCI, Admiral Hillenkoetter. A special subcommittee chaired by Clarence Brown (R-Ohio) investigated why the intelligence system failed to coordinate as designed; in news reports, Brown exploited the moment by referring to the event as a "South American 'Pearl Harbor.'" Representative Edward Devitt (R-Minnesota), according to the *Washington Post,* "demanded a complete overhaul of the Nation's espionage set-up," claiming that "the Bogotá revolt was a 'fiasco' of American intelligence." Taking further aim, Devitt told the *Post* reporter, "Intelligence is the most neglected and incompetent aspect of our national defense. It is equal to, if not greater, in importance than atomic energy."[12]

The aim of the first hearing, held on April 15, 1948, while the American delegation was still in Bogotá, was to determine why the CIA failed to provide the State Department with any advance warning of the possible threat. Hillenkoetter, the first witness to testify at the hearing, staunchly defended the Agency's handling of the intelligence. He told Brown that he had indeed issued warnings to the State Department via the embassy. He further explained that he had not issued the warning directly to Robert Lovett, the deputy secretary of state, because that would have violated a national security protocol, NSCID 2, which precluded the DCI from communicating the intelligence to senior State Department personnel on his own. Given this new information, Brown began to question the State Department's role in the matter. In the end, he exonerated the Agency and assigned most blame to the State Department. In defense of the CIA—an agency he helped to establish—Brown declared: "Our Central Intelligence Agency must be protected against censorship or intimidation by any arm of the Executive Branch. . . . Otherwise, one might as well turn the intelligence agency over to the State Department and let those dumb clucks run it."[13]

Houston remained confident that the bill would still pass because the committee exonerated the CIA. In a May 7 memo to Hillenkoetter, Houston told the DCI that he "believed that the Bill, as submitted, would have the support of all the executive departments and substantial support in Congress." Neither the Bogotá affair nor the congressional inquiry were mentioned in the memo. However, when the bill failed to pass in the House over a month later, most Agency insiders, including Houston, Walter Pforzheimer, and Darling, blamed the unanticipated outcome on the Bogotá affair.[14]

The SASC chairman, John C. Gurney, felt confident that S. 2688 would easily pass when it reached the floor of Congress on June 19, 1948, for he knew that he had the bipartisan support of every member of the SASC. But the clock was ticking. Congress was scheduled to begin its summer recess on June 20, and the bill would have to pass in both the Senate and House on that same day.

He discussed the matter with Senate Majority Leader Kenneth Wherry, who agreed to fast-track the bill based on Gurney's assurances. Wherry then stood before the chamber and requested a speedy passage of the bill: "I am told by the distinguished chairman of the Committee on Armed Services that there is no controversy involved. I am also told by the distinguished Senator that he would like to ask unanimous consent that the unfinished business be temporarily laid aside and that the Senate proceed to the consideration of Calendar No. 1340, S. 2688."

It was now Gurney's turn to explain why the bill had to be expeditiously shepherded through the Senate without debate. He spent approximately one minute on the Senate floor speaking to his colleagues: "Hearings on the matter were conducted in executive session because the confidential nature of the Agency's functions was deemed to be such as to require the discussions to be so held. The committee carefully considered all sections of the bill, and, after such consideration, is satisfied that all provisions of the proposal are justified and necessary to the efficient operation of the intelligence service of United States." He ended his uninspiring sales pitch by urging fellow senators to pass the bill without objection or further questions: "The bill has the unanimous approval of the committee, and I ask for its immediate adoption." Gurney purposely kept his words brief. Instead of laying out a stronger case, he put on his best poker face and played the national security card. The presiding officer then asked, "Is there objection?"[15]

Brien McMahon, the young Democrat from Connecticut who two years earlier had chaired the Special Committee on Atomic Energy, stood up to object, citing his uneasiness with Section 7b on the DCI's confidential funds authority. McMahon surely must have recalled Lindsay Warren's decisive testimony before the special committee he chaired as he now made his statement on the Senate floor:

> It is with great reluctance that I rise to object. I should like to call the attention of the chairman of the committee to section (b) of the bill, which reads as follows: "The sums made available to the Agency may be expended without regard to the provision of law and regulations relating to the expenditure of government funds; and object of a confidential, extraordinary, or emergency nature, such expenditures to be accounted for solely on the certificate of the Director and every such certificate shall be deemed a sufficient voucher for the amount therein certified." Mr. President, it is with reluctance I would move to strike this section from the bill. . . . I am slightly Scotch about it, and I have my doubts.

McMahon wanted to let some time pass in order to see how the CIA functioned without Section 7b, which would leave open the possibility of revisiting the issue in the future. It was a worst-case scenario from the CIA's standpoint, which considered Section 7b the most important provision in the bill.[16]

Now, suddenly, S. 2688 was in deep trouble, for there was no time left to achieve a workable compromise with McMahon. And even if it passed in the Senate, the House still had to vote on the bill that night without debate. Stunned by the turn of events, Gurney conceded defeat: "Mr. President, in view of my promise to the Senator of Missouri that I should not delay debate, I am compelled to accept the amendment, in the hope that we can get the bill over to the House and secure its passage in the House tonight, where a similar bill is on the calendar. I, therefore, accept the amendment." However, other senators, along with "a visibly angry Walter Pforzheimer," confronted McMahon, and a tense exchange ensued on the Senate floor. It is unknown how an observer of the proceedings, such as Pforzheimer could have convinced McMahon to change his mind; but, when the powerful senator returned to the floor, he announced, "I have resolved that the thing to do is to withdraw the objection." Forty years later, in 1987, Houston recalled this chaotic moment in a letter to DCI Robert Gates: "As it was, in 1948, Senator Brien McMahon moved on the floor to strike that provision, and it was stricken. However, after a rather bitter dispute with Mr. Pforzheimer outside the Senate chamber immediately thereafter, to his credit Senator McMahon returned to the Senate floor and restored the stricken provision." The resolution was then unanimously passed and sent over to the House for a vote.[17]

Gurney succeeded in fast-tracking the bill through the Senate, barely averting disaster on the Senate floor, but the effort to pass the legislation in the House was far less successful. S. 2688 died on the House floor that night without being prioritized for an uncontested vote, leaving the bill in limbo for another year.

THE OFFICE OF POLICY COORDINATION

Statutory recognition for the CIA was just the first step toward the development of a much larger and more powerful intelligence agency. Ambiguous wording in the 1947 charter in key areas that involved espionage, foreign counterintelligence, and covert action left the language open to interpretation by the NSC. In 1968, Richard Bissell, the former deputy director of the CIA clandestine services (1958–1962), spoke to an elite group at a secret session of the Council on Foreign Relations at the Harold Pratt House in New York City. The highly esteemed speaker explained to the audience that "CIA's full 'charter' has been frequently revised, but it has been, and must remain, secret. The absence of a public charter leads people to search for the charter and to question the Agency's authority to undertake various activities. The problem of a secret 'charter' remains as a curse, but the need for secrecy would appear to preclude a solution." The dilemma for the CIA, as Bissell so aptly laid out, was that its public charter was purposely ambiguous, while its secret charter was never made public. The secret charter, via NSC directives, defined the legal boundaries imposed on the CIA's foreign activities, and those boundaries affected where the unvouchered funds were being directed.[18]

At the time the CIA was created, James Forrestal, the secretary of defense, asked Hillenkoetter whether the "CIA would be able to conduct covert cold-war activities, such as black propaganda, commando-type raids, sabotage, and support of guerrilla warfare." The OSS, of course, had engaged in these kinds of activities during World War II. Forrestal and other senior-level hawks in the Truman administration looked to Section 102(5)(d) for the necessary authority. Hillenkoetter turned to Lawrence Houston for a legal opinion. Houston thought that the NSC had the authority to direct the CIA to perform "other functions and duties related to intelligence" only in the special case in which the national security of the United States was at stake. On unvouchered funds and their use by the CIA, Houston said: "Aside from the discussions of normal departmental expenses for CIA as a whole, approval was given to the unvouchered funds requested by the Director of Central Intelligence mainly for the specific purposes of conducting clandestine intelligence operations outside the United States. We believe that there was no intent to use either the vouchered or unvouchered funds for M. O. or S. O. work."[19] Houston admonished Hillenkoetter: "It is our conclusion, therefore, that neither M. O. nor S. O. should be undertaken by CIA without previously informing Congress and obtaining its approval of the functions and the expenditure of funds for those purposes."[20]

Houston conceded that perhaps some "black" operations could be financed by channeling money to foreign resistance groups, as the OSS had done during World War II. But he strongly advised Hillenkoetter to "go to Congress for authority and funds" in special cases involving covert action. Such activity was a gray area in international law. When was covert action on foreign soil legally justifiable? The claim, whether entirely true or not, can always be made that one nation is protecting its national security against a potential threat posed by another. But when covert action is carried out abroad without direct provocation, it can justifiably be considered an act of war, or at the very least, a serious national security violation. Although Houston's reply was probably not what Forrestal wanted to hear, it influenced the evolution and pace of NSC directives over the next couple of years. Forrestal's dilemma was partly circumvented by interpreting vague terms like "intelligence," "national security," and "plausible deniability" in the broadest possible way, which allowed the CIA to expand its covert operations on foreign soil through a series of NSC directives.

Development of a covert action wing of the CIA was furthered by NSC 4-A and NSC 10/2, which were issued in the Agency's first full year of operations. NSC 4-A authorized the CIA to carry out psychological operations abroad; it was the first major NSC policy directive to increase the legal boundaries of covert action in peacetime. According to Darling, "The importance of NSC 4-A in the history of Central Intelligence and relationships between the collection of secret intelligence and subversive activities overseas is not to be underestimated, especially at the date of this writing in January 1953 when some of those activities have been badly exposed." NSC 4-A initially defined the relationship between passive intelligence gathering and "subversive activities" aimed at politically destabilizing a targeted political regime.[21]

NSC-4A was a legal test of the NSC's authority. As usual, Hillenkoetter found himself on the other side of the fence from key NSC members, such as Forrestal. Hillenkoetter thought that NSC-4A had dangerous implications for the CIA because Congress had never considered covert field operations when it passed the National Security Act.

According to Darling, Hillenkoetter felt that

> the administration of the Agency had developed along two determining lines. The first was that matters of personnel, support services, and budgets should be centralized to serve all components of the Agency. Second, controls were established to maintain those budgets, ensure against illegal

transactions, avoid waste and duplication in expenditure, and adhere to standards required by security, the Civil Service Commission, the Bureau of the Budget and the General Accounting Office. No agency, he said, regardless of its nature, and "most emphatically" none that handled confidential funds of the Government, could possibly avoid such controls.[22]

By the spring of 1948, the NSC was planning for the creation of a new autonomous intelligence field unit that would carry out acts of political warfare and other subversive activities. It was anticipated that the CIA would pay all the bills and assume legal responsibility for the proposed off-the-books special ops outfit. But the NSC, not the DCI, would have control of the organization and its agenda. Hillenkoetter opposed this development, but to no avail. James Forrestal, the new secretary of defense, led the initiative, but it was George Kennan, head of the State Department's Policy Planning Staff, who drafted the directive that became known as NSC 10/2. Internal NSC debate focused on whether to create a totally new organization or a new department inside the CIA. In the end, they effectively did both, as contradictory as that may sound.

In a multi-page memo, the "problem" was defined as "the inauguration of organized political warfare." That is, how to intervene in the political and economic affairs of another country without getting caught. The memo set the stage for the planning and execution of covert action by the CIA in peacetime. In the NSC, a consensus grew in support of extending covert operations into the legally murky area of low-grade political warfare; still, the principal members remained divided on the fundamental question of how to create a new organization for special covert operations without informing Congress. The Policy Planning Staff's first draft proposal for a new intelligence directive, submitted on May 5, called for the creation of a new organization that functioned under the authority of the NSC.[23]

NSC 10/2 created an autonomous organization called the Office of Special Plans and left the CIA responsible for funding and housing it:

> The Central Intelligence Agency is charged by the National Security Council with conducting espionage and counter-espionage operations abroad. It therefore seems desirable, for operational reasons, not to create a new agency for covert operations, but in time of peace to place the responsibility

> for them within the structure of the Central Intelligence and correlate them with espionage and counter-espionage operations under the over-all control of the Director of Central Intelligence.[24]

Unvouchered funds would be channeled from the CIA to the Office of Special Plans, but its operational agenda would be carried out under the direction of the secretaries of the State and War Departments. NSC 10/2 was approved the day before Congress voted on S. 2688, apparently in the belief that the bill would pass.

Based on that approval, the NSC directive also sanctioned covert action under Section 102(d)(5):

> Therefore, under the authority of Section 102(d)(5) of the National Security Act of 1947, the National Security Council hereby directs that in time of peace: A new Office of Special Projects shall be created with the Central Intelligence Agency to plan and conduct covert operations; and in coordination with the Joint Chiefs of Staff to plan and prepare for the conduct of such operations in wartime. A highly qualified person, nominated by the Secretary of State, acceptable to the Director of Central Intelligence and approved by the National Security Council, shall be appointed as Chief of the Office of Special Projects. The Chief of the Office of Special Projects shall report directly to the Director of Central Intelligence. For purposes of security and of flexibility of operations, and to the maximum degree consistent with efficiency, the Office of Special Projects shall operate independently of other components of the Central Intelligence Agency.[25]

The Office of Special Plans began operations on September 1, 1948, but its name was changed to the Office of Policy Coordination (OPC) "to ensure plausibility while revealing practically nothing of its purposes." The CIA, as designed, functioned as the OPC's paymaster, which left the DCI to assume accountability for OPC activities. If something went wrong, the CIA, not the NSC, would be held responsible. Arthur Darling explains, "The Department of State and the Military Establishment insisted upon placing OPC in the Agency because neither wanted the other to have it. Both sought the cover of the Agency for it because neither wanted the responsibility. If it failed, they could disown it."[26]

Frank Wisner, a former OSS commander in Eastern Europe, was

chosen to head this new covert arm of the intelligence community. Wisner, like Donovan and Dulles, had been a Wall Street lawyer prior to joining the OSS. Upon resuming his role as full partner at the firm of Carter, Ledyard after the war, he became restless and longed for the kind of adventure he had experienced in war-torn Europe. In the summer of 1947, an old business connection offered him a State Department job serving as the assistant secretary for occupied areas. This special branch had a close liaison with the National Military Establishment in the US-occupied regions of Germany, Austria, Korea, Japan, and Trieste.[27] Wisner[28]met all of Kennan's desired qualifications, right down to his strong anti-communist leanings and his active membership in the Council on Foreign Relations.[29]

In his memoir, Lyman Kirkpatrick, assistant director of the Office of Special Operations (OSO), describes the OPC as "one of the weirdest organizational concepts in Washington—a city that has seen plenty of weird concepts." The coexistence of two CIA-supported intelligence outfits quickly incited intense internal rivalry. Making matters worse, the OSO and the OPC did not coordinate their activities. In some instances, OSO and OPC case officers found themselves competing to recruit the same foreign agents. This acrimony persisted until Bedell Smith, Hillenkoetter's eventual successor, took charge of the situation and amalgamated the two outfits into a single clandestine directorate.[30]

The chain of command between the CIA and the OPC was confusing and ambiguous. Wisner demanded unfettered access to senior officials at the State and Defense Departments; he argued "that the new head would require 'broad latitude' in selecting his 'methods of operations,'" and would need to have "continuing and direct access" to the State Department and the military establishment "without having to proceed through the CIA administrative hierarchy in each case." Hillenkoetter was caught in the middle of this power struggle, largely because the CIA was expected to covertly fund the OPC without asking too many questions. It was all part of the plan. According to Arthur Darling:

> Hillenkoetter believed that NSC 10-2 made a bad situation worse. He was responsible under NSC 4-A for operations which he did not want the Agency to conduct. But he had full authority then, so long as he kept close touch with the Department of State. His was the responsibility to the Council. He

had full control over his subordinates in a chain of command. He could direct them as he saw fit. Now under NSC 10-2 he could not choose his own chief of operations; he could merely accept someone offered to him by the Department of State."[31]

The OPC presented the NSC with a new option in the Cold War, namely, covert action. NSC 10/2 was crafted while S. 2688 was taking shape in the House and Senate armed services committees. With the secret issuance of NSC 10/2 on June 18, most anticipated that the CIA would soon have the necessary authority to channel unvouchered funds to the OPC. This funding strategy, of course, depended entirely on the passage of S. 2688 on the following day.

THE GAO, THE OPC, AND THE DCI'S CONFIDENTIAL FUNDS AUTHORITY

The champagne corks were likely already popping at the CIA after S. 2688 passed in the Senate. When the bill failed to pass in the House, the NSC was suddenly confronted with a serious legal dilemma. The CIA was supposed to function as a surrogate for the OPC, supplying funds and housing to a new organization that had neither. NSC 10/2 authorized the CIA to direct unvouchered funds to the OPC under the auspices of the DCI's confidential funds authority, but that authority depended entirely on the bill's passage. If the bill had passed in the House, the CIA could have channeled unvouchered funds to the OPC without informing the GAO or Congress.

No one inside the CIA knew for sure what the implications were, but the hope was that the GAO would allow some basic changes to the rules governing the working fund. When the bill failed to pass, Houston scheduled a meeting with the GAO on June 28 to discuss CIA funding for the upcoming year under the working fund arrangement. Attending from the CIA were Houston, Walter Ford, Edward Saunders, Kenneth Woodring, and Walter Pforzheimer; on the GAO side, attendees were Lyle Fisher, E. W. Bell, chief of GAO's Auditing Division, and "Mr. Taylor," the special GAO auditor assigned to the CIA.[32]

Houston explained to Hillenkoetter in a June 29 memo, "In view of the failure of Congress to pass the legislation needed for administrative support of the CIA, a discussion was held today on procedures to be followed in the administration of CIA funds for fiscal year 1949." Houston hoped that the GAO might still recognize the main fiscal provisions in the DCI's confidential funds authority as part of the working fund arrangement. It was an audacious strategy, considering that the bill had just failed to pass. Houston first recited the history of the working fund and the reasons the bill had failed to pass. Presumably, he attributed the failure to the politics surrounding the Bogotá riots, but this part of the memo was redacted. The GAO, however, saw the situation differently and rejected Houston's proposal. According to Houston, "Mr. Fisher stated that, while it was regrettable that the necessary authorities had not been granted, it was clear that Congress intended CIA to continue functioning as presently constituted and that there were adequate grounds on which the GAO could continue its informal support of CIA until legislation was finally enacted."[33]

Houston then asked "whether it would be possible to have the appropriation section of the bill established as the basis on which CIA vouchered funds would be expended during the interim period." Section 7 of the bill stated, "The sums made available to the Central Intelligence Agency may be expended without regard to the provisions of law and regulations relating to the expenditure of Government funds," which technically applied to either vouchered or unvouchered funds. The GAO rebuffed this request as well. According to Houston, "Mr. Fisher felt that this would be impossible and that we should continue to operate under procedures now in effect." The next fourteen lines of the memo are redacted, but given that the memo was to the DCI, it seems likely that Houston analyzed the impact on the Agency's funding of the OPC based on the GAO's informal ruling.[34]

The focus of the meeting next switched to a discussion of the nature of the covert operations allowed under the working fund:

> It was specifically pointed out to Mr. Fisher that, even though CIA did not have legislative authority to perform certain acts which the bill would have authorized, it might become necessary, in order to support CIA operations, to perform such acts during the interim period, and if the Director determined that such necessity existed [rest of sentence deleted]. Mr. Fisher ac-

> knowledged the possibility of such a situation, and though it is felt that it would be impossible for him [next three lines deleted] in law.[35]

While Fisher acknowledged "the possibility of such a situation," the GAO had no legal basis for arbitrarily modifying the accounting rules, procedures, or authorities established for the administration of the working fund in line with S. 2688. The working fund was set up to meet the CIA's stringent security requirements, which gave the CIA more fiscal latitude than any other agency in the federal government. On July 1, the secretary of state, secretary of the army, and secretary of the navy signed a letter addressed to the comptroller general requesting that the "same authorities and arrangements apply for the activities and funds of the Central Intelligence Agency as existed during 1947 and 1948 fiscal years."[36]

THE OPC, THE CIA, THE GAO, AND THE MARSHALL PLAN

The failure of S. 2688 to pass left the OPC without any appropriations of its own; under the working fund there was no legal mechanism—other than gaining the approval of the comptroller general or Congress—for surreptitiously siphoning off unvouchered funds and directing them to the OPC. Nonetheless, Frank Wisner still managed to scrape together enough sponsorship to keep the OPC functioning on a minimal budget until the passage of the CIA Act of 1949. One of Wisner's key quasi-government sponsors was the European Cooperation Agency (ECA), which was directing Marshall Plan funds to rebuild Europe.[37]

Congress appropriated over $12 billion in loans and grants (mostly grants) to the European Economic Recovery Program and created the ECA to oversee the transfer of American dollars to the recovery effort. The ECA coordinated its activities with the State Department from its headquarters in Paris. Not coincidentally, the ECA began its operations in July 1948, at about the same time that the NSC was secretly establishing the OPC. George Kennan's Policy Planning Staff drafted both NSC 10/2 and the Marshall Plan. NSC 10/2 was crafted with the Marshall Plan in mind.

Declassified CIA records show that the ECA, with a nod from the State Department, served as a conduit to finance the OPC's covert operations. This was probably not the original intention, but when S. 2688 failed to pass, the NSC needed a plan B. Richard Bissell, the ECA's assistant director of administration in Washington, was Wisner's first point of contact. Bissell, a Yale PhD in economics, served as the chief economist for the Office of War Mobilization and Reconversion (OWMR) during World War II. In his memoir, published posthumously in 1994, Bissell says that he first learned about the OPC from Frank Lindsay on "one very foggy December evening" in 1948. Stationed in Europe as an OSS field officer, Lindsay had participated in SI and SO operations behind enemy lines. He worked at the ECA under Bissell until Wisner recruited him to serve as the OPC deputy chief. Lindsay informed Bissell at the time that "he was leaving to work for Frank Wisner" and that Wisner "was forming and heading the Office of Policy Coordination, a covert-action organization that was soon merged into the newly constituted Central Intelligence Agency."[38]

Wisner "unexpectedly" paid Bissell a visit "sometime thereafter" and quietly informed him that "he needed money." Wisner asked Bissell to help finance "OPC's covert operations by releasing a modest amount from the 5 percent counterpart funds." Counterpart funds were "local currency funds generated by Marshall Plan countries as a condition of their participation in the European Recovery Program." According to Bissell, for each dollar in US aid received, the recipient had to contribute an equal amount in local currency, 95 percent of which would be used for Marshall Plan programs. The other 5 percent (counterpart funds) would be used by the US government and, in particular, the ECA to finance administrative and other miscellaneous costs. Bissell openly admitted this in an interview with Burton Hersh. "'I suspect that for a couple of years it was a principal source of funding for the OPC,' Bissell will now concede. 'How this was handled administratively, and in terms of accounting at the Treasury, I don't know. . . . Frank Wisner was very reticent with me about what he was doing, and properly so.'"

The advantage of counterpart funds was that they could be readily transferred to the OPC on short notice in most any European currency. The SFB foreign exchange division performed a similar function for the OSS clandestine services during World War II.[39]

The interagency relationships among the ECA, the CIA, the OPC, and the GAO under the Marshall Plan can be partly reconstructed from declassified documents and insider accounts. A declassified top secret memo from the CIA Finance Division reveals that

> certain portions of the 5% Counterpart funds of ECA are made available to CIA for the purpose of furthering the Marshall Plan by [word deleted] combating Communist elements in participating counties. It is our understanding that, originally, each grant of funds was made available for a specific purpose, such as the subsidization of a foreign labor or political group. Further, that in every instance the proposed activity had the mutual concurrence of the Administrator, ECA, the American Ambassador concerned and the Director, CIA.[40]

This same memo, which was dated a few short months after the passage of the Central Intelligence Agency Act of 1949, confirms that the GAO was involved in the approval process. There were formal rules and guidelines to follow in accounting for counterpart funds: "We have also just been advised that the GAO has approved the expenditure of these ECA funds by CIA for approved ECA purposes, with the assumption that the CIA would expend and account for these funds in the same detail and in accordance with the same policies as it does its own funds." The memo suggests that the GAO believed the CIA to be the spending agency. It seems unlikely that the GAO knew about the creation of the OPC early on.[41]

But the following declassified memo, with subject header "CIA Responsibility and Accountability for ECA Counterpart Funds Expended by OPC," suggests that even the covert side of CIA's Budget Office had little knowledge of how OPC's confidential funds were being utilized:

> It is also understood that ECA prescribes no specific policies or regulations to govern the expenditure of these funds, but merely requires acknowledgment of receipt of the funds by CIA, a summary statement of funds expended, and the return of any balances not expended for the approved purposes. It was our original understanding that CIA assumed accountability and responsibility for these funds only as the agent of ECA; that CIA was merely the temporary custodian and transmitting agent of these funds for ECA. Accordingly, the Finance Division has maintained a separate set of fi-

> nancial records for these funds, based upon reports received from their CIA custodians, showing monies received, disbursed, and balances on hand. The Finance Division has also confirmed these reports by examining receipts obtained from either the principals of subsidized groups or receipts from the operational principals disbursing the funds. OPC, however, presumably has in its files detailed operational reports and/or financial accountings disclosing the purposes, approvals, and amounts of monies expended for each individual transaction.

The CIA Finance Division presumed that the OPC was keeping detailed accounting records and reports, but it was hard to know that for sure because there was no coordination between the OPC and the CIA Finance Division in the form of internal controls and standardized accounting and auditing procedures.[42]

Hillenkoetter probably welcomed the GAO's approval because it provided him with some much-needed political cover. This memo suggests that the DCI was seeking a measure of accountability for the OPC: "Lastly, we have just been informed by the Budget Officer that the DCI wishes a monthly report on all subsidy expenditures. Since the bulk of the ECA fund activities of OPC are in the nature of subsidies, it is assumed that such a report should include these funds." This part of the memo explains that the OPC was receiving the "bulk" of its ECA money in the form of "subsidies" and that CIA's Budget Office could not account on its own for how the OPC was spending that money. Hillenkoetter hoped to exert some authority by requiring Wisner to provide monthly expense reports.[43]

Although knowledge of the funding loop was restricted to a few people, complete concealment from the most senior people involved in the ECA was impossible. In a rare interview with Sallie Pisani, Bissell elaborates on the informal relationship between the ECA and the OPC:

> The OPC was formed right after the Marshall Plan, but there was no connection for some months. It was a complementary operation to secure Western Europe. Harriman, Foster, and Katz knew about it. But I doubt that the Marshall Plan people knew or were double personnel. Some people Wisner may have had under ECA cover. But Hoffman would have resisted that as he was thoroughly committed to economic measures. . . . Hoffman probably knew but didn't like it. Didn't want to know. But he had been told by higher

> authority it was approved use. It was probably known in the planning community after the Italian elections. When I was deputy administrator of the Marshall Plan, counterpart funds were funneled to the OPC. Wisner came for the funds but said I didn't have to know what for. My feeling was that we needed this procedure because we needed a political arm.[44]

Bissell provided Wisner with ECA funds, but he did not know how they were being used. Paul Hoffman, chief administrator for the ECA, was one of the people who knew where the money was going, but Bissell claims that he had no influence over the matter. The mere existence of the OPC increased the demand for unvouchered funds, but until the passage of the CIA Act of 1949, there was no administrative mechanism for disbursing unvouchered funds to the OPC, nor did the DCI have the statutory authority to certify those disbursements.

10. The Central Intelligence Agency Act of 1949

UNTOLD LEGISLATIVE HISTORY

When S. 2688 died on the House floor, the OPC was left hanging without an operational source of unvouchered funds. On February 18, 1949, Subcommittee No. 3 of the HASC convened to discuss the new spy bill in closed session.[1] Carl Durham (D-North Carolina), the committee chair, five congressmen, and one professional staff member attended the meeting. The two main witnesses on the first day of testimony were CIA Deputy Director Edwin K. Wright and OGC's legislative counsel, Walter Pforzheimer. No stenographers were present to record their testimony, but the House Rules Committee gave the CIA "permission to make notes of the Committee hearings." The bill's language was ironed out at this meeting with senior CIA officials.[2]

Nothing was left to chance this time. The House and Senate armed services committees did their part by keeping the hearings secret. The House Rules Committee also did its part by introducing special rules that limited the scope and duration of open floor debates. Some of the bill's provisions could not be debated or discussed on the floors of either chamber. Moreover, non-committee members could not submit amendments to the bill.[3]

The new bill, titled H.R. 2663, read much the same as S. 2688, but it had one new eye-opening provision on immigration—Section 8. Section 8 had been part of the CIA's original proposal in 1948, but it had been yanked out of the bill by the State Department due to the potential controversy it might arouse in Congress. Section 8 stated:

> Whenever the Director, the Attorney General, and Commissioner of Immigration shall determine that the entry of a particular alien into the United States for permanent residence is in the interest of national security or essential to the furtherance of the national intelligence mission, such alien and his immediate family shall be given entry into the United States for permanent residence without regards to their inadmissibility under the immigration or any other laws and regulations pertaining to admissibility.

When the new bill reached the State Department in late December 1948, Secretary of State George Marshall was at Walter Reed Hospital recovering from major surgery to remove one of his ailing kidneys. About to officially resign, Marshall was no longer running the department. In his absence, Robert Lovett, the under secretary of state, was filling in as acting secretary—but Lovett had also recently announced his intention to resign. Dean Acheson was slated to succeed Marshall as secretary of state.

Park W. Armstrong, the special assistant for research and intelligence, briefed Lovett on the status of the CIA legislation ten days before Acheson's confirmation and recommended that he "sign the attached letter concurring in the CIA legislation." There is reference to a discussion between Lovett and Hillenkoetter, in which Lovett agreed to include the "immigration clause."

> With respect to the immigration clause which permits the bringing into the United States of up to 100 individuals without regards to immigration statutes, the following is pertinent:
>
> (a) In discussion with Admiral Hillenkoetter, it is understood that you gave informal approval to this clause.
>
> (b) The Visa Division has concurred in this clause of the legislation and, in fact, in consultation with CIA representatives has suggested improvements in the phraseology which have been adopted by the CIA according to the attachment.

Adding the attorney general and the commissioner of immigration to the list of approving authorities helped to smooth over objections from the bill's critics, even though it doubled the number of fast-tracked immigrants permitted per year, from 50 to 100. On other points, the admission process for immigrants was highly secretive—the attorney general and the commissioner were technically the only people outside of the CIA with a need to know.[4]

Armstrong's memo to Lovett also alludes to Section 10b,[5] dealing with the DCI's confidential funds authority; he notes that it was added at the request of the GAO: "The specific grants in powers of this legislation are being sought by the CIA now as a result of requests by the General Accounting Office, and are in accordance with their specifications. It is understood the Bureau of the Budget also concurs in the need for such modifications to the CIA enabling legislation." Armstrong does not show a clear understanding of this matter. The GAO had an interest in severing the comptroller general's authority from the DCI. This conflict in the authority structure went back to the working fund agreement at the August 1946 conference. The GAO objected to the fact that, although the comptroller general bore fiduciary responsibility for the DCI's certifications, he could not look behind his certificate without evidence of a major fiduciary impropriety. This unconventional delegation of authority was viewed as a provisional step, not a permanent one. Armstrong's memo, furthermore, says nothing about the eleventh-hour change to the bill that took place the year before. The GAO was still unaware of that change when this memo was written.[6]

As mentioned earlier, in the previous year three changes were made to the statutory language in Section 7b. As first worded, this confidential funds authority was assigned to the NSC—a group that included the president. Next, the NSC was scratched, and this extraordinary authority was transferred to the budget director, a senior official who coordinated the funding of the executive branch. In one final change, just before the bill was approved in the Senate, the budget director was removed from Section 7b and replaced with the DCI, the spender of unvouchered funds. This last tweak was, without question, the most controversial; yet Houston decided on the spur of the moment not to inform the GAO of the change in good faith. It seems fair to speculate here that this was a calculated decision based on the strong sense inside the CIA that the bill would pass. Houston did not want to risk a show-stopping response from Warren so close to the finish line.

After the new bill was submitted, the budget bureau instructed Houston "to inform the comptroller general in view of the rewording of Section 7 (b)." On February 7, Houston met with Lyle Fisher to inform him of the change and to explain why the change had been made at the last minute in the previous year. Houston must surely have gone into the meeting hoping to smooth over the awkward situation privately. A memorandum, written by Houston that day to document the meeting, starts by explaining why he went to Fisher instead of formally submitting the new bill to the comptroller general for review: "Rather than submit the new bill for formal clearance by the Comptroller General, I discussed the situation with Mr. Fisher, his General Counsel." Houston would have been concerned about Warren's reaction to the change, which had been made after his formal endorsement of the bill in a letter to Webb. Hillenkoetter had also used quotes from Warren's letter in his testimony to the HASC the year before.[7]

According to Houston, "Mr. Fisher stated that in accordance with their normal approach to such matters, they would prefer to have some control outside the Agency over the amount which would be beyond the audit powers of GAO. I stated that we were in agreement with the principle that there should be some control, either in the NSC or the Bureau of the Budget, but that in view of the express intent of the Senate Committee in 1948, the Bureau of the Budget did not wish to go back to the wording of the legislation submitted last spring."[8]

Although Lyle Fisher did not endorse the change that he was only now being informed about, he did not reject it, either. Houston's memo suggests that, although speaking off the record, Fisher was extremely careful in stating the GAO's position on Section 7b, saying that

> he could not speak officially for the Comptroller General, but felt that in view of our past relations with his office, and our special needs, the comptroller general would not be compelled to object strenuously to the wording of Section 7(b) as redrafted by the Senate Committee. He was, therefore, not approving submission of this wording for himself or the Comptroller General but was taking the position that they did not feel it necessary to object to its submission. I stated that we would not quote him as approving, and would understand fully that if Mr. Warren were called to testify on this situation, he might feel it necessary to state his position to such blanket authorization of unvouchered funds.[9]

Fisher knew that his boss would have trouble supporting the altered provision, but in this extraordinary case, he convinced Warren in confidence to modify his previous position by remaining neutral, neither endorsing nor rejecting it on the record. Nine years later, Houston reminded Dulles of Warren's decision to remain neutral on the bill:

> [The comptroller general's] support was a strong influence in obtaining our statutory authorities. If he had opposed our confidential funds authority, we

> might well not have been given it as the Atomic Energy Commission was refused such authority on the opposition of the Comptroller General. However, Mr. Fisher emphasized our unique role and the world situation which made it so important and obtained the Comptroller General's approval of granting such authority to the CIA.[10]

Outside of Washington, the CIA lobbied its powerful supporters in the media in a semi-clandestine effort to gain an undercurrent of public support for the bill. Declassified CIA calendar notes from February 25, 1949, indicate that Walter Pforzheimer discussed the legislation privately with media moguls and CIA-friendly reporters:

> [Name blacked out] cleared Mr. P's talking with Miss Clay of 'Newsweek' and also Whitelaw Reid of the New York Herald Tribune re: on H.R. 2663. . . . Spoke with Mr. Whitelaw Reid, Vice President of the New York Herald Tribune, regarding their editorial concerning CIA. Informed him that we would be most anxious to have his support and that I would like to explain to him the matters involved in the House enabling bill. He promised to arrange appropriate appointments for me.

Collectively, OGC calendar notes and private communications with ranking members of the armed services committees suggest that the CIA choreographed this entire sequence of events.

A note from March 4 says that Pforzheimer "talked with Mr. Connery of CBS regarding the material of Sec. 8 H.R. 2663 for the Edward R. Murrow broadcast." Edward R. Murrow, a highly respected journalist and the head of CBS news, strongly endorsed the immigration provision in his nightly radio broadcast on April 4, several days before the House voted on the bill:

> This is essentially an underground railroad for first-class passengers only, up to 100 a year. It will be confined to people of the highest caliber, morally and mentally, who have to get out of their own countries on short notice or face arrest, torture, or execution, people whose background, information, and services are so valuable to us that it would not be safe to keep them for any prolonged length of time even in countries of western Europe.[11]

The *Washington Post* reported on March 5 that the HASC was considering a "hush-hush measure giving legal basis for the Nation's spy system," and that the bill would "give permanent, statutory authority to the Central Intelligence Agency, and exempt it from normal auditing and Civil Service regulation to keep operations secret." It also reported that the House Rules Committee was fast-tracking the bill for passage by approving "closed" rules that limited debate on the bill to one hour.[12]

Calendar notes from March 5 reveal that the CIA provided Durham with all his talking points on the House floor: "Prepared text of statements to be delivered on H.R. 2663 by Cong. Sasscer and Durham in support of bill." Durham and Lansdale Sasscer (D-Maryland) essentially parroted endorsements conveniently scripted by the CIA. Both of their emotionally charged statements were peppered with nationalistic overtones, and Durham's statement alluded to Murrow's radio broadcast from a few days earlier:

> There are many people all over the world who believe in this country and what it stands for implicitly. Many of them are living in police states. Some of them may have formerly been highly placed in the service of their government. Some of them may even be there now. Many of them have important intelligence information to make available to this country, and such information may be of vital importance to our nation security and our policies. These people, be they soldiers or statesmen or scientists, can only approach a representative of America once. If they are seen talking to an American, it may mean the concentration camp or in some instances death itself.[13]

The House floor debates on March 7 lasted only about forty minutes; most of the dissenting opinions took aim at the unprecedented secrecy surrounding the bill. The immigration provision—the only provision that Congress in plenary could deliberate on—also took attention away from Section 10b and the DCI's special confidential funds authority. A small minority of congressmen, nevertheless, did express their dissatisfaction with the bill. Emanuel Celler (D-New York), the powerful chairman of the House Judiciary Committee, was angry that the immigration provision was not brought up before his committee. Celler's committee had jurisdiction over immigration law, and he bitterly complained about the House rules in his floor speech:

> In the first place, if there had not been a closed rule, I would have made the point of order to strike out this provision because it is exclusively within the

> province of the Committee on the Judiciary and is not the business of the Committee on the Armed Services. The Committee on the Armed Services has nothing to do with immigration. Now this provision I have read throws out of the window, at the discretion of the Director . . . and the Attorney General, all the legislative immigration restrictions that we have built up over the years. It throws them to the wind, and if the Attorney General and the Director wish to admit Fascists, Communists, Hitler sadists, morons, moral perverts, syphilitics, or lepers, they can do it. I think the House ought to know what it is legislating about, and I think, in a measure, this indicates how the cold war is unhinging the nerves of our high military authorities.[14]

Celler, who voted for the measure, patronized the armed services committee's highly secretive handling of the legislation:

> Certainly if the members of the Armed Forces Committee can hear the detailed information to support this bill, why cannot our entire membership? Are they the Brahmins and we the untouchables? Secrecy is the answer. What is secret about the membership of an entire committee hearing the lurid reasons? In Washington three men can keep a secret if two men die. It is like the old lady who said, "I can keep a secret but the people I tell it to, cannot."[15]

Only four members of the House voted against the bill. Outspoken dissenter Vito A. Marcantonio (I-New York) focused his opposition on the bill's unprecedented secrecy. He felt that the HASC had hijacked the legislation and was using secrecy as a justification to engineer its passage. In his floor speech, Marcantonio argued that the legislative process was undemocratic and had shifted power to a small minority of congressional members:

> What are we doing here? First of all, as to the secrecy with which the committee has been operating, it admits that its members have the information which they are withholding from the House. . . . Yet, we are told that the information the committee has must be kept a secret from the Members of the House. What is worse, the committee informs us through its report that the Members of the House must pass this bill without any explanation of all of its provisions. This makes every single section of this bill suspect. No member of Congress has been informed. No Member of Congress has

> been given the full explanation of all of the provisions of the legislation to which the representatives of the people are entitled before voting on any legislation. Only the member of the Armed Services, we are told, have been given the explanation. . . . I do not care what the reason is. There has never been and there can never be any justification at any time for the representatives of the people, who are elected to Congress, to abdicate their function of legislating with full knowledge on the matters which come before them. This bill suspends that function and says, "You must not have knowledge of all of the provisions of the bill." It says, "You must vote blindly and must take the word of a committee."

Marcantonio's floor speech did little to change the outcome, but he did force a roll call that required all House members to vote on the record. The bill passed in the House on March 7 by a margin of 384 to 4.[16]

Indeed, there were heated discussions about Section 10b inside the GAO. On March 4, three days before the House vote, the chief of the Accounting and Bookkeeping Division, J. Darlington Denit, alarmed by the extraordinary wording of Section 10b, sent an urgent memo to Lindsay Warren:

> The general application of existing laws and the authority and responsibilities vested in this Office over the control and review of the financial transactions of various government agencies would be completely nullified insofar as the transactions of the Central Intelligence Agency were concerned and that the legal effect of such a provision places the agency in an autonomous position from the standpoint of accountability for the funds that may be appropriated or transferred to it.[17]

Denit recommended that the language in Section 10b be changed to read: "Of the sums made available to the Agency amounts shall be specified which shall be expended for objects of confidential, extraordinary, or emergency nature, such expenditures to be accounted for solely on the Certificate of the Director and every such Certificate shall be deemed a sufficient voucher for the amount therein certified." Denit's proposal removed the clause "may be expended without the provisions and regulations relating to expenditure of Government funds."[18] Lindsay Warren told Denit in his reply on March 14 that it "was deemed unnecessary to make any other comment on the bill at this time." Warren gently told Denit to stay out of it by referring him to his March 12, 1948, letter to James Webb from the previous year.

Frank Weitzel, Warren's top assistant in the office of the comptroller general, also expressed his misgivings in a letter to Fisher that recommended the GAO file an abuse report on the bill prior to passage. Weitzel felt that the GAO should go on the record to strengthen its position in the event that an abuse by the Agency was eventually discovered. An internal CIA memorandum helps to illuminate these internal discussions:

> Mr. E. L. Fisher, General Counsel, on March 10, 1949, wrote Mr. Weitzel . . . and recommended that we not make a voluntary report on these bills. Mr. Fisher stated that he honestly believed that nothing could be accomplished by such a report and we could jeopardize ourselves against an "abuse report" later on. He stated that we can watch the operations under the bill and be in a better position to make an "abuse" report later on if we are not disregarded on a voluntary report now.[19]

With senior GAO officials voicing concerns inside the agency, Fisher called Houston on March 10 to discuss the language of Section 10b. Houston documented their conversation in a March 11 memorandum for the record:

> [Fisher] said several members of the Comptroller's office had raised questions concerning this unlimited availability and he wished to refresh his recollection. I rehearsed the history stating that we had initially proposed outside control, first in the National Security Council, and then in the Bureau of the Budget, and were still of the opinion that such outside control was desirable in principle and practice. I stated that the control by the Bureau of the Budget had been specifically and intentionally eliminated by the Senate last year when they passed our Bill, and that when we were clearing our Bill through the Bureau of the Budget for presentation this year, the question had been raised as to what language would be used in this Section, and it was determined that the language passed by the Senate would be used, if it would not be objectionable to the Comptroller General's Office.

Houston then reminded him of their conversation in early February: "I recalled my earlier conversation with Mr. Fisher, in which I explained substantially the same situation, and that he had stated while he could not approve the language for the Comptroller, he did not feel the Comptroller would be forced to object strongly to the submission of such language to Congress." According to Houston, Fisher "agreed that this was a clear statement of his position and said that he was not now changing the position but wished to refresh his memory on the facts for explanation to the Comptroller's Office." Moreover, he "repeated that if the Comptroller's opinion were asked by the Senate, he would probably be forced to state his basic principle in such matters that no such blanket authority should ever be given." Houston assured him that "if the Bill were enacted as passed by the House, that there would be no change in the Agency's policy towards, or use of, unvouchered funds and that it would not, in any way, alter the auditing agreement which had been in force with GAO since CIA's conception. It would rather simplify and assist the audit made by their representative."[20]

The road to passage was a bit bumpier in the Senate, where individual senators had the power to filibuster and modify bills. This time around, Senator William "Wild Bill" Langer (R-North Dakota) stood in the way of the bill by placing a hold on it that lasted for over two months. Langer was an old-school Republican with an isolationist perspective. He supported the creation of the CIA, but his fears were aroused because the secretive spy bill transferred extraordinary authorities to the Agency in key areas of government administration (e.g., financial, immigration, and personnel).

Senator Pat McCarran (D-Nevada), an anti-communist zealot and chairman of the Senate Judiciary Committee, was also unhappy with the CIA and the SASC, for the same reason as Celler: his committee had been bypassed. McCarran, too, threatened to block the bill's passage, and on March 11, several days after the floor debate in the House, he wrote Senator Millard Tydings, chairman of the SASC, to express his displeasure: "In view of the fact the Senate Committee on the Judiciary has not had occasion to consider the above-mentioned provision of the bill, I am constrained to object to consideration and passage of the bill."[21]

Hillenkoetter met with McCarran on March 17, hoping to alleviate his concerns. The next day, he sent the senator a letter thanking him for "the opportunity to discuss with you and your staff . . . the problems arising out of the proposed Section 8 of H.R. 2663." His letter added:

> I am quite in accord with the thought that your Committee should be appraised of the operation of Section 8 of this proposed bill once it has become law. Therefore, I will send to you personally, as Chairman of the Committee, a quarterly report of the operations of this section for your confidential use. As I told you yesterday, we will be more than happy to cooperate with our Committee staff in furnishing you information on a confidential basis which you may from time to time request.

In this, Hillenkoetter could only have been speaking informally for himself, for nothing in the law required the DCI to provide the chairman of the Judiciary Committee with a quarterly report. After his meeting with Hillenkoetter, McCarran sent a letter to Tydings, removing his objection and promising to support the bill's passage: "Since writing to you, I have made a careful study of the provisions of the bill, which were of special concern. . . . I no longer desire that an objection be interposed to the consideration and passage of this bill, and am pleased to lend my support to its early consideration and passage." The stage was now set for the first vote in the Senate.[22]

The Senate passed H.R. 2663[23] unanimously without any major theatrics, much to the relief of the CIA and its major supporters. Afterward, Hillenkoetter sent a letter to Senator Tydings to express his "sincere appreciation" for "shepherding" the CIA legislation to passage. On the following day, the *Washington Post* reported: "The Senate yesterday passed without opposition a closely guarded bill to strengthen the Central Intelligence Agency and protect its agents abroad. In the brief debate prior to passage, few details of its contents were revealed. No public hearing had been held by the Armed Services Committee which recommended its adoption." Langer told a reporter afterward, "This is probably the first time that Congress has been asked to pass a bill without knowing what all of its provisions meant."[24]

After its passage in the Senate, the bill was sent back to the House for reconciliation, which was more of a formality. Marcantonio, the only House member to vote against the bill, called its passage "dangerous and subversive of our Bill of Rights." President Truman signed the Central Intelligence Agency Act of 1949 into law on June 20, 1949.[25]

FIRST REORGANIZATION OF SUPPORT FUNCTIONS UNDER THE CIA ACT OF 1949

The CIA Act of 1949 provided a statutory basis for building a clandestine financial administration for concealing the movement of government funds to field operations around the world. Vouchered and unvouchered funds were generally viewed as exclusive categories of spending. In practice, however, jurisdictional authority was often murky, especially when vouchered funds were used in support of secret foreign intelligence operations. In this not-uncommon situation, there was a question about which agency had audit jurisdiction over the expenditures. Because the two jurisdictions were not mutually exclusive in practice, the CIA and the GAO coordinated informally to handle these special cases.

Hillenkoetter sent a formal letter to Warren on August 17, less than two months after the passage of the CIA Act, stating that the new act "granted to the Agency and myself certain very broad and unusual powers in several respects. Passage of this legislation, therefore, emphasized rather than reduces the responsibilities which are placed on me and which I am keenly aware of." He assured Warren, "We have attempted to keep your General Counsel, Mr. Fisher, aware of our general procedures and policies and wish, particularly, to express our appreciation for his able assistance and support." At the end of the letter, he promised Warren that "so long as I hold this position, these policies and my attitude toward the Government funds under my control would in no way be changed by legislative grants of power to me." Hillenkoetter mostly kept his word, but he could not speak for his successors.[26]

Soon after the Agency was created in 1947, Hillenkoetter began moving covert support services into the OSO. By mid-1948, the OSO had an administrative support directorate consisting of three staff units: Personnel, Special Funds, and Transportation and Supply. Emmett Echols remained the special funds chief during this transitional period. A declassified top secret review of the CIA's financial operations reports: "The transfer of the Special Funds Division to OSO was based upon the premise that that office must have complete control and jurisdiction over all administrative service elements necessary for its support. However, there was a fundamental cleavage of opinion on this point within the agency." This experiment in covert administration would come back to haunt Hillenkoetter a year later, following the creation of the OPC.[27]

The DCI now sought to more efficiently compartmentalize the overt and covert administrative functions. On September 20, three months after the act's passage, Hillenkoetter ordered a major reorganization of the CIA, largely to gain greater fiscal and operational control over the OPC. Hillenkoetter moved the administrative support functions in the OSO back under the CIA executive but left sharp organizational divisions between the overt and covert administrations. The overt and covert auxiliary staffs that handled personnel, finance, and logistics were subsequently headed by different people. The SFB, under Eck Echols, was moved from the OSO to the Special Support Staff; vouchered funds, on the other hand, became part of the Administrative Support Staff.[28] The new organizational chart also included a budget office, headed by Edward Saunders, that was compartmentalized into covert and overt subdivisions.[29]

These reforms were the first step toward the centralization of CIA's budget and accounting functions; they had the immediate effect of increasing the Agency's fiscal and budgetary control over the OPC. Hillenkoetter's reorganization shortly after the passage of the CIA Act also set the stage for Bedell Smith—his successor—to fully incorporate the OPC into the CIA. According to Darling, "Hillenkoetter drew the budgeting and accounting of the new Office of Policy of Coordination closely under his central administration." Under this new administrative system,

> The Office of Policy Coordination was to operate "independently of other components" of the Agency, for security and "flexibility of operations." OPC was to do so to the "maximum degree consistent with efficiency." But it was the Director of Central Intelligence who was to make that decision. Hillenkoetter's judgment was that his responsibility to Congress for the use of vouchered and unvouchered funds made it incumbent upon him to maintain central control over the financing of those operations.

Frank Wisner, on the other hand, wanted the financial administration integrated into the clandestine services under the OPC head. He considered Hillenkoetter's restructuring of the financial administration to be a usurpation of his administrative authority.[30]

National emergencies did not fit neatly into a normal budgetary cycle. Funds simply had to be made available when needed. In one of Hillenkoetter's last major actions as DCI, he set up a modest $4 million emergency reserve fund to provide a mission-ready source of discretionary unvouchered funds for operations of an extremely urgent nature. The CIA reserve fund account, which increased by orders of magnitude during the 1950s, was a key part of the Agency's financial system. This special fund allowed circumvention of the normal congressional protocols associated with supplementary budget requests. In a memo to Echols, Hillenkoetter explained that the "amount of the reserve fund may be communicated only to the minimum number of employees on your staffs who must have such knowledge to administer the fund, and to the following CIA officials." He copied the executive, deputy executive, general counsel, chief of inspection, security staff, and the chief of the audit division.[31]

The highest intelligence priority in 1949 was to attain information on the state of the Soviet Union's nuclear program. Because the Soviet Union was a closed society, most of its secretive military programs were difficult to spy on. On August 29, 1949, just two months after the passage of the CIA Act, the Soviet Union successfully tested its first atomic bomb. Three days later, air force "sniffer" planes off the Kamchatka Peninsula detected radiological evidence of the blast. President Truman announced in a prime-time speech on September 23, "We have evidence that within recent weeks an atomic explosion occurred in the USSR." The Soviet's "First Lightning" test was arguably the single most important event of the Cold War.[32]

PART FOUR
THE CIA, THE GAO, THE COLD WAR, AND THE CIA ACT OF 1949

11. The Military-Intelligence-Industrial Complex

THE CIA ACT OF 1949 AND THE COLD WAR

In his groundbreaking book *The CIA and Congress*, David Barrett investigates the early history of the CIA and its relationship to the four big committees that controlled its budget. He reports: "After Fiscal Year 1949, the CIA attempted to create budgets in which the costs of covert action and other Cold War activities were fully planned for as part of its 'normal' budget." The numbers speak for themselves. From 1950 to 1953, CIA's annual budget grew from $52 to $587 million. By 1953, about 75 percent of the total budget was earmarked for covert action programs, up from about 25 percent in the late 1940s. The CIA, of course, was not the only beneficiary of Cold War funding during the 1950s. The defense budget averaged about 10 percent of the gross national product per year during the 1950s—in 1953, it took a large spike to about 15 percent. This alarming increase in defense spending helped to fund the emergence of a rich and powerful military-intelligence-industrial complex.[1]

The CIA Act of 1949 not only facilitated the integration of the OPC into CIA's administrative infrastructure under Bedell Smith but also factored into CIA's planning under Hillenkoetter. Notes from CIA's historical staff allude to the impact of the OPC on the agency's financial operations:

> The creation of this office was to have a significant and far-reaching effect upon the budget and fiscal as well as other administrative support activities of the Agency. However, immediately following its activation, OPC was engaged primarily in planning activities; and the budget impact and logistic and financial support requirements of that office did not make themselves felt until much later. In retrospect, it appears clear that too little attention was given during this period to the establishment of adequate financial and administrative support staffs which were later required to implement the broad programs planned by OPC.

The OPC was eventually absorbed into CIA's clandestine services; during the 1950s this arrangement impacted the allocation of financial resources to covert action.[2]

PRESIDENT EISENHOWER AND THE MILITARY-INDUSTRIAL COMPLEX

President Dwight D. Eisenhower must have been thinking about his future legacy as he prepared his final speech to the American public, given on January 17, 1961. On national television, Eisenhower proclaimed to the citizenry and the world:

> Our military organization today bears little relation to that known by any of my predecessors in peacetime, or indeed by the fighting men of World War II or Korea. Until the latest of our world conflicts, the United States had no armaments industry. American makers of plowshares could, with time and as required, make swords as well. But now we can no longer risk emergency improvisation of national defense; we have been compelled to create a permanent armaments industry of vast proportions. . . . We annually spend on military security more than the net income of all United States corporations.

The former five-star general had witnessed two world wars and the rapid growth in the US national security establishment in the postwar era. Eisenhower warned the public of the ominous threat posed to American society by the growing influence of the defense industry on the federal government and its budget:

> This conjunction of an immense military establishment and a large arms industry is new in the American experience. The total influence—economic, political, even spiritual—is felt in every city, every Statehouse, every office of the Federal government. We recognize the imperative need for this development. Yet we must not fail to comprehend its grave implications. Our toil, resources and livelihood are all involved; so is the very structure of our society.

The conflation of military and business interests, according to Eisenhower, posed an insidious threat to the basic organization and structure of American society. "In the councils of government," he declared, "we must guard against the acquisition of unwarranted influence, whether sought or unsought, by the military-industrial complex. The potential for the disastrous rise of misplaced power exists and will persist." It hardly needs to be said that most of the game-changing technological innovations of the Cold War were not developed on the cheap. The technological limits of warfare were, in fact, being pushed toward the extremes of scientific possibility, placing extravagant demands on the US Treasury. Eisenhower promulgated the idea that the best defense against the military-industrial complex was a vigilant citizenry knowledgeable of the possibilities: "We must never let the weight of this combination endanger our liberties or democratic processes. We should take nothing for granted. Only an alert and knowledgeable citizenry can compel the proper meshing of the huge industrial and military machinery of defense with our peaceful methods and goals, so that security and liberty may prosper together."[3]

The CIA Act of 1949 played an instrumental role in fomenting this new threat by enabling the Agency to insulate the flow of unvouchered funds from the US Treasury to field operations all over the world. The financial system was designed to support the rapid movement of funds, people, and supplies to anywhere in the world on a moment's notice. Under the CIA Act, the Agency could secretly embed its employees in key positions at other departments, namely, the State and Defense Departments. This extraordinary level of access gave the CIA leverage over the administrative and operational affairs of other departments. During the 1950s and 1960s, senior officials chaired or served on most of the major interdepartmental committees involving intelligence and national security. By the early 1960s, CIA analysts were giving personal briefings to the president. The Agency could never have become such a powerful force in government without the CIA Act of 1949.

The CIA-GAO liaison continued to evolve during the 1950s, driven mainly by their mutual interest in the jurisdictional boundaries for vouchered and unvouchered funds, about which the CIA Act was purposely vague. In 1981, the CIA's deputy general counsel, David Addington, described the early history of the liaison in an internal CIA memo:

> Beginning in August 1946, the General Accounting Office conducted audits of the Central Intelligence Group, the institutional predecessor of the CIA,

> under arrangements agreed upon between the GAO and the CIG. Audits continued under these arrangements after creation of the Central Intelligence Agency by the National Security Act of 1947. With the passage of the Central Intelligence Agency Act of 1949, the Agency acquired broad powers to expend its appropriations without regard to statutes regulating government expenditures, and where necessary for reasons of confidentiality, to make unvouchered expenditures accounted for solely by the Director's certificate of the amount expended.

According to Addington, "The GAO limited its audit to a review of vouchered expenditures of appropriations to determine whether the Agency spent the funds in accordance with applicable statutes. The GAO made no reports concerning its audits to anyone outside CIA." Section 10b created jurisdictional divisions between vouchered and unvouchered funds, and it was these statutory divisions that precluded the comptroller general from looking behind the DCI's certification of unvouchered funds.[4]

CONFIDENTIAL FUNDS AND THE EARLY US PRESIDENTS

Lawrence Houston was well aware that one badly blown covert operation in a foreign country, or the discovery of nefarious illegal activity involving the misuse of unvouchered funds, would be likely to set in motion a full-scale congressional investigation of the Agency's financial operations. If broad enough, such an investigation could expose the inner workings of the Agency's stealth financial system, which, in turn, could bring about legal reforms that would limit its freedom and ability to operate abroad. That may have been a worst-case scenario, but Houston prepared a legal defense of the CIA Act just in case a constitutional challenge ever arose.

In the early 1950s, the office of the CIA's general counsel wrote a legal brief, "Historical Study of the Use of Confidential Funds," about the DCI's confidential funds authority under Section 10. According to Houston,

> The objective of this study is to correlate such historical and judicial materials relating to the use of confidential funds as are available and to examine

> them for whatever light they may throw upon the expenditure of the confidential funds granted it by Congressional appropriation. Implicit in such a study, of course, is the search for possible guideposts to assist those responsible in determining the purposes for which those appropriations may properly be spent.

Houston prepared a legal defense of Section 10b that considered early statutory precedents in US history back to Revolutionary times:

> Section 10(b) is the critical section for this present discussion. It can logically be sub-divided into two parts. The first part authorizes expenditure of funds without regard to provisions of law or regulations. This extraordinary authority technically applies to both audited and confidential funds. . . . The second part of Section 10(b), after the semicolon, authorizes the Agency to expend funds for objects of a "confidential, extraordinary, or emergency nature," such expenditures to be accounted for solely on the certificate of the Director and every such certificate to be deemed a sufficient voucher for the amount therein certified. The words "extraordinary or emergency" enlarge greatly the traditional concept of confidential funds. CIA is thus given the widest authority for expenditure of unvouchered funds in peacetime.[5]

The "audited" funds Houston refers to are the vouchered funds that were audited by the GAO. He also distinguishes between peacetime and wartime authority, for during World War II the OSS director was delegated similar authorities.

The final report concluded, "The recorded instances in the history of the United States of the use of confidential funds in the intelligence area are not many. There are, however, sufficient documentations to establish that their use dates to American Revolutionary times. Criticism of such use goes back nearly as far."[6] Houston, however, did find a statutory precedent from the constitutional era that involved the use of confidential funds on foreign affairs by the executive branch. This one law placed the CIA Act of 1949 on far more secure legal footing.

President George Washington established a rudimentary intelligence function in the State Department during his two terms in office. Once in office, Washington looked to Congress to establish a special discretionary fund with which he could hire secret executive agents for unofficial diplomatic missions. In his first State of the Union address at Federal Hall in New York City on January 8, 1790, he made his case to Congress:

> The interests of the United States require, that our intercourse with other nations should be facilitated by such provisions as will enable me to fulfill my duty in that respect, in the manner, which circumstances may render most conducive to the public good: And to this end, that the compensations to be made to the persons, who may be employed, should, according to the nature of their appointments, be defined by law; and a competent fund designated for defraying the expenses incident to the conduct of foreign affairs.[7]

Washington was careful not to use the words "spy" or "diplomat" in his written speech. The "persons" that he had in mind were not exactly spies or foreign service officers. Instead, he loosely referred to these executive agents as persons employed "according to the nature of their appointments." This subtle ambiguity, though probably intended, caused considerable confusion in the congressional committee that later drafted the legislation.

The drafting committee sought answers to fundamental constitutional questions pertaining to the nature of the employment. Should the persons hired by the president be classified as unofficial spies or state diplomats? For instance, if they were not state diplomats, could they secretly conduct foreign negotiations on the nation's behalf without diplomatic authority and the advice and consent of the Senate? And what limits should be imposed on their compensation? On July 1, 1790, the First US Congress passed a statute creating a discretionary fund known as the "contingent fund of foreign intercourse" and appropriated $40,000 to it, a whopping 10 percent of the federal budget at that time.[8]

Washington had already dispatched the savvy Gouverneur Morris to London with confidential instructions even before he delivered his State of the Union to Congress. Washington paid him out of his own pocket during the first year of his assignment. Morris, who had a wooden leg and liked to dance, was effectively the first secret executive agent of the United States of America. He departed for Great Britain without diplomatic status. The first official payment of $2,000 was made to Morris on December 19, 1790, almost six months after the creation of the fund. Washington, however, did not notify Congress of Gouverneur Morris's special assignment in England until February 14, 1791. Although most senators deferred to Washington's personal integrity on the matter, Senator William Maclay, from Pennsylvania, later wrote in his private journal: "He has acted in a strange kind of capacity, half pimp, half envoy, or perhaps more properly a kind of political eavesdropper about the British court, for some time past."[9]

State-sponsored piracy in the Mediterranean Sea threatened the future of American trade with Europe. One of Washington's top foreign policy goals was to end the capture of American merchant ships by the Islamic city-states along the North African coast: Morocco, Algiers, Tunis, and Tripoli, known collectively as the Barbary States or Powers. Captured American ships, their cargo, and their seamen were typically held hostage until obscenely large ransom demands were paid. The United States had no navy when Washington was elected, nor had it established diplomatic relations with the Barbary States. Without a military option, Washington sought a diplomatic solution, using the contingent fund of foreign intercourse. It was a dirty little secret, but all the major European powers paid peace tributes to the Barbary States and, to that end, maintained small consulates at each of the four Barbary capitals for conducting official state diplomacy. Although paying tributes to pirates was morally repugnant, it was better than embroiling the nation in an expensive and unpopular war.[10]

In August 1990, as the United States prepared to open diplomatic relations with Portugal, President Washington appointed David Humphreys as chargé d'affaires in Lisbon. That was his official cover; his confidential mission was to open diplomatic relations with the Barbary States. Humphreys had been one of General Washington's most trusted aides during the Revolutionary War. Years earlier, Washington had lobbied hard to get Humphreys nominated for the important position of secretary to the Commission for Negotiating Treaties of Commerce with Foreign Powers, where he served alongside John Adams, Thomas Jefferson, and Benjamin Franklin. Jacob Read, a delegate from South Carolina, obviously shared Washington's opinion of Humphreys, remarking in a personal letter at the time, "You know the abilities and genius of Colo[nel] Humphreys."

Washington's desire that Humphreys keep a low profile while serving as chargé d'affaires was upended when, at about that time, the queen of

Portugal sent a minister resident (i.e., ambassador) to the United States. The queen refused to conduct foreign relations in the royal court with a chargé d'affaires, which pressured Washington to reciprocate by nominating Humphreys to serve as minister resident—the highest position at the embassy. Washington explained this change to the Senate as a measure taken to minimize cost. True, perhaps, but he was also trying to keep the mission as discreet as possible. Over the next decade, in each capital city, Humphreys skillfully set up consulates, each headed by a consular agent. These agents conducted state business using money from the contingent fund of foreign intercourse.[11]

On February 9, 1793, Congress passed legislation to amend the 1790 statute so that it more clearly linked the fund's expenditures with the employment of secret executive agents "for the purposes of intercourse or treaty with foreign nations." Under the amended law, the president could classify expenditures from the fund as either public or confidential. Public expenditures were "to be duly settled annually with the accounting officers of the Treasury" like all other expenditures in the government. Confidential expenditures, in turn, were handled differently. For these, the law authorized the president or the secretary of state[12] "to make a certificate or certificates of the amount of such expenditures, as he may think it advisable not to specify; and every such certificate shall be deemed a sufficient voucher for the sum or sums therein expressed to have been expended." Houston surely realized he had struck gold with the discovery of this 1793 statute, which he interpreted as the "statutory authority for the employment of confidential funds" in the brief.[13]

To help further Washington's negotiations with the Barbary States, Congress appropriated $1 million to the fund in 1794. In a separate but related bill passed in the same year, funds were appropriated for the construction of six naval vessels to support a federal navy to defend US maritime interests in the Mediterranean. According to the statute, "the depredations committed by the Algerine corsairs on the commerce of the United States render it necessary that a naval force should be provided for its protection." These ships, nevertheless, took years to build, and in the meantime presidents George Washington and John Adams had few alternatives other than to agree to treaties under extremely unfavorable terms. Instead of guaranteeing peaceful relations, the clandestine payments to the Barbary States demonstrated that the United States was willing and able to pay, which, contrary to producing a lasting peace, compounded the financial demands on the US Treasury. In 1800, for example, the consular agent in Tunis reported that the US Navy "furnished the navy of Algiers, on various accounts, a frigate of 32 guns, a brig of 22, one schooner of 18, one of 14, and one of a smaller size." After delivering its annual cargo to Algiers, USS *George Washington* "sailed for Constantinople, in service of the Dey, wearing his flag, and carrying his ambassador and regalia to the Sublime Porte," the seat of Islamic political power.[14]

In 1792, on behalf of the president, Secretary of State Thomas Jefferson presented the first financial report to Congress on the status of the fund. For the most part, though, Congress showed little interest in the fund until the Democratic-Republican party took control of Congress in the early nineteenth century. There are no similar reports to Congress about the fund until Jefferson's presidency.[15]

In 1802, Congress summoned a report on the contingent fund of foreign intercourse from the president. The new Congress showed a sudden, acute interest in finding out what had happened to the boatloads of money secretly delivered to the Barbary governments as a diplomatic means of preventing attacks against American merchants. The Treasury secretary, Albert Gallatin, admitted in the report that most of the accounts remained unsettled: "The greater part of the accounts being yet unsettled, and several of the most important, not having yet been rendered, it is not practicable to state, with precision, in what manner the whole of the sums drawn out of the Treasury has been ultimately applied." Along with his official statements, Gallatin provided the committee with a comprehensive balance sheet that accounted for all the historic payments to the Barbary States from the contingent fund of foreign intercourse.[16]

That same year, a committee chaired by Joseph Nicholson (R-Maryland) launched a congressional investigation of the Treasury Department "to inquire and report [on] whether moneys drawn from the Treasury have been faithfully applied to the objects for which they were appropriated," and to ascertain "in what manner and under what checks, moneys were drawn from the Treasury of the United States and were afterwards expended and accounted for." Numerous irregularities discovered during the investigation led the committee to single out the contingent fund of foreign intercourse in its report. They found an alarming number of unsettled accounts in the State Department during the tenures of secretaries Edmund Randolph (1794–1795) and Timothy Pickering (1795–1800). Randolph's unsettled accounts were still tied up in litigation, and Pickering was unable to account for $78,588, part of which had allegedly been misapplied to unapproved expenditures.

The committee also discovered that the war secretary had assumed authorities only legally vested in the president or the secretary of state. Regarding these "improper" expenditures,[17] the final report stated:

> The policy of this law, the committee does not intend to question, but it is clear that it extends only to cases of compensation, for what are usually termed "secret services" that may be rendered to the United States in their intercourse with foreign nations. . . . But in every law on the subject, it has been expressly confined to foreign intercourse. It has not, therefore, been without considerable surprise that the committee have seen the same principle applied to the expenditures of the War Department.[18]

The historical record shows that the first two generations of US presidents used the contingent fund of foreign intercourse for a variety of purposes that did not fit neatly into the foreign affairs of the State Department. These unconventional matters of foreign policy included the commencement of foreign relations with new countries, restoration of foreign relations (that had been broken off), initiation of foreign intercourse with unrecognized states, and attendance at international conferences. In addition, the fund provided a large reserve of money for peace tributes and special situations.[19]

In 1803, for example, President Thomas Jefferson was in negotiations with France and Spain for the purchase of New Orleans. Napoleon, desperately in need of fast cash to fight his bloody wars in the Caribbean, offered Jefferson's negotiators the whole Louisiana Territory for a bargain price that barely exceeded what the United States was prepared to pay for New Orleans alone. To help close the deal, Congress appropriated $2 million to the contingent fund of foreign intercourse. The Treasury Department in previous administrations had established a special funding system that used Amsterdam banks to disburse money to agents; in this case, the fund provided a financial mechanism for transferring a large sum of money to France. Though a mere footnote in US history, money from the contingent fund of foreign intercourse was used to finance the famous Louisiana Purchase, one of Jefferson's signature achievements[20] as president.[21]

In 1810, Madison's secretary of state secretly dispatched an unofficial executive agent, Joel Poinsett, to South America with confidential instructions. Poinsett, the first executive agent sent to open diplomatic relations with an unrecognized state, arrived in Buenos Aires "disguised as an Englishman aboard a British merchant vessel." He later famously wrote to Secretary of State James Monroe: "All South America will be separated from the Parent country. They have passed the Rubicon." Joel Poinsett was one of several executive agents sent to South America during the presidencies of Madison and Monroe. As a foreign agent of the United States, Poinsett fought with the Chilean junta and later participated in the writing of their national constitution. He served six presidents and enjoyed a long career in American foreign politics. After Poinsett, Madison and Monroe dispatched executive agents to open diplomatic relations with other new governments throughout South and Central America. This innovative US foreign policy using secret executive agents culminated with the Monroe Doctrine in 1823.[22]

During Madison's presidency, members of Congress first began privately referring to the contingent fund of foreign intercourse as the "secret service fund"; in the years to come, the term found its way into public debates on the House and Senate floors, typically used in a pejorative sense. The early investigations of the contingent fund of foreign intercourse not only alerted Congress to chronic accountability problems but also revealed a hidden political agenda.

In the lead-up to the War of 1812, Madison paid $50,000 from the secret service fund—the entire appropriation for that year—to two foreign con artists in exchange for incriminating intelligence against his political adversaries in Boston. The two had fooled Madison into thinking that they had documentary proof of treason, and, as part of the deal, the men and their families were safely sent back to Europe just before the documents were released to Congress.

The documents that Madison presented to Congress were authentic but did not prove anything. According to Samuel Morison,

> Josiah Quincy, member of Congress for the Boston district, was wise enough to see that the documents were genuine, and clever enough to direct a vigorous probe of the affaire that proved very embarrassing to the administration. By tracing the Treasury warrants, Quincy not only discovered the price paid to Henry, but the fact that the transaction was completed ten days before the date of Henry's published letter in which he pretended to donate them to the government out of pure, disinterested patriotism.

When the true story came out, the *Independent Chronicle* in Boston published a front-page article on March 23, 1812, with the eye-catching headline: "$50,000 Dollars!"[23]

In 1816, a committee headed by Benjamin Huger (F-South Carolina) investigated the management of the secret service fund by the state department. Huger's committee focused its investigation on the relationship between the secretary of state and the comptroller of the Treasury. On the continuing problem of unsettled accounts, the final report states, "Although prepared to meet many difficulties, in the proposed investigation of unsettled balances, they had by no means anticipated that these difficulties would have been so serious."[24]

The State Department was not set up to function like the Treasury Department, yet it spent money all over the world that needed to be accounted for. In the special case of the secret service fund, the secretary of state certified the settlement of accounts. The investigation revealed that many settled accounts failed to specify the purpose or object of the expenditures. Lump sums were simply approved without preserving any accounting record of the purpose of the disbursement or expenditure records. The report recommended that an "office of accountant in the Department of State" be established, and it directed that "regular accounts be rendered by foreign ministers and agents." With a better accounting division, the State Department promised to institute "greater system and uniformity in the final adjustment of different accounts" that would provide "frequent and regular settlements."[25]

In 1828, a committee chaired by John Blair (R-Tennessee) conducted perhaps the most comprehensive investigation of the secret service fund ever. It learned that money was first withdrawn from the Treasury with warrants signed by the secretary of state and was then deposited into the

Bank of the United States. A single clerk at the State Department certified both the withdrawals and deposits from the fund. The report stated, "The check upon him, (it is said,) that after making his quarterly disbursements, an account thereof is furnished the Secretary of State, who writes his approval, which is understood to be an approval of the objects only." The secretary of state approved the general disbursal of funds, but not at the voucher level; he considered the propriety of an expense only when an official ruling was required. The report concluded that the auditor could not objectively corroborate the veracity or legality of expenditures based on the information provided by the agents.[26]

In January 1829, just prior to the inauguration of Andrew Jackson, whose military record raised some concern, the chairman of the House Retrenchment Committee, William Rives (D-Virginia), introduced a bill that would "prohibit the use of secret service money in time of peace and for other purposes." Rives's bill stated, "Moneys drawn from the Treasury on account of the contingent expenses of foreign intercourse to be accounted for 'by making a certificate of the amounts of such expenditures as he may think advisable not to specify,' shall hereafter be construed and understood as extending and applicable only to periods when the United States may be engaged in hostilities with some foreign nation." The bill failed to pass.[27]

Congress had originally created the secret service fund to strengthen the president's hand in conducting foreign policy. Over time, presidents found ways to exploit ambiguities in the statutory language in a semi-clandestine effort to broaden the legal notion of executive privilege. The existence of the fund also compartmentalized diplomatic initiatives inside the executive branch and left the Senate in the dark on the country's foreign policy. Although Congress held onto the purse strings, it was unable to monitor the fund's expenditures. Appropriations to the fund declined for the first time during Monroe's presidency and, thereafter, remained capped at around $30,000 to $40,000 per year, while the federal budget continued growing.

12. The GAO and the Cold War

THE BUDGET AND ACCOUNTING PROCEDURES ACT OF 1950

The federal government grew exponentially in size and complexity during the twentieth century—as measured by federal spending—in response to World I, the Great Depression, and World War II. As the government grew by leaps and bounds, parts of it were becoming more secretive and difficult to audit. By the end of the war, there were 136 separate war agencies in the federal government. This increasing administrative complexity forced the GAO to rethink its role in the federal government, with the aim of improving how it measured government accountability.

When World II ended, the GAO, stuck in the weeds of corroborating the accuracy and legality of all the vouchers in the federal government, was not seeing the bigger picture. In the late 1940s, the federal audit system required that all government vouchers be physically shipped to the GAO Headquarters in Washington, DC, for examination and storage. A GAO staff paper from 1947 reports that in a single year the GAO and the US comptroller general:

- Maintained 100,000 appropriations and limitation accounts, 44,000 personal accounts with accountable officers, and about 270,000 other accounts;
- Countersigned 60,000 Treasury Department Warrants and approved 14,000 requisitions for disbursing funds;
- Audited 93,000 accountable officers' accountings, containing 35 million vouchers, 5 million transportations vouchers, 1.5 million contracts, 260 million postal money orders, 57 million postal notes and 26 million postal certificates;
- Settled 108,000 accountable officers' accounts, 35,000 postmasters' accounts, and 773,000 claims;
- Reconciled 490 million checks;
- Issued 1,300 reports on inspections, surveys, and special investi-

> gations, made 6,200 replies to miscellaneous inquiries from members of Congress, issued 400 reports to the President, Congress and the Bureau of the Budget, and issued 7,400 decisions of the comptroller general and 2,200 reports to the attorney general.[1]

Considering the mind-boggling amount of bookkeeping involved, it no longer made sense for the GAO to examine and verify every single financial transaction in the federal government.

In the latter part of 1947, the GAO, the Treasury Department, and the Bureau of the Budget held a series of high-level meetings in a concerted effort to modernize the federal government's budget and accounting system.[2] A pilot program led by the GAO, known as the Joint Accounting Improvement Program, was tested in the early postwar era; it culminated with the institution of a new audit paradigm known as the "comprehensive audit."

Warren announced the program and described its purpose on October 20, 1948, in a letter to the heads of all government agencies: "This program contemplates the full development of sound accounting within each agency, as a working arm of management, in terms of financial information and control. At the same time, it envisions an integrated pattern of accounting and financial reporting for the Government as a whole responsive to executive and legislative needs." Lindsay Warren embraced the idea that the department head was better suited to oversee the accounting records of his or her department. Shifting more responsibility for accountability to the executive department freed up time and resources for the GAO to focus its audits on higher level accounting systems. Walter Frese, the GAO's director of the Accounting Systems Division, spearheaded this ambitious effort, which he characterized as "the verification of assets, liabilities, and operating results, combined with a voucher audit with power to take exceptions, aimed at the proper level, such power to be used with discretion." In practice, the audit was not truly comprehensive; as GAO scholar Frederick Mosher explains, "The GAO could not focus at once on every financial and managerial aspect of an agency's operations; a comprehensive audit would direct its attention to areas of prime importance or where there was reason to expect some deficiency. Therefore, a comprehensive audit was selective, not total as the adjective suggests."[3]

This new type of audit was based on a top-down review of spending, administration, and inventory and involved a broad examination of the department's accounting system and administrative operations. According to Trask,

> The comprehensive audit procedures included
>
> (1) a review of laws and legislative history to ascertain congressional intent on the agency's activities, the way in which they were to be conducted, and the extent of the agency's responsibility and authority;
>
> (2) a review of agency policies to see that they conformed to congressional intent and carried authorized activities efficiently and reasonably;
>
> (3) a review of agency internal controls to determine how well they ensured control of expenditures, revenue, and assets; ensured the accuracy of financial data; promoted operational efficiency; ensured compliance with laws, regulations, and decisions, and conformed to prescribed policy;
>
> (4) a review and analysis by activity of revenue, spending, and asset utilization, to evaluate the effectiveness of the application of public funds and the reliability and completeness of the agency's financial data;
>
> (5) an examination of transactions, confirmation of balances, and physical inspection of property to provide assurance that transactions are legal, assets have been correctly accounted for, and the agency's control processes are functional effectively; and
>
> (6) the full explanation of deficiencies discovered and presentation of recommendations for correction to Congress, the agency head and other interested agencies.[4]

The Joint Accounting Improvement Program paved the way for the passage of the Budget and Accounting Procedures Act of 1950 (BAPA), which, in turn, brought about a major reorganization of the GAO and its audit activities. In this reorganization, the once powerful Accounting and Bookkeeping Division, headed by J. Darlington Denit, was completely eliminated because the individual expense records were no longer the primary focus of the audit. Clerks were replaced by certified public accountants. The establishment of the comprehensive audit throughout the federal government began a new era of the GAO's institutional history.[5]

The Budget and Accounting Act of 1921 transferred the comptroller and audit functions from the Treasury Department to the GAO, but deeply rooted administrative connections kept the two agencies joined at the hip. The Treasury Act of 1789 required the countersigning of treasury warrants by the secretary of the treasury and the comptroller general. Duplicate accounting records were maintained at both agencies. BAPA eliminated this vestige of the original treasury system. The countersigning of warrants was left to the discretion of the comptroller general but was no longer mandatory. The new law improved efficiency by eliminating inefficient, outdated controls.

The GAO had served as a repository for all the financial records and vouchers in the federal government since its establishment in 1921; however, like the CIA, its people were spread out in various buildings across Washington. It did not have a large headquarters with the storage capacity for all its records. Plans to construct a central headquarters had been in the works since the GAO's early days, but it was not until after World War II that Congress selected a site on Judiciary Square and appropriated money to the project. Construction began in 1948 and was completed on September 11, 1951. In President Harry Truman's speech to the crowd gathered at the dedication of the building, he remarked that "the General Accounting Office has handled the biggest auditing job in the history of mankind and has done it well." With the digital age still years away, GAO's need for storage capacity (of paper records) was projected decades into the future. Under BAPA, most of GAO's activities took place on-site, so a large percentage of the building was empty in the early 1950s.[6]

After BAPA passed, the GAO established twenty-three new field offices across the United States and Europe to accommodate the demands of the comprehensive audit and the postwar expansion of the federal government's operations abroad. The GAO opened the European branch in response to Congress's desire for more oversight of the public money directed to Marshall Plan projects in Europe. Under Lindsay Warren, the GAO opened offices in London (1952), Rome (1952), Frankfurt (1953), and Madrid (1954). In 1956, Joseph Campbell—Warren's successor—opened GAO's first Asian outpost in Tokyo.[7]

The statutory language of the CIA Act of 1949 was rooted in the old audit system, which focused on verifying the accuracy and legality of vouchered expenditures. These audits differed from a normal GAO audit in that the entire audit was conducted on-site. That feature was consistent with the new approach, but otherwise the two approaches to accountability were fundamentally different. Houston, Saunders, and others at the CIA sat on the sidelines but watched with great interest as the bill to reform the GAO made its way through Congress in 1950. About a month after the act's passage, a fiscal inspector sent a memo to the chief of the Fiscal Division that assessed the impact of BAPA on the CIA. The inspector pointedly noted that the act "has not had a great effect on present fiscal activities since enumerable regulations required thereunder have not been issued by the General Accounting Office thereby making it too early to resolve the overall effect that the law will have at this time. However, the Act and regulations to be issued conceivably will have great effect on a number of divisions." Houston was concerned about the potential future impact of BAPA and was unsure what effect it might have on the director's confidential funds authority—if any. There is no CREST record of any meeting between Houston and Fisher to discuss the impact of BAPA on GAO's vouchered audit of the CIA. Houston probably did not want to raise the issue, for the CIA Act had only been in effect for one year. In the early 1950s, the GAO was busy making the transition to the comprehensive auditing approach, which proved especially challenging inside the Defense Department. The comprehensive audit was shunned by the national security establishment, for it required far more access to classified information. The GAO was an outsider with a need to know. BAPA, nonetheless, still required the national security establishment to comply with GAO auditor requests, which were often challenged, leading to unnecessary delays.[8]

THE GAO AND THE NATIONAL SECURITY ESTABLISHMENT

The National Security Act of 1947 placed the navy, army, and air force under a unified military command, known in the act as the National Military

Establishment, headed by the secretary of defense. The three secretaries of the US Armed Forces retained a strong voice in the president's cabinet and continued to function with considerable autonomy. The act did not formally unify the military departments under singular leadership, for the defense secretary was not yet truly the head of all three. Shortly after the passage of the CIA Act of 1949, Congress formally unified the army, navy, and air force under the Department of Defense, headed by the secretary of defense, in an amended version of the National Security Act of 1947. Truman signed the act into law on August 10, 1949—less than two months after the passage of the CIA Act of 1949.

Under Title IV, the new law centralized the financial administration of the Defense Department by shifting more fiscal responsibility to the secretary. Title IV created the Office of the Comptroller, headed by a comptroller appointed at the level of an undersecretary of defense.[9] The Defense Department comptroller was responsible for establishing sound accounting and auditing procedures and for certifying budget estimates. Warren was a strong supporter of the bill and considered Title IV to be one of the early accomplishments of the Joint Accounting Improvement Program. The increased fiscal autonomy of the Defense Department, nevertheless, created problems for the GAO under the new system of oversight.[10]

Not wanting a repeat of the accountability debacle that the GAO stumbled onto after World War II, Warren sent a memo to his division chiefs at the onset of the Korean War, proclaiming:

> With the national debt standing at over a quarter of a trillion dollars, it is essential to our economic survival not only that the national defense be strengthened but that this be done as effectively and as economically as possible in terms of expenditures. The nation cannot afford to repeat the mistakes and extravagance which were permitted in World War II under the guise of necessity to the war effort.

Warren directed his senior staff to "seek out excesses, waste, and extravagance including those in procurement and contracting"; but, not wanting to deter the prosecution of the war, he instructed GAO supervisors to "actively cooperate with and assist the defense fiscal staffs to meet their monumental problems of organization, method and control." His biggest concern was the Defense Department's preference for negotiated contracts.[11]

In a letter to Marshall, he cited recent legislation that amended the First War Powers Act of 1941, emphasizing that this "will result in extraordinary power being given to the Department of Defense, particularly with respect to the making, performance, amendment and modification of contracts." With hindsight, Warren hoped that "the abuses of similar authority which occurred during World War II are reduced to a minimum or entirely eliminated." According to Robert Trask, "GAO had a serious problem with the DOD during the Korean War period on access to records." These bureaucratic obstacles impeded the GAO's efforts to apply the comprehensive audit in the Defense Department during the 1950s.

According to Mosher, "Public concern was enhanced by widespread reports of excessive profits of defense contractors, cost overruns, delays, inadequacies, and sometime outright failures in the carrying out of contracts. It was further agitated by alleged 'buddy' relationships of military and civilian officials in the military establishment and related agencies, such as the Atomic Energy Commission, with private industries, particularly those whose business in large part depended upon defense contracts." Warren's successor, Joseph Campbell, made the auditing of the defense sector a top GAO priority. Soon after his arrival, he reorganized the GAO into Civil and Defense Divisions.[12]

Lyle Fisher appeared before the HASC in 1955 to give testimony about GAO's experience with the Armed Services Procurement Act of 1947. He criticized the Defense Department for its reliance on negotiated contracts. Recounting his role in the legislative history of the act, he told the committee:

> Prior to World II, most purchases were required to be made by advertising. When World War II started, there was obviously an emergency. Procurements were made immediately for a lot of items that they could not make specification on. And the first War Power Act was passed, Title II, which authorized negotiation. That went on through the war, until at least after the actual conflict, and a draft was prepared of [the] Armed Services Procurement Act. That was presented to the General Accounting Office through the Bureau of the Budget for our comment before it ever reached the Hill. And

> we took violent exception to that draft. Thereafter, I personally spent hours and days with the people from the military departments revising that draft, to put in certain revisions, eliminate certain features, to the point where we got it substantially as it was enacted. A number of these so-called exceptions were exceptions that were recognized under the competitive bidding statutes. We had no particular problem with those. A number were not accepted under the general law and we discussed those many, many times, and those are the ones that have the restrictions as to making findings and determinations—a written record that anybody could look at and say, "Why are you doing this without advertising?" Reports have to be made to Congress, so the Congress could see periodically what they are doing under that exception.[13]

He testified that the GAO rejected earlier versions of the Armed Services Procurement Act[14] because it did not restrict the use of negotiated contracts by the military strongly enough:

> [The] authority we thought and were told at the time was to be used in case of some sudden emergency such as World War III, so that they would not have any delay getting to Congress and getting legislation. It was certainly not for the normal situation. Under that authority, the President declared a state of emergency in 1950, after the outbreak of the Korean war, and they are still operating under it. . . . There may be some justification for it. I think that is up to the Department to establish to your satisfaction, if they can. We are pleased that the committee is looking into the matter. We do not feel in the General Accounting Office that the departments are advertising as much as they could, and I don't believe that they will contend to you that they are.[15]

In a speech given at a lawyer's convention several years after his retirement from the GAO, Fisher more candidly elucidated his view on negotiated contracts:

> This business of what to do about procurement is very fluid and very elusive. I am sure it will surprise you to hear that shortly before my retirement from the General Accounting Office [in 1958] some of the high-level accountants came to me and said they were going to propose doing away with formal advertised bidding because their observation had been that negotiated pro-

> curements resulted in the best deal for the Government. I was horrified and let them know in no uncertain terms that I would oppose any such proposal. Then what happened—a so-called "Horror" case arose where, under a negotiated contract, a contractor made a pricing mistake in his favor. The rest is history. Now the GAO is opposed to negotiated contracts. I have tried to point out some of the problems inherent in any attempt to modernize and simplify defense procurement. You have probably concluded that I am rather pessimistic on this subject—I am.[16]

The Defense Department was uncomfortable with highly trained GAO accountants arriving on-site to conduct audits of its financial system, for these audits required broad access to its administrative, financial, and property records. In a need-to-know administrative setting like the military, it was highly unconventional for an outsider like a GAO auditor to start asking for information that was classified. GAO auditors frequently came face-to-face with mid-level departmental supervisors, military and civilian, who lacked an adequate understanding of the GAO's investigative powers. According to Robert Trask, in January 1952 William Ellis, the GAO chief of investigations, told an investigating committee that "in some instances when his staff examined military installations, considering among other things fiscal and accounting methods and business practices, local commanders responded to their suggestions by making immediate changes." But in other situations, Ellis reported, "GAO and the military did not get along well." The Defense Department was able to exert its power and authority to decide what information would be provided to the GAO, in line with internal policy directives issued by the defense secretary.[17]

The GAO was hindered in its effort to audit the Defense Department when its auditors were not on the need-to-know list. In response to GAO complaints, policies were modified slightly in 1957. But GAO auditors still encountered administrative barriers to gaining access to classified information during their audits. On July 9, 1958, the GAO was called to testify before the HASC about its access to the classified information it required to perform its comprehensive audits of the Defense Department. Lyle Fisher, who was less than two months away from retirement, appeared with Robert F. Keller, his anointed successor, and the director of GAO's Defense Accounting and Auditing Division. Keller provided most of the testimony from the GAO side. He explained to the committee,

> Our need for access to records, generally, and to classified defense information, was increased considerably [under BAPA]. . . . The effect was that many and varied interpretations began to be made at all levels within the military departments on whether or not we should have access to classified defense information. Questions which could not be settled locally were forwarded to higher echelons and our representatives were confronted with frequent delays and impairment of our audit efforts.

He estimated that "as much as 80 percent of the activity areas in which we were currently devoting our efforts involve a need for access to classified defense information." He argued that the delays incurred in gaining access to information impaired the effectiveness of the audit and were completely unnecessary:

> We also mentioned that we had been frequently delayed in the accomplishment of our objectives, and, even when arrangements for clearance at the secretarial level had been made. . . . We believed the "sensitive area" concept had operated in a manner which impaired the efficient accomplishment of our audit responsibilities, and on one occasion had prevented us from performing our statutory responsibility. We also stated that the need-to-know theory in relation to our audits was largely academic, inasmuch as there is always a need-to-know all information which is relevant to the areas of audit interest.[18]

The problem of gaining access to classified information was exacerbated by the fact that the GAO was part of the legislative branch. Separation of power issues went to the heart of the Constitution. Whose authority took precedence on matters of protecting national security information, the secretary of defense or the comptroller general?

The broader concept of a US intelligence community had the insidious long-term effect of bringing military intelligence under the CIA Act of 1949. A 1981 declassified brief by the CIA's deputy general counsel, David Addington, alludes to some of the legal obstacles faced by the GAO during the 1950s in its effort to obtain information from the National Security Agency—an autonomous branch of the Defense Department:

> Since 1955, GAO has conducted financial site audits of the National Security Agency (NSA) through a small, cleared GAO site audit staff. NSA and GAO have agreed that NSA may regulate the access of GAO personnel to classified and compartmented information, but GAO maintains that NSA may never completely deny GAO access to NSA information, arguing that statutory restrictions on disclosure of NSA information, apply only to disclosure to the public and not disclosure to GAO.

This legal position suggests that the GAO was willing to work with other members of the intelligence community but that the CIA Act could not be legally extended to other members of the intelligence community. Addington makes another important legal distinction between disclosures to the public and to the GAO, regarding the classified status of the materials requested by the GAO.[19]

Addington reveals that the GAO eventually ceased its audits of intelligence operations in the Defense Department due to the restrictions precluding the release of required information:

> GAO audits of the Department of Defense have not reviewed DOD intelligence operations; GAO cites restrictions on access to information as precluding worthwhile review. GAO audits of the Department of State have touched on some intelligence matters but have not focused on the Bureau of Intelligence and Research. In auditing the Federal Bureau of Investigation, GAO has access to all but the most sensitive individual investigative files and certain unvouchered expenditures records when the Attorney General has certified the expenditures.

Addington's brief suggests that the rest of the intelligence community operated under the statutory umbrella of the CIA Act of 1949.[20]

The public funding of military and intelligence committees, boards, and think tanks was another costly outgrowth of the military-intelligence-industrial complex during the 1950s. Some of these organizations existed in the public sector, such as the National War College (1946), whereas others, such as the RAND Corporation (1945), operated within the private sector. In both cases, such groups and organizations were funded with government money while they also served as advisory experts and consultants to the federal government. The GAO was not well positioned to oversee this developing trend due to high levels of secrecy, legal limits on government oversight of the private sector, and the fact that there was nothing fundamentally illegal about spending public money on think tanks. Military-intelligence think tanks provided a powerful intellectual foundation for the military-intelligence-industrial complex to flourish.

The Psychological Strategy Board (PSB) offers a perfect example. This shadowy, highly classified interdepartmental committee was established in August 1950 to coordinate and plan psychological operations. The PSB was created "to provide for more effective planning, coordination and conduct of psychological operations within the framework of approved national policies." Chaired by the CIA and financed in equal parts by the CIA, the State Department, and the Defense Department, the board quickly outgrew its mandate. The size of its budget was beginning to raise questions, and, on top of that, the board expressed reluctance to share any operational information with the congressional committees.[21]

The PSB also caught the attention of the GAO. In early January 1952, Houston met confidentially with Lyle Fisher to discuss GAO's view of the board's status. One internal CIA memorandum reports that Houston

> further explained that Mr. Edwin L. Fisher, General Counsel of the General Accounting Office, is of the opinion that the Board is rapidly becoming an independent agency and had the characteristics of one; therefore it would be necessary to secure some Congressional recognition of the Board either through the means of an enabling statute or at least a recognition of its existence through the means of appropriations of funds for its activities.

Although Eisenhower terminated the PSB in September 1953, it by no means disappeared. Rather, its coordinating functions were transferred to the Operations Coordinating Board (OCB), which was an organizational element of the NSC bureaucracy.[22]

BAPA was on the GAO's side, but the military culture, in its efforts to block the release of classified information to GAO auditors, delayed its audits and impeded the modernization of GAO's audit system around the comprehensive audit. The congressional watchdog was too busy with the Defense Department to worry about the CIA. When it finally challenged the status quo at the end of the decade, the CIA and its financial system were too deeply rooted in the national security establishment for the GAO to bring about any of its desired reforms, but it was not from a lack of trying.

13. 1950

NSC 68

NSC 68 was issued in April 1950, a couple of months before the outbreak of the Korean War. This momentous directive elevated the United States' superpower role in its Cold War standoff with the Soviet Union, and it started a rapid and costly build-up of political, economic, and military strength. Based on a sixty-six-page policy paper by the NSC Study Group, which was chaired by George Kennan's understudy Paul Nitze, the directive's strategic goal was to contain the expansion of the Soviet Union without dragging the nation into a nuclear war. To achieve this, secret wars that exploited the use of covert action emerged as the most risk-averse and cost-effective operational strategy. Covert operations, furthermore, were designed to conceal the role of the US government, which provided the president and the CIA with plausible deniability.

Dean Acheson, Truman's secretary of state, wrote in his memoir: "NSC 68 lacked, as submitted, any section discussing costs. This was not an oversight. To have attempted one would have made impossible all those concurrences and prevented any recommendation to the President. It would have raised at once the extent and tempo of the program deemed necessary to carry out the conclusions and recommendations." Without a credible cost analysis, however, there was no way for Congress, the Budget Bureau, or anyone else to gauge whether the recommendations for a rapid military build-up were realistic from a budgetary or national security point of view. NSC 68 was the first major stimulus to increase the flow of unvouchered funds overseas.[1]

The development of innovative Cold War strategies during the 1950s offered a strong policy rationale for increasing the funding for CIA-sponsored intelligence activities. Under Bedell Smith and Allen Dulles, the synergy between the CIA Act of 1949 and the Cold War precipitated a major restructuring of CIA's administrative system around covert action. The CIA was originally designed in 1947 for the collection, evaluation, and reporting of intelligence; its mission began to change in

1950, as the Agency became more deeply involved in covert operations in peacetime, considered to be in the gray area of CIA's charter.

THE KOREAN WAR

The Korean War was another major budgetary stimulant that fit neatly in with the goals of NSC 68. It was also an urgent national security situation that required a healthy source of unvouchered funds. North and South Korea were born from the carnage left behind by the Japanese occupation of the Korean Peninsula. As in Germany, Soviet and American forces played a vital role in the liberation of Korea, leading to the formation of North and South Korea in 1948. The Berlin Wall divided the city of Berlin into East and West; in Korea, the 38th parallel created a geopolitical fault line between North and South. The new countries were separated by a narrow region known as the demilitarized zone. The conventional wisdom at the time suggested that the young North Korean leader Kim Il-sung took his orders from Moscow and would never order an invasion of South Korea without the approval of Joseph Stalin. CIA intelligence reports estimated that North Korea had the capability to start a war but lacked the will and authority to launch a full-scale attack on the South. This overly simplistic analysis proved naïve and shortsighted; the CIA failed to see the attack coming until it was well under way. The North Korean Army proceeded to invade South Korea on June 25, 1950.

Just two days earlier, at a secret hearing of the House Foreign Affairs Committee, Hillenkoetter, when asked about his confidence in the intelligence coming out of Korea, had not given any hint that the United States was about to be dealt a major foreign policy crisis. Styles Bridges (R-New Hampshire), the ranking Republican on the Senate Appropriations Committee, spoke before the Senate the day after the attack and assured his colleagues, "Neither the State Department nor the Department of Defense was informed by the Central Intelligence Agency of the impending attack." Bridges made it clear that the committee would be examining the matter "in some detail." At an impromptu appearance before the Senate Appropriations Committee, Hillenkoetter fielded a barrage of emotionally charged questions from confused and disgruntled senators. Once again, the CIA found itself on the hot seat.[2]

On the following morning, the Appropriation Committee heard testimony from Secretary of State Dean Acheson and Defense Secretary Louis Johnson, who both said they had received no warning from the CIA of an imminent attack. Johnson called it a "complete surprise." Bridges asked Johnson: "Why wasn't the Central Intelligence Agency on the job?" Then, after blurting out how much money the Agency had received from Congress that year, Bridges again questioned him: "What are they doing with it [i.e., the money]?" Johnson replied: "You'll have to ask Admiral Hillenkoetter."[3]

Tensions were running high, with many in Congress afraid this could be the first domino to fall. Hillenkoetter appeared before Congress to explain why the CIA seemed as surprised by the attack as the rest of Washington. The DCI withstood a grilling, but everyone knew by then that he was on the way out. By October, a World War II icon would be heading the Agency, and with a new DCI, this intelligence failure was quickly forgotten. In the early 1950s, the CIA began to fortify its operational presence in Asia under the cover of the Korean War and the CIA Act of 1949.

THE DULLES REPORT, NSC 50, AND BEDELL SMITH

On January 13, 1948, the NSC commissioned a three-person panel known as the Intelligence Survey Group (ISG) to make a "comprehensive, impartial and objective survey of the organization, activities, and personnel of the Central Intelligence Agency." James Forrestal handpicked Allen Dulles, William Jackson, and Matthias Corea to lead this highly classified review of the CIA. The three were considered to be among the nation's top intelligence experts, though they all had returned to the private sector after World War II. Allen Dulles, who headed the ISG, had been the OSS station chief in Bern during the war. Jackson had trained at Bletchley Park and, after D-Day, had served as a G-2 intelligence officer, overseeing OSS special counter-intelligence units in X-2. He had returned to work as an investment banker for the venture capital firm of J. H. Whitney &

Company. Corea had served as a US attorney for the Southern District of New York before the war and as a counterintelligence officer for the OSS during the war. He was now working under Forrestal as a special assistant to the secretary of the navy. The ISG submitted its final report to the NSC on January 1, 1949, which served as the blueprint for NSC 50.[4]

The so-called Dulles report was merciless in its evaluation of the organization and its leadership, concluding that "the CIA had failed in its responsibilities with regard to both the coordination of intelligence activities and the production of national intelligence estimates, and it attributed those failures to a lack of understanding and leadership on the part of the Director of Central Intelligence." The report strongly recommended a major restructuring of the CIA and its intelligence activities. One of the report's main targets, Hillenkoetter, was initially in charge of spearheading the recommended reforms. NSC 50 was issued on July 7, 1949, shortly after the enactment of the CIA Act of 1949. Unlike its handling of NSC 10/2, the NSC waited for the bill's approval in Congress before it issued the directive.[5]

The release of NSC 50 foreshadowed the coming of a new DCI, and it would be left to Hillenkoetter's successor to implement the recommendations of the directive. The outbreak of the Korean War provided the perfect catalyst for this much-anticipated change. Hillenkoetter, who was as ready for his tenure to end as anyone, was now able to make a graceful exit from a job that had never been a good fit. And the NSC was eager to appoint a person of their own choosing. After Hillenkoetter submitted his resignation, he was reinstated in the Pacific fleet at his previous rank of rear admiral.

Hillenkoetter had many critics, but it would be a mistake to underestimate the importance of his three-year tenure. He oversaw the transition between the CIG and the CIA, and he served longer than his first two predecessors and his immediate successor. During his tenure, he led the CIA through major administrative transitions that came about on the heels of the National Security Act of 1947, the creation of the OPC, and the CIA Act of 1949. Hillenkoetter, and many who followed in his footsteps, including Allen Dulles, served as convenient fall guys for systemic problems inside the Agency, problems that were bigger than they were.

Lieutenant General Walter Bedell Smith succeeded Hillenkoetter as

DCI. Smith's confirmation in the Senate was as close to a slam dunk as one could hope for. The hard-nosed, three-star army general had served as secretary of the JCS during World War II and had played a key role in establishing the OSS as an operational arm of the JCS. He later served in England as General Eisenhower's chief of staff. After the war, Smith served three years as the US ambassador to the Soviet Union in Moscow. Well-respected in the military and around Washington, "Beetle" Smith, though a popular choice, was not in the best of health. He was still recuperating from an operation that had removed most of his ulcerated stomach when Hillenkoetter resigned. By early August, Smith was on the road to recovery, and, although heading the CIA was probably the last thing he wanted, Truman reportedly ordered him to accept the position. He was sworn in on October 7, 1950.[6]

Bedell Smith served for a little over two years. His tenure, brief though it was, shaped the future CIA as much as that of any director in its history. Ludwell Montague writes that "the history of US intelligence is clearly divisible into two distinct eras, before Smith and after Smith." Lyman Kirkpatrick, assistant director for Special Operations under Smith, similarly wrote in his memoir: "The year 1950 was one of the most momentous changes for and in the Central Intelligence Agency. Two major events had far-reaching effects on the organization. The first was the outbreak of the Korean War on June 25; the second was the appointment of "Beetle" Smith as director of Central Intelligence."[7]

Smith's greatest impact on the CIA was, arguably, the organizational changes that he orchestrated. Soon after he took charge, he enticed Allen Dulles to come on board as a consultant on a six-week commitment. He then coaxed him into heading the new operations directorate that he was in the process of creating. Dulles readily accepted the offer and took charge of the directorate in January 1950. Dulles was assigned to oversee the absorption of the OPC into the CIA's clandestine services. Smith also recruited William Jackson, another of the authors of the Dulles report, to serve as the deputy director of Central Intelligence (DDCI). Montague says, "Smith never felt the same confidence in Allen Dulles and Frank Wisner that he did in William Jackson. During 1951, he had Jackson investigate the offices under Dulles's supervision because he came to suspect that Dulles and Wisner were actually pursing a policy contrary to his own." Smith was not a total advocate of covert action because he did not think that was how the CIA should be spending its money. According to Montague, in a memo dated May 8, 1951, "Bedell Smith argued that the scope of the CIA's covert operations already far exceeded what had been contemplated in NSC 10/2 (1948) and that still greater increases would be required to discharge the missions now proposed by State, Defense, and the JCS, and implicit in NSC 68."

When Jackson left the Agency after serving less than a year, Smith promoted Dulles to DDCI, the number two position at the Agency. Dulles's background in the OSS was rooted in secret intelligence. It appears that Smith was taking advantage of Dulles's reputation in both intelligence and foreign relations, while also pulling him away from Wisner and the early development of CIA's covert operational agenda. As the number two man at the Agency, Dulles was then just one step away from the position that he most coveted.[8]

14. Clandestine Financial Administration

CIA ADMINISTRATION DIRECTORATE

On October 7, 1950, Walter Bedell Smith arrived at CIA headquarters; dismayed by the Dulles report, he set to work immediately to reform the CIA's administration around NSC 50. Since his confirmation in August, Smith had carefully reviewed NSC 50 and discussed the directive privately with Allen Dulles and William Jackson. Two weeks into his tenure at the CIA, he announced at a meeting of the Intelligence Advisory Committee that major organizational changes were coming. The minutes of the meeting report, "General Smith stated that NSC 50, giving effect in substance to the recommendations of the so-called Dulles Committee Report, had not yet been carried out by the Central Intelligence Agency, but that it was his intention promptly to carry out this directive."[1]

A major criticism raised by the report was that control over the intelligence functions went from the DCI through the CIA executive, an administrative official; the administrative hierarchy "necessarily resulted in policy control over intelligence offices by those not qualified in intelligence." Smith's reorganization plan split command and control across three top-level directorates, Plans, Intelligence, and Administration; each of these was headed by a deputy director who reported to the DCI. The operational directorate, Plans, included subdivisions for covert action, foreign espionage, and foreign counterespionage.

The OPC was absorbed into the CIA as a subdivision of the Plans Directorate without resistance from the NSC. The rapid growth of the Plans Directorate during the 1950s placed enormous pressures on the CIA's administrative functions. New office staffs were created during this period, tasked with finding better techniques and methods to account for all the money, personnel, and equipment being secretly transported all over the world. According to CIA's historical staff, "In addition to the increase in the volume of disbursements, many of the new projects and programs undertaken involved the development of new principles and techniques of financial support." Even with more people, money, resources, and greater centralization, the CIA support functions struggled mightily to keep pace with the rapid growth of Plans under Smith and Dulles.[2]

The Administration Directorate controlled a diversity of support functions essential to running an international spy agency. Separate divisions were established for handling finance, personnel, procurement, legal, medical, internal security, and logistics. Smith appointed Murray McConnel, a businessman with a long career in investment banking, to be the first deputy director of administration (DDA) on October 16, 1950. Smith's reorganization sought to modernize the developing administrative infrastructure and to give it the best of both worlds: centralization and compartmentalization.

The Administration Directorate formed informal political liaisons with other federal agencies; this practice opened a back-door conduit for insider information on virtually every important political, economic, and military development in the federal government. Confidential liaisons were established with the NSC, the Pentagon, the State Department, the Bureau of the Budget, Congress, the GAO, and the Treasury Department. No other agency in the federal government had more access to power and information, or was more deeply entrenched in the national security establishment, than the CIA.

Executive Director[3] Captain Clarence Winecoff resigned in April 1950 after having served under Hillenkoetter for just over a year. L. T. Shannon, his deputy, served as acting CIA executive until McConnel's arrival. Once Smith arrived, Shannon became McConnel's deputy. Shannon, another former OSS officer who had a long career at the CIA, was by most accounts an effective administrator. However, according to Montague, he ended up in the middle of a power struggle between the clandestine services and administration.[4]

The position of CIA's top administrative official, the third most senior Agency official, was a job that entailed fighting many unpleasant bureaucratic battles inside the Agency. McConnel was the third to serve in the position since the creation of the CIG. When he accepted the position, he agreed to serve for six months only; true to his word, he stepped down in the middle of Smith's initial reorganization of the Agency. He was replaced by Walter Wolf, another investment banker. Noting that Wolf had "no experience in the management of an operating enterprise," Ludwell

Montague suggests that Ted Shannon was running the administration behind the scenes.[5]

In December 1951, Smith appointed Lawrence "Red" White to be assistant deputy director of administration.[6] Shannon settled into a new coordinator position, functioning as a senior liaison officer with the Plans Directorate. Red White, the son of a poor Presbyterian minister from Tennessee, attended West Point, fought in World War II, and returned home a highly decorated army soldier. After joining the CIA in 1947, he ran the Foreign Information Branch in the semi-covert Office of Operations. White proved to be an effective administrator that got along with everyone. His presence stabilized the directorate at the top during Wolf's brief tenure. When Wolf left the CIA shortly after Allen Dulles became DCI, White was appointed to the position.[7]

Under Hillenkoetter, the organizational chart instituted a firewall between overt and covert operations, making interoffice coordination on essential administrative matters difficult and inefficient. CIA's early liaison with the GAO probably influenced this organizational structure. The decision to merge the overt and covert divisions under a single chief aroused considerable controversy inside the Agency at the time. Jackson and Claussen report, "The detailed organizational arrangements of the new DD/A group called for a degree of compartmentalization between overt and covert administrative matters, which seemed to provide at least a temporary solution for reconciling the conflicting demands for centralized administration and operational autonomy."[8]

Senior members of the clandestine divisions forcibly argued that OSO and OPC should handle all their own finances without any support from the administration. The Dulles report advised against centralizing the administrative functions, "since secret operations require their own separate administration." Dulles strongly believed that the clandestine services should control their own administrative functions. Senior advisors to Smith, such as William Jackson, also argued that "the administrative offices had been 'running the show' and recalled that he and the Director both exerted the 'strongest pressure' to have the group 'serve' rather than 'control' the Agency's substantive activities." Financial management and audit control of the clandestine services, indeed, were briefly transferred to the OSO shortly after its creation. However, declassified records from this period reveal that as the Agency expanded the size, scope, and complexity of its covert operations, it failed to establish adequate methods to control and account for unvouchered funds. The absorption of the OPC further complicated this arrangement.[9]

One aim of Smith's 1950 reorganization was to bring a proper balance of power and control among the different parts of the CIA. Competing interests and the need for compartmentalization worked against the centralization of basic support functions in administration. On February 12, 1951, Smith consolidated the executive office and budget staff into a new office in the OSO under Harry W. Little, another former OSS officer with past connections to special funds. These offices furnished basic administrative support and acted as a liaison between Plans and Administration. The OPC reportedly established administrative support functions, but Jackson and Claussen have little to say about that, simply noting: "There was also a separate administrative staff in OPC, but this unit did not appear on the organizational chart."[10]

It may have made practical sense to place administrative offices in the OSO and OPC, but it created jurisdictional ambiguity over which directorate, Plans or Administration, controlled the handling of highly sensitive intelligence business. In August 1952, Smith appointed Shannon to the new position, chief of administration in Plans. Montague writes, "The clandestine services came to appreciate Shannon's talents when he went to work for them. He had a long and successful career in DD/P."[11]

OFFICE OF THE COMPTROLLER

Smith's reorganization established an Office of the Comptroller that united the overt and covert financial operations under the authority of one person: the CIA comptroller. The first to be appointed to the position was Edward Saunders; he was the head of CIA's Budget Office and had previously served as a top budget man for the OSS, SSU, and CIG. The CIA Office of the Comptroller had subdivisions for different operations: budget (Budget Division), vouchered funds (Fiscal Division), and unvouchered funds (Finance Division).

Hillenkoetter's reorganization of CIA's financial administration, shortly after passage of the CIA Act, had not gone nearly far enough. Although it had succeeded in returning fiscal control of unvouchered funds to the administrative components of the CIA, the increasing amounts of unvouchered funds that flowed overseas created serious accountability problems in the understaffed Finance Division of the Special Support Staff. Echols, who still headed the division, asked that a survey be done due to the

> physical inability [of the Finance Division] to fulfill its responsibilities and duties under a greatly increased workload without serious curtailment of services and impairment of the standards of fiscal control desired by the Agency. For many months a back log of work has been accumulated and day-by-day fiscal requirements of the Covert Offices have been met only at the expense of the physical welfare of employees and lower work standards. This in turn has resulted in increasing errors, technical deficiencies and inadequate documentation.[12]

The CIA executive subsequently sent a memo to Hillenkoetter to recommend a substantial increase in the staffing of the Finance Division, Special Support Staff.[13] Two reasons were cited: "Greatly improved policy guidance and control provisions to safeguard the utilization of confidential funds" and "OPC support requirements which have grown considerably beyond any previous conception." The management survey revealed the inadequacy of the accounting standards and controls for unvouchered funds:

> While operating as the Special Funds Branch, Office of Special Operations, the processing of financial transactions was accomplished with a minimum review which determined that a transaction had been directed, was properly approved, and the expense appeared to be reasonable. Later the Division was transferred to the jurisdiction of the Budget and Finance Office with an entirely new concept and under much more detailed regulations without any increase in personnel.[14]

Of course, the CIA's Financial Division could not recruit staff by putting an employment ad in the newspaper. This action item went all the way up to the DCI because the handling of unvouchered funds demanded a unique skill set. As underscored in a subsequent memo to Hillenkoetter from Shannon, acting CIA executive, "The very nature and type of financial administration required for Confidential Funds requires unusual integrity, judgement and initiative on the part of employees of all levels. In the necessary absence of precise regulations governing operational expenses, and necessary lack of precise and formalized accounting procedures, forms and standards, the highest type of personnel are essential to ensure effective and efficient financial processing and administration."[15]

These issues were addressed in Smith's reorganization, which unified overt and covert financial administration under the CIA comptroller. According to Jackson and Claussen, Edward Saunders was responsible for planning, directing, and supervising "all budgetary and financial operations of the Agency on a world-wide basis" and was also involved in "CIA's financial support and funds control." The latter included four types of financial operations: budgeting, disbursing and monetary, accounting, and auditing and inspection. One CIA official in 1951 described the comptroller's responsibility as "an obligation—a peculiar obligation—to be damned careful what he is doing with a hell of a lot of money." Smith's 1950 reorganization elevated the CIA comptroller to one of the most powerful positions[16] in the Agency.[17]

Saunders had his hands full, for the CIA was far from prepared to oversee all the unvouchered funds flowing into intelligence activities overseas. In 1950, in contrast with the Fiscal and Finance Divisions, which had some 140 employees, the Budget Staff had only about fifteen, a number that doubled over the next three years. In a memo to Saunders from the deputy comptroller (name deleted) early in his tenure, he writes, "As we have discussed on several occasions, it is imperative that we take appropriate steps to establish a staff of high-level accountants to accomplish the large amount of staff work of the Comptroller's Office." He then alludes to the systemic nature of the problem:

> At the present time too much of your and my time is devoted to developing answers to accounting, audit and financial problems that occur daily which involve policy determinations and decisions, but which require hours of research and development. . . . The accounting and financial problems of CIA that occur daily and the accounting and financial projects of the Agency which require development in adequate and meaningful reports and finan-

> cial statements, are unique and complex; they involve the application of both governmental and commercial accounting techniques and methods and the development of finance methods for which there is frequently no precedence.[18]

In response, the comptroller's office added two more organizational elements in June: the Technical Accounting Staff and the Programs Analysis Staff.[19] These offices helped the Agency adapt administratively to the growing demands and stresses on the financial system.[20]

Eck Echols, the former SFB theater chief in Kandy, ran the Finance Division. This special division handled diverse financial operations, including budgeting, disbursement, certification, contracts, and the regular auditing of unvouchered funds. Truly a global enterprise, it had offices all over the world for disbursing funds to the clandestine services. Still, the nature of unvouchered funds raised eyebrows. Jackson and Claussen discuss the dilemma of properly accounting for unvouchered funds, noting that "their confidential and somewhat unaccountable character, and the need of protecting the secrecy of CIA's operations financed by them, made the problem of funds control even more necessary and more complex." They infer that, as a result, "a multiplicity of practices and procedures, not normally found in other Government agencies, were developed and applied in CIA by its financial-management organization."[21]

The role of the Monetary Branch, at the center of CIA's global operations, was essentially the same as that of the SFB Foreign Exchange Branch during World War II. It was responsible for providing funds in a multitude of currencies for use in the field. In 1952, a memorandum for the record reported: "Events of the past few weeks indicates that it is necessary that we review our procedures for handling the increasingly large sums of cash now being processed through the Monetary Branch." The memo emphasized the need to improve fiscal controls: "Greater control could be exercised if insofar as possible those persons actually handling the money were to assume responsibility therefore." The principle of individual accountability was fundamental to the GAO's operation. The bulk of the memo was an argument for the institution of sounder certification procedures. It also addressed the procedures used for the "cleaning" of confidential disbursements transferred to overseas field stations. Approving officers were important points of control in ensuring "these funds are maintained pending completion of the cleaning operation and return of the notes to [place deleted]." The "cleaning" referred to in the memo, as one might surmise, was the laundering of unvouchered funds disbursed overseas in order to conceal their link to the US Treasury.[22]

An internal review of the Office of the Comptroller conducted in the mid-1950s concluded that major accountability problems continued to plague the financial management of covert programs. The declassified report was especially critical of senior level management and the fiscal controls applied to unvouchered funds. The report concluded:

> The establishment of a strong comptrollership is being retarded by a number of factors: (a) senior officials have not exercised sufficiently determined leadership in developing sound financial management; (b) too often supervisors have not enforced the clear-cut responsibilities for expenditures set forth in Agency regulations; (c) operating components have neither fully accepted nor effectively used fiscal management as an integral part of their machinery for controlling and directing their activities; (d) a sizeable portion of the funds expended for clandestine activities have been exempted from adequate control; (e) and the office of the Comptroller has not been sufficiently aggressive in recommending policies and procedures for better control of funds and in initiating effective action to expose and correct situations where fiscal management is inadequate.[23]

The review had discovered that Allen Dulles was issuing "blanket waivers of all fiscal controls normally exercised by the Comptroller"; the report concluded that such "waivers are prima facie evidence of a belief that normal Agency standards, procedures, and security are inadequate to meet the requirements of certain sensitive covert projects." This internal investigation found that the administrative system of regulations, policies, and standards was often subject to the whims of division chiefs, based loosely on operational security requirements. Its most scathing criticisms were aimed at the Agency's fiscal management and control of advances for covert programs; the investigation found that 137 of 180 accounts were delinquent. Chronic financial accountability problems continued to plague the Agency throughout the 1950s. This was part of the learning curve involved in running a multibillion-dollar international spy agency, in which security requirements always took precedence over financial accountability.[24]

AUDIT OFFICE

In 1947, Hillenkoetter established an Audit Branch in the Inspection and Security Office (ISO) to conduct postaudits of secret programs. Even within the CIA, little is known about the early history of the secretive ISO, which handled all matters of internal security. As with the office he headed, little is known about Sheffield Edwards, who remains a shadowy historical figure. Even the CIA historical staff struggled to find scraps of information on the institutional history of ISO. A brief footnote on ISG, found in Jackson and Claussen, states, "Unlike most of the other offices in the D/A Group, this office has no history on file . . . and there are relatively few historical records on it, for 1950–53, in the DCI's Executive Registry." The ISO had four divisions—Audit, Security, Inspection, and Special Security—along with four staffs for Administration, Counterintelligence, Alien Affairs, and Security Control. To make the audit function independent from ISG, in April 1951, Smith formed a new office directly under the DDA, devoted to postaudits of covert projects under the CIA Act of 1949.[25]

Captain T. Veach was appointed by Smith to head the office in April 1951, but his tenure was short. About a year later, Smith reorganized the audit function, and appointed an auditor in chief to head the new office, who was "responsible to the DCI 'through the DD/A.'" Major General Eugene Foster, the CIA's first auditor in chief, was responsible "for the audit . . . of all finance, fiscal, and property matters not under General Accounting Office procedures, and for assuring that appropriate current audits are made." His authority included the audit of unvouchered funds and was "only limited by the requirement that operational security be maintained, and that intelligence sources and methods be adequately protected." Foster reorganized the division around the audit system he innovated, and he actively recruited experienced government accountants and career-oriented college graduates to work overseas as CIA auditors.[26]

In a later interview with the CIA's Historical Staff, Foster explained that the audit staff "performs for unvouchered funds what GAO does for other parts of the Government. [The Audit Office] audits all overseas funds since they are unvouchered." The clandestine divisions, however, still maintained a fair amount of control over the release of sensitive information to members of the audit staff. If an auditor requested information deemed to be too operationally sensitive, Frank Wisner could simply deny the request, claiming the auditor had no need to know. In one case, Wisner sent a memo to Allen Dulles asking him to block the audit staff from reviewing information in a sensitive file. He argued that the "auditor does not need-to-know the identity of the recipient or the actual operating details in order to complete the audit." Although the Audit Office in this case was acting within its authority, the DCI had the power under Section 10b of the CIA Act to overrule the auditor in chief.[27]

Compared to the Finance Division, the Audit Office was a small-time operation. In 1950, when it was still a division of the ISO, its working staff consisted of just nine employees. The audit staff grew to twenty employees under Smith, but then, over the next two years, only managed to add eight more employees; by contrast, during the same period, the Agency's budget grew elevenfold. How could a staff of twenty-eight people oversee the covert budget and accounting system of an agency that was spending hundreds of millions of unvouchered dollars per year on covert operations carried out all over the world?[28]

The powerful Finance Division, under the CIA comptroller, managed the day-to-day financial operations of the clandestine services and was responsible for periodically auditing its covert programs. In most cases, certifying officers in the Operations and Liaison Branch performed the audit functions "subject only to the eventual post audit by the Audit Staff." The Finance Division performed "examinations and audits of vouchers, accounts, and records" and conducted "such site audits and inspections of financial activities at installations or field locations as may be necessary to assure the administrative competence and fidelity of individuals in connection with the expenditure of funds for proper official purposes in accordance with established agency policies." Red flags were going up long before Congress finally got involved. A report from the general counsel's office in the early 1950s raises concerns related to the control of unvouchered funds: "The complexity and geographical dispersion of our financial transactions, and the degree of flexibility and tolerance which must be observed, for security reasons, in connection with our accounting requirements, presents opportunities for indolent and unethical financial practices to flourish behind a screen of 'security.'" Ironically, the strict security concerns of the clandestine services opened the door to the internal misuse and theft of unvouchered funds.[29]

Finding the proper balance between security and accountability remained a hugely important administrative matter. Some early studies by the financial divisions found irreconcilable informational gaps in the "unvouchered accounting data." One early report faults the administrative connection "between the expenditure data reflected in the existing accounting records and accrued financial commitments entered into by the agency." This report underscored the need for more financial information on the disbursal and expenditure of unvouchered funds: "additional unvouchered information is an urgent requirement that can no longer be disregarded irrespective of increased cost." Financial information was the "link between accounting control and budgetary control." The root of the problem was the inherent conflict between the need-to-know security protocols of the clandestine divisions and the recommended accounting standards of CIA's Office of the Comptroller and the comptroller general of the United States.[30]

Between 1953 and 1956, the Audit Office[31] expanded and established new field sites in the Far East, Europe, and the Middle East. As the Agency's projects grew in number and complexity, new cutting-edge auditing methods were introduced. According to declassified notes from the CIA's historical staff, "with improved training and enlargement of the Audit Staff it has been practicable to extend the audit into a more comprehensive type than it has been practicable prior to this period." The Audit Staff "found many things needing correction which would not have been discovered through the procedures previously in effect whereby accounts were audited on the basis of records submitted to Headquarters."[32]

The Audit Office was also involved in auditing CIA-run corporations that operated in the private sector. CIA was "able to maintain a current program of auditing propriety projects" in the 1950s that entailed "the audit of all propriety projects once each year." It is noted, however, that there were some exceptions. For example, in a limited number of cases, public accounting firms were employed "where the cover division or the interested operating division was of the opinion that it was inadvisable, for cover reasons, for the Audit Staff personnel to make the audit." The CIA's auditing function evolved over time and, in many respects, paralleled changes that were taking place at the GAO.[33]

GAO auditors working on-site were closely monitored. Until the CIA moved into its new building at Langley in 1962, the Agency and its employees were housed in a large building complex that encompassed twenty-eight different buildings. This arrangement was notoriously bad from the standpoint of internal security; however, with respect to GAO site audits, it allowed sensitive areas associated with espionage and covert ops to conveniently be sealed off from the Fiscal Division by locating them in a different building.

An eleven-page internal FAQ document from the early Dulles era explains the Agency's policies on GAO site audits. This list of questions and answers was used to train CIA employees how to handle GAO audits. Red White, Houston, Saunders, and the deputy comptroller contributed to this FAQ sheet, which sheds light on how carefully the CIA choreographed its liaison with the GAO. Here is a small sampling of the questions and answers:

> Q. Will the GAO auditors be given full freedom of movement throughout the Comptroller's Office?
>
> A. (Col. White) Not initially, they should be escorted: however, impression should not be given that they are being restricted. Maybe after four to six months or so as the audit progresses this will be modified.
>
> Q. Will all Comptroller Instructions and Notices and Division Operating Procedures be made available?
>
> A. No as a general rule.
>
> Q. Will information be made available as to the funding of the Agency's operations through other Government Agencies?
>
> A. No. They know that our funds are buried in other Agency appropriations and this is all they need-to-know.
>
> Q. Will information be made available that reflects the overall accounting

system of the Agency's activities and the relationship of the vouchered and confidential funds accounting controls?

A. So long as they relate solely to overt activities.

Q. Will the Agency budget be made available to the GAO? If not the budget document itself, will summary data reflecting the total dollar amount of the budget document be revealed?

A. a. No.

b. Yes, summary data only by organizational segments of major component for DD/I [Intelligence Directorate] and DD/S [Support Directorate]. DD/P [Plans Division] total only.

Q. Will any of the confidential funds records be made available? Any Accounting reports? Any information with respect to confidential funds payroll?

A. No.

The GAO could not even review the official policies of the CIA comptroller on the handling of unvouchered funds. GAO auditors obviously faced numerous obstacles, and this situation only worsened with time.[34]

CIA INSPECTOR GENERAL

The Office of the Inspector General was created in late 1951 to fill a missing niche in the internal oversight of the Agency. Other than the DCI, no one at the Agency had investigative authority over all three major directorates. Smith placed DDCI William Jackson in charge of conducting investigative surveys of the Plans Directorate after his arrival. Jackson, who resigned in August 1951, stayed on as a special assistant to the director and oversaw Plans under the auspices of Smith. Montague dubbed Jackson the CIA's "first Inspector General" because he performed the duties generally assigned to the position; however, he carefully notes that Jackson "never bore the title."[35]

Officially, fifty-two-year-old Stuart Hedden, a graduate of Wesleyan

University and Harvard Law School, was named as the CIA's first inspector general (IG) on January 1, 1952. Hedden had previously served as the finance chairman of Wesleyan University in Middletown, Connecticut. Smith interviewed Hedden and was greatly impressed by his demeanor. Montague says that Jackson opposed the appointment but, under pressure from Smith, finally agreed to take Hedden under his wing. On October 30, 1951, Hedden began to conduct sensitive investigative work inside Plans under Jackson's tutelage.[36]

Montague's firsthand account characterizes Hedden as "General Smith's personal handyman." Hedden was responsible for a broad range of ad hoc administrative duties, which were not clearly defined at first. His jurisdiction and authority were at the pleasure of the DCI, and his main function was to serve as an ombudsman to CIA employees. When directed by the DCI, Hedden also had the authority to investigate matters of financial accountability, but the investigative powers of the IG were limited by its small size.[37]

On April 14, 1952, a *US News & World Report* correspondent called the director's office "to size up story prospects for a treatment of the US intelligence system." The atmosphere inside the CIA was tense in the early 1950s, and this reporter wanted to write an investigative piece that uncovered "a dozen or more 'intelligence failures.'" Hard to believe, perhaps, but this reporter was seeking corroboration from the CIA's front office. Jackson, who was on the receiving end of the enquiry, sent a memo to Hedden that same day expressing his concerns.

In the memo Jackson told Hedden, "I do believe we have safely diverted him from that approach." He was especially concerned by the reporter's interest in "the agency's lack of public accountability" and noted that the reporter had asked: "Is there anyone . . . who knows enough about what you're doing to determine whether you're doing a good or bad job?" Jackson cavalierly explained to Hedden, "Aside from the Bureau of the Budget, obviously, there is not. CIA has grown to be a half-billion-dollar pig in a poke."

Jackson further railed about problems of accountability that he saw as plaguing the Agency: "Once before I referred to the danger implicit in this lack of accountability. The statement was made in a memo of mine on November 22nd":

> Admittedly CIA is a super-sensitive agency—but it is also an executive agency with characteristics common to all executive agencies of government. It acts (like others) in the public interest; it is supported (like others) by public funds. And like all others, CIA is accountable in the end to public opinion.
>
> Because CIA is a sensitive agency, it is exempted from the ordinary scrutiny to which most agencies are subjected. However, this exemption is a privilege, not a right; and like most privileges it entails obligations. If CIA would warrant this exemption, then CIA must also establish such standards of integrity and performance that it can conscientiously claim the confidence it contends it must have.

Jackson continued, "High standards, however, are not enough. The Director is still, to all intents and purposes, his own and only overseer. Since he is not required to account in detail to anyone other than the Bureau of the Budget, perhaps he should recommend some form of accountability that he need not be compelled to carry this half-billion-dollar bag alone."

His concern was well placed, but pulling the lid off the CIA's financial operations would require far more than a few blown operations and an internal lack of accountability.[38]

Stuart Hedden resigned and left the Agency before the arrival of Allen Dulles. Dulles appointed Lyman Kirkpatrick as the CIA inspector general. Kirkpatrick had formerly headed CIA's Office of Special Operations. He was also a former OSS officer and an original CIG member. Kirkpatrick had recently returned to the CIA following a long, painful bout with polio that left him partially paralyzed and reliant on a wheelchair. It was a magnanimous gesture on Dulles's part, perhaps, but Kirkpatrick's paralysis obviously would have made it cumbersome, to say the least, for him to continue to oversee the CIA's worldwide operations. Just before Hedden left the Agency, he advised Kirkpatrick to "insist that Allen agree that you are responsible only to him."[39]

In his sanitized memoir, Kirkpatrick wrote, "Even though Mr. Dulles had named me IG, it soon became obvious that he didn't intend to require all of the units to submit to inspections, and we settled into what became a fairly intensive jurisdictional struggle." He continues:

> It took nearly two years before we finally were able to establish the work of the inspector general on a sound basis in the Agency. We were consistently

> blocked from doing any inspections in the operational area and it was only by dint of persistence that finally it was opened to our inspections and we were able to review the work of all of the components in the Agency on a systematic basis. Obviously, some of our inspections were better than others.

If the DCI's handpicked inspector general had these kinds of problems, one can only imagine how difficult it was for GAO's auditors to gain access to classified financial information.[40]

FRONT COMPANIES

During World War II, the OSS used front companies to hide the transfer of money, people, and supplies to field operations conducted behind enemy lines. Section 10 of the CIA Act of 1949 exempted the Agency from a minefield of federal laws and regulations. Elimination of these operational constraints allowed some part of the Agency to function like a private corporation, without disclosing its business relationships to the US government. This opened the door for the CIA to covertly purchase and own companies in the private sector. A front company is a subsidiary or shell company used to shield another company from liability or scrutiny. The CIA used such companies as operational support for conducting clandestine activities. In this context, the US government, the CIA's sponsor, functions as the parent company, and the front company offers plausible deniability for the geopolitical effects of the Agency's covert actions carried out on foreign soil.[41]

By 1950, government corporations had been around for at least fifty years. For example, the Panama Canal Company (1903), the Reconstruction Finance Corporation (1932), the Tennessee Valley Authority (1933), the Federal Deposit Insurance Corporation (1933), and the Commodity Credit Corporation (1933) are all government corporations that existed before World War II. Created by statute, they functioned autonomously and generated their own revenue just like private businesses. Because they generate revenue, public companies are not heavily subsidized by Congress, unlike executive agencies.

In the early years, government corporations did not recognize the comptroller general's authority over their financial accounts. Roger Trask writes, "One of the most difficult audit problems GAO faced in the 1920s and 1930s was dealing with government corporations," for its statutory authority over government corporations was not clearly spelled out in the Budget and Accounting Act of 1921. Although these corporations were supposed to adhere to all federal laws and regulations, there was legal ambiguity because the GAO's authority was not specified in the originating legislation. Government corporations like Tennessee Valley Authority simply ignored requests for financial records until Congress finally stepped in. Congress passed the George Bill (the War Mobilization and Reconversion Act) in 1944 and the Government Corporation Control Act in 1945, which brought government corporations under the authority of GAO's charter. The GAO, in turn, established a Corporate Audits Division, which applied auditing methods that were more compatible with overseeing the financial operations of a private corporation. CIA-owned front companies were supported by unvouchered funds and, therefore, were exempt from the GAO's audit.[42]

The first major business venture for the CIA and Echols's Finance Division was the purchase of a small airline operating in China called Civil Air Transport (CAT), a few months after passage of the CIA Act. Two Americans, Claire Chennault and Whiting Willauer, started CAT in 1946. During the war, Chennault, a former air force lieutenant general, had commanded a famous squad of fighter aircraft known as the Flying Tigers; the unit functioned as part of the Chinese Air Force under Generalissimo Chiang Kai-shek. The squadron's fighter jets, known for their noses painted with an open tiger shark's mouth with gleaming white teeth, were flown by trained US army pilots. Willauer had spent the war in China, serving as executive secretary of the China Defense Supplies, Inc., where he coordinated the purchase and transfer of military supplies from the United States to Chiang Kai-shek and the Chinese Nationalists.

Chennault and Willauer were both personal friends of Chiang Kai-shek. After the war, as private citizens, they established the airline to continue their support of the Chinese Nationalists. They used CAT to transport Chinese refugees from regions that were coming under the control of Mao Zedong's People's Liberation Army. By the summer of 1949, the business operations of CAT were in free fall. Given the financial risk and political uncertainty, no profit-minded businessman or company would have seriously entertained the idea of buying CAT and assuming its liabilities, but the CIA had other plans for the company.

CAT was valuable to the Agency. It offered financial cover for the CIA's Far East operations; and, logistically, it provided a secure means of transporting case officers, refugees, cash, weapons, and cargo to and from hotspots around the Far East. Agency interest in purchasing CAT peaked when it became clear that the airline could not survive much longer on its own. Without Agency intervention, the most probable scenario was that the communists would take control of CAT's remaining assets in mainland China. The CIA had to act quickly: employees from other airlines in China had already defected and coopted planes to the People's Liberation Army. In the summer of 1949, Chennault was in the United States looking for congressional support for the Chinese Nationalists. He and Pat Corcoran, a politically connected financial backer of CAT, met with senior CIA representatives to discuss the company's situation. A declassified top secret CIA memo recounts the summer meeting: "We urged them to hold the airline together because of the potential usefulness to this country of its fleet of planes, its trained pilots and its capabilities from an operational point of view. . . . Through summer and early fall, they therefore held the airline together although its losses were substantial."[43]

On November 1, 1949, in a secret deal with CAT representatives, senior CIA officials agreed to pump money into the company through subsidies. The Agency moved cautiously to keep the airline operational and to limit its financial exposure to incurring liability for CAT's mounting debt. The decision on whether to purchase the company outright was put off for almost a year. A month before the deal was made, on October 3, Frank Wisner dispatched Alfred Cox, an OPC special operations officer, to Hong Kong on an important cover assignment. Cox had been an OSS special operations expert; he retired from the military in 1946 but returned to the OPC in 1948. Cox's assignment in Hong Kong was to coordinate CIA covert operations with CAT operations in China. According to Cox, "there were no OPC Stations as such in the Far East area" when he arrived.[44]

In the official declassified history, Cox describes what CIA accountants from the Finance Division found when they arrived on the scene to review CAT accounting records:

> Its fiscal records and accountings were in an almost unbelievably chaotic condition. Many of the records had been lost, and such records as were kept were incomplete. Various stations upcountry, holding out until the last minute and then having to flee precipitously, were not able to furnish the home office with the accounts documenting the cash flow and expenditures of the office. The accounting situation was further complicated by the wild inflationary effects of the fall of the mainland and the problems of converting foreign currency into US dollars.[45]

Cox's report says that the General Counsel's Office and the Finance Division participated in the negotiations to purchase the company. Emmett Echols, the head of the Finance Division, likely attended the meetings in China, for he is prominently mentioned in Cox's chronology. From the CIA's vantage point, the contract signed between the CIA and CAT representatives served two purposes: "to subsidize CAT by underwriting its operating losses so that it would be available for Government use" and "to finance the establishment of a new operating base at Sanya Basin on the southern end of Hainan, a site chosen by Government." The CIA agreed to pay CAT at commercial rates for the passengers it transported, as a way of financing the company's operations. As specified in the secret agreement signed on November 1, the Agency could earn discounts on the air travel to "the extent that CAT was able to carry cargo to help pay for the flights."

According to Cox, "Echols stated that in time it would be necessary to provide a financial technician for the project who would ensure that adequate financial records were maintained so as to provide data that was essential to the administration of the contract." It would also be necessary "to obtain concurrence of the OPC Chief of Field Activities that the items directly chargeable to the government accounts were operationally necessary, and to act as OPC Finance Officer for confidential funds." Echols, concerned about CAT's growing liabilities, foresaw that a CIA accountant was needed to oversee the company's financial operations, to protect the Agency from potentially massive financial losses. A secret ownership agreement could eventually lead to litigious claims against the US government by the company's creditors. Moving cautiously at first, the Agency gradually took over the company's operations during the next year, clearing the way for the purchase of the airline. Chennault and Willauer continued to run CAT, giving the appearance that nothing had changed, even as CIA operatives moved into cover positions inside the company. The Far East Division of the OPC managed the company and embedded its officers in the corporate structure.[46]

Shortly after reaching an agreement with CAT representatives, the CIA hired a financial analyst and instructed him "to proceed to the Far East and undertake a study of the financial aspects of the CAT operation." Cox reported that "just prior to [this analyst's] departure on 14 November 1949, he turned over several classified books, unwrapped, to a hotel clerk instructing him to call the Agency and have someone pick up the books. It's not too hard to see how this was considered a serious breach of security." Even more comically, the company had just recently moved its corporate headquarters to Hong Kong, and as Cox explains, the new building was a "large completely glass-enclosed office on the mezzanine of the Gloucester Hotel"—called the "Goldfish Bowl"—that "provided no privacy from the causal onlooker."[47]

An internal CIA audit of CAT conducted after the purchase of the company showed that from November 1, 1949, to January 31, 1950, the government had not paid CAT for its flight time. The lost revenue had contributed to the airline's continuing financial woes, and the auditor's report said that the company "is entitled to payment for the flying time used by Government order and for which it has never been paid." The CIA refused to pay its mounting bills because CAT could not precisely account for the billed hours of flight time and only provided an approximate number. These outstanding claims, which extended back to before the CIA purchased the company, were still unresolved by the end of 1951. Inspector General Stuart Hedden reported in a memo dated January 2, 1952, that "our agreement provided that CAT should make no decisions with respect to financial arrangements, scope of business operations or related activities or employment of executive personnel without prior approval of the Government's designated field agent, and that all CAT's records were to be open to our inspection." In other words, CAT's top officers could not make any decisions without government approval, while at the same time the CIA was stiffing the company for the cost of the flights it was ordering. The company's financial losses were further compounded when it lost the entire Hainan base following the island's takeover by communists.[48]

CIA financial analysts, nonetheless, eventually determined that the company had some real book value in addition to its value as a front company. Top Agency officials concluded that, despite CAT's financial difficulties, it had been "one of the most successful projects CIA has undertaken" on operational grounds. The Agency subsequently exercised its option to purchase CAT outright after a private auditing firm calculated that the company's assets exceeded the CIA's total investment. The airline was officially incorporated in Delaware on July 10, 1950, a few weeks after the outbreak of the Korean War.

This first airline purchase was just the beginning. During the 1950s, the CIA formed a holding company, the Pacific Corporation, which consisted of several airlines that serviced the CIA in different parts of the world. CIA-owned planes provided logistical support to the Agency's covert operations. As far as the GAO and the rest of the federal government were concerned, CIA's business enterprises were completely off the books. CIA-owned airlines even won contracts to service the military departments, which helped with the business side of the company. In an interview with Sallie Pisani during the 1980s, Lawrence Houston explained, "Early covert operators believed that the lessons of free enterprise might well be learned by government. Even when their primary concern was fighting Communist subversion, their secondary aim was to show bureaucracies how it might be done efficiently and cheaply. When the CIA finally liquidated the airline in the early 1970s, it had to turn over a $30 million profit to the American government."[49]

15. CIA–GAO Liaison under the CIA Act of 1949

BEHIND THE SCENES

When the working fund was created in 1946, the CIG and the GAO formed a liaison that revolved around the audit of vouchered and unvouchered funds. There were many times under this extraordinary arrangement when the audit jurisdiction of a particular expenditure was uncertain. Matters such as this required coordination between the two agencies in good faith on a case-by-case basis. The declassified CIA records show that meetings between the two general counsels served as an outlet for discussing fiduciary matters of mutual concern. The goal of these meetings in the early years was to engender a legal consensus on the matter at hand.

From September 5, 1946, to June 20, 1949, the joint audit system functioned according to the original 1946 arrangement. After that, it came under the CIA Act of 1949. The CIA's increased involvement in covert action programs during the 1950s was directly coupled with sharp increases in the amount of unvouchered funds flowing into field operations all over the world. It became a problem for the GAO when the Agency began to spend vouchered funds on covert programs with more frequency, while concealing the expenditures behind the DCI's certificate.

Lawrence Houston and Lyle Fisher, the general counsels of the two agencies, continued to meet on an intermittent basis during the 1950s, as they had earlier, to discuss a variety of legal questions that existed solely because of the CIA Act of 1949. In early November 1950, shortly after Bedell Smith's arrival, Houston, Saunders, and Fisher met to discuss "the payment of a telephone bill installed in a private home." Houston solicited the GAO's opinion on a fiduciary matter involving a small expenditure of vouchered funds. In this case, the Agency sought to treat the telephone bill as an unvouchered expenditure that would not be audited by the GAO. Houston anticipated that if he raised the issue with Fisher in good faith, then the GAO would accept CIA's desired treatment of this very small expense.

Afterward, Houston sent a memo to the new DDA, Murray McConnel, to brief him on their meeting: "We mentioned that the problem had arisen before, specifically in the case of the Coordinator of Information, whose funds were contained in an appropriation to the President containing broad language similar to that." According to Houston's account:

> Mr. Fisher stated that a somewhat broader approach had been taken to statutory language of this type in the last few years, and that the earlier opinion to the Coordinator of Information would not necessarily be binding. He did state, however, that we should not submit the question for an official ruling at this time, but authorized us to notify the GAO auditor that the problem involved in this particular telephone bill should not be raised as a formal issue. I feel the inference in Mr. Fisher's remarks to be that we should not risk an adverse ruling on such a small point as it might rise to plague us on larger questions in the future.[1]

The "earlier opinion" Houston alludes to would have been the War Powers Act of 1941, which granted the president extralegal authority over the president's emergency fund. Those powers, of course, expired six months after the war ended.

The CIA got most of what it wanted, but Fisher dissuaded Houston and Saunders from shifting expenses from the vouchered to the unvouchered side of the budget simply "to avoid questions." Recounting their conversation, Houston wrote,

> He said he felt sure he would be compelled to rule in some cases that, while the law as stated seemed to give almost unlimited authority, the payments involved could not be made. I feel he was encouraging us in such cases to make the same type of informal approach we have occasionally taken in the past. He did state that he was in agreement that items of this sort should not be put on the unvouchered side merely to avoid questions.[2]

In the following year, a similar question came up, again related to the installation of a phone at a private residence. An internal memo states that the situation "has arisen in the past" and cites the previous meeting with the GAO: "installation was made in accordance with the understanding that if any question were to arise in the future, it should be referred to Mr. Fisher[3] for his handling." It was decided, however, to treat the installation as an unvouchered expense without informing the GAO:

> The present regulation, [one word deleted] although technically within the normal prohibitions against the provision of such service is in [several words deleted] application of the above informal understanding. (No new reference has been made to Mr. Fisher in the premises, however). Although the regulation may be subject to technical legal criticism, it is the feeling of this office that little or no actual criticism of this action will be forthcoming.

Because the expense was small and had been given special treatment once before, it was viewed as improbable that it would ever be subject to criticism. It appears here that this favorable GAO decision, informally solicited in confidence, was afterward treated as precedent inside the Agency.[4]

Houston told GAO's general counsel at that earlier meeting that the "new regime" under Bedell Smith would continue to "maintain close supervision over the unvouchered side and would insist that funds be properly spent for necessary official operations." A year later, Smith sent a formal letter to Comptroller General Lindsay Warren to seek an official ruling on Section 10b relating to the confidential funds authority of the DCI. According to Darling, Smith asked Warren "if he might be authorized under the extraordinary powers granted by Congress, by his freedom from statutory controls over expenditure and accounting, to raise the pay of the Agency's employees retroactively." Without a doubt, it was a bold move by Smith, given Warren's well-known views on unvouchered funds.[5]

Warren predictably rejected the request and, in his usual style, declared in his ruling that "to adopt the view suggested in your letter would be equivalent to concluding that your Agency is authorized to grant retroactive increases, bonuses, or other prerequisites to any or all its employees with such frequency, or at such times, as desired, contingent only on the availability of funds," to which he rhetorically concluded: "I cannot attribute any such intention to Congress." Years later, in a 1958 memo to Allen Dulles, Houston writes: "[Fisher] was forced to rule against us when a pay raise was made retroactive, but we were not given the retroactive authority specifically. I have no quarrel with his law on this point." Like the previous matter involving the phone bill, the question of retroactive pay raises came up again in 1956 during the tenure of Allen Dulles. The two general counsels met to discuss whether the comptroller general's previous ruling might be revised based on the Executive Pay Act of 1956. Fisher said he would consider it, but after discussing the matter with some of his staff, he told Houston that he "could find no distinction between" the two situations and "that he sympathized with our desire to make the raises retroactive and would like to find in our favor, but would be compelled to take the same legal position" as before.[6]

On January 29, 1952, Houston, Walter Pforzheimer, and Fisher met to discuss a draft proposal by the CIA to amend the CIA Act of 1949. The Agency sought to repeal Sections 3 and 5 and to expand "Section 10 (a)(2) to include procurement and travel expenses." Section 3 covered expenditures related to procurement, and Section 5 covered travel. This proposal placed procurement and travel squarely under the DCI's confidential funds authority. According to Pforzheimer's internal memo written afterward: "We pointed out to Mr. Fisher that it now appeared necessary to expand our procurement authorities in Section 3, particularly in the field of research and development, and to amend several of the subsections of Section 5; and that it appeared particularly in connection with Section 5 that this would be a recurring problem as Congress amended and changed various statutes in this general field."[7]

The subtle, but substantive, change that the CIA was proposing to Section 10a would decouple CIA's procurement from the Armed Services Procurement Act and also simplify the administration of CIA's travel expenses, a major area of expenditure growth at the CIA. According to Pforzheimer:

> Mr. Fisher stated that while he and the comptroller general felt that CIA should have the broadest possible powers, the comptroller general was reluctant to extend these powers where not essential, and that if we could proceed with the alternative of amendments, they would consider it highly preferable. Mr. Fisher offered the services of members of his staff to assist us in revising Section 5 and redrafting our procurement section, with a view of writing a full procurement section directly into our Act.

Fisher offered GAO assistance in the redrafting of Sections 3 and 5 to satisfy both the CIA's security concerns and the GAO's administrative concerns, but that was not what the CIA was looking for.[8]

Also in 1952, in early summer, the Agency was dealing with a serious administrative problem. Several temporary buildings in the CIA complex lacked air-conditioning; the sweltering heat was damaging morale and, in some cases, causing employees to be sent home early. The Agency had no vouchered funds left in the budget to purchase the necessary air-conditioning equipment, and the General Services Administration had previously denied the release of any funds for this purpose.

On June 26, 1952, when Houston and Saunders met with Fisher to discuss the problem, the outcome was so controversial that Houston meticulously detailed the minutes in a later memo. He first outlined the nature of the problem: "The Bureau of the Budget had tentatively approved release of the necessary funds, but that it left to us the question of whether such funds could legally be spent for the desired equipment in view of the statutory restrictions on procurement. I also noted that since we did not get an annual appropriation act, we could not logically ask for specific language authorizing the expenditure." The lack of vouchered money available in the budget only left one viable option: the use of unvouchered funds. Houston and Saunders clearly did not want to be the ones suggesting that simple solution, and so they looked to Fisher for advice. He did not initially offer an informal ruling but instead "asked if it would not be possible for us to utilize our authority for expenditure of unvouchered funds." The CIA Act was ambiguous on matters such as this. Looking for a middle road, Houston stated that "as a matter of principle we did not wish to do this unless it was clear that the expenditure was the type for which unvouchered funds were provided, that there was no clear indication here of Congressional intent." Unvouchered funds were only supposed to be used on the CIA's most sensitive and highly classified expenditures. On this point, Houston "stressed [to Fisher] that our appropriation matters were handled in a most confidential manner with the very minimum number of Congressmen who must necessarily be aware of our activities, and that the key members of Congress in this case would be Representative Mahon on the House side and probably Senator O'Mahoney on the Senate side."[9]

Fisher told Houston in no uncertain terms that "he did not see how he could approve use of vouchered funds which would be audited by the GAO, but that he would have no objection to our expenditure of unvouchered funds for procurement of the necessary air conditioning equipment provided we had the specific approval of the appropriate members of Congress, presumably Mr. Mahon and Senator O'Mahoney." Effectively giving Houston and Saunders the green light, Fisher, in this case, deferred the matter of congressional intent to Congress. As long as the purchase did not use vouchered funds, the GAO would not object.[10]

It appears here that in the interest of arbitrating a solution, Fisher issued an informal ruling without first consulting with the comptroller general. He probably was not anticipating that such a practical ruling would contribute to blurring the jurisdictional distinction between the CIA's vouchered and unvouchered funds. Houston, though, was extremely appreciative of the GAO's support and at the end of the memo wrote:

> We agreed that this was a satisfactory solution and that we could continue in the future to utilize unvouchered funds for anything we thought appropriate for covert operations, but would not use them for this type of administrative expense without prior discussion with his office. I consider this another example of the outstanding cooperation we have received from Mr. Fisher in the past which is based primarily, I believe, on his confidence in the manner in which we are utilizing the extraordinary financial powers granted to us by Congress.[11]

Shortly after Fisher's retirement in 1958, Houston recounted this intriguing episode in a memorandum to Allen Dulles:

> He approved our purchase of air-conditioning equipment for the temporary buildings without specific authority in the face of a statutory prohibition. On this his law was probably wrong and he certainly took a considerable chance to help us with this problem. This, however, was typical of his normal common sense handling of the matters we took up with him. I feel we owe him a considerable debt for his support and the manner in which it was given.[12]

The air-conditioning matter came up again about a year later in a memo from Red White, who recounted the circumstances to Dulles:

> About mid-July 1952, I had several discussions with the Director [i.e., Smith] concerning the expenditure of unvouchered funds to air condition our temporary buildings. . . . I advised the Director that the Bureau of the Budget would release the funds and that the General Accounting Office would not object to such an expenditure, provided the Agency had specific approval from appropriate members of Congress. I suggested that the Director get approval from Representatives Mahon and Taber and Senators O'Mahoney and Ferguson. He advised me later that he had contacted each of these individuals and that they had given their approval for this expenditure. . . . In each case General Smith merely told the Congressmen that we were losing a tremendous number of man hours due to dismissals because of excessive heat in our temporary buildings and that morale and efficiency were deteriorating rapidly. In each case the Congressmen gave their approval without hesitation.[13]

Allen Dulles surely would have viewed this information with great favor as he prepared next year's unvouchered budget proposal for the House and Senate Appropriations Committees.

NO YEAR FUNDING

In early December 1953, senior officials from the CIA and the Budget Bureau met to discuss a legal strategy for obtaining no-year treatment for CIA's entire budget. Most congressional appropriations expire after a fixed period of one or five years. Any unexpended funds must be returned to the Treasury at the end of the fiscal period. In the case of no-year funding, there is no expiration date. With no-year status, the CIA could function more like a bank. For example, if the agency was spinning up a new covert operation in a remote place like Angola, but there were no funds yet in the pipeline to support the project, it could divert funds from somewhere else. It was a good old-fashioned transfer that the early US presidents took advantage of in the days before Congress adopted the doctrine of specific appropriations. No-year status would give the CIA the spending power to obligate money against almost any account at the Agency because, in principle, none of its funds would ever expire and have to be remitted to the Treasury. Money could then be freely directed from the reserve fund or other operations with a surplus of funding.[14]

Everyone at the December meeting agreed that it would be a mistake to move too fast, considering all the political pressure on the CIA at the time. In an internal memorandum, Houston reports:

> At a conversation between the Central Intelligence Agency and the Bureau of the Budget the subject of no-year treatment for CIA appropriations came up. Present were Colonel White, [name deleted[15]] and Mr. Houston for CIA and Messrs. Perry and Hamilton for the Bureau of the Budget. It was agreed that it would be premature to request no-year authority for the regular portions of the budget as we are not prepared yet with detailed justifications. It was also agreed, however, that it would be more secure, practical, and sensible to consider the unexpended portions of the reserve on a no-year basis so that such portions could be carried over from year to year for expenditure under the policies applying to use of the reserve and so that appropriations would be made each year only in an amount necessary to replenish the reserve and to keep it up to the authorized level. The Bureau of the Budget was in favor of presenting this proposal to the Appropriations Committees, but asked whether we had authority to use funds on a no-year basis. I said our authorities might be wide enough as stated in the law, but as this proposal had not been contemplated when the law was enacted, we could not say that it was clearly the intent of the Congress to authorize us to carry funds in this manner. It was agreed, therefore, that I would consult with the Comptroller General's Office to see if he felt the laws pertaining to no-year appropriations and our law would prevent handling the reserve in the desired manner.

Ambiguity in Section 10 of the CIA Act allowed the CIA to interpret the law pretty much as it wanted. Lawrence Houston, reluctant to push the envelope too far, recommended that they first solicit the informal opinion of Lyle Fisher.[16]

Houston reported that he spoke at length on the subject with Fisher, who said that "it made sense to him to handle the reserve on a no-year basis" but that he "was not sure whether we had the requisite authority." Fisher requested "a day or two to look into the matter, stating that even if we technically had the authority he might need something in writing from the Congress to indicate their intent to have our authorities applied in this manner." They discussed GAO's decision on the phone on December 9. The memo recounts,

> That while some of Mr. Fisher's staff doubted whether we had clear-cut authority to handle funds in a no-year manner Mr. Fisher took the position that he would approve of treatment of the reserve on this basis provided we got some expression of intent in writing from the Congress, presumably from the House Appropriations Committee, which would clarify their intent in this respect. . . . I saw Mr. Fisher informally a few days later, and he repeated that he had had to overrule some technical objections presented by members of his staff." Houston concluded: "if the Committee passes on this specific point and approves, there is no one who can logically question the procedure.[17]

After gaining the GAO's support, the CIA received approval from the House and Senate appropriations committees. In a letter to Gordon A. Nease, a senior staff member for the Senate Appropriation Committee, Saunders explained: "It is the desire of the Agency to secure approval of both the Senate and House Appropriation Committees to have the contingency reserve fund designated as a 'No-Year' fund." The letter revealed that the Agency's budget for fiscal year 1955 totaled $335 million, with "$225 million for normal operations and a contingency reserve fund of $110 million for unforeseen emergencies."[18] Both committees approved the request.[19]

A year later, the CIA tried to run with the same script that had proved so successful in the previous year, but this time it approached Fisher looking to receive the GAO's blessing on no-year status for its entire budget. Only a few people outside of the Agency had access to detailed budgetary information on the CIA. Moreover, its funding was channeled through hidden accounts established in other federal agencies such as the Defense and State Departments. No-year treatment of the CIA's entire budget promised to remove all remaining fiscal constraints.

As before, the CIA approached the GAO before going to Congress. On March 7, 1955, Houston and Saunders met once again with Lyle Fisher, hoping to gain a favorable opinion from the GAO on the new proposal. Houston documented the meeting two days later: "We explained the reason for wanting this as increasing the security of our funding and incidentally reducing the new authorization for Fiscal Year 1956." The central thrust of Houston's legal argument was that no-year treatment of CIA's budget promised to improve its operational security for administering unvouchered funds. It was not much of a legal argument, and it failed to consider that CIA's budget and accounting system was far more secure than that of virtually every other agency in the federal government. On this occasion, Houston may have pushed the envelope a little bit too far. He recalls:

> Mr. Fisher was somewhat doubtful whether he could agree with the Bureau of the Budget's suggestion that the committee authorize all funds now or hereafter made available as being on a no-year basis, but after discussion he said he was willing to recommend to the comptroller general that it be done as proposed above for Fiscal Year 1956 alone. He said he must clear this with the Comptroller General, however, in view of the fact that he was new to the job and not yet confirmed and might have some reservations, particularly as Mr. Fisher was not prepared to say that there was clear-authorization in our statute.

Fisher discussed the matter privately with the new comptroller general, Joseph Campbell, and with Assistant Comptroller General Frank Weitzel. He called Houston the following day and told him that the comptroller general was "not prepared to accept [CIA's] proposal in light of the absence of any specific legal authority." It is doubtful that Fisher lobbied hard for the CIA in this case. It seems far more likely that his face-to-face meeting with Houston and Saunders had left him taken aback by the CIA's persistence, and so he left the decision to Joseph Campbell, an outsider to the CIA–GAO liaison. By this time, two major investigations of the Agency were already under way.[20]

16. The Annual Budget Ritual

THE CIA AND THE BUDGET BUREAU

Federal agencies cannot perform their statutory duties without operational funds to cover future expenses. Budgets are designed to project operational costs at least one year into the future. A budget combined with a postaudit of expenditures provides a way to measure an agency's financial performance against its institutional record. Because there is no public record of the CIA's operations, there is, in the end, no public accountability in any practical sense. In this case, government accountability becomes more a matter of faith.

In the 1950s, the CIA's budget system involved liaisons with three external government entities: the Bureau of the Budget, Congress, and the NSC. There is a whole section in the Dulles report on the budgetary process, which Allen Dulles almost certainly authored—most of it still remains classified. The first page summarizes how the budget process worked in 1948. This overview provides a good introduction to CIA's annual budget ritual:

> The budget proposals, as approved by the Director, are submitted each year with the authorization of the National Security Council to the Bureau of the Budget where they are handled by one official who has full security clearance. Then the budget is supported before special sub-committees of the Appropriations Committee of the two Houses of Congress. After approval, arrangements are made with the Bureau of the Budget so that various parts of the budget are appropriated to other departments. Thus, there is no official appropriation to the Central Intelligence Agency, but there are a number of separate blanket and unidentified appropriations to other departments, which act as the vehicles for transmitting the funds to the Central Intelligence Agency. Both Congress and the Bureau of the Budget have refrained from examining in detail the internal workings of the Central Intelligence Agency in order to determine the justification for the budget. It is important that such discretion and security be continued, and that special treatment be

> accorded. However, in order to justify this, it is necessary that the National Security Council continuously assure itself as to the proper management and operations of the Central Intelligence Agency, serving as the informed sponsor of the Agency and as the protector of its security.

Congress and the Budget Bureau were kept in the dark on the "internal workings" of CIA's financial system and its interconnections to other federal departments.[1]

Like all other federal agencies in the 1950s, each year the CIA submitted a budget proposal to Congress that attempted to project its expenditures on foreign intelligence operations one year into the future. All the most senior officials in CIA's administrative directorate were involved in this budgetary process, which began long before the DCI's formal presentation of the budget to the small congressional subcommittees that considered the details. There is no more important administrative activity at the CIA than its annual budget proposal to Congress; and the DDA, DDP, DDCI, comptroller, general counsel, and the heads of the Budget, Finance, and Fiscal Divisions were all involved.

The Budget Bureau was wired into the national security establishment through its administrative relations with the CIA and the NSC. The budget director wielded the most authority over the development of a comprehensive budget proposal for the CIA and the rest of the intelligence community. Under Eisenhower, the NSC expanded administratively in support of the proliferating national security complex. Members of the Budget Bureau supported two key NSC boards: the OCB and the Planning Board. The Planning Board was responsible for making policy recommendations, whereas the OCB used those recommendations to advise the CIA and other defense organizations that supported the US national security establishment.

The budget director—the federal government's top budget man—gave final approval to CIA's budget before sending it to Congress. To some extent, the bureau held the purse strings connected to CIA's most cherished foreign projects. The director regularly attended NSC meetings and was "called upon whenever the budget effects of contemplated actions became important." The director also served as a permanent member of the Planning Board and supplied technical staff to the OCB. It was a demanding job, and during the 1950s, there were six different budget directors, spanning two presidencies.[2]

The budget bureau oversaw CIA's budget proposal to Congress from beginning to end, but this important liaison was highly compartmentalized. Financial information was restricted to a small number of people at the bureau on a need-to-know basis. During the 1950s, Robert Macy and Hart Perry served as Budget Bureau liaisons to the CIA, working directly with the Agency's top budget men to ensure that the proposal remained in line with the president's foreign policy agenda. In Allen Dulles's first year, he informed the deputy directors of Plans, Intelligence, and Administration in a memo to his top senior staff: "I wish to call your attention to the fact that all liaisons by this Agency with the Bureau of the Budget must be controlled and supervised by the Comptroller."[3]

The Budget Bureau closely monitored the growth of the intelligence and defense budgets during the 1950s. A special committee was established inside the intelligence community to review the most recent report from the bureau and make recommendations for the development and presentation of intelligence cost estimates. This committee, known as the "Working Group," was chaired by Edward Saunders, CIA's comptroller. The other members of the committee included representatives from the office of the secretary of defense, joint chiefs of staff, army, navy, air force, AEC, FBI, and CIA. Their meetings led to the creation of a Costs Estimates Committee, headed by Saunders. This committee became responsible for producing a report for the upcoming fiscal year. The development of a complex administrative infrastructure was instrumental in preparing the CIA budget proposal for just a few eyes in Congress.[4]

THE CIA AND CONGRESS

Congress plays a completely different role in the annual budget ritual. It is Congress that pays the Agency's bills; and, to fulfill its constitutional duty, lawmakers need to know something about the nature of CIA's intelligence activities. But is it really necessary that every member in the House and Senate know the budgetary and operational details of every one of CIA's covert programs? In a pure democracy, every congressional vote carries the same weight; practically speaking, however, not every member of Congress can be equally trusted to keep a secret. In politically controversial situations, some holders of sensitive information in a free society, whether for reasons of self-interest or moral conscience, will choose to publicize that information or leak it to the public surreptitiously. The handling of classified information at the committee level in the early 1950s was considered a serious national security matter, and public leaks by committee members were not tolerated. A leaker, if identified, risked expulsion from the committee.

The most compelling justification for the use of unvouchered funds by the government was the need to protect the United States and its citizens from a surprise nuclear attack. The advent of intercontinental missile systems made the nation vulnerable to attack from anywhere on the face of the earth at any time, whether the country was at war or at peace. The emergence of the intelligence community in parallel with the CIA brought about fundamental reforms in how Congress appropriated money to the national security establishment. During the 1950s, four standing committees controlled the defense and intelligence budgets: the House and Senate each had an appropriations and an armed services committee. In those years, these powerful committees established a secret legislative system to fund the national security establishment. Under this system of congressional oversight, black budgets became the norm.

Legislative power in a congressional committee was centrally concentrated in the chairman, who controlled the committee's agenda, its schedule, and its protocols. In the case of the CIA, the chairman also decided what information, if any, could be disclosed to other members of the committee, which was determined via private consultation with senior CIA officials. The committee chairman was the most important contact in the information loop. The chairman and his committee coupled the intent of Congress to the executive branch. Oversight of the CIA in each of the four committees was further compartmentalized within a special CIA subcommittee.[5]

Occasionally, the chairmen of the four big committees would throw their weight around, to make sure the CIA understood who really controlled their budget; but, in the end, the CIA generally got what it asked for. Although the full Congress registered their votes for appropriation bills on defense and intelligence, the passage of the intelligence budget was based entirely on the recommendations of the four oversight committees. As a practical matter, because most congressmen were not cleared to view the itemized budget, there was little room left for debate.

This is not to suggest that all members of Congress were happy with these legislative protocols on national security spending. But most congressmen, in the interest of national security and love of country, accepted the new system as a necessity of the times. This disposition gradually changed during the 1950s. The huge spike in national security spending during the Korean War did not go unnoticed, and defense and intelligence budgets continued at wartime levels long after the armistice agreement between North and South Korea was signed. Taxpayer dollars just kept flowing into the military-intelligence-industrial complex without much federal oversight or a clear assessment of the national security benefits. Most congressmen during the early years of the Cold War knew absolutely nothing about the Agency's covert operations abroad. With so much secrecy, how was Congress supposed to measure the peace benefits of national security spending against the enormous cost to society?

The CIA managed to keep most of its congressional critics at bay for a number of years; however, beginning in the early 1950s, some congressmen began to speak out. The first to shatter the code of silence was the anti-communist zealot Senator Joseph R. McCarthy (R-Wisconsin), who feared that the nation's premier spy Agency was being infiltrated by communists. After the political defections of Donald Maclean and Guy Burgess to the Soviet Union in May 1951, the notorious senator took direct public aim at the CIA. Both Brits had been working for years as double agents for the Soviets, while they enjoyed high-level diplomatic assignments at the British embassy in Washington. Maclean and Burgess were also longtime friends of Kim Philby, the British double agent that ran the Soviet Division of MI6 (British foreign intelligence).

The success of these double agents raised the alarming idea that KGB agents could penetrate the CIA and gain access to the nation's most sensitive national security information. The director of the CIA, Bedell Smith, inadvertently threw more fuel on the fire. During testimony before McCarthy's House Un-American Activities Committee, on an unrelated matter, Smith candidly told the committee that he believed Soviet agents had probably infiltrated his Agency. This gaffe further emboldened the McCarthy underground, not to mention the national media. McCarthy was at the apex of his career, a political force to be reckoned with in Washington. In his memoir, Lyman Kirkpatrick, CIA's IG during the Dulles years, recounted the political tactics of the McCarthy underground:

> The "McCarthy Underground" consisted of a group of individuals who were supporters of the Senator, who were not on his payroll, but who in some instances were subsidized by money from wealthy friends of McCarthy, and who made it their full-time occupation to be investigators of alleged Communism or subversion in the government. . . . One "McCarthy Underground" technique was a not very subtle form of blackmail. Within the CIA we had cases where individuals would be contacted by telephone and told that it was known that they drank too much, or were having an "affair," and that the caller would make no issue of this if they would come around and tell everything that they knew about the Agency.[6]

Many in Washington may have privately repudiated McCarthy's ruthless political tactics and outrageous accusations. Still, he had ruined many careers and had to be taken seriously. In the middle of Dulles's first year as DCI, he appointed William Bundy, a Yale graduate and former Skull and Bones member, to the CIA's elite Board of National Estimates. This hire infuriated McCarthy; his informants reported that Bundy had donated $400 to Alger Hiss's defense fund. Hiss, a high-ranking State Department official, had been convicted of perjury for lying about his communist associations. McCarthy publicly accused Bundy of being a communist sympathizer and demanded that he appear before his committee. This confrontation triggered a flurry of letters between McCarthy and Dulles; and the matter was further complicated by the fact that Bundy was the son-in-law of Dean Acheson, the former secretary of state.

In a letter to Dulles, McCarthy wrote: "Your insistence that Congress is not entitled to obtain information about improper conduct on the part of your top officers is extremely revealing—doubly so in view of the material which has been coming to me within the past few weeks." Dulles assured him that Bundy would be fully investigated by internal security, but McCarthy dismissed this as a mere fig leaf. The powerful senator, adept at the game of politics, retaliated to the rejection of his demand by threatening to launch a full-scale congressional investigation of the Agency. Finally, President Eisenhower intervened to keep the dispute from escalating into a full-scale media circus. To put the matter fully to rest, the president grudgingly agreed to allow two independent investigations of the CIA, one by the executive branch (president) and one by the legislative branch (Congress).[7]

OVERSIGHT AND ACCOUNTABILITY

President Eisenhower appointed Lieutenant General James Doolittle to lead the executive branch investigation. The other members of the Doolittle Committee were William Franke, Morris Hadley, and William Pawley. The congressional investigation of the CIA was led by General Mark Clark. The Clark Task Force was a five-person board of consultants that formed an investigative component of the Second Hoover Commission. President Eisenhower, the NSC, and the DCI all had an interest in controlling these investigations as much as possible.

In a three-page letter to Doolittle, Eisenhower said he expected his committee to "conduct a study of the covert activities of the Central Intelligence Agency," adding that, because "these sensitive operations are carried on pursuant to National Security Council action approved by me, I desire that your report be made to me personally and classified TOP SECRET." Doolittle was instructed to focus his investigation on the clandestine services: "You will deal with the covert activities of the CIA as indicated . . . and your report will be submitted to me. General Clark's Task Force will deal largely with the organization and methods of operation of the CIA and other related agencies within the limits prescribed in the law. I will determine whether or not the report or any part thereof should have any further dissemination."[8]

The assessment of the CIA in the committee's written report is kinder than it was in the oral version given to Eisenhower. Like the Dulles Report, the Doolittle Report severely criticized the Agency and its senior leadership: "The weakness of the CIA is in the organization—it grew like [a] topsy, sloppy organization. Mr. Dulles surrounds himself with people in whom he has loyalty but not competence. There is a lack of security consciousness throughout organization. Too much information is leaked at cocktail parties."[9]

The report's more serious criticisms were reserved for CIA's accounting system and its compartmentalized handling of budgetary information. The committee observed poor communications between the Office of the Comptroller and the clandestine divisions on matters relating to purely administrative functions in which the comptroller and the chief of the finance division had a clear need to know:

> Due to [the Deputy Director of Plans] present secrecy policies with respect to Foreign Intelligence projects, the Comptroller of the Agency is unable to maintain meaningful records showing the expenditures made for individual projects in this category. The Foreign Intelligence Staff keeps certain records of such expenditures but on the basis of a calendar rather than a fiscal year. We believe that the Comptroller should be furnished with information which will enable him to record, control and account for the costs of the individual projects of this element of the Agency. Adequate protection for security purposes can and should be provided within the Office of the Comptroller. Certain other projects in the political and psychological and paramilitary areas, of a sensitive nature are occasionally developed and processed without full information with respect thereto being given to the Deputy Director for Administration and the Comptroller.[10]

The Doolittle Report concluded that the comptroller was bound to find out about the existence of covert operations because all the funds released to the different agency components had to pass through the comptroller:

> It is inevitable that [the Comptroller] will have knowledge that operations of this nature are being conducted and it is unlikely that more specific information relating to the projects can long be kept secret from him. In one particular instance where substantial sums were expended, the Comptroller was called upon to make the expenditure with no supporting data being furnished to him at the time or at any future date. When we requested breakdowns of costs of the operation, we found that they were available only in the area division involved and that they were incomplete and unsatisfactory. We are of the opinion that this deviation from the normal procedure of placing upon the Comptroller the responsibility of accounting for expenditures

> is unsound and is not justified by the claim that the security of the operation is improved by this deviation.[11]

The Doolittle Report recommended that the comptroller be furnished "with sufficient information on all covert projects to enable him to exercise proper accounting control on a fiscal year basis."[12]

The report from the Clark Task Force complimented Dulles's selfless enthusiasm for the spy business; but, overall, it was critical of his performance and of the Agency. It recommended "a sweeping reorganization of CIA to help overcome what it called a 'serious lack' of adequate intelligence data on Russia, Red China and other Communist nations." Although the task force was not supposed to focus its investigation on CIA's clandestine operations, the two studies did overlap on the issues of CIA's budget and accounting system. One important part of Clark's mandate was to examine CIA's administrative operations, which included the Office of the Comptroller. In its final report, the Clark committee complained that "the Task Force was considerably hampered in its investigation of the intelligence community by the fact that the security restrictions around CIA were such that they could not adequately collate their report between agencies." These complaints probably stemmed from differences of opinion on the extent of the study's congressional mandate. Any overlap of the study with CIA's covert operations or with the investigative domain of the Doolittle committee would also have been closely scrutinized by ISO.[13]

Senator Mike Mansfield (D-Montana) was the first member of Congress to introduce legislation aimed at improving congressional oversight of CIA's budget and operations. In his late forties, Mansfield already had a long record of public service; he had joined the US Navy in 1918 and served in the Marine Corps from 1920 to 1922. Mansfield had served in the House since 1943 and had been elected to the Senate for the first time in 1952. He did not dispute the need for the CIA, but he did criticize its lack of accountability. In July 1953, the senator proposed the creation of an eighteen-member Joint Congressional Intelligence Committee, like the Joint Atomic Energy Committee, with an even number of members selected from the House and Senate. His resolution faced fierce resistance from the CIA, the president, and the four big committees. Though soundly defeated, Mansfield was not deterred; he introduced a similar proposal in

1954, which was again defeated. His legislative proposal was starting to gain traction in the Senate, however. By the early part of 1955, thirty-two other senators endorsed his proposal, representing one-third of the Senate body. Seven of his cosponsors this time were members of the SASC.[14]

The *Washington Post* interviewed Mansfield: "As things now stand, he said, there is no way for Congress to check up on the hush-hush spy agency. Until a committee of the kind I am proposing is established, there will be no way of knowing what serious flaws in the Central Intelligence Agency may be covered by the curtain of secrecy in which it's shrouded." He continued to argue that a joint congressional CIA oversight committee was desperately needed to "'keep a constant check' on the Central Intelligence Agency." He told the reporter, "The present method of letting a few top members of Senate and House committees check the super-secret agency 'is a hodge-podge system.'" His perennial bill to improve congressional oversight of the CIA once again failed to pass.[15]

In January 1956, President Eisenhower announced the creation of the President's Board of Consultants on Foreign Intelligence Activities (PBCFIA) "to keep tabs on the super-secret CIA." The new board was made up of eight "distinguished citizens outside the government" that were "qualified on the basis of achievement, experience, independence, and integrity." The PBCFIA was given the authority to conduct high-level reviews of the CIA's foreign intelligence programs and report its findings to the president. Eisenhower chose James Killian, the president of MIT, to serve as the board's chairman. The other members were an eclectic mix that included former political heavyweights, former high-ranking military officers, and leaders of the corporate community. The PBCFIA was expected to meet "at least once every six months."[16]

The PBCFIA was yet another board added to a growing list of boards and think tanks created to advise and oversee the CIA. Created to rectify the fundamental disconnect between the intelligence community and the American public, the PBCFIA had access to the unflattering reports of the Doolittle Committee and the Clark Task Force. Two members of the board, David Bruce and Robert Lovett, took charge of the PBCFIA's first investigation of the CIA. Bruce had served as Donovan's chief of secret intelligence for the OSS in World War II; in the postwar era, he had served as the US ambassador to France, West Germany, and the United

Kingdom. Lovett was part of the inner circle of advisors who contributed to shaping the military and intelligence arms of government during the late 1940s and early 1950s. He was also a full partner at the Wall Street investment banking giant Brown Brothers Harriman. Dulles knew Bruce and Lovett well and could not have handpicked two men more likely to throw their support behind the Agency. Dulles biographer Peter Grose describes Bruce as one of "Allen's oldest and closest friends."

Bruce and Lovett soon learned that covert action programs were consuming the bulk of the CIA's resources, amounting to "more than half of CIA personnel and over 80 percent of the budget." According to Grose, Bruce was "very much disturbed" by the amount of money being spent on operations designed to meddle in the political affairs of other countries. He asked the rhetorical question that many would ask for years to come, "What right have we to go barging around into other countries, buying newspapers and handing money to opposition parties or supporting a candidate for this, that or the other office?"[17]

The Bruce–Lovett report overwhelmingly found that the CIA had gone beyond its original mandate: "We are sure that the supporters of the 1948 decision to launch this government on a positive [psychological and political warfare] program could not possibly have foreseen the ramifications of the operations which have resulted from it. No one, other than those in the CIA immediately concerned with the day-to-day operation, has any detailed knowledge of what is going on." According to the report, the country's most sensitive covert programs were being run by "a horde of CIA representatives (largely under State or Defense cover), . . . bright, highly graded young men who must be doing something all the time to justify their reason for being."[18]

The Bruce–Lovett Report was released on the heels of the Doolittle and Clark investigations. Although none of these reports were widely circulated, all three uncovered chronic problems of accountability at the CIA and raised questions about the nation's investment in covert operations. Still, nothing changed in the way the CIA did business; and, in fact, two of its biggest operations were yet to come. Both proved to be colossal failures: Indonesia and the Bay of Pigs.

17. Secret Programs under the CIA Act of 1949

CIA programs tend to remain highly classified, never seeing the light of day. If information does leak into the public domain years after the fact, it is nearly impossible to link the operational funding with the operations themselves. To evaluate the costs and the benefits of the CIA Act of 1949 to American society, the use of unvouchered funds will be investigated for three illustrative historical examples: MKULTRA, the U-2 Project, and the National Reconnaissance Office (NRO).

MKULTRA

In 1953, the new DCI, Allen Dulles, started a research and development project known as MKULTRA that was financed entirely off-the-books with unvouchered funds. MKULTRA studied the effects of lysergic acid diethylamide (LSD) and a host of other powerful psychedelic drugs on human subjects. Little was known about LSD and its mysterious psychological properties at the time. The CIA sought to harness the psychological powers of hallucinogenic drugs like LSD so that they could be used in the field against enemy targets. Dulles authorized experiments on unwitting human subjects as a means of speeding up the learning curve. It was the CIA Act of 1949 that made all this ethically dubious research possible.

MKULTRA was first approved by CIA's Project Review Committee (PRC) under Bedell Smith in June 1951. The PRC was a high-level committee responsible for vetting special funding requests before they ever reached the DCI. Allen Dulles, the DDCI, chaired the PRC under Smith. Its other members included the DDP, the DDA, the general counsel, and the top financial administrators from the comptroller's office. The project was proposed by the Technical Services Staff (TSS), a small and obscure division in the Plans that recruited highly trained experts in a multitude of scientific and engineering fields. Bedell Smith would never have approved unvouchered funding for a risky project like MKULTRA, but that decision was left to Allen Dulles.

Richard Helms, the deputy director of Plans, sent a memo to Dulles on April 3, 1953, briefing him on the original TSS proposal. Only 6 percent of the TSS funding proposal involved what Helms characterized in his memo as "Extremely Sensitive Research and Development." It was this part of the proposal that received the cryptonym MKULTRA. Helms now looked to Dulles to start apportioning unvouchered funds to this newly conceived project. He also recommended that it be carried out under the technical direction of the head of the TSS Chemical Division, Sidney Gottlieb.[1]

The CIA suspected that the Soviet Union was weaponizing drugs like LSD for possible use in interrogations of enemy spies. On April 7, just four days after he read Helm's memo, Dulles gave a speech to a group of Princeton alumni, titled "Brain Warfare." The DCI warned his audience about a new emerging front in the Cold War:

> I wonder . . . whether we realize how sinister the battle for men's minds has become in Soviet hands. We might call it, in its new form, "brain warfare." The target of this warfare is the minds of men both on a collective and on an individual basis. The aim is to condition the mind so that it no longer reacts on a free will or rational basis but responds to impulses implanted from outside. If we are to counter this kind of warfare, we must understand the techniques the Soviet Union is adopting to control men's minds.[2]

Describing a scenario that could have come from George Orwell's gloomy book *1984* (1949), Dulles ominously admonished his audience: "Parrot-like the individuals so conditioned can merely repeat thoughts which have been implanted in their minds by suggestions from the outside. In effect the brain under these circumstances becomes a phonograph playing a disc put on its spindle by an outside genius over which it has no control."[3]

Three days later, on Monday April 13, Dulles sent a memo to Walter Wolf, the DDA, authorizing $300,000 for "research" and "operating costs" for a new program. Helms had been emphatic in his earlier memo, "It is highly undesirable from a policy and security point of view that contracts should be signed indicating Agency or Government interest." Key lines from Helms's memo made it into Dulles's memo to Wolf. Dulles insisted that no formal contracts would be signed and that the CIA grants would be based on secret oral agreements with the grantees. His instructions to Wolf stated: "No further documents will be required to justify payment of the invoices. Exacting control will be maintained over the Project by TSS." Anticipating that some highly valued grantees would want documentary evidence of an agreement, he left open the possibility of an "informal agreement":

> Although no formal contract will be signed, it will occasionally be possible for TSS to sign an informal agreement with the individual or concern performing the work. In such cases, TSS will retain in its files all documents. TSS will endeavor wherever possible to obtain documentary support of invoices, such as cancelled checks, receipted bills, etc., and these will remain in TSS files. Such documents at best will only cover a portion of the total expenditures, and regular audit procedure will not be followed.[4]

By an informal agreement, Dulles meant a memorandum of understanding with the person conducting the work. It was not a formal contract. In this special case, the grantee's agreement with the Agency would remain hidden away in Gottlieb's secret files and would not be shared with the CIA comptroller. The comptroller was primarily involved in approving the release of funds in bulk amounts to a small budget office in TSS that was established to handle the approvals, disbursements, and accounting for MKULTRA. Audits by the Finance Division were restricted to a cursory examination of the approvals and certifications corresponding to disbursement requests. Its primary oversight role was to verify that the financial policies of the Agency were properly followed—and these could be modified by the DCI for special situations. The TSS Budget Office[5] effectively managed the finances of these programs. Its accounting system was based on the notion of "memorandum accountability," and all this funding was totally off the books. Sidney Gottlieb, incidentally, destroyed the documents under his control before he left the CIA in 1972; only a few records remain. Moreover, communications between the TSS Budget Office and Echols's Finance Division were probably face-to-face in most instances.[6]

The funding of subprojects under MKULTRA required certifying signatures of approval from the TSS research director, the executive secretary of the Research Board, and the chief of the TSS Chemical Division. Dr. Willis Gibbons, the TSS research director, certified "that the invoice applies to Project MKULTRA and that the conditions outlined in the DD/P memorandum for DCI dated 3 April have been complied with." Louis deFlorez, the executive secretary of the Research Board, next certified "that the scope of the program has been approved." Lastly, Sidney Gottlieb certified "that the work has been satisfactorily performed from a technical point of view and has been carried out in accordance with the understandings reached between TSS and the individual or concern doing the work." These three signatures appeared on all official memos to the comptroller to request the start-up of new accounts and to direct funds to MKULTRA subprojects.[7]

MKULTRA generated a whole new market for research grants, but unvouchered funds could not be handed out to the beneficiaries in the usual way. An internal administrative system was developed that used cut-outs as intermediaries in the transfer of money between the Agency and its recipients. A cut-out was an "entity or individual used by [TSS] for the sole purpose of providing covert funding channel for MKULTRA activity." Research foundations that tacitly supported the goals of the Agency, such as the Josiah Macy Jr. Foundation and the Geschickter Fund for Medical Research, knowingly functioned as cut-outs by providing administrative cover to the Agency's funding of MKULTRA. The grantee was the "ultimate recipient of funds for research provided under MKULTRA activity"; and "control over funds held by grantees will be exercised through the use of memorandum accounts."

Gottlieb started disbursing unvouchered funds to high priority subprojects soon after Dulles authorized the program. On April 27, 1953, Gottlieb sent a memo to the CIA comptroller (Saunders) that opened a clandestine account for subproject 1: "Under the authority granted in the memorandum dated 13 April 1953 from the DCI to DD/A[8] and the further authority granted in the memorandum dated 17 April 1953 from DD/A to the Comptroller on the subject, 'DD/P-TSS Project MKULTRA,' to subproject 1 has been approved, and $2000.00 of the over-all Project MKULTRA funds have been obligated to cover the subprojects expenses." The long list of funding requests that followed had the same wording, with different subproject numbers and amounts.[9]

Some of these subprojects are real eye-openers. Subproject 2—another very high priority project with a budget of $4,650—investigated methods "for the administration of drugs without the knowledge of the patient."

The final objective was the "preparation of a manual" for testing "methods which have been used by criminals for surreptitious administration of drugs" and for observing and analyzing "the psychodynamics of situations of this nature."[10]

Subproject 3, with an overall budget of $8,875, was headed by George White, a former OSS officer who worked for the Federal Bureau of Narcotics after the war. Gottlieb requested that the first payment of $4,132 from the Finance Division be made in cash. He received the payment three days later and sent it to White "for services rendered." Gottlieb requested a second payment for an additional $4,235 on June 15. In that case, a check was made out to someone else, possibly White, though the name of the recipient has been redacted. This extraordinary subproject was designed to test LSD, and other drugs and drug combinations, on unwitting subjects in an uncontrolled experimental setting. White set up two adjacent apartments in Greenwich Village in Manhattan, using CIA money to pay for the furnishings and other supplies for his cool village pad, which included liquor and drugs for entertaining his guests. He lived in one of the two apartments, posing as a street artist and seaman known locally as Morgan Hall. Morgan Hall lured unsuspecting visitors to his CIA "safehouse" in Greenwich Village to participate in social drug experiments that were being filmed and recorded in the room next door. Once White had loosened them up with a little alcohol, he would slip them 100 micrograms or so of LSD without their knowledge. The legal protections afforded by the CIA Act helped to create an institutional culture where ethical concerns such as these were ignored or covered up inside the TSS Budget Office.[11]

Guaranteeing its own supply of LSD while preventing the Soviet Union from obtaining large quantities of the drug was considered a serious matter of national security inside the CIA. In the early 1950s, Sandoz, the company that discovered the drug, only produced it in small quantities for research purposes. Because LSD had no known medicinal benefits, its marketplace was limited to a small group of researchers. For a while, Sandoz, as the only producer, had a monopoly over a powerful mind-altering drug that was in very short supply.[12]

The CIA initially attempted to purchase Sandoz's entire stock of LSD but learned that the drug was only produced in small quantities, exclusively for controlled research. Through secret negotiations, Sandoz agreed to supply the CIA with 100 grams of LSD weekly. Sandoz, as a foreign drug company, had no real interest in playing a major role in the Cold War for the benefit of the CIA. The CIA, on the other hand, wanted to dominate the marketplace by purchasing the world's supply of the drug, which at this time was 100 grams per week.[13]

MKULTRA subtasks were set up to increase production of the drug. Gottlieb entered into secret negotiations with Eli Lilly & Company, an American business, to develop a new process for synthesizing LSD and its derivatives in large quantities. Gottlieb sent a memorandum to the comptroller on June 1, 1953, requesting that $5,000 be obligated to cover the project expenses in the first year. On December 1, 1953, $400,000 under Subproject 18 was earmarked for the purchase of Eli Lilly's production quota of LSD.[14]

It was just a matter of time before something went terribly wrong, and, indeed, disaster struck seven months later at a top secret interagency retreat in the backwoods of Western Maryland. The retreat at the Deep Creek Lodge brought together senior people from TSS and the Army Chemical Corps Special Operations Division, based in Fort Detrick, Maryland; it was an opportunity to discuss projects of mutual interest in a relaxing, rustic atmosphere far away from Washington. On the second night, Thursday, November 19, all but two of the men had a Cointreau cocktail that had secretly been spiked with LSD. Gottlieb asked the men after about twenty minutes if they noticed anything different. The drugged subjects later acknowledged noticing changes in their psychological state once Gottlieb posed the question to them. The meeting continued for a short while longer before devolving into laughter and desultory conversations. Most of the men endured the experience without any lasting effects. Dr. Frank Olsen, a bacteriologist and an expert in biological weaponry, had a bad trip, however. While his Fort Detrick and CIA colleagues found ways to connect with the others in the room, he said little to his fellow attendees. After he sat there for hours feeling isolated, he began to suspect that his colleagues were making fun of him.

In the days that followed, Olsen's erratic, paranoid behavior at home and at work caught the attention of his wife and his supervisor (who had been at the retreat). Gottlieb and his deputy, Robert Lashbrook, attempted to get Olsen psychiatric help while they also sought to cover up the whole episode. Their effort to keep the matter quiet ended disastrously at about 2 a.m. on November 28, 1953, when Olsen crashed through a window at the Statler Hotel in New York City and fell ten floors to his death.[15]

The ISO and the IG both investigated the matter afterward to assess the collateral damage to the Agency and to determine whether Gottlieb and Lashbrook should face reprimand or punishment for their actions. During questioning by the IG, it came out that Gibbons, the TSS head, and James Drum, his deputy, had known about Gottlieb's experiment in advance and had at least tacitly approved it. As was generally the case in these situations, nothing was in writing. Wisner and Helms both flatly denied knowing about it in their interview with Kirkpatrick; however, they also tried to dissuade Kirkpatrick from recommending serious disciplinary action. DeFlorez, the research director, also opposed handing out reprimands to the two most culpable people. At the end of his investigation, Kirkpatrick issued letters that mildly denounced their actions, but these phony reprimands had no lasting effect on MKULTRA or Gottlieb's career. Higher up the chain of command, both men were informally told that the letters should not be considered a reprimand and would not be placed in their permanent file. The incident did little to slow Gottlieb's career path. In fact, in 1967, just a year after the termination of MKULTRA, the new DCI Richard Helms appointed Gottlieb head of the Technical Services Staff. This institutional culture was another unintended consequence of the CIA Act and the unfettered use of unvouchered funds.[16]

Although Allen Dulles flatly acknowledged that the Agency could not possibly account for all the unvouchered money disbursed to MKULTRA's many subprojects, he still insisted that a regular audit could not be performed for security reasons. This reasoning was used to stop the CIA's auditor in chief from conducting postaudits of the various subprojects started under MKULTRA. It was the McCarthy era after all, and there was no telling what Joe McCarthy might do with information about a top secret CIA program to control the mind with a new super drug. While the Olsen affair was playing out, Major General Eugene Foster, the auditor in chief, conferred with the TSS about examining its financial records, noting that he had a particular interest in "the financial aspects of MKULTRA." Red White, the acting deputy director of administration, insisted that Foster conduct the audit himself and that all TSS documents be "examined on an 'Eyes Only' basis." Only part of Foster's report has been declassified, but this portion of the report exposes some of the serious accountability problems festering in the accounts of MKULTRA. In one case cited by Foster, he states:

> Over 150 cash memoranda were submitted to [name redacted] in the form of sales slips, cash register slips and notations signed by the individual that sums were spent. These numerous cash memoranda were listed by [word redacted] and applied to the total cash he received. At the time of the audit there was no cash on hand, and, accordingly, [name redacted] had to assume that all of the cash had been spent, though the cash memoranda did not equal the cash he had received. There was no record maintained of expenditures, so that the disbursements made for which no receipts were obtainable appears to cause the unaccounted for balances.

A report like this generally would have been followed up with a point-by-point written commentary focusing on areas of the report where there were strong disagreements. Instead, White sent a brief response to Foster on April 14, requesting they meet privately "to chat." In his reply, he pointedly noted, "The thing that concerns me is whether an auditor should report on the conditions of an account as he finds them or accept oral explanations." Incidents like this had a chilling effect on the CIA's audit system. In the interest of protecting MKULTRA from scrutiny, Dulles chose to short-circuit all the established accountability protocols in place.[17]

In late 1956, Dulles finally authorized the IG, Lyman Kirkpatrick, to conduct a five-year survey of TSS, including an examination of MKULTRA. Kirkpatrick requested Foster's report from the Audit Staff, but it was initially withheld from him until White gave the auditor in chief "permission to make his audit reports available to the Inspector General on Project MKULTRA." Kirkpatrick's report, submitted in April 1957, criticized the program on many grounds. The report was strongly rebutted inside of Plans, however, and it had little, if any, effect on the future activities of MKULTRA.[18]

John McCone succeeded Dulles as DCI in 1962. He instructed the new IG, John Earman, to conduct a comprehensive audit of MKULTRA and the Technical Services Staff. Earman, given far more access than Kirkpatrick, identified many serious accountability problems, which he weighed against any redeeming benefits that could be excavated from the research. He concluded that MKULTRA contributed little to the operational capability of the CIA. In his final report he wrote, "Weighing possible benefits of such testing against the risks of compromise and of resulting damage to CIA has led the Inspector General to recommend termination of this phase of the MKULTRA program. Existing checks and balances on the working level management of such testing do not afford the senior command of CIA adequate protection against the high risks involved." Attempts to improve the recordkeeping and fiscal controls helped rein in the program in its later years, but with a new senior level staff in control of the CIA, the original enthusiasm for MKULTRA was gone. The last of the program's subprojects was terminated in 1966, the year that Richard Helms succeeded William Raborn as DCI.[19]

Considering the high risk involved, it seems fair to ask whether the program was worth the cost. Like most of the CIA's R & D programs, MKULTRA was designed to deliver operational capability. The original plan was to innovate delivery systems for LSD and other drugs, and to prescribe methods for their use in the field. It does not appear that any of the CIA's goals for MKULTRA were ever achieved because the mystical properties of the drugs could not be harnessed. There are no published results that document any of the studies conducted by the experts. In the end, the program was a total waste of taxpayer dollars, without any documented benefit to national security. Worst of all, for years the program encouraged illegal experiments to be performed on unwitting individuals, placing the health and safety of its victims in the United States and other parts of the world in danger. MKULTRA was made possible by the CIA Act of 1949.

U-2 PROJECT

In the mid-1950s, US planners foresaw a brief window of opportunity to penetrate Soviet airspace, risk free, using an aircraft that could fly above the range of Soviet surface-to-air missiles. Designed for this purpose, the U-2 spy plane was jointly developed by the CIA, the air force, and the navy. This strange-looking airplane with its long, flimsy wings started a revolution in an emerging and highly valued area of intelligence collection known as Imagery Intelligence or IMINT. From altitudes of seventy thousand feet, the U-2 was able to collect photographic imagery of Soviet military infrastructure on the surface. The spy plane's overflights of the Soviet Union ended after several years, when pilot Gary Powers was shot down while flying through Soviet airspace and was captured on May 1, 1960. Satellite-based systems seamlessly supplanted the fragile, high-flying aircraft in the early 1960s.

The U-2 project offers another good example of how the CIA Act of 1949 was exploited to fund a highly classified project under the control of a small inner circle of CIA senior officials, with little external oversight. This top secret project was spun up in November 1954 using an injection of seed money from the CIA reserve fund. Allen Dulles, Air Force Chief of Staff Nathan Twining, Assistant Chief of Staff for Research and Development Donald Putt, and Secretary of Defense Charles Wilson met with Eisenhower at the White House to discuss the funding of the project. Richard Bissell, the U-2 project manager, recounted this event in his memoir:

> Andrew Goodpaster, Eisenhower's staff secretary,[20] noted in a memorandum of that meeting: "Authorization was sought from the President to go ahead on a program to produce thirty special high-performance aircraft at a cost of about $35 million. The President approved the action. Mr. Allen Dulles indicated that his organization could not finance this whole sum without drawing attention to it, and it was agreed that Defense would seek to carry a substantial part of the financing."

The entire program, code-named Project AQUATONE, was financially managed by the CIA for reasons that will become clear shortly.[21]

On December 1, 1954, the CIA signed a contract with Lockheed Aircraft[22] to design and develop the plane. The financial management of the project involved a secret partnership among the CIA, the air force, the navy, and Lockheed Aircraft. To conceal the project, every dollar spent on it went through CIA's Finance Division. The Agency functioned as the sole procurement agent for the project, which was critical, for all funding from the CIA, the air force, and the navy was pooled in a CIA-controlled account under the DCI's certificate (i.e., unvouchered). The enabling of the navy and air force was not covered under Section 10b of the CIA Act;

their funding was still subject to GAO audit control. Since the original seed money came out of the reserve fund, no one in Congress needed to be informed about the new project. It is the CIA's financial management of the project that begs legal scrutiny here.[23]

Allen Dulles waited until the U-2 was operationally ready before he informed a few select members of Congress on the four big oversight committees. Leverett Saltonstall, chairman of the SASC, was the first member of Congress to be told of the U-2 project; on February 24, 1956, when the plane was ready for its first operational flight, Dulles divulged more information at a subsequent meeting with Saltonstall and Richard Russell, the ranking member of the minority party. Three days later, at their request, Dulles met with the two leaders of the House Appropriations Committee, Clarence Cannon (D-Michigan) and John Taber (R-New York) to inform them. The U-2's first overflight of the Soviet Union on July 4, 1956, was greatly celebrated back in Washington.[24]

The CIA men who ran the program clearly knew that their handling of unvouchered funds fell in the gray area of the CIA Act. Houston discussed this esoteric legal matter beforehand with the general counsel of the air force and "various Air Force fiscal and procurement officials." His memo to Bissell on July 26, 1957, outlined his view:

> This Agency has been acting as Procurement Agent for the Air Force and the Navy for supplies, equipment, material, undertaking this role, we considered carefully the legal basis for so doing and the legal problems. . . . It is my understanding that we are in agreement on the legal aspects and believe that the role of the Agency as Procurement Agent under these circumstances and the manner in which it carries out its role are consistent with applicable law.[25]

Houston saw nothing technically wrong with the CIA coordinating with other departments and acting as the project's financial administrator during the U-2's early development; he considered it to be consistent with the Armed Services Procurement Act of 1947 and the CIA Act of 1949. His opinion, however, as so often is the case in the intelligence business, was heavily nuanced. Houston supported this line of reasoning in his memo, "We have also reviewed the manner in which the various procurement contracts under these arrangements are being negotiated and administered. In my opinion we have not and will not exercise any procurement authorities which are not available to the Air Force and the Navy, and we are not, therefore, through these arrangements circumventing any legal prohibitions on those services." The military departments, like the CIA, could engage in negotiated contracts under the Armed Services Procurement Act; and these contracts were, by design, more secretive. That is what Houston seems to be suggesting here.[26]

Houston explained that the expenditures of the military agencies were, however, under the GAO's audit jurisdiction: "The one area in which our arrangements depart from those normally authorized for services is in connection with methods of payment and audit. We have arranged channels and methods of payment required by security which normal services' practices would be unable to follow. Also, the funds involved are certified by the Director and are not subject to General Accounting Office audit other than a review of his final certification."[27]

Bissell wrote to Dulles to ask if his confidential funds authority could be extended to cover all the project's funding. Realizing he was in a little over his head, Dulles looked to Houston for a more formal opinion. Houston wrote back to Bissell on August 26 with a pointed response: "I understand the Director wanted to be informed whether our acting as agent for the Navy and the Air force on procurement matters circumvented any legal restriction they might otherwise operate under." He asserted: "There is, in my opinion, one point which may cause difficulties and which we should keep in mind with the lessening security problem." The remainder of this paragraph—about eight lines of text—is redacted. According to CIA's general counsel:

> From the audit point of view I have no particular concern about a General Accounting Office review of the contracts involved. Inasmuch as the security considerations are far less restrictive than in the initial stages, and so far as procurement is concerned will continue to reduce, we should give consideration to permitting a General Accounting Office audit at some future date. This could be done by either opening all contracts to their inspection or else authorizing the Air Force and the Navy to make available their portion of the procurement to GAO.[28]

It was Bissell's intention, however, to keep the GAO completely out of the accountability loop, if possible. He wanted to avoid setting any new jurisdictional precedents involving GAO oversight of secret programs under the CIA Act. Bissell candidly wrote about the secrecy aspect of the project in his memoir: "Larry Houston recalls how adamant I was that we keep knowledge of the project limited to just a few individuals—even in the CIA. I called him later and said I wanted him and no one else in his office, to do the legal work. In carrying out my instructions, he had to handle a wide variety of tasks, from fund transfers to contract negotiations." Bissell explains that he and Kelly Johnson

> cut through layers of red tape and reporting procedures that would have slowed the project down. We kept our regular monthly progress reports to about five pages, for example; had the same program been developed for the air force, it would have required the preparation of a document one inch thick. . . . The agency's way of working, as it evolved, was a dramatic contrast and an effective one. . . . All this day-to-day business was facilitated by the covert manner in which the agency was able to operate. I worked behind a barrier of secrecy that protected my decision making from interference.[29]

Bissell was open to meeting directly with the comptroller general if the GAO found out about the project and started asking questions. He discussed this possibility in a later memo to Dulles:

> The first step . . . might well be a discussion with the comptroller general himself in which, without any allusion to AQUATONE, the main relevant circumstances surrounding our procurement for the Navy and the Air Force could be explained. . . . It could be explained to the comptroller general that, even in the absence of overriding security requirements, there could have been no question of opening the Air Force and the Navy procurement to competitive bids, since the quantities required by these two Services were small and could undoubtedly be furnished under more advantageous terms and more speedily by the Agency's contractors who were already producing times in acquisition. Finally, the main features of the contracts could be outlined to the comptroller general to make clear that they were prudently drawn in such a manner as to give full protection to the Government. . . . Should you desire that I contact the GAO on your behalf to explore this problem, please advise me.[30]

Bissell clearly lacked an understanding of the legislative history of the CIA Act and the long-term liaison between Houston and Fisher. Though Houston accepted Bissell's position, he saw sharing the information with the GAO as a continuing sign of good faith. Here, the CIA was knowingly violating the spirit of the law. Houston was concerned that if the GAO learned that they were cut completely out of the loop on an important fiduciary matter, it might perturb their long-term liaison. Joseph Campbell, the US comptroller general, was still an unknown quantity to the CIA, and Houston thought it more prudent to inform the GAO in good faith, since the security risk was significantly lower. Acquiescing, in the end, to Bissell's preferred treatment, Houston conceded in a November 4 memo to Bissell:

> The main point of my original suggestion has been amply considered. I had no fixed views on whether or not we should open the Air Force and Navy portion of the AQUATONE procurement through General Accounting Office. I merely wished the question to be seriously studied and a determination made. I am quite satisfied with the reasons for recommending that these contracts not be opened to General Accounting Office audit and will join in the recommendation. I believe that such a determination would serve to answer queries from General Accounting Office or the Comptroller General. This being the case I believe we should not approach the comptroller general unless we have some indication that he is aware of and bothered by the problem. If the Comptroller General's office raises the question it will almost certainly come to me through Lyle Fisher, the CG General Counsel, with whom we have had a long and highly satisfactory liaison. Further, if for any reason we decided to approach the Comptroller General's office, I would feel strongly that our approach should be made through Mr. Fisher. He has a keen understanding of our legal problems but also of our operational and security problems and has demonstrated time and again that he is as little legalistic as his position permits and will support a sound practical determination.

Houston, though, suggested in the memo that if the GAO learned about the arrangement, it could be interpreted as bad faith: "Mr. Fisher would be somewhat unhappy as a matter of principle that Army and Navy contracts will not receive General Accounting Office audit due to the utilization of our Agency as a procurement office, as he has raised this point before."[31]

Here is another case where the CIA's legal position seems to have rested on the calculated assumption that no one outside of the inner circle of AQUATONE would ever know about it. Houston concurred with Bissell that "we are unanimous in recommending against opening the contracts for audit," but he added the caveat, "If any problem arises in connection with the General Accounting Office or the comptroller general you and I will handle it preferably in the first instance with Mr. Fisher or if necessary, with the comptroller general himself."[32]

The U-2 proved to be a spectacular success, thoroughly disproving the infamous missile gap theory. The missile gap conjecture, as it should be called, was based on the patently false premise that the Soviet Union's nuclear arsenal greatly exceeded US stockpiles. Some might point to the success of the U-2 program as a justification for deciding not to inform the GAO, but there is an inherent problem with this view. By not informing the GAO, the CIA acted in a way that could be considered bad faith, and it established a secret precedent that arbitrarily expanded the DCI's authority under the CIA Act to encompass any project or program that arguably involved national security. One only needs to extrapolate a decade or two into the future to see the effects of precedents like this. Lastly, there is no reason to think that the project would not have been just as successful if the comptroller general and his general counsel had been informed of the joint contracts after the first operational flights, as Houston initially recommended.

THE NATIONAL RECONNAISSANCE OFFICE

In the late 1950s, while the U-2 was still conducting successful overflights of the Soviet Union, President Eisenhower approved funding for two programs to develop a satellite reconnaissance system, one run by the CIA and the other by the US Air Force. The two programs, codenamed CORONA (CIA) and SAMOS (air force), were designed to develop a spaceborne photographic system. Both programs, however, ran up against technological barriers and cost overruns in the race to develop a successful prototype. The CIA's first thirteen Corona flights, for example, failed to achieve orbit and were aborted. Lockheed was appointed as the lead contractor; because the project was so complex, subcontractors were also hired to innovate and install niche technologies essential to building a prototype system as quickly as possible.[33]

Secret CIA programs always run the risk of accidental discovery by the press or another government agency, such as the GAO. Near the end of the program's first year, a GAO auditor approached the Fairchild Camera & Instrument Company and began asking questions about the Itek Corporation. Itek was a secret CIA subcontractor with a sole-source contract to develop a camera system for the first spy satellite. From there, it proliferated into a multimillion-dollar company that, for a short while, was a darling on Wall Street, though no one really knew how the company made its money.[34]

Someone from the Corona Program, anxious about the GAO's line of questioning, contacted the CIA's security office and recommended that "the General Accounting Office auditor be restricted in his efforts"; but the person offered the security office no reason why it should intervene. A security officer then contacted Saunders and asked for his opinion. Saunders replied to the security officer, the DCI, the DDP, and the DDS:

> There are several obvious questions and/or observations that would be raised by the General Accounting Office should they be contacted with a request that they recall their auditor from his cost examination at Fairchild Camera & Instrument Company. They would want to know what security objection could possibly be involved if the General Accounting Office auditor was aware only that he was examining costs in Fairchild Camera Instrument Company that pertain to a contract held with ITEK[35] Corporation. The auditor would not need-to-know of the ultimate user of the end product and he should not ask or be told. The General Accounting Office auditor would possibly be satisfied to the extent that he would not even approach ITEK Corporation, but even should he pursue his functions into ITEK, he should not learn anything about the Agency unless some witting employee in ITEK should be careless.

Saunders argued against taking any preemptive action, for even if the GAO did investigate, the CIA would have ample opportunity to handle the matter with the GAO behind the scenes. He recommended that the Security Office "not contact the General Accounting Office in an attempt to lessen their cost audit examination until we have reached a point where there is security danger." Saunders was willing to take the matter up with the GAO if there was a serious risk of exposure.[36]

Eisenhower eventually combined the two satellite reconnaissance programs into a joint program called the National Reconnaissance Program. This top secret program was spun up in the Defense Department but was jointly managed by the CIA and the air force. Once operational, it was renamed the National Reconnaissance Office (NRO). Everything about the organization, even its name, was kept classified until the 1990s. Today, the NRO is one of the three largest intelligence organizations in the US government—the CIA and the NSA are the other two. The NRO manages the financial operations of the nation's satellite reconnaissance programs and today spends roughly 10 billion taxpayer dollars per year.

The establishment of the NRO exploited the legal protections offered the CIA under Section 10. The CIA's continued involvement with the new organization ensured that its budget would remain under the director's confidential funds authority. The NRO, though, was technically an autonomous part of the Defense Department. The CIA was understandably averse to delegating the director's authority to an outsider; the air force, too, wanted administrative control of the new organization. A power struggle ensued between the two for control of the new intelligence office. It was finally agreed that the DDP, Richard Bissell,[37] and Joseph Charyk, the air force undersecretary, would serve as codirectors. Bissell, by virtue of his official connection to the Agency, could then be delegated confidential funds authority under the CIA Act. The NRO became an extension of the CIA for budgetary purposes and fiscal control.[38]

The CIA also wanted its funding priorities factored into the NRO budget. By this time, John McCone had replaced Allen Dulles. The CIA comptroller Edward Saunders[39] was another casualty of the Dulles era. McCone replaced Saunders with John Bross, an OSS veteran with a long career in intelligence. His tenure began about the time when the CIA's role in the funding of the NRO was being debated. The problem, as Bross characterized it, was in "determining whether funds for CIA projects under the NRO should be included in the CIA Budget as part of the CIA appropriation or whether they should be included as projects undertaken by CIA under NRO for which reimbursement is requested." It was decided that the NRO would be responsible for the preparation of budget requests for all NRO programs and would present the budget proposal to "the Secretary of Defense and the Director Central Intelligence, the Bureau of the Budget and Congressional Committees." A special exception was made for the CIA's unvouchered funds, which fell under the statutory authority of the CIA Act. The exception states, "Funds expended or obligated under the authority of the Director of Central Intelligence under Public Law 110[40] will be administered and accounted for by CIA." The NRO's charter prohibited these unvouchered funds from being diverted to non-CIA projects. John McCone recommended that the CIA direct funds to NRO projects that would be considered part of the CIA budget. Bross pointed out that the "control vested in CIA by an appropriation may be more apparent than real, as NRO will, to a very considerable degree, exercise centralized control over the administration and funding of projects."[41]

The director's special authorities under Section 10 gave the CIA considerable leverage in the financial management of the NRO. The CIA desired more internal control over the development of satellite reconnaissance, but a major CIA satellite program would not have gone unnoticed by Congress. In this case, there was in fact a massive public investment in space reconnaissance, and it went almost completely unnoticed by Congress, the holder of the purse strings.

18. The Dulles Letter

THE CIA AND THE YEAR 1958

Lyle Fisher suffered a major heart attack shortly after his fiftieth birthday. By the time he returned to work, Robert Keller, who had been appointed the acting general counsel in his absence, was being groomed as his successor. Keller had begun his career at the GAO in 1935 and was a top legal assistant to Lindsay Warren and Joseph Campbell. Keller worked as an attorney in the general counsel's office between 1946 and 1950, so he and Fisher must have known each other well. In 1950, he moved over to the Office of the Comptroller General to serve as one of Warren's top legal assistants. In his final year at the GAO, Lyle Fisher spent most of his time mentoring Keller. It can be reasonably inferred that Keller first learned about the history of the CIA–GAO liaison during this transitionary period.

Lyle Fisher retired from the GAO on August 31, 1958. Shortly after that, Lawrence Houston invited Fisher downtown for a special luncheon at CIA headquarters on October 16. Fisher had been the GAO's sole liaison to the CIA since the creation of the working fund in 1946, and the Agency formally recognized him for his formative role in the establishment of CIA's special financial system for handling unvouchered funds. The Dulles letter, where this story all began, alludes to his two most important contributions: the establishment of the working fund prior to the creation of the CIA and his influence in advising the comptroller general to remain neutral on the CIA Act of 1949. The luncheon was a flattering gesture, of course, but the CIA–GAO liaison had cooled by then. Direct communication between the two general counsels had waned—and perhaps had ceased altogether—even before Fisher's heart attack in 1957. Why then did the Agency decide to recognize his contributions so many years later? The letter suggests that his retirement factored into the decision, and clearly it did, but the answer to the question in this case is not as simple as it may seem on the surface.

The year 1958 turned out to be one of the worst in the history of the Agency and that, too, seems to have factored into the decision. A hapless chain of events started on October 4, 1957, with the Soviet's successful launch of Sputnik 1, the world's first earth-orbiting satellite. The CIA, basking in the early success of the U-2 program, was mostly caught off guard by this historic event. Over the next year, the Agency fell victim to a perfect storm of intelligence failures that rocked it to its core. This organization, which shrouded itself in secrecy, never confirming or denying reports about its alleged intelligence activities, was struggling mightily in 1958 to contain the public fallout.

Shortly after the launch of Sputnik 1, Senator Henry Jackson (D-Washington) spoke of "a week of shame and danger for America." Decrying the missile gap, Jackson proclaimed, "We are behind and we are falling further behind . . . abdicating world leadership to the Soviet Union." Sputnik 2 was launched a month later, followed by Sputnik 3 on May 15, 1958. Many Americans, fearing World War III was imminent, invested their hard-earned money on the construction of backyard underground bomb shelters.[1]

With the United States and the Soviet Union investing heavily in Cold War operations, the geopolitical world order was in a state of flux. In Indonesia, a political hotspot, there were pockets of civil resistance and social instability. At a press conference on April 30, 1958, Ray Scherer, a news correspondent from NBC, asked President Eisenhower for his reaction to recent statements by President Sukarno, who accused the "Americans" of "flying rebel planes" in support of the anti-government insurgency. Eisenhower's initial response was defensive; he said he was not ready to comment publicly. Saying he had only been briefed on Sukarno's remarks that morning, the president nonetheless felt compelled to tell Scherer, "When it comes to interstate difficulty anywhere, our policy is one of careful neutrality . . . so as not to be taking sides where it is none of our business."[2]

Eisenhower knew far more than was acknowledged at the time. For one thing, he knew that Sukarno was telling the truth, for he personally had authorized the overthrow of the Indonesian government on September 25, 1957. Under his authorization, the CIA's involvement was limited to the secret transfer of weapons and supplies to the anti-government insurgents. When, by April 1958, the insurgency was rapidly losing ground to government forces, the CIA resorted to desperate measures in a last-ditch effort to salvage its original foreign policy objective—the overthrow of

Sukarno. With rebel forces near collapse, the fateful decision was made to send the Agency's own pilots on bombing missions against government targets. These CIA-led sorties commenced on April 19, prior to the Eisenhower press conference, which would suggest that the president was aware of the situation when he was questioned by Ray Scherer. By then, Frank Wisner was personally running the operation from a secret headquarters in Singapore. The mission took a predictably disastrous turn on May 18, when Sukarno's forces shot down a CIA case officer who was piloting a US-made B-26 bomber over Ambon City. The pilot, Allen Pope, safely parachuted to the ground after ejecting himself from the aircraft and was quickly captured by government troops.[3]

It is standard procedure for the US government and the CIA to deny any association with case officers captured while on a covert mission. CIA case officers are trained not to carry documents and identification that could betray their association to the US government. For example, Gary Powers had been given a poison pill to take in case of his capture during the U-2 overflights, but he decided not to take it. In this case, Pope brought classified documents with him that proved he was a CIA agent, to avoid being killed as a mercenary. Sukarno used the incident to his political advantage by parading the disgraced CIA officer before the world media, much to the chagrin of the president and the CIA.[4]

While the CIA was assisting the Indonesian rebels in late April, Vice President Nixon embarked on a highly publicized goodwill trip to South America. The United States had many critics in Latin American countries; they denounced its support of corrupt and autocratic dictators who ruled with an iron fist. In Peru, demonstrators got close enough to Nixon to spit saliva in his face. On May 13, when Nixon and his entourage arrived in Caracas, Venezuela, the last stop on the tour, their motorcade was attacked by a mob of angry protesters. The limousine that carried the vice president and his wife was surrounded; they were showered with spit and shouted at while they huddled nervously inside their vehicle. The motorcade hastily departed from the airport but immediately got held up in bumper-to-bumper traffic. When the protesters caught up with the motorcade, they shook the car carrying Nixon and his wife and began smashing its windows. For a few moments, the vice president and his wife appeared to be in grave danger.

It was later reported that the CIA and the State Department, headed by the two Dulles brothers, were aware of at least three death threats against the vice president prior to the trip. Congress naturally wanted to know why they had not done more with the intelligence they allegedly had. Representative Prince Preston (D-Georgia) spoke angrily on the House floor about the "unbelievable amount" of money Congress gave the CIA "with no questions asked." In an attempt to mitigate the CIA's complicity, John Taber (R-New York), the powerful chairman of the House Appropriations Committee, tried to shift some of the blame to the State Department, pointing out that "the CIA had the information and gave it to the State Department." This strategy had worked ten years earlier, after the Bogotá riots. The Senate Foreign Relations Committee met on May 20 to "find out . . . whether the Administration knowingly gambled on violence." Allen Dulles appeared in a closed hearing to answer questions about the trip.[5]

The situation, it seemed, could not possibly get any worse. But on July 14, 1958, the pro-American monarchical government of Iraq, under King Faisal II, fell to a military coup. Faisal, the crown prince, the prime minister, and other members of the royal family were brutally assassinated. In the congressional hearings that followed, the CIA reluctantly admitted that it had received no intelligence suggesting that a coup d'état was imminent. Representative Charles Brownson (R-Indiana) "called Iraq the 'final straw' in a series of intelligence failures."[6]

Frank Wisner, who suffered from bipolar personality disorder, took this sequence of events especially hard. The failed operation in Indonesia may have pushed him over the edge. Severely depressed, he checked himself into Sheppard Pratt, a CIA-approved psychiatric hospital in Baltimore, where, among other things, he received electroshock therapy. His health problems forced him to resign as the DDP at the end of the summer.[7]

Lawrence Houston summarized this unprecedented year in a memo to Allen Dulles, dated September 24, 1958:

> The basic problem of satisfying the requirements of the Congress for information about the Agency and about intelligence matters generally within the proper security limitations was somewhat intensified [this past year].

> On the one hand, the Agency appeared more frequently before congressional committees, provided more information, and made more official contacts with the Congress than in prior years. On the other hand, continuing high pressure of international affairs and certain specific instances, such as the Venezuelan riots during the Vice President's visit and the coup in Iraq, aroused increased congressional interest in the intelligence performance of the Executive and in the activities of the Agency.

To this assessment, Houston adds, "Considerable criticism of the Agency was expressed by various member of the Congress, and there was rather widespread dissatisfaction at the amount of information available." On a more positive note, he adds: "Specific briefings . . . were on the whole well received, and the revival of proposals for a Joint Committee on Intelligence was not pressed to an issue." Houston was referring to Senator Mansfield's multiple attempts to establish a permanent Joint House–Senate Intelligence Committee.[8]

LUNCH AT THE CIA: OCTOBER 16, 1958

The CIA was struggling to survive one of the worst years in its brief eleven-year history when Lyle Fisher retired from the GAO. If, near the end of his career, he harbored any lingering doubts about the CIA Act of 1949, the events of 1958 would have done little to ease his mind. Fisher must have known about the CIA's troubles; they were splashed across the morning newspaper. On June 29, an editorial written by John Scali about the CIA appeared in the Sunday edition of the *Washington Post*. Scali, a popular ABC news correspondent, colorfully described the secrecy and lack of oversight underlying the CIA's funding system in "The $350-Million-a-Year CIA Writes Its Own Tight-Mouthed Ticket":

> The CIA is unique among American governmental agencies. Its estimated budget of $350 million is little better than a reasonably good guess. No one outside the highest official circles can say for sure. But if the estimate is correct, it is $130 million more than the State Department spends on its 282 diplomatic outposts around the world. Only a handful of top Government

> executives know exactly how many people work for the CIA. The State Department has about 16,000 American employees. It has been estimated that the CIA has almost as many.

More pointedly, Scali next turned to the DCI's special powers under the CIA Act and the ad hoc legislative system that funded the Agency's operational agenda:

> Allen Dulles's job is unique in at least one respect. He can write a check for a million dollars without telling even the General Accounting Office exactly why he is spending the money. Most Congressmen, who watch financial matters like a detective eyeing a pickpocket, have only a vague idea of how much the CIA spends and what it spends it for. Yet each year the agency's budget is appropriated promptly.

Here was another classic case of the fox guarding the henhouse. By this point in his career, Lyle Fisher surely must have realized that Scali had hit the nail on the head and that, worst of all, there was nothing he could do about it. His career in public service was about to end.[9]

Lyle Fisher probably did not anticipate that the CIA would invite him downtown for a special lunch in his honor. Houston hastily organized the luncheon in early October, soon after Wisner stepped down. In preparation, he sent Dulles a formal invitation on October 9, 1958, requesting his attendance: "I have invited Mr. E. Lyle Fisher for lunch on Thursday, 16 October. I hope you can join us as he was a firm and powerful friend through our growing years. The attached memorandum indicates his support more specifically. We are holding this date on your pad."[10] In the memo that Houston cites, the history of the liaison is recounted: "Mr. Fisher was General counsel to the comptroller general from the last days of OSS and through the beginnings and growth of the agency. . . . He was a firm friend of the agency throughout his tenure with the Comptroller General, and all our major dealings with that office were through him."[11]

Fisher's retirement represented a major personnel change from the CIA's standpoint. The torch was now being passed from someone the Agency knew and trusted to Robert Keller, an unknown quantity. Had Fisher's support for the Agency wavered over the years? Did he still support Section 10b of the CIA Act? The shackles of public service were off,

CENTRAL INTELLIGENCE AGENCY
WASHINGTON 25, D. C.

OFFICE OF THE DIRECTOR

16 OCT 1958

Mr. Edwin Lyle Fisher
5122 Wessling Lane
Bethesda 14, Maryland

Dear Mr. Fisher:

Since you have recently retired at the end of a distinguished Government career, it is appropriate that we express to you our appreciation of the guidance, understanding, and support you gave to this Agency throughout its growing years.

Before the Agency was recognized by statute, it was only through techniques worked out with you that the Central Intelligence Group was able effectively to lay the foundations for the future Agency. Once formally established, the Agency was faced with a requirement for the authorities necessary to carry out its functions. Again your understanding of our responsibilities and the problem of undertaking them in the cold war era was a powerful influence in the passage of the Central Intelligence Agency Act of 1949. This act is now time tested, and our experience has shown that the wide authorities granted to this Agency are essential to its ability to perform effectively.

Many other times you have considered our problems, some of them perhaps unique in Government, and always we found your counsel constructive. It was therefore with great regret that we saw you leave the Government, but we extend our best wishes for a long career in the comparatively simple life of private industry.

Sincerely,

Allen W. Dulles
Director

The Dulles letter presented to Lyle Fisher at a private lunch at the CIA on October 16, 1958.

allowing him to speak his mind more freely. He had many friends and connections in Congress and, through his liaison with the CIA, had acquired an insider's knowledge of its stealth accounting system. It was a powerful combination of factors.

The guest list for the luncheon included the DCI, the DDCI (Cabell), the DDS (White), the ADDS, the comptroller (Saunders), chief of the audit staff, the legislative counsel (Pforzheimer), and of course, Lawrence Houston. Red White noted in his diary on October 16, "With Mr. Dulles, General Cabell and others I lunched with Lyle Fisher, former General Counsel in the Office of the Comptroller General, who is now retired." The brief entry ended on a reflective note: "Mr. Fisher is most anxious to be of any assistance he can." That sentence was the only personal remark in this diary entry. Among other things he could have mentioned, he chose to emphasize Fisher's willingness to be of future assistance. The remark comes across as somewhat speculative and cursory because White did not know Fisher nearly as well as Houston did. Fisher probably felt humbled by being honored in a confidential setting surrounded by the top administrators of the CIA. White's pointed interest in Fisher's disposition toward the CIA seems noteworthy. Based on circumstantial factors, it appears that the organizers of the event used the face-to-face meeting to feel Fisher out and influence his future actions. Given the pressure that the Agency was under, the last thing it needed was for the GAO's former general counsel to speak out in criticism of the CIA's audit system.[12]

Although Houston, White, and Dulles may have been interested in how Fisher might act in the future, it seems more than likely that the real damage had already been done in the months before that lunch took place. Lyle Fisher had been part of the system for many years. Although he could no longer spearhead any major GAO reforms of the CIA audit, he was still well positioned in his last year to influence and advise Robert Keller, the incoming general counsel. Even as a lame duck, his recommendations to Keller in regard to the future handling of the CIA could have had some influence on the GAO's future actions regarding its audit of the CIA.

19. The End of Public Accountability

COLLISION COURSE

The GAO modernized the federal audit system during the 1950s, based on the comprehensive audit approach. By the end of the decade, even the Defense Department had succumbed to this new top-down metric for evaluating government accountability. By contrast, the congressional watchdog's audit of the CIA had not changed at all since the working fund was created in 1946. By the end of the decade, only about 25 percent of the CIA's total budget fell within the GAO's jurisdiction. Prior to the CIA Act, vouchered funds had made up closer to 75 percent of the budget. This complete reversal in the budgetary pie chart for vouchered and unvouchered funds can be attributed to the establishment of the OPC and the passage of the CIA Act of 1949. CIA's expenditure patterns also changed as vouchered funds were used on covert programs; those expenditures were shielded from the GAO's special auditor under the authority of the DCI's certificate.

Although, under Section 10b, vouchered funds could be spent without regard to the laws and regulations of the federal government, they were still to be audited by the GAO's special auditor. The provision kept the GAO from questioning the legality of the expenditures it audited, although it routinely did so in all its other audits of the federal government. But the numbers, nevertheless, still had to add up and meet certain accounting standards. Even in this extraordinary legal environment, GAO audits continued to uncover suspense items. These fiduciary anomalies got reported to Saunders for action on CIA's side, but there was little follow-up. That's the way the system worked.

By the end of the decade, Comptroller General Joseph Campbell had seen enough; he requested a closed-door hearing with the HASC CIA subcommittee that was chaired by the conservative Texas Democrat Paul Kilday. On March 2, 1959, senior GAO representatives met confidentially with Kilday's subcommittee to discuss the comptroller general's plan to modernize GAO's audit of the CIA. After a second, more substantive, meeting on May 15, Campbell followed up with a strongly worded letter to Kilday, in which he recounted the legislative history of the CIA Act of 1949 and noted the problems that diverging interpretations of Section 10b had caused for the GAO during the 1950s:

> Following the enactment of the Central Intelligence Agency Act of 1949, the then Director of the Agency [Hillenkoetter] requested that notwithstanding the very broad and unusual powers granted to the Central Intelligence Agency by the Act an audit of expenditures at the site, as previously performed by the General Accounting Office, be continued. Accordingly, the General Accounting Office has continued to make audits of vouchered expenditures, under the same arrangements that were in effect with the predecessor Central Intelligence Group. However, in view of the provisions of section 10 of the Central Intelligence Agency Act, no exceptions have been taken to any expenditures. In those cases where questionable payments come to our attention, we refer the cases to the CIA Comptroller's Office for corrective action. In using the term questionable payment, we mean any expenditures which, except for section 10 (a) of the Act, would appear to be improper or illegal either under law or under the decisions of the Comptroller General.

Sections 10a and 10b, taken together, technically permitted all CIA's expenditures to be made without regard to the laws and regulations of the federal government. As Campbell lobbied to customize the comprehensive audit for the CIA, he also said: "At this time we don't recommend any change in section 10 of the Central Intelligence Agency Act." Nor did he rule this possibility out, if nothing changed.[1]

The GAO of 1959 was not the same agency it had been at the end of World War II, and Campbell emphasized how it had changed in the next part of his letter:

> Since the enactment of Central Intelligence legislation we have generally broadened the type of audit we make of the activities of most Government agencies. Under our comprehensive audit approach, our basic purpose is to review and evaluate the manner in which the agency or activity under audit carries out its financial responsibilities. We construe financial responsibilities as including the expenditure of funds and the utilization of property and

personnel in the futherance only of authorized programs or activities in an effective, efficient, and economical manner.

The rest of Campbell's letter explained why the federal government and the CIA would be better off if the GAO were to apply a comprehensive audit approach:

> We believe that a broader type of audit is appropriate for our work at the Central Intelligence Agency and is more likely to be productive of evaluations of the administrative functions which would be helpful to the Congress and the Agency Director. We have accordingly concluded that it would be desirable to expand our audit work at Central Intelligence Agency more in line with our regular comprehensive audit approach. The expanded work would include an examination of vouchered expenditures, and, at the outset, the controls and procedures used in processing unvouchered expenditures. Also we would propose to make a limited examination of the support for unvouchered expenditures in accordance with such agreement as to access as can be worked out between the CIA and our office.[2]

Campbell was not challenging the DCI's authority over unvouchered funds—even though it may sound that way. The law precluded the comptroller general from looking behind the DCI's certification of unvouchered expenditures; that's not what he was asking for. The times had changed. With the comprehensive audit, the GAO was focused not so much on vouchers as on higher-level administrative functions that did not require a review of the vouchers and certifications. Section 10b said nothing about these financial operations. Although not explicit in his letter, Campbell strongly implied that Section 10b could not be arbitrarily extended to components of the financial system other than the certification of vouchers; these other components remained under the authority of the comptroller general of the United States. When the written law is not clear, general counsels seek clarity in the original intent of Congress, which ties the legislative history of the act to the spirit of the law. In this case, it was Kilday's subcommittee that had to decide what those original intentions were.

Kilday's power as subcommittee chairman was derived from his central role in the CIA's funding process. He probably did not fully comprehend the kind of changes that Campbell was advocating. To his credit, though, the committee chairman initially supported Campbell's reforms in a June 18 letter to Dulles. He also attached a copy of Campbell's letter. The powerful congressman, not wanting to alarm the DCI, reassured Dulles that the "Subcommittee fully appreciates the legal exemption of the Central Intelligence Agency from audit by the General Accounting Office." Then he listed the primary issues that had arisen from their discussions with GAO officials:

(1) the degree of audit of vouchered funds performed by GAO representatives in the Central Intelligence Agency was considerably less than had been thought;

(2) for the protection of the Agency and the assurance of the Congress, the audit function should continue;

(3) that more senior representatives of the General Accounting Office should be assigned to this function; and,

(4) that the Chairman of the Subcommittee should seek the formal opinion of the comptroller general with respect to this matter.[3]

The first point addressed the critical issue of what constituted vouchered and unvouchered spending under the law. These arcane definitions no longer had any meaning because the spending category was not decided by Congress or the GAO, but rather by the DCI. The long-term effect of Section 10b was to blur the legal distinction between vouchered and unvouchered funds. Kilday also seemed surprised by the small number of GAO representatives involved in the audit. That was a design feature of the audit system that the CIA originally had a big say in. The CIA also maintained a policy of keeping interagency interactions informal, which left few records behind to document that a relationship ever existed.

Kilday urged Dulles to arrange a meeting with GAO representatives, clearly hoping that the two agencies could agree to make some changes to the system on their own without a protracted battle. Trying to appease Dulles, Kilday wrote: "The question now arises as to the action that will be taken with reference to this matter. Inasmuch as the General Accounting Office participates in the activities of your Agency by invitation, it is my opinion that it would be both appropriate and desirable for you to initiate a conference with the comptroller general in an effort to clarify the existing situation." Nothing in the CIA Act of 1949 said anything about the GAO needing an explicit invitation from the CIA to audit its vouchered expenditures. At the August 1946 conference, it was the GAO that had all the decision power in the design of the working fund, which the CIG, and later the CIA, both formally signed off on.[4]

Campbell's letter raised serious concerns in the mind of Allen Dulles. The easygoing, pipe-smoking DCI was right at home in his dealings with the egocentric chairmen of the oversight committees; he was not in a similar comfort zone with the comptroller general. The CIA, after all, had spent the past decade developing a covert financial system for secretly disbursing money anywhere in the world at any time without anyone outside the CIA knowing about it. His interest was in keeping the GAO from learning anything about how that financial system operated, from the top down.

On June 30, Dulles sent a letter to President Eisenhower stating his concerns on the record:

> The comptroller general notes that since the enactment of Central Intelligence Agency legislation the General Accounting Office has generally broadened the type of audit made of activities of most Government agencies but that with the Central Intelligence Agency it has continued to make only a voucher audit of vouchered funds and no audit of confidential funds. He, therefore, recommends " . . . a change in the scope of our audit work at CIA . . ." by broadening the General Accounting Office's audit while recognizing that "Any broadening of audit activities should not include an evaluation of the intelligence activities of the Agency."

Dulles insisted that he "put as much of our expenditures on the 'vouchered' side as possible and still protect sensitive activities" and that these "expenditures have been subject to a voucher audit by representatives of the General Accounting Office." He also insisted that "all other expenditures have been subject to the strictest kind of internal control and auditing by our own Audit Staff and Comptroller." It may have seemed that way to him, but in practice the system was full of loopholes and exceptions, as programs like MKULTRA clearly demonstrated.[5]

Dulles argued that the CIA was an executive agency directly involved in foreign policy: "The Central Intelligence Agency is a particularly sensitive arm of the executive branch of the Government in the general field of foreign relations, and would not wish its usefulness to be impaired in any way by accepting from a body responsible to the legislative branch or from the legislative branch a measure of control or supervision detrimental to its effectiveness." Here he seems to be making a separation of powers argument. The letter, however, fails to explain how improving the audit would "impair" the Agency's "usefulness" or how it would be "detrimental to its effectiveness." Counting on Eisenhower's support, Dulles ended his letter by drawing a line in the sand: "I would be pleased to continue with these procedures; however, if there is a broadening of the General Accounting Office's review into a comprehensive audit of the vouchered side, we will encounter serious problems as such an examination would necessarily extend into the field of intelligence sources and methods unless its scope were limited at our direction."[6]

In July, Adolph Samuelson, the head of the GAO's Civil Accounting and Auditing Division, met with Red White, DDS of the CIA. White discussed this developing matter afterward at a deputies meeting on July 24, 1959, where he threw out the idea of inviting Campbell and Samuelson "over for lunch and a briefing on Agency activities in the near future." He hoped to "convince them [i.e., GAO] of the fact that the unvouchered funds activities of this Agency are so sensitive in fact they will not wish to attempt to audit these funds." The minutes of the meeting reveal that "White undertook to discuss with Mr. Helms and others in DD/P the projects and activities which should be presented in this briefing" and "undertook to look into the relations and manner in which the NSA handles its audit problems with the General Accounting Office."[7]

On July 30, CIA representatives met with Campbell[8] and Samuelson to discuss the possibility of a comprehensive audit by the GAO and the necessary restrictions CIA would impose on such an audit. On October 16, 1959,[9] Dulles sent Campbell a letter stating his position. It started off pleasantly by suggesting there existed some common ground for expanding GAO's audit: "I believe that the General Accounting Office can expand its current audit activities in a considerable portion of the Agency, and in moving forward in this direction I feel that we should reach agreement on certain fundamental aspects." The rest of the letter is far less conciliatory, for Dulles adamantly opposed the development of a comprehensive audit, believing that it would usurp his confidential funds authority under the CIA Act:

> The Congress, recognizing some of the unique problems involved in the conduct of intelligence activities, provided broad authorities over the expenditure of and accounting for Agency funds. In particular, [Section 10b] of that Act provides that expenditures for objects of a confidential, extraordinary, or emergency nature are to be accounted for solely on the certificate of the Director and every such certificate shall be deemed a sufficient voucher for the amount therein certified.

Dulles then formally stated his legal view on unvouchered funds to the comptroller general: "While all funds appropriated to the Agency are technically on an 'unvouchered' basis, it has been my policy and that of my predecessors to limit the exercise of this special authority to those activities which in the national interest should have the maximum-security protection."[10]

His claim that all funds appropriated to the Agency were "technically" unvouchered was inconsistent with the original intent of Congress, regarding the jurisdictional boundaries of vouchered and unvouchered funds. When the CIA Act of 1949 passed, vouchered funds exceeded unvouchered funds in the budget. Dulles conceded that vouchered funds were often expended on "activities, not in themselves sensitive but conducted solely in support of highly confidential operations." When vouchered funds were used on covert operations, he believed that his authority gave him the discretion to treat the expenses as unvouchered for accounting purposes. "The comprehensive audit," Dulles demurred, "would have to be limited so as to remain outside the area of sensitive security operations."[11]

What Dulles was offering fell far short of what Campbell was proposing. To add insult to injury, he ended his letter by patronizing the normally stone-faced comptroller general: "In view of the statutory background, I trust that you will agree with the position set forth above. If you have any question I would be delighted to discuss the subject with you at your convenience." Dulles was not offering Campbell much more than a reformulation of the status quo, while leaving little room for disagreement.[12]

Joseph Campbell promptly replied to Dulles five days later and made no attempt to refute the contents of his letter. Instead, he clarified the key point where his interpretation of Section 10b diverged. In Campbell's opinion, the reforms he proposed had no effect on Dulles's statutory authority, for a comprehensive audit could be performed without any review of the sensitive vouchers certified by the DCI. The language of the CIA Act referred only to vouchers; and, therefore, it could not be arbitrarily extended to the higher-level functions and operations of the accounting system under GAO's new 1950 charter. Much to the DCI's chagrin, Campbell saw no problem with setting up a comprehensive audit at the CIA that did not compromise the director's confidential funds authority as stated in Section 10b:

> In our comprehensive audits, we examine the organization structure, agency policies, and agency practices and procedures, together with selective examination of actual transactions as a means of appraising the application of agency practices and procedures. As a result of the discussion with your Staff it seems possible for the General Accounting Office to expand its audit at the Central Intelligence Agency into a considerable part of the Agency's activities, even though our reviews would be outside the area of sensitive security operations. Despite the limitations, we believe as a result of the reviews we could make evaluations of a substantial part of the administrative functions.[13]

But Campbell also made it clear that if the two agencies could not find a mutually agreeable arrangement, he might consider terminating the audit altogether: "In the event it appears after a trial period that our reviews are limited to such an extent that we cannot effectively and constructively accomplish any worthwhile objectives, we will have to consider whether the audit should be continued."[14]

On November 16, 1959, Adolph Samuelson and Eugene L. Pahl met with Red White, H. Gates Lloyd, the assistant deputy director of support, and Houston to discuss what the GAO had in mind. Samuelson was the director of the Civil Accounting and Auditing Division, and Pahl was the supervisor of the CIA audit. Pahl led the GAO's review of the audit; in an internal memo, he briefed Samuelson on his meeting that day with CIA officials, at which "future audit work at the CIA" was discussed. He sounds optimistic about the prospects for a comprehensive audit at the CIA:

> After obtaining a general knowledge of the organization, our initial work would be to review the CIA financial management program to determine whether the CIA effectively and efficiently controls the funds entrusted in its care and does so within the scope of the authority of the legislation and executive orders under which CIA operates, and [a] review and evaluation of the internal checks, such as internal audit and inspection operations of the CIA.[15]

On March 22, 1960, just a few months later, Samuelson and Pahl met again to discuss how things were progressing. Pahl explained that the CIA intended to impose severe restrictions on the audit, limiting its viability and usefulness: "1. The audit will have to remain outside the area of sensitive security operations. 2. The Agency regulations setting forth the policies, procedures, and practices under which CIA activities are conducted are not available to GAO."

Pahl emphasized that the first restriction meant that "the GAO [would] not be permitted to review or audit the CIA clandestine activities or the activity of an administrative organization whereas the activity of such organization is in support of a clandestine activity." With these restrictions, the GAO could not possibly conduct a credible review of the comptroller's office. They were even restricted from reviewing of the internal policies and regulations issued by Dulles (DCI), White (DDS), and Saunders (CIA comptroller). The GAO was offered access to general organizational charts, but nothing more. Pahl was advised that the restrictions on vouchered funds were "necessary because the policies and procedures on both clandestine and overt activities are so intermingled in the regulatory issuances that it is not possible to sterilize them for GAO use." Pahl concluded from his initial review that "only a very limited comprehensive audit would be possible."[16]

A final report on Pahl's review of the audit was sent to Red White on January 11, 1961. It did not go over well and sat on White's desk for about a month without a formal reply. That is, until Pahl reached out and requested a response. He promptly received a letter from White's deputy,

H. Gates Lloyd, who reported that White was out of the country and that he had not quite finished his review. But Lloyd divulged that White's

> immediate reaction on scanning the report was that it fails to acknowledge in any way the various steps which have been taken to place the GAO audit team in a position to do a comprehensive audit of the overt activities of the Agency. Instead, the report makes repeated assertions that the GAO auditors have less access now than they did before we attempted to expand their activities in the Agency.[17]

THE LAST STRAW

In March 1960, President Eisenhower approved funding for the infamous plan to invade Cuba, using a CIA-trained force of Cuban exiles. The recruitment and training of exiles was well under way when John F. Kennedy was elected president. Kennedy expressed strong reservations about the logistics of the plan and insisted that the United States maintain plausible deniability for its role in the covert op to overthrow the Fidel Castro government. Kennedy still signed off on the operation — despite his misgivings — apparently hoping to get something out of CIA's substantial investment of unvouchered funds. On April 17, 1961, fourteen hundred Cuban exiles invaded Cuba at the Bay of Pigs. The invasion was quickly put down by Castro's waiting army. The subsequent actions by the comptroller general suggest that the failed Bay of Pigs operation played a decisive role in the GAO's two-year effort to reform its audit of the CIA.

An investigative piece by Drew Pearson of the *Washington Post* criticized the Agency's lack of financial accountability. The article pointedly alludes to the director's authority under the CIA Act of 1949, but most readers—as the article insinuates—probably missed what he was getting at:

> One aspect of the Central Intelligence Agency which few people realize is that it is the only Government agency which doesn't have to submit its expenses to an accounting. Its books are not scrutinized by the General Accounting Office and the Congressional Appropriations Committees do not make the Agency justify its funds as with other branches of Govern-

> ment. This makes for reckless, irresponsible spending, sometimes by Ivy Leaguers who have had little experience in hiring ships, buying arms, and masterminding political revolutions as in Cuba. It also tends to make the CIA representative in foreign capitals more important than the American Ambassador. The CIA has an unlimited bankroll; the ambassador expenses are carefully restricted. The man with the money usually has the greatest influence, and word soon gets around in most capitals that the man to talk to is not the American Ambassador but the CIA man.[18]

The GAO's discreet audit reform initiative was moving along at a snail's pace behind the scenes when the sordid details of the failed operation began to hit the front pages of newspapers around the world. After two years, with little progress to show for GAO's effort, Campbell attempted to gain further leverage by exploiting the situation.

On May 16, Campbell sent official letters to Kilday and Dulles vehemently expressing his displeasure with CIA's intransigence. In his letter to Kilday, longer and more detailed than the one he sent Dulles, Campbell said: "It is our view that under existing security restrictions on our audit of CIA activities, we do not have sufficient access to make comprehensive reviews on a continuing basis that would be productive of evaluations helpful to the Congress." Though still insisting on "comprehensive reviews" of the Agency, Campbell bitterly complained about the restrictions and threatened to terminate the audit if the CIA refused to allow for an expansion of the audit:

> We limited our review to selected overt activities as the covert (confidential) activities of CIA was denied us. We have had no access whatsoever to the Plans Component, and we cannot effectively review and evaluate the activities of the Support Component because the confidential and overt activities of this component are integrated to such an extent that we cannot make reasonably comprehensive audits. We have been given sufficient access to make reasonably comprehensive reviews of the overt activities of the Intelligence Component, but such reviews, in our opinion, will not be productive of significant evaluations because we cannot feasibly evaluate the extent to which needed overt information is available for [rest of sentence redacted].[19]

When people request classified information from the CIA—or any other government organization—it is, in general, hard for them to know whether they have been given everything pertinent to the request. They are left to accept in good faith that they have been given everything, unless there is evidence to the contrary. That seems to have been one of Campbell's concerns.

Kilday had done what he could to let the two agencies resolve the audit matter without getting his subcommittee involved. But, understanding that Campbell's threat had to be taken seriously, he forwarded Campbell's letter up the chain of command to Carl Vinson, the powerful chairman of the HASC, seeking guidance on how to handle the matter. From that point onward, Vinson handled the correspondence between the HASC and Campbell. Vinson was an icon of the American political establishment and had served in Congress since 1914. All the big decisions related to the CIA and armed services went through him.

Considering recent events, it was no time for the auditing arm of Congress to pull out due to inaction on the part of the House committee overseeing the CIA. So, two days later, with the underlying goal of salvaging the status quo while appeasing Campbell, Vinson sent him a letter that defended CIA's position based on the need for security restrictions—as though the GAO had not heard that line many times before. The letter did not refute Campbell's innovative interpretation of Section 10b: "Mr. Kilday and I have discussed the contents of your letter at some length and in view of the course of action, which you contemplate, I feel it incumbent upon me to promptly express my judgment on this matter." Vinson opines that Congress originally intended that there be "certain restrictions on the scope of the audit by the General Accounting Office" and that such "restrictions were inherent in a relationship of this nature." There is some truth to his opinion here, but Section 10b is ambiguous. The resolution of that ambiguity is to determine congressional intent, which is linked to both the statutory language and the legislative history.

Conspicuously, neither the GAO nor the US comptroller is named anywhere in the CIA Act. No matter how many times one reads Section 10b, the provision fails to explicitly transfer certification authority for unvouchered funds from the comptroller general to the DCI. Rather, it assigns that authority to the DCI without reference to the comptroller general of the United States. The DCI's confidential funds authority applied to the certification of unvouchered funds; that was it. Nothing is said that would preclude a top-down audit of the CIA's dualistic financial system by a federal watchdog like the GAO.[20]

Vinson conceded that the audit "should be the subject of future discussions between the HASC, the General Accounting Office and the Central Intelligence Agency"; but he gave no assurances that any of Campbell's recommendations would ever see the light of day. Vinson and Kilday considered a termination of the GAO audit unwise; the audit provided the HASC and the CIA with much-needed administrative cover. Vinson told Campbell that "even a limited audit of overt accounting actions would serve a worthwhile purpose" and adamantly discouraged him from terminating GAO's vouchered audit: "I cannot recommend too strongly against the course of action which you propose." Vinson argued in favor of maintaining the status quo: "I trust you will agree with my firm belief that there is nothing in this situation which requires precipitous action." The GAO's role in the audit, however, was not to provide the HASC and the CIA with administrative cover for the funding of covert operations that used unvouchered funds.

The Bay of Pigs, and the presidential investigation that followed in its wake, spelled the end for Allen Dulles. Dulles, DDCI Charles Cabell, and DDP Richard Bissell were each asked to resign in the aftermath of the Taylor investigation ordered by Kennedy. Dulles resigned from the Agency on November 29, 1961.

Campbell may have sensed a small window of opportunity, under the auspices of a new DCI, for the GAO and the CIA to move forward. In the spring of 1962, John Bross, the new CIA comptroller, urged Campbell not to terminate the audit. A proposed meeting between the two was abruptly canceled after Campbell learned that the new DCI favored the status quo, like his predecessor. Samuelson and Pahl met with Bross and his deputy for the last time on June 8 to explain why the GAO "could not make a worthwhile contribution, either to the Congress or the agency, commensurate with the investment of . . . professional resources."[21]

On June 21, 1962, in a three-page letter to Carl Vinson, Campbell said that after three years of GAO effort "despite the severe limitations," he had decided that "under the current security restrictions on our audit of CIA activities we do not have sufficient access to effectively accomplish any worthwhile audit objectives at CIA on a continuing basis." Tired of being strung along, Campbell now made good on his promise to pull the GAO out of the audit. In his final letter, Campbell reflected on GAO's long effort to reform its audit of the CIA:

> During the ensuing 30 months we undertook to make reviews of selected overt activities as access to the covert activities was not made available to us. In this connection, access to the activities of the Support Component in which we could be expected to be most effective in our reviews was significantly limited because covert and overt activities of this component are integrated. We were not able to review sufficiently financial management, property management, contracting, procurement, and similar activities for any effective appraisal of the administration of these activities. . . . We had no access whatever to the work of the Inspector General; therefore, we were not able to appraise the internal review mechanisms with the Agency.[22]

Campbell remained steadfast in his insistence that the GAO could "perform a reasonably comprehensive review of CIA activities" but that a comprehensive audit required the kind of information that Allen Dulles and the Agency wanted to keep secret.[23]

Vinson allowed some time to pass before he replied. The only surviving copy of his letter is found in a declassified draft letter dated on July 11. He hoped that Campbell would reconsider but had no tricks left in his bag. He assured Campbell that Director John McCone intended to take "the reorganizational steps" to strengthen "the comptroller and internal audit functions in the Agency." McCone planned to move the Office of the Comptroller, the Audit Staff, and the Office of General Counsel from SD to the Office of the Director. The GAO had heard this kind of thing before. Vinson was trying to sell Campbell on the idea that the CIA could oversee its own finances—all on the heels of the Bay of Pigs. Reluctantly accepting Campbell's decision, Vinson conceded that "since you feel confirmed in your opinion that it is not a worthwhile effort, I am agreeable that you withdraw from further audit activities in the Central Intelligence Agency." With that letter, the GAO's oversight of the CIA, which began with the creation of the working fund in 1946, quietly ended without anyone seeming to notice.[24]

20. Hidden Costs

THE DCI AND THE CIA ACT OF 1949

The CIA Act of 1949—Public Law 110—enabled a decade of organizational changes at the CIA aimed at centralizing administrative control over the agency's compartmentalized overt and covert support functions. These organizational reforms by Hillenkoetter, Smith, and Dulles helped to spawn a powerful support directorate to handle the CIA's administrative operations. These changes better integrated the covert funding of the Agency into the administrative infrastructure of the clandestine services. In the early years, prior to the passage of the CIA Act, Hillenkoetter tried to set up the covert administrative functions as subdivisions inside the clandestine services. Indeed, in 1947, shortly after the creation of the CIA, Hillenkoetter transferred Eck Echols's special funds division to the OSO and placed its financial administration under its chief. This failed early experiment in covert financial management was made administratively impossible the following year by the creation of the OPC.

Hillenkoetter orchestrated the first major reorganization of the CIA's administrative functions under Public Law 110, just a few months after its passage. Although substantive, these changes stopped well short of the centralization of the overt and covert administrative divisions that was accomplished by his successor. Smith's legacy in shaping the future of the CIA speaks for itself. In 1950, a year after Hillenkoetter's organizational reforms, Smith centralized all the administrative support functions under a directorate headed by a single individual: the deputy director of administration. Additionally, he centralized the budget and finance operations under the Office of the Comptroller, headed by Edward Saunders, and further established an independent Audit Office, headed by an auditor in chief—who was not under Saunders's authority—to conduct postaudits of CIA programs and operations. In addition to all that, Smith appointed the CIA's first IG, who in principle oversaw all three directorates under his authority. Allen Dulles inherited this administrative system. Once in charge, Dulles assumed an inordinate amount of personal control over the checks and balances that Smith had tried to institutionalize in his brief tenure. Dulles added some incremental reforms of his own, but these cursory organizational changes seem mostly intended to underscore administration's support role with respect to the clandestine services. Dulles and others, such as William Jackson, thought that the primary role of administrative functions was to support, not control, the clandestine services.[1]

Admiral Roscoe Hillenkoetter served as director of both the CIG and the CIA. During his tenure, he exchanged few communications with Lindsay Warren. More than Smith or Dulles, he understood the history of the CIA–GAO liaison and realized the importance of maintaining a good working relationship through their chief legal counsels. Under the CIA Act of 1949, Hillenkoetter assumed essentially the same powers as earlier, with one main difference: his authority no longer depended on a delegation of authority from someone else. Although Hillenkoetter, ostensibly, did not try to push the limits of his authority under Section 10 beyond Congress's original intent, the two following DCIs went much further.

Early in his tenure, Smith tried to expand Section 10b's nebulous boundaries by issuing a retroactive pay raise to CIA employees using unvouchered funds. In this unusual case, a formal ruling from the comptroller general was requested from Warren, who rebuked Smith for even making the request. Smith, to his credit, treated the GAO as a coequal partner in the matter and accepted Warren's opinion as the final authority. In 1956, Houston met with Lyle Fisher—clearly at Dulles's request—to ask whether the GAO would reconsider its previous ruling on the retroactive pay raise using unvouchered funds. The GAO again found no compelling justification and rejected the proposal for the same reasons.[2]

Allen Dulles was more surreptitious than Hillenkoetter and Smith; in his interpretation of Section 10b, the DCI's confidential funds authority was absolute. Shortly after he assumed the position in 1953, he fully committed the agency to the MKULTRA project and then single-handedly eliminated all the oversight controls that were in place. The death of Frank Olsen can be traced back to his early decision to authorize the program and leave oversight of it to Sidney Gottlieb. Congress did not catch wind of MKULTRA for another two decades, and by then Gottlieb had destroyed all the incriminating documents under his control. A proper investigative audit of MKULTRA by the CIA inspector general, in fact, was not carried out until 1963—after Dulles had left the agency. Results of the audit led to the termination of the program and to the conclusion that MKULTRA was a highly risky venture that produced no tangible benefit to national security.

Dulles's legal view remained an enigma until the GAO launched its spirited audit reform initiative in 1959. In his letter to President Eisenhower, Dulles formally stated his legal opinion on the record: "In view of the close interrelation of all of this Agency's activities, I believe it could have been correctly argued that all of the funds of the Agency should be expended under the authority of this section so that none of them would be subject to outside audit." Prior to that, Dulles's actions spoke much louder than his words. For Allen Dulles, what mattered most was not whether the funds were earmarked as vouchered or unvouchered, but whether the money supported overt or covert operations. In his opinion, Congress intended those decisions to be made entirely at the discretion of the DCI. In his view, there were no gray areas that would require the DCI to request a formal decision, as Smith had done, or to consult informally with the GAO's legal counsel on how to best handle the matter, as Houston had done. Dulles's position empowered the Agency by shifting a much larger fraction of its budget from the audit jurisdiction of the comptroller general to the DCI.[3]

Dulles's actions help explain why the CIA–GAO liaison ended so badly. The Agency's recalcitrance paid off and handed Allen Dulles exactly what he wanted. How did the United States benefit from shifting such extraordinary authority to a political appointee like Allen Dulles? On his watch, major covert projects and operations—MKULTRA, Iran, Indonesia, and the Bay of Pigs—were funded with unvouchered funds. They may have looked good on paper, but in reality they were quite costly, politically and financially. Even some that were considered successes at first appear, retroactively, to have been total failures. A fundamental problem with transferring confidential funds authority to the DCI is the lack of uniform standards in the audit and settlement of unvouchered funds. This is the same problem that the Treasury Department faced in the nineteenth century when it had two comptroller generals. Most people in the position of DCI have had very little experience in accounting and finance, and their tenures of office have varied greatly. By contrast, the comptroller general of the United States is confirmed to a fifteen-year term.

Lawrence Houston, a major figure in the legislative history of the National Security Act of 1947 and the CIA Act of 1949, understood the history of the informal CIA–GAO liaison better than anyone else at the Agency. He understood the importance of Section 10b to the CIA's foreign agenda and the DCI's potential culpability for the expenditure of unvouchered funds. In his time at the CIA, Houston served both the Agency and the DCI. With the exception of the president, no one other than Houston, whether inside or outside of the Agency, was in a position to say no to the DCI. In his interpretation of Section 10b, a provision that Houston himself recognized as "extraordinary," he seemed to be quite flexible and acquiescent to the fringe views and opinions of the DCI, especially Allen Dulles. Houston understood that the CIA operated behind a wall of secrecy and that, without evidence of major financial abuses of its charter, it was highly unlikely that the four powerful congressional committees that oversaw the CIA would ever initiate a major investigation. He had a tendency not to push back against the extreme positions of the DCI, and that is what made him the enabler.

THE YEAR OF INTELLIGENCE: 1975

The CIA weathered three major investigations in the mid-1950s, but the final reports from those nascent probes were highly classified and apparently never led to any significant reforms. The well-publicized intelligence failures of 1958, though embarrassing, also seem to have had little effect on the way the Agency conducted its business. The CIA's track record with the GAO was not much better; in 1962, the comptroller general terminated the GAO's audit, which left the CIA to manage and oversee its own finances right on the cusp of the Vietnam War. Although there were clearly festering problems, more than a decade passed after the Bay of Pigs without a comparable intelligence fiasco—until 1975. That year is remembered as the Year of Intelligence because, as in the mid-fifties, three separate investigations of the Agency were carried out after journalists alleged that the CIA was egregiously violating its founding charter.

On December 21, 1974, as the Vietnam War neared its anticlimactic end, the *New York Times* published a front-page article by the Pulitzer Prize–winning investigative journalist Seymour Hersh: "Huge C.I.A. Operation Reported in U.S. against Antiwar Forces, Other Dissidents in Nixon Years." The article alleged that the CIA had conducted domestic intelligence operations against antiwar groups in the United States during the Nixon years.[4]

With Congress under pressure, President Ford appointed Nelson Rockefeller to head a committee to investigate CIA political activities inside the United States. The Senate and the House of Representatives also launched their own major investigations of the CIA's operations and its financial system. Frank Church (D-Idaho), a conservative Democrat, led the Senate investigation to determine whether the Agency had violated its founding charter, as alleged. As with Watergate, the Church Committee hearings captured the undivided attention of the American public, as the so-called family jewels were exposed. Even Lawrence Houston got called out of retirement to give testimony. It is the disastrous House investigation by the Pike Committee, however, that stands out as most relevant to this discussion.

The House investigative committee was initially chaired by Lucien Nedzi (D-Michigan). However, because presidential and senatorial CIA investigations had already been announced, Nedzi decided against having the House launch a third investigation. This was not well received by the rest of the committee, and a mutiny arose within his own party. Five committee members called for his resignation, and he obliged in June 1975. Under a new House committee, chaired by Otis Pike (D-New York), a full-blown investigation was launched into the Agency's financial administration and the movement of public funds between the Treasury and CIA operations abroad. As it turned out, only the Church Committee report ever made it into the official public record. The Pike Committee report, arguably far more revealing and damaging, was never certified by Congress and so was never publicly released.

The Pike Committee investigated all aspects of the CIA's financial system, but it faced numerous obstacles to obtaining the highly classified information it demanded. The credibility of the investigation was diminished by disputes and acrimony between the CIA and the committee. Although the branches were coequal, Pike treated CIA senior officials with antagonism, an attitude that did not help resolve disputes. The trouble started shortly after Pike was named chairman of the committee. A letter that Pike sent to William Colby reveals his subtle contempt for the CIA in its very first sentence: "First of all, it's a delight to receive two letters from you not stamped 'Secret' on every page." The letter then explained his goals as chairman: "I am seeking to obtain information on how much of the taxpayer's dollars you spend each year and the basic purposes for which it is spent." Colby, who had a legal responsibility to protect CIA sources and methods, initially tried to control the dissemination of classified materials to the committee. Pike rejected Colby's overtures and declared that his committee would enforce its own security measures. More alarmingly, Pike claimed that he had the authority to unilaterally declassify anything he thought should be shared with the public.[5]

On July 31, 1975, Otis Pike explained the goals and investigative approach of his committee in his opening statement at the first hearing:

> We start by looking at the cost. It is not easy. The Constitution of the United States, article I, section 9, says, "No money shall be drawn from the Treasury but in consequence of appropriations made by law and a regular statement and account of the receipts and expenditures of all public money shall be published from time to time." It does not say "some public money." It says "all public money."

He next zoomed in on the CIA budget:

> I have looked hard, but the results are spotty. We have, according to the budget, an FBI, but I can find no CIA, no NSA, no DIA. There is a line item on page 73 of this book under the Department of Defense for 7.3 billion for intelligence and communications. But I don't know what that means. I get the uneasy feeling I am not supposed to know what it means. We shall find out. As we learn what the costs are, we will look at the benefits achieved as well as the risks created by gaining this intelligence. What benefits have we the right to expect?[6]

Comptroller General Elmer Staats was the first witness to testify before the committee. Staats succeeded Joseph Campbell in 1966. Much of Staats's testimony related to the GAO's early involvement in CIA's financial system. The GAO, after all, was the only external government agency that had ever overseen the spending of the CIA. The committee wanted to better understand the history of the CIA–GAO liaison before calling other witnesses. Staats recited the history of the GAO audit and the reasons that had led Campbell to terminate the audit in 1962. Indeed, it was the Pike Committee that resurrected the revealing series of correspondences between the CIA, the GAO, and the HASC between 1959 and 1962.

Staats first reviewed GAO's oversight authority with respect to the CIA:

> In general, we have not pressed for reviews of intelligence operations on our own initiative for the simple reason that our legal authority is quite limited and the problems of access to information have been such as to cause us to conclude that efforts to review these activities would have little practical result. GAO's basic audit authority is contained in the Budget and Accounting Act of 1921 and the [Budget and Accounting Procedures] Act of 1950, the Legislative Reorganization Act of 1970, and the Congressional Budget and Impoundment Control Act of 1974. These statutes authorize GAO to audit the activities of most executive branch agencies and grant it access to the records of the agencies necessary to the discharge of this responsibility. However, certain restrictions on our audit authority are also provided for by law, including instances where moneys are accounted for solely on certification by the head of a department or establishment. For example, expenditures of a confidential, extraordinary or emergency nature by the CIA are to be accounted for solely on the certificate of the Director.

Here, Staats was obviously referring to Section 10b and the director's confidential funds authority. According to Staats, the restrictions on the GAO extended to "all agencies involved in intelligence gathering or analysis namely the need and desire to maintain close security so as to reduce the risk of leakage by minimizing the number of people having access to such matters."[7]

Congressman David Treen (R-Louisiana) enquired about the DCI's certification authority and asked Staats a few arcane questions about GAO oversight that went beyond the scope of most people's understanding.

First, Treen alluded to the GAO's secret audit of the Manhattan Project. He then asked about the DCI's confidential funds authority and what it meant from a legal perspective:

> STAATS. In the case of CIA there is a specific provision in its organic act, as you know, which authorizes the Director to make expenditures on his own certificate, which means we do not have any authority to go behind—
>
> TREEN. I would like to examine that a little bit legally. I have never examined into this area before, but when Congress says that the head of an agency may expend money on his own certificate, of course that means that he then is given a great deal of discretion in how that money is spent, but do you interpret that to mean that you cannot then look at how it was spent?
>
> STAATS. That is correct.
>
> TREEN. He is given the authority to spend it?
>
> STAATS. That is correct. Legislation has been introduced in the House . . . which would at least authorize us to go behind the certification to the extent of making a judgment as to whether it was in fact a justifiable certificate in the sense of being secret or confidential.
>
> TREEN. You don't think you have that authority now? Are there any court decisions upon which you base that opinion?
>
> STAATS. No, sir.
>
> TREEN. It seems to me the discretion to spend on the certificate of a head of an agency doesn't mean that you can't examine that expenditure; at a very minimum you can—you can total up the amounts he has spent on his own certificate, can't you?
>
> STAATS. We may not even be permitted to know the amount.[8]

Section 10b precluded the GAO from looking behind the DCI's certificate, and Staats explained what that meant.

The Pike Committee was also surprised to learn that for many years the DCI had been serving as the budget man for the intelligence community. The DCI made the funding pitch to Congress on behalf of the intelligence community's members. Without any statutory mandate, his authority over unvouchered funds had arbitrarily been extended to the whole intelligence community. According to the Pike Committee report:

> The DCI presents the entire foreign intelligence budget to Congress and the President, but he only has authority for CIA's budget. Defense officials testified that a substantial part of their intelligence budget is considered the responsibility of the Secretary of Defense. The DCI, they say, merely reviews their work. . . . Fragmented authority and coordination leave the budget wide open to distortions. Each agency applies its own budget standards.

Many congressmen knew barely anything at all about the existence of the other two behemoths in the intelligence community: the NSA and the NRO.[9]

Once the veil of secrecy was removed, the Pike Committee found hidden accountability problems just about everywhere it looked. On the important matter of cost oversight and expenditure control, the committee reported that the CIA's "audit staff is undermanned for a comprehensive review of complex and extensive agency spending that takes place worldwide." For decades, covert programs had been subjected to significantly looser standards, and, in some cases, critical financial information was withheld from the CIA's own auditors:

> They are allowed to balance books, but they are not always allowed to know the exact purpose of expenditures. Only five percent of all vouchered transactions are checked even though these add up to 20 percent of CIA's entire budget. Substantive corroborating records are not kept. Their audits deviate from the standards of professionally certified Public Accountants, and CIA has not compiled a list of these exceptions to control deviances. These and other shortcomings in audit and control, for both foreign and domestic intelligence agencies lead to an inevitable result—spending abuses.[10]

The committee also discovered a "close, almost inbred relationship between OMB officials and intelligence budgetmakers." Only six people in OMB were assigned to work on CIA's budget, and three of them had formerly worked at the CIA: "In turn, the CIA official in charge of the Agency's budget [had] recently arrived from OMB, where he had primary responsibility for CIA's budget." Summarizing its findings, the committee concluded: "All this adds up to more than $10 billion being spent by a handful of people, with little independent supervision, with inadequate controls, even less auditing, and an overabundance of secrecy."

These were just a few of the take-home messages from the Pike Committee Report, which was leaked to the public by the *Village Voice* after it failed to gain certification. The Pike Committee[11] recommended that the GAO and the CIA coordinate to establish a comprehensive audit of the Agency. As earlier, this recommendation went nowhere. Still, the combined effect of all three investigations resulted in some meaningful government reforms. The Year of Intelligence led directly to the creation of the Permanent Select House (1977) and Senate (1976) Intelligence Committees, a move that the CIA had fiercely resisted in the 1950s. The egregious lack of oversight that had been exposed also led to the creation of the Foreign Intelligence Surveillance Court in 1978 and the act of 1978, albeit the CIA was initially exempted from the act. Fourteen years later, though, in the aftermath of the Iran–Contra Affair, Congress amended the law to require that the CIA Inspector General be nominated by the president and confirmed in the Senate, consistent with the Inspector General Act of 1978.[12]

THE CIA AND THE GAO: FORTY YEARS LATER

Under the CIA Act, unvouchered funds[13] are used to move extraordinarily large sums of money from the public to the private sector without any external government oversight. Government accountability is the public domain of the GAO. Nothing about the relationship between the GAO and the CIA seems to have changed since Joseph Campbell abruptly terminated the vouchered audit of the CIA in 1962. In light of the major congressional investigations of the 1970s and 1980s, involving coordination between the White House, the NSC, and the CIA (e.g., Vietnam War, Watergate, and Iran–Contra), it almost defies reason to explain why Congress, acting in the public interest, has not expanded the GAO's audit authority over the national security establishment.

In 2001, almost forty years after Campbell terminated the GAO's vouchered audit of the CIA, Henry Hilton, the managing director of

Defense Capabilities and Management, testified before a congressional subcommittee about access to the records of CIA programs and activities. When asked about the GAO's relationship to the CIA, he told the subcommittee:

> We face both legal and practical limitations on our ability to review these [CIA] programs. For example, we have no access to certain CIA "unvouchered" accounts and cannot compel our access to foreign intelligence and counterintelligence information. In addition, as a practical matter, we are limited by the CIA's level of cooperation, which has varied through the years. We have not actively audited the CIA since the early 1960's, when we discontinued such work because the CIA was not providing us with sufficient access to information to perform our mission. The issue has arisen since then from time to time as our work has required some level of access to CIA programs and information. However, given a lack of requests from the Congress for us to do specific work at the CIA and our limited resources, we have made a conscious decision not to further pursue the issue. Today, our dealings with the CIA are mostly limited to requesting information that relates either to government wide reviews or analyses of threats to U.S. national security on which the CIA might have some information. The CIA either provides us with the requested information, provides the information with some restrictions, or does not provide the information at all. In general, we are most successful at getting access to CIA information when we request threat assessments and the CIA does not perceive our audits as oversight of its activities.[14]

GAO oversight had never led to the leaking of top secret information. The GAO, after all, had audited the Manhattan Project during World War II, and not even Congress knew about it. One thing this story clearly demonstrates is that the GAO can keep a secret.

In 1946, Lindsay Warren told a friend just how cynical he had become about government accountability in a personal letter:

> I have now decided that when I was in Congress my knowledge of the Government was almost nil. To see and to know and to evaluate what our Government is, one must be Comptroller General. In this position I see it the few times at its best and most of the time at its worst. I see scheming, plot-

> ting and conniving men holding high office who think first forever about themselves and the country last; men who are sitting up late at night trying to circumvent the Congress, and who don't wish their acts audited and checked. I see daily the most unbridled waste and extravagance and a "hell and don't care" attitude on the part of most administrators. I have no power or authority to stop it. I report it to the Congress so much that it is almost a joke, but they don't give a damn and are almost impotent to prevent it anyway. . . . I will admit that what I daily see makes me somewhat cynical, but above all it makes me wish to wash my hands of all of it and fold my tent and leave.

Warren's words seem just as timely and relevant today as they did seventy-five years ago.[15]

Lawrence Houston was a central figure in the legislative history of the CIA Act of 1949 from the very beginning. He understood as well as anyone that Section 10b was without precedent and that the DCI's confidential funds authority should be viewed as a privilege, not a right. Just three years after the passage of the CIA Act, under Bedell Smith, Houston wrote,

> A literal interpretation of Section 10 invests the Director of Central Intelligence with absolute power to control the expenditure of confidential funds allocated to the Agency. Behind this facade of power, however, there lies a history of Congressional, judicial and other inquiries into the area of such expenditures which inescapably leads to the conclusion that constant vigilance is necessary to guard against abuse of the power. If knowledge of such an abuse is obtained outside the Agency, in view of the Congressional propensity to investigate, it will likely precipitate an inquiry possibly followed by statutory revision which might seriously impede, if not effectively halt, certain of the Agency's operations.

Section 10, in effect, was a statutory privilege without any deep constitutional roots.[16]

To assess the benefits of the US intelligence apparatus to American society, one must weigh the costs and the risks of maintaining this vast infrastructure against the accrued benefits to American society, both tangible and intangible. This calculation turns out to be an ill-defined problem because there are hidden costs to society. There are, of course, the unavoidable financial costs, which are hidden behind a wall of secrecy. These costs are exacerbated by blowback, the unintended political and financial costs of covert action. But it is the social and opportunity costs, harder to quantify and account for, that impact everyone's quality of life in the long-term. Opportunity cost can be qualitatively understood as the net cost of directing money to secret intelligence programs rather than some other program more justifiably in the public interest. For instance, imagine the cost of stockpiling military hardware that might never get utilized because it becomes outdated or unsuitable for future warfare. What a colossal waste of public resources that would be.

Epilogue

I have gotten to know my grandfather over the past twenty years through my research and the telling of this previously untold story about the CIA. Of course, I had no idea how the story was going to turn out when I began this project. There were admittedly some anxious moments early on, as I wondered about the nature of my grandfather's liaison with the CIA. Once I knew the whole story, my interest gravitated to understanding how Lyle Fisher's legal view of the CIA Act of 1949 continued to evolve during the 1950s, once the transfer of certification authority took effect. That was the critical period when, all of a sudden, the Agency began disbursing unvouchered funds in large amounts to covert action programs all over the world. The GAO was not supposed to know anything about that. Still, it is hard to imagine that the congressional watchdog was completely oblivious to the precipitous increases in unvouchered spending levels—despite not being provided any financial information from the CIA about its budget or its use of unvouchered funds.

By the mid-1950s, there was good reason to suspect the existence of serious accountability problems at the Agency involving the handling of unvouchered funds, which remained hidden behind the DCI's certificate. The CIA Act of 1949 never received a formal endorsement from the comptroller general of the United States. As this story reveals, Section 10b was hotly debated inside the GAO prior to the bill's passage. Darlington Denit, who headed the Accounting and Bookkeeping Division, suggested that Warren insist on a rewording of Section 10b, while his top legal advisor, Frank Weitzel, recommended the filing of an abuse report prior to passage. Other than Warren's letter to James Webb in 1948, the comptroller general remained conspicuously silent while the bill was being shepherded through Congress in the following year. That letter to Webb is an important part of the legislative history, but it should not be considered an endorsement of Section 10b in any way, shape, or form. Warren, in fact, endorsed a different version of Section 10 that agreed to transfer confidential funds authority to the NSC—which was chaired by the president. He never endorsed a permanent transfer of his certification authority to the DCI, but he also did not vehemently oppose the 1949 bill before Congress. His neutral position was clearly not intended as an endorsement.

Warren would never have accepted this legal advice from my grandfather without some very heated discussion about his cardinal views behind closed doors. In retrospect, the GAO's position on Section 10b appears to have been part of a long-term legal strategy. The CIA played its hand extremely well right from the beginning. At the hearings on the National Security Act of 1947 and the CIA Act of 1949, the DCI graciously expressed appreciation for the invaluable assistance of the comptroller general and the GAO in establishing the working fund. By all accounts, the working fund up until then had been a great success. Furthermore, the informal liaison formed between the two agencies at the August 1946 conference was amicable and seemed to be working effectively as designed.

Section 10b was extraordinary and unprecedented in every way, and GAO insiders at that time understood that if the DCI's confidential funds authority was mishandled, it could potentially impact the US treasury system. There is no denying that, but the times had changed, and the smart money was on the bill passing. The CIA was also promoting the idea that nothing much would change in practice when Section 10b went into effect. It was supposed to simplify the administration of CIA's funds in ways that were better for everyone.

I now firmly believe that my grandfather had begun to seriously question the agency's good faith near the end of his career. In my opinion, the most notable shift in his legal disposition occurred on March 7, 1955, at a private meeting with Lawrence Houston and Edward Saunders. It was at this meeting when Houston and Saunders asked him to support no-year status for CIA's entire budget. A year earlier, he had supported a similar proposal that involved establishing the reserve fund on a no-year basis. In that special case, the reserve fund consisted entirely of unvouchered funds, meaning that all expenditures from that fund would have to be made under the DCI's certificate. The reserve fund also had a fiscal cap that was set by Congress. That's about as black and white as it gets with Section 10b. In that particular case, he thought the authorization should come from Congress, not the GAO. The request for no-year funding for the entire budget affected both vouchered and unvouchered funds. That was a whole different matter; and Houston and Saunders—of all people—should have realized that. Houston's description of the meeting suggests that "Mr. Fisher was somewhat doubtful whether he could agree with Bureau of the Budget's suggestion that the committee authorize all funds now or hereafter made available on a no-year basis." He was not initially on board and was probably thinking to himself, "If the budget bureau feels that strongly, then why wasn't anyone from the bureau at the meeting?" It was only "after discussion" that he agreed to support their proposal on a provisional one-year basis. Their proposal was flatly rejected by the comptroller general the next day. It was an audacious move for the CIA to make on such a significant legal matter. On top of the shear impudence of the request, the Agency at that time was being investigated by the executive (Doolittle Committee) and legislative branches (Clark Task Force).

There were other things that he more than likely did not know about but would have had a serious problem with if he had known about them. My grandfather, for instance, would have been most disappointed to learn that his informal opinions, solicited confidentially behind-the-scenes by Houston, were being treated as legal precedents inside the CIA. He never intended for his informal rulings to serve as precedents for deciding future cases, but as this story reveals, favorable rulings tended to be treated that way. I also have to presume that he never found out about Houston and Bissell's decision in the summer of 1957 not to inform the GAO about the U-2 project and the secret financial arrangement between the CIA, the air force, and the navy. Although Houston seems to have been in favor of informing the GAO of the arrangement, the fact remains that the DCI, the general counsel, and the U-2 project manager decided to cut the GAO out of the loop by consensus. The written correspondences between Houston, Bissell, and Dulles offer solid anecdotal evidence of the diminishing importance of the CIA's liaison with the GAO.

According to family members, my grandfather never seriously considered retiring from the GAO until after he suffered his first heart attack in 1957. That was about a decade before the advent of blood pressure medication, quadruple bypass surgery, and heart transplants. It was during his long recovery that he begrudgingly announced his retirement; and, on

August 31, 1958, his last day, he was honored at a ceremony attended by Joseph Campbell.

That summer, he received a personal letter from Lindsay Warren, who had just heard about his old colleague's impending retirement. Warren, a mentor and a friend, had done more than anyone else—except possibly his predecessor John McFarland—to help launch his career. This letter surely meant a great deal to him at the time:

> My dear Friend:
> I got word that you are retiring and I hate to hear it. Not because I appointed you as General Counsel of the General Accounting Office, a fact in which I have always taken the greatest pride, but time after time I have generally stated that I considered you the ablest general counsel in the entire government. You have a brilliant and distinguished record. I can never recall a time when I wavered in my support of you for I quickly recognized that you were a devoted public servant and that I had a great legal mind to advise me. Aside from that, I like you as a man and as a friend.[1]

Their relationship at the GAO stretched over many years, and Warren clearly trusted his legal advice. However, at this point in the story, I should probably mention that they had a major falling out in 1953, near the end of Warren's fifteen-year term.

On June 29, Assistant Comptroller General Frank Yates suffered a fatal heart attack, and that sad event was the catalyst for a short-lived power struggle in the senior ranks of the GAO. While the agency mourned the death of Warren's deputy, my grandfather privately informed Warren that he intended to seek President Eisenhower's nomination to succeed Yates. Official records, obtained from the Dwight D. Eisenhower Presidential Library, show that he ran a vigorous campaign, but there was one major obstacle standing in his way. His primary competition for the nomination was Frank Weitzel, the person Warren planned to nominate. Upon hearing that his own general counsel intended to compete for the nomination, he scheduled an impromptu meeting with President Eisenhower, which he documented afterward in a personal memo. In that memo, he describes my grandfather's intention as "grossly lacking in propriety." Eisenhower, to no one's surprise, nominated Weitzel, another career GAO employee. Although the nomination was eventually confirmed, Eisenhower initially appointed Weitzel while Congress was in recess. Weitzel served as the assistant comptroller general until 1966.[2]

My grandfather's career was beginning to plateau by this juncture. He apparently saw the death of Yates as an opportunity to advance to the number two position in the agency. It's hard for me to imagine how such a bold move could have turned out well for him. Warren and Yates, though, were at the end of their terms in office, and I suspect that he was already thinking about pursuing one of those two positions. Like everyone else, he was caught off guard by the sudden death of his good friend. His failure to win the nomination, according to his oldest daughter, was one of the biggest disappointments of his life. The important thing for me here is that Warren's letter suggests that he had moved on from the incident and had forgiven my grandfather for his unfettered ambition.

After his retirement, he took a position as a legal counsel in the Aircraft Division of the Glen L Martin Company.[3] The job was less demanding and paid more than he ever made as a government lawyer, but from what I've heard, he didn't enjoy this work. According to my Aunt Joan, he was "bored to death" and "they didn't have enough for him to do (I think they hired him because of his government contacts)." In the last few years of his life, with his career and health in decline, he became more depressed. He died on July 11, 1962, from a massive heart attack suffered at his Bethesda home. Strangely enough, he died on the twenty-first anniversary of Bill Donovan's appointment as the COI. It was also the same day, as I learned through my research, that Carl Vinson penned the letter that led Joseph Campbell to formally end the GAO's audit of the CIA.

As the general counsel of a major legislative agency, my grandfather got to know plenty of congressmen and other general counsels in the executive branch. Some of his former government friends, upon hearing of his death, wrote bereavement letters to my grandmother to pay their respects. I found these old letters in the same box that I pulled the Dulles letter out of. Warren Burger, an old friend from the Justice Department and future chief justice of the US Supreme Court, wrote:

> Dear Mrs. Fisher
> It was with great sadness that I learned of Lyle's death and I send heartfelt sympathy. I had a profound admiration for him as a lawyer and a public ser-

> vant of the highest quality. His passing is a great loss to the legal profession he served so well. His loved ones can take great pride in his splendid career and his fine record.
>
> Sincerely
> Warren E. Burger[4]

Another intriguing letter from an old government associate named Daggett Howard, who my grandmother had never met, enigmatically alluded to his involvement in classified projects of national importance:

> Dear Mrs. Fisher:
> The news about Lyle came as a very deep shock to me. I knew him for many years in the Government, and have kept in touch with him in a business way since he went into private life, although I have never had the pleasure of meeting you. I have always considered Lyle one of the finest people I knew, and have sincerely felt that there are few, if any, men who have made a contribution comparable to his. I know, first hand, that innumerable projects of the greatest national interest and importance would have foundered but for his constructive understanding of them when he was in the Comptroller's office. He carried the same wisdom and integrity into his private life after leaving the Government.
>
> I had arranged just the other day to have lunch with him and renew old times. You have my most profound sympathy. Please do not hesitate to ask me if there is anything I can do to be of help.
>
> Sincerely yours,
> Daggett Howard[5]

I was unable to determine what professional connection my grandfather had to Daggett Howard, but the letterhead indicates that Howard was an attorney at the law firm of Cox, Langford and Brown.

Who could have predicted Lyle Fisher's life trajectory? An impoverished kid from the Midwest came to occupy the third most senior position at the GAO. In his dealings with the CIA, my grandfather confronted confounding legal problems that sometimes required him to make spur-of-the-moment decisions, with virtually no statutory precedents to rely on. Obviously, the CIA was careful about which cases they sought informal rulings on. Most of the time when Houston solicited his informal opinion, he sought practical legal solutions aimed at balancing the need for secrecy and expediency against the need for government accountability. The DCIs pushed the legal boundaries of Section 10b as far as they could. I find it noteworthy that the GAO rejected the DCI's two most extreme proposals: Smith's intent to issue a retroactive pay raise to employees using unvouchered funds and Dulles's initiative to gain no-year funding for the agency's entire budget.

The advent of nuclear weapons and the threat they posed to the nation impelled the GAO to serve the national interest by designing and participating in a financial audit that would ensure accountability for public funds and protect the security interests of the CIA and the country. Initially, the passage of the CIA Act came as a relief to the GAO, because it extricated the comptroller general and the GAO from incurring liability for the DCI's certifications under the working fund. The GAO never intended to provide administrative cover for covert operations certified by the DCI.

Like Lindsay Warren, my grandfather was cynical about the government on matters of accountability. He gave the CIA considerable latitude when they came to him and explained their situation in good faith. He also never opposed the policy of informally addressing legal questions that arose on a case-by-case basis. It appears that in the beginning, out of necessity and the spirit of the times, there really was good faith on both sides. But that spirit changed in the decade that followed the passage of the CIA Act. My grandfather continued to accept the CIA's good faith at face value, even when, especially during the tenure of Allen Dulles, he was probably being played. Over time, the GAO and the CIA drifted apart, as coordination between them became constrained to perfunctory audits of the CIA's most innocuous vouchered accounts.

Someday I would like to find out whether my grandfather influenced the GAO's decision to reform its audit of the CIA. He mentored his successor Robert Keller for about a year and was the only person at the GAO capable of briefing Keller on the history of the informal liaison between the two agencies. If he had any deep-seated concerns about the audit, that would have been the time to bring them up. Up until his official retirement, he was still technically in charge and in a position to influence his own legacy.

My grandfather died just four years after that lunch at the CIA took place, and it's impossible to say what he might have done had he lived another two or three decades. My grandmother never discussed his CIA liaison with anyone that I know of, suggesting that he never talked about it with her. I've discussed the Dulles letter with my father and his two sisters. Other than having read the letter that remained in the family, they cannot recall anything about his relationship with the CIA. As far as I know, this story remains a secret, even in my own family, and so it appears to me that he took all those secrets with him to his grave.

Notes

DESCRIPTIVE NOTES ON REFERENCES

CREST Citations:

The CREST citations can be viewed at the CIA web site https://www.cia.gov/readingroom/advanced-search-view. The ESDN number attached to each CREST citation can be inserted into the advanced search box labelled Document Number/ESDN.

OSS Textual Citations:

The National Archives and Records Administration (NARA) is the custodian of the OSS textual documents. The entire OSS archive is contained in Record Group 226. These documents are located according to Box no. (B), Stack no. (St), Row no. (R), Compartment no. (C), Shelf no. (Sh) and Entry no (E). The notation used in the endnotes is B, ST/R/C/Sh. (e.g. box 3, 190/38/23/07, entry UD 169). This notation can be used to complete the pull slips at NARA.

The OSS personal files were declassified in 2007. This relatively new source of information is cited in the notes according to the box number. All the personnel files can be located under Entry: A1-224. A complete listing of the OSS personnel on file can be found at https://www.archives.gov/files/iwg/declassified-records/rg-226-oss/personnel-database.pdf. The OSS Special Funds Branch history is a particularly significant document that helped me to connect the wartime history of the Special Funds Branch to the worldwide disbursement of unvouchered funds during World War II. This important eighty-four-page document is found in box 63, 50 64/23/07, entry A1-210, 5–6, NARA 210, RG226, NARA. The CIA recently made the Special Funds Branch history available on the CREST system; its ECN number is 00038955, though this document is heavily redacted and some of the copied pages are impossible to read.

Congressional Records:

The early records of Congress and Executive branch cited in the endnotes are provided by the Library of Congress, A Century of Lawmaking for a New Nation website at https://memory.loc.gov/ammem/amlaw/.

Acronyms and Abbreviations:

CREST CIA ReSearch Tool (https://www.cia.gov/readingroom/advanced-search-view)

FRUS	Foreign Relations of the United States: Emergence of the Intelligence Establishment 1945–1950
HBPB	History of the Budget and Procedures Branch (OSS)
MFR	Memorandum for the Record
NARA	National Archives and Records Administration
SFBH	OSS Special Funds Branch History

PROLOGUE

1. Maarja Krusten began as a staff historian under the chief historian, Roger Trask. She retired from the GAO in 2016. Krusten formerly worked on the Nixon Tapes at NARA.

2. B-Files are part of the GAO's archiving system and apply to information that came to the attention of the GAO's Office of the General Counsel. All of the GAO documents in my collection have B-File reference numbers.

3. The ESDN uniquely identifies a document in the CREST database. For example, copy CIA-RDP80-01240A000100140093-5 into the ESDN box at https://www.cia.gov/readingroom/advanced-search-view, and read the associated document.

4. In 2003, it cost seventy-five cents per page to use the photocopiers in the textual records section on the second floor.

1. THE PROBLEM OF FUNDING A NATIONAL INTELLIGENCE SERVICE

Epigraph: Robert H. Alcorn, *No Bugles for Spies* (New York: Popular Library, 1964), 58.

1. US Congress, *United States Code: First War Powers Act, 50a U.S.C. §§ 601-622 1946*. 1946. Periodical. https://www.loc.gov/item/uscode1946-004050a009/.

2. National Security Act of 1947, Pub. L. No. 80-253, 61 Stat. 495 (1947). https://catalog.archives.gov/id/299856. The CIA's statutory charter is contained in Section 102 of the act.

3. Comptroller General Lindsay Warren to Director of the Budget Bureau James Webb, March 12, 1948, CIA-RDP78-05246A000100010001-3, CREST, NARA.

2. THE GENERAL ACCOUNTING OFFICE

1. Roger Trask, *Defender of the Public Interest: The General Accounting Office, 1921–1966* (US Government Printing Office, Washington, DC, 1996), 6–7.

2. Frederick Mosher, *The GAO: The Quest for Accountability in American Government* (Baton Rouge: Louisiana State University Press, 1984), 26; Act of September 2, 1789. 1st Cong., 1st Sess., chap. 12: An Act to Establish the Treasury Department.

3. A Treasury warrant is an order in the form of a check that authorizes the withdrawal of Treasury funds.

4. Joseph Nourse, the first register of the Treasury, served in this position under the first seven presidents; he finally retired in 1928 shortly after the election of Andrew Jackson.

5. Act of September 2, 1789, chap. 12, sect. 2–6 *Stat. 1*, 12.

6. James Madison or Alexander Hamilton, "The Federalist No. 58, [20 February 1788]," *Founders Online,* National Archives Federalist, https://founders.archives.gov/documents/Hamilton/01-04-02-0207.

7. There was considerable debate at the Constitutional Convention on the practical issue of whether the second part of Clause 7 belonged in a founding constitutional document. James Madison, the secretary at the convention, resolved the stalemate by proposing that the temporally precise word "annually" be replaced by the more flexible phrase "from time to time."

8. St. George Tucker, *Blackstone's Commentaries with Notes of Reference to the Constitution*, (Philadelphia: William Young Burch and Abraham Small, 1803), 1:note D, pt. 9.

9. "Debate in Massachusetts Ratifying Convention," document 9 in *The Debates in the Several State Conventions on the Adoption of the Federal Constitution as Recommended by the General Convention at Philadelphia in 1787. . . .* 5 vols, edited by Jonathan Elliot, 1888, 2d ed. repr. (New York: Burt Franklin, n.d.), 2:52. http://press-pubs.uchicago.edu/founders/documents/a1_5s9.html.

10. Trask, *Defender of the Public Interest*, 13.

11. Trask, 10–12.

12. Trask, 14–16; Mosher, *The GAO*, 32–34.

13. Trask, *Defender of the Public Interest*, 17–18; Mosher, *The GAO*, 34–36.

14. Lucius Wilmerding Jr., *Spending Power: A History of the Efforts of Congress to Control Expenditures* (New Haven: Yale University Press, 1943), 250. For additional quotes and commentary, see Wilmerding, 250–252; Trask, *Defender of the Public Interest*, 14, 19, 16, 24.

15. Trask, 35–42.

16. The Bureau of the Budget's name was changed in 1970, to the Office of Management and Budget (OMB).

17. Throughout the rest of this story, the formal title, comptroller general of the United States, will be abbreviated as the comptroller general.

18. Only Supreme Court justices serve longer: they receive lifetime appointments.

19. Charles G. Dawes, *The First Year of the Budget of the United States* (New York: Harper and Brothers, 1923), 8–9; Percival Brundage, *The Bureau of the Budget* (New York: Praeger, 1970), 14–15.

20. Frederick Mosher, *A Tale of Two Agencies: A Comparative Analysis of the General Accounting Office and Office of Management and Budget* (Baton Rouge: Louisiana State University Press, 1984), 4.

21. Wilmerding, *Spending Power*, 259, 284.

22. Budget and Accounting Act of 1921, Pub. L. No. 67-13, 42 Stat. 20, S. 1084 67th Congress, June 10, 1921. Sections 312 and 313.

23. Frederick Mosher, *The Quest for Accountability in American Government* (Boulder, CO: Westview, 1979), 86–87; Trask, *Defender of the Public Interest*, 58.

24. John R. McCarl, "Government-Run-Everything," *Saturday Evening Post*, October 3 and 17, 1936; Jason W. A. Bertsch, "John Raymond McCarl: Budget Hawk at the GAO," Profiles in Citizenship, *Policy Review*, November 1, 1997, https://www.hoover.org/research/profiles-citizenship-6; Trask, *Defender of the Public Interest*, 64.

3. THE OFFICE OF STRATEGIC SERVICES

1. Thomas Troy, *Donovan and the CIA: The History of the Establishment of the Central Intelligence Agency* (Frederick, MD: University Publications of America, 1981), 11–13; Sallie Pisani, *The CIA and the Marshall Plan* (Lawrence: University Press of Kansas, 1991), 19–20.

2. Douglas Waller, *Wild Bill Donovan: The Spymaster Who Created the OSS and Modern American Espionage* (New York: Free Press, 2011), 14–15, 22–23.

3. Troy, *Donovan and the CIA*, 69–70, app. C; "Colonel Will Soon Be Named Coordinator of Intelligence for the Government," Information Post, *New York Times*, July 10, 1941.

4. The acronym COI corresponds to both the head of the organization and the organization itself. The intended meaning can be inferred from the context.

5. Records of the Budget and Planning Office, History of the Budget and Procedures Branch (hereafter, HRBPO), box 1, 190/007/022/02, entry UD 130, rec. group 226, US National Archives and Records Administration (NARA).

6. Troy, *Donovan and the CIA*, 74.

7. HRBPO, 1; *War Report of the OSS*, 1:12 (New York: Walker, 1976); Troy, *Donovan and the CIA*, 88.

8. Troy, *Donovan and the CIA*, 42.

9. HRBPO, 3.

10. HRBPO, 4.

11. Troy, *Donovan and the CIA*, 112. A photocopy of the COI's first budget submitted November 7, 1941.

12. HRBPO, 4–7; *War Report of the OSS*, 1:85; see Troy, *Donovan and the CIA*, 106–107.

13. General Accounting Office, Accounts and Procedures Letter No. 4923, July 16, 1942, box 1, 190/007/022/02, entry UD 130. General Accounting Office, Accounts and Procedures Letter No. 3428, December 18, 1941. Box 1 contains several Accounts and Procedures letters issued by the comptroller general authorizing the COI's use of unvouchered funds withdrawn from the president's emergency fund. These letters established precedent setting guidelines on the user of unvouchered funds in wartime. The letter dated on December 18, 1941—the day Congress passed the War Powers Act of 1941—is not in box 1, but is formally referenced as an original precedent in the July 16 letter.

14. A voucher here represents a documented record of an expenditure, containing enough information to track and account for the expense (who, what, where, when, and how much).

15. *War Report of the OSS*, 1:84.

16. Donald Downes, *The Scarlet Thread* (Great Britain: Love & Malcolmson, 1953), 85.

17. Special Funds Branch History (SFBH), Sources and Methods, box 63, 250/64/23/07, entry A1-210, rec. group 226, NARA; the SFBH is an official historical account written by Lieutenant Colonel John Williams. It took me ten years to find this report, for it was a later release that was not included in the original OSS finding aids.

18. SFBH, 23–25; *War Report of the OSS*, 1:85.

19. SFBH, 24.

20. William Rehm to G. F. Allen, March 25, 1942; William Rehm to Francis J. Rue, vice president of Bankers Trust Company, which is also signed by G. F. Allen (chief disbursing officer of the Treasury Department, March 25, 1942, box 140, 250/64/23/07, entry A1-210; OSS personnel files of William L. Rehm, box 637, 230/86/39/02, entry A1-224, Robert Goddard, box 278, 230/86/31/07, entry A1-224, Douglas M. Dimond, box 188, 230/86/30/01, entry A1-224, Charles Lennihan, box 445, 230/86/35/03, entry A1-224, and Emerson Bigelow, box 56, 230/86/27/03, entry A1-224, rec. group 226, NARA.

21. Bradley Smith, *The Shadow Warriors* (New York: Basic, 1983), 125–126.

22. *War Report of the OSS*, 1:85, 248–252.

23. Troy, *Donovan and the CIA*, 136.

24. Troy, 136.

25. Troy, 150–153; Military Order of June 13, 1942, Offices of Strategic Services, appendix E, 427.

26. SFBH, 1–2; William Donovan to G. F. Allen November 17, 1942, OSS personnel files of Douglas M. Dimond, box 188, 230/86/30/01, entry A1-224 and Emmerson Bigelow box 56, 230/86/27/03, entry A1-224, rec. group 226, NARA.

27. Troy, *Donovan and the CIA*, 14, 140.

4. THE OSS SPECIAL FUNDS BRANCH

1. *War Report of the OSS* (New York: Walker, 1976), 1:121.

2. Special Funds Branch History (SFBH), OSS Sources and Methods, 5–6, box 63, 250/64/23/07/, entry A1-210, rec. group 226, NARA; See also http://libertyladybook.com/2010/09/09/oss-headquarters/.

3. SFBH, 23–24; *War Report of the OSS* 1:143.

4. Robert Hayden Alcorn, *No Bugles for Spies* (New York: Popular Library, 1964), 56–58.

5. Alcorn, *No Bugles for Spies*, 5, 57–58.

6. *OSS London Special Funds Branch War Diary, London office* (SFB London War

Diary), 18, OSS London, box 3, 190/038/023/05/, entry UD 169, rec. group 226; *War Report of the OSS* 1:147; SFBH, 44–46.

7. Robert Hayden Alcorn, *No Banners, No Bands: More Tales of the OSS* (Philadelphia, PA: D. McKay, 1965), 112.

8. *War Report of the OSS* 1:143.

9. SFBH, 26; OSS Personnel file of Colonel William L. Rehm, box 637, 230/86/39/02/, entry A1–224, rec. group 226, (all OSS personnel files are in the same rec. group), NARA.

10. SFBH, 24, 56–58; OSS Personnel file of Edgar Lucas, box 465, 230/86/35/06/, NARA (three-page history of SFB's accounting branch).

11. SFBH, 57.

12. These statements can be found in the personnel files of the key OSS paymasters held at the national archives. See personnel files for William Rehm, Douglas M. Dimond, Emmerson Bigelow, etc.

13. Lennihan left the SFB permanently in the fall of 1944 and died before the end of the war.

14. SFBH, 30–33, 56–57; personnel file of Robert Goddard, box 278, 230/86/31/07, entry A1-224, NARA.

15. SFBH, 35.

16. SFBH, 7, 28; John W. Chambers II, "A Wartime Organization for Unconventional Warfare," in *OSS Training in the National Parks and Service Abroad in World War II* (Washington, DC: US National Park Service, 2008), 61. https://www.nps.gov/parkhistory/online_books/oss/index.htm.

17. SFBH, 11–12, 44–45; *War Report of the OSS*, 1:147.

18. SFBH, 11, 37–41; *War Report of the OSS*, 1:149.

19. Emmerson Bigelow to George Gorin, February 12, 1945, box 229, 190/010/012/07, entry UD 199, rec. group 226, NARA.

20. SFBH, 71–72; *War Report of the OSS*, 1:248. Allen Dulles started out in the New York office under the COI; he was dispatched to serve as the head of SI in Bern, Switzerland, shortly after the establishment of the OSS.

21. SFBH, 7, 73.

22. *War Report of the OSS*, 1:144.

23. SFB London War diary, 1–2; *The Overseas Targets: War Report of the OSS*, vol. 2 (New York: Walker, 1976), 23.

24. SFBH, 43–45; *War Report of the OSS* 1:147–152; Alcorn, *No Bugles for Spies*, 49–53.

25. Alcorn, *No Bugles for Spies*, 31–32.

26. Alcorn, 78.

27. OSS personnel file for Robert Alcorn, box 8, 230/86/26/04/, entry A1-224, rec. group 226, NARA; Alcorn, *No Banners, No Bands*, 113.

28. Alcorn, *No Bugles for Spies*, 57.

29. SFBH, 9; Bradley F. Smith, *The Shadow Warriors: O.S.S. and the Origins of*

the C.I.A. (New York: Basic, 1983), 146; OSS personnel file of Edward Fay, box 230, 230/86/30/07/, entry A1-224, rec. group 226, NARA.

30. SFBH, 9–10; OSS personnel file for John W. Williams, box 810, 230/86/43/03/, entry A1-224, rec. group 226, NARA.

31. OSS personnel file for David Crocket, box 351, 230/86/29/03/, entry A1-224, rec. group 226, NARA.

32. Lieutenant Holt Green was later declared missing in action in the Balkans and by the end of the war was presumed dead.

33. SFBH, 9–10; *Overseas Targets: War Report of the OSS*, 2:47.

34. OSS personnel file for Thomas Bland, box 60, 230/86/27/04, entry A1-224, rec. group 226, NARA.

35. Example of letter signed by Thomas Bland and G. F. Allen in records of the SFB office in Cairo, box 145, 190/010/012/07/, entry UD 199, rec. group 226, NARA.

36. OSS personnel file of Nick Steichen, box 742, 230/86/41/03/,entry A1-224, rec. group 226, NARA.

37. SFBH, 45–46.

38. SFBH, 10, 45.

39. SFBH, 43–44, 48; *War Report of the OSS*, 1:151; Alcorn, *No Bugles for Spies*, 51–53.

40. SFBH, 10, 49; Douglas Waller, *Wild Bill Donovan: The Spymaster That Created the OSS and Modern American Espionage* (New York: Free Press, 2011), 286.

41. SFBH, 15; Waller, *Wild Bill Donovan*, 159–160.

42. OSS personnel file for Robert Alcorn, box 8, 230/86/26/04/, entry A1-224, NARA.

43. James Srodes, *Allen Dulles: Master of Spies* (Washington, DC: Regnery, 1999), 222–227; Peter Grose, *Gentleman Spy: The Life of Allen Dulles* (New York: Houghton Mifflin, 1994), 148–152.

44. Memorandum from William Donovan to President Roosevelt, May 27, 1942, PSF box 106, OSS files, Roosevelt Presidential Library, Hyde Park, NY; Srodes, *Allen Dulles*, 217.

45. SFBH, 45; Report from SFB field auditor William Peratino (1006) to William Rehm (128) on Bern financial operations, May 5, 1945, OSS Sources and Methods, box 160, 250/64/23/07/, entry A1-210; William Rehm to Charles Dyar, November 11, 1944, OSS Sources and Methods, box 140, 250/64/23/07/, entry, rec. group 226, NARA; Memorandum from W. Donovan to President Roosevelt, May 27, 1942, PSF box 106, OSS files, Roosevelt Presidential Library, Hyde Park, NY. Most of the information on Agent 227 comes from the SFB Bern office records.

46. Thomas Bland (1062) to Nick Steichen, February 13, 1945, OSS personnel file for Thomas Bland, box 60, 230/86/27/03/, entry A1-224, rec. group 226, NARA; SFBH, 70–71, 77.

47. Thomas Bland (1062) to William Rehm (128), April 19, 1945, OSS Sources and Methods, box 160, 250/64/23/07/, entry A1-210, NARA; Thomas Bland (1062) to

William Rehm (128), May 4, 1945, OSS Sources and Methods, box 160, 250/64/23/07/, entry A1-210, NARA.

48. Rehm's trip report to Donovan, box 60, 190/006/009/07/, entry A1-99, rec. group 226, NARA. Rehm briefly mentions Halliwell in his trip report, referring to him as "Comdr. Halliwell." The Honolulu office is not even mentioned in the official SFB history.

49. Memorandum from William Rehm to William Donovan, attached trip report chronicling Rehm's world tour of special funds operations, December 15, 1944, box 60, 190/006/009/07/, A1-99, rec. group 226, NARA. Smith, *The Shadow Warriors*, 129, 195–196; Waller, *Wild Bill Donovan*, 231–234.

50. Smith, *The Shadow Warriors*, 194, 255–256; Waller, *Wild Bill Donovan*, 216–219; R. Harris Smith, *OSS: The Secret History of America's First Central Intelligence Agency* (Berkeley: University of California Press, 1972), 244.

51. Historical report on the OSS China-Burma-India theater of operations to 26 October 1944, box 58, 190/006/009/07/, entry A1-99, rec. group 226, NARA; Smith, *The Shadow Warriors*, 131; Waller, *Wild Bill Donovan*, 214–215.

52. George Gorin Special Funds Report to OSS Commanding Officer, Detachment 101, Special Funds Report, May 22, 1945, box 71, 190/010/012/07/, entry UD 199, rec. group 226, NARA.

53. Gorin's Special Funds Report.

54. Gorin's Special Funds Report.

55. Gorin's Special Funds Report; Trip Report chronicling Rehm's world tour of SFB operations, William Rehm to the Director (Donovan), December 15, 1944, box 60, 190/006/009/07/, entry A1-99, rec. group 226, NARA.

56. Gorin's Special Funds Report; Commander Joseph Leete to William Rehm, May 27, 1944, box 56, 190/010/012/07/, entry UD 199, NARA.

57. Donovan did manage to establish an intelligence network in China that involved businessmen and front companies. This intelligence network was the brainchild of Cornelius V. Starr, an insurance magnate and international investor with business roots in China. According to Douglas Waller, it received money from the OSS. The SFB was probably involved in disbursing unvouchered funds to at least one of the front companies, Metropolitan Motors Overseas Incorporated, which operated out of Kunming. Waller, *Wild Bill Donovan*, 209–210.

58. Chungking is today known as Chongqing.

59. Joseph Leete to William Rehm, August 10, 1944, box 56, 190/010/012/07/, entry UD 199, rec. group 226, NARA.

60. Rehm to the Director, Trip Report, December 15, 1944, box 60, 190/006/009/07/, entry A1-99, rec. group 226, NARA.

61. Joseph Leete to William Rehm, August 10, 1944, and R. H. Goddard to Joseph Leete, August 24, 1944, box 56, 190/010/012/07/, entry UD 199, rec. group 226, NARA.

62. William Rehm to George Gorin, February 10, 1945, box 56, 190/010/012/07/, entry UD 199; Joseph Leete to William Rehm, August 10, 1944, and Robert Goddard

to Joseph Leete, August 24, 1944, box 56, 190/010/012/07/, entry UD 199, rec. group 226, NARA. Note in OSS personnel file for Joseph Leete.

63. Rehm to the Director, Trip Report, December 15, 1944, box 60, 190/006/009/07, entry A1-99, rec. group 226, NARA.

64. Emmerson Bigelow to George Gorin, February 12, 1945, box 229, 190/010/012/07/, entry UD 199, rec. group 226, NARA.

65. OSS personnel file for Emmett Echols, box 211, 230/86/30/05/, entry A1-224, rec. group 226, NARA.

66. OSS personnel file for Emmett Echols.

67. Emmett Echols to the Director, Office of Strategic Services, Emmett Echols to George Gorin, June 16, 1945, rec. group 226, NARA.

68. The matter of transfers in CIBTO is discussed in memos and reports between Washington and Detachment 404; also see Gorin's Special Funds Report, box 71, 190/010/012/07/, entry UD 199, rec. group 226, NARA.

69. OSS personnel file for 190/010/012/07/, entry UD 199, rec. group 226, NARA.

70. OSS Personnel file for R. G. White, box 833, 02/43/86/230, entry A1-224, rec. group 226, NARA.

71. William Rehm to Robert Alcorn, January 26, 1944, box 3, 190/38/23/07/, entry UD 169, rec. group 226, NARA.

72. James B. Donovan to G. E. Buxton (Acting Director), June 3, 1944, OSS Sources and Methods, box 349, 250/64/23/07/, entry A1-210, rec. group 226, NARA.

73. James B. Donovan to G. E. Buxton; William Donovan to Lindsay Warren, OSS Sources and Methods, box 349, 250/64/23/07/, entry A1-210, rec. group 226, NARA.

74. SFBH, 63; *War Report of the OSS*, 1:128, 145.

75. *War Report of the OSS*, 1:145; SFBH, 3.

76. This special category of vouchered funds applied to all CIA's vouchered funds under the CIA Act of 1949.

77. Memorandum from the Board of Review to Strategic Services Officers, June 20, 1944 and Memorandum from Board of Review to Theater Boards of Review, September 27, 1944, box 145, 190/010/012/07/, entry UD 199, NARA; SFBH, 69–71.

78. Memorandum from Edgar Lucas to Robert Alcorn, June 20, 1944, box 27, 190/38/24/05/, entry UD 197A, NARA.

79. SFBH, 69–71.

80. Richard Park, Report on his OSS Investigation, NARA. Larry McDonald, a NARA archivist, took me into a back room, pulled the Park Report out of a drawer, and handed it to me so I could take pictures. I don't have the specific reference for it. I did not ask to see it, nor had I any familiarity with it. He wanted me to see that document.

5. THE CENTRAL INTELLIGENCE GROUP

1. Exec. Order No. 9621, 10 Fed. Reg. 12033 (September 20, 1945), document 14, Foreign Relations of the United States, 1945–1950, Emergence of the Intelligence

Establishment, https://history.state.gov/historicaldocuments/frus1945-50Intel (hereafter, FRUS); President Truman to Secretary of State Byrnes, September 20, 1945, document 15, FRUS; Harry Truman to William Donovan, September 20, 1945, CIA-RDP90-00610R000100200006-9, CIA Research Search Tool (CREST).

2. Director of the SSU (Magruder) to Assistant Secretary of War (McCloy), October 9, 1945, document 96, FRUS; Memorandum to the SSU branch and office chiefs from the assistant secretary of war, September 29, 1945, CIA-RDP83-00036R0 01000040016-2, CREST.

3. The order for this reorganization came down on May 11, a few days after the surrender of Germany.

4. Woodring was formerly the chief of the OSS Finance Branch. His personnel file is empty; apparently its contents remain classified. If files are removed due to classification, NARA generally states that on the folder. Edward Saunders's OSS personnel file is completely missing. No one at NARA could explain why. *War Report of the OSS* (New York: Walker, 1976), 1:145; Records of the Budget and Planning Office, History of the Budget and Procedures Branch (HRBPO), box 1, 190/007/022/02, entry 130, rec. group 226, NARA; Special Funds Branch History (SFBH), Sources and Methods, 78, box 63, 250/64/23/07, entry A1-210, rec. group 226, NARA.

5. SSU Office of General Counsel to the SSU Strategic Director, Certification of Vouchers for the Expenditure of Confidential Funds, October 12, 1945, CIA-RDP57-00384R000400110213-2, CREST. This memorandum was written before Lawrence Houston took over as SSU general counsel in November.

6. Emmett Echols to Robert Barker, March 27, 1947, OSS personnel file for Robert Barker, box 36, 230/86/27/01/, entry A1-224, rec. group 226, NARA.

7. The personnel files of all these people are available at: Office of Strategic Services Personnel Files from World War II, NARA.

8. Robert Alcorn to Lois Frauenheim, May 8, 1946, personnel file for Robert Alcorn, box 8, 230/86/26/04/, entry A1-224; rec. group 226, NARA; "Historical Notes Re: Budget and Finance Activities CIA and Predecessor Organizations Period: 20 September 1945–28 January 1952," CIA-RDP83-01034R000200140004-1, CREST (hereafter, CIA, "Historical Notes").

9. The Budget and Finance Branch was renamed the Finance Branch when Saunders became head. It still included separate divisions for special funds, fiscal, and budget.

10. HRBPO, 23–24; CIA, "Historical Notes." CIA, "Historical Notes;" George S. Jackson and Martin P. Claussen, The DCI Historical Series: "Organizational History of the Central Intelligence Agency Chapter X Conduct of the Agency Business," 149 (fn 3), box 4, 190/25/08/07/, entry A1-21, rec. group 263.2.2, NARA, also available online at https://drive.google.com/file/d/1bDopKpGMbVuWuZtdy9ROPJ48r8ifp1jG/view.

11. Presidential Directive on Coordination of Foreign Intelligence Activities, to the Secretary of State [Byrnes], Secretary of War [Patterson], and Secretary of the Navy [Forrestal], January 22, 1946, document 71, FRUS; Arthur B. Darling, *The Central*

Intelligence Agency: An Instrument of Government, to 1950 (University Park: Pennsylvania State University Press, 1990), 71.

12. Presidential Directive on Coordination of Foreign Intelligence Activities, document 71, FRUS.

13. CIA, "Historical Notes."

14. Thomas Troy, *Donovan and the CIA: A History of the Establishment of the Central Intelligence Agency* (Frederick, MD: University Publications of America, 1981), 346, 351.

15. NIA Directive No. 1, February 8, 1946, Doc. 141, FRUS; NIA Directive No. 2, February 8, 1946, Doc. 142, FRUS; Troy, *Donovan and the CIA*, 354–355.

16. National Intelligence Directive No. 4, April 2, 1946, Doc. 106, FRUS. See also FRUS Doc. 107–108.

17. David F. Rudgers, *Creating the Secret State: The Origins of the Central Intelligence Agency, 1943–1947* (Lawrence: University Press of Kansas, 2000), 112.

18. DCI Sidney Souers to the National Intelligence Authority, June 7, 1946, Doc. 154, FRUS.

19. Lawrence Houston to Hoyt Vandenberg, June 13, 1946, Doc 196, FRUS.

20. Houston to Vandenberg; John Ranelagh, *The Agency: The Rise and Decline of the CIA* (New York: Simon and Schuster, 1986), 106.

21. See Draft of National Intelligence Authority Directive enclosed in memorandum from Vandenberg to the Intelligence Advisory Board, June 20, 1946, Doc. 156, FRUS.

22. Director of Central Intelligence's Executive (Wright), July 11, 1946, Doc 114, FRUS; CIA, "Historical Notes."

23. Minutes of the Fourth Meeting of the National Intelligence Authority, July 17, 1946, document 198, FRUS.

24. Minutes of the Fourth Meeting, document 198.

25. Memorandum from the Director of Central Intelligence (Vandenberg) to the National Intelligence Authority, July 30, 1946, document 199, FRUS.

26. Memorandum from the Director of Central Intelligence (Vandenberg), document 199.

27. "Memorandum on Central Intelligence Agency," CIA-RDP80-01240A00010 0140093-5, CREST.

6. PUBLIC OVERSIGHT OF THE ATOMIC BOMB

1. Excerpts from congressional testimony from Lindsay Warren to the Special Committee on Atomic Energy, April 4, 1946, on atomic energy. A Bill for the Development and Control of Atomic Energy, S. 1717, 79th Cong. (1946). See Appendix F in Historical Study of the Use of Confidential funds, CIA-RDP78-05246A000100010001-3, CREST.

2. Appendix F in Historical Study, CIA-RDP78-05246A000100010001-3.

3. Appendix F in Historical Study, CIA-RDP78-05246A000100010001-3.

4. Appendix F in Historical Study, CIA-RDP78-05246A000100010001-3.

5. Appendix F in Historical Study, CIA-RDP78-05246A000100010001-3.

6. Appendix F in Historical Study, CIA-RDP78-05246A000100010001-3.

7. Warren might have taken the provision more seriously if the law had also created the statutory position of AEC comptroller independent of the commission.

8. Lawrence Houston, Memorandum for Record, GAO and Unvouchered Funds, April 22, 1946, CIA-RDP62-00631R000200100068-6, CREST.

9. Appendix F in Historical Study, CIA-RDP78-05246A000100010001-3; Roger Trask, *Defender of the Public Interest: The General Accounting Office, 1921–1966* (US Government Printing Office, Washington, DC, 1996), 273.

10. Leslie Groves, *Now It Can Be Told: The Story of the Manhattan Project* (Cambridge, MA: Da Capo, 1962), 360–361.

11. Trask, *Defender of the Public Interest*, 274; Groves, *Now It Can Be Told*, 39–55.

12. Groves, 48–54.

13. Groves, 57–58.

14. Groves, 57–58; Trask, *Defender of the Public Interest*, 275. The person at the GAO who best fit the description of the principal assistant was J. Darlington Denit, head of the Accounting and Bookkeeping Division. He had a need to know, and he was not shy about bluntly stating his opinions to Warren.

15. Trask, *Defender of the Public Interest*, 275, See fn. 82, 85.

16. Groves, *Now It Can Be Told*, 361.

17. Once Congress was on board, General Groves invited congressmen Clarence Cannon, Gene Snyder, George Mahon, John Taber, and Albert Engel to visit the Oak Ridge facility.

18. Groves, *Now It Can Be Told*, 362–363.

19. Groves, 362–363.

7. ORIGINAL SIN

1. Michael Warner, *Central Intelligence: Origin and Evolution* (Washington, DC: Center for the Study of Intelligence, Central Intelligence Agency, 2001), 4.

2. Director of Central Intelligence (Souers) to the National Intelligence Authority, June 7, 1946, document 154, Foreign Relations of the United States, 1945–1950, Emergence of the Intelligence Establishment, https://history.state.gov/historicaldocuments/frus1945-50Intel (hereafter, FRUS).

3. National Intelligence Directive (NID) no. 4 Policy on Liquidation of the Strategic Services Unit, April 2, 1946, CIA-RDP84-00022R000400090009-3, CREST; Supplies and Equipment, Central Intelligence Group [Assistant Secretary of War (H. Peterson) to the Chief, Strategic Services Unit (Brigadier General J. Magruder)], March 8, 1946, CIA-RDP54-00177A000100010002-9, CREST, NARA; Historical Notes Re: Budget

and Finance Activities CIA and Predecessor Organizations Period: 20 September 1945–28 January 1952, CIA-RDP83-01034R000200140004-1, CREST.

4. Memorandum from the Director of Central Intelligence to the National Intelligence Authority, July 30, 1946, document 199, FRUS.

5. Reorganization Act of 1945, Sec. 7, December 20, 1945; document 199, FRUS.

6. CIG Executive for Personnel and Administration (Ford) to the Director of Central Intelligence (Vandenberg), the CIG Executive to the Director (Wright), the CIG Assistant Executive Director (Dabney) and the Assistant Director for Special Operations (Galloway), August 7, 1946, CIA-RDP57-00384R000200080120-1, CREST; Memorandum on Central Intelligence Agency, CIA-RDP80-01240A000100140093-5, CREST.

7. Memorandum from Walter Ford to Hoyt Vandenberg, August 7, 1946, CIA-RDP57-00384R000200080120-1.

8. The Economy Act of 1932, June 30, 1932, 31 USC 1535.

9. Military Appropriation Act, 1947, July 16, 1946, ch. 583, 60 Stat. 541, https://www.govinfo.gov/content/pkg/STATUTE-60/pdf/STATUTE-60-Pg541.pdf; Naval Appropriation Act, 1947, July 8, 1946, ch. 543, title 1, 60 Stat. 481, https://www.govinfo.gov/content/pkg/STATUTE-60/pdf/STATUTE-60-Pg481.pdf.

10. Lyle Fisher initialized all memos and formal documents with all his initials, ELF. The most important documents involving the CIA-GAO liaison bear these initials, generally with a small note.

11. Troy's allusion to the August 1946 conference (and Fisher's participation) is the only reference to the conference that I've found in any published literature on the early establishment of the CIA.

12. Memorandum on Central Intelligence Agency, CIA-RDP80-01240A000100140093-5; Thomas Troy, *Donovan and the CIA: A History of the Establishment of the Central Intelligence Agency* (Frederick, MD: University Publications of America, 1981), 371.

13. CIG Executive Walter Ford to Lindsay Warren, August 15, 1946, CIA-RDP78-05844A000100140051-0, CREST.

14. The CIA executive was the most senior administrative CIG official under the DCI.

15. Walter Ford to Lindsay Warren, CIA-RDP78-05844A000100140051-0.

16. Memorandum from Lawrence Houston to Allen Dulles, October 9, 1958, CIA-RDP80-R01731R000100160041-3, CREST.

17. Memorandum from the Director of Central Intelligence (Vandenberg) to the National Intelligence Authority, August 21, 1946, document 200, FRUS; Comptroller General (Warren) to the Director of Central Intelligence (Vandenberg), August 28, 1946, CIA-RDP78-05844A000100160051-8, CREST.

18. National Intelligence Authority to the Comptroller General (Warren), September 5, 1946, CIA-RDP78-05844A000100140041-1, CREST.

19. Historical Notes Re: Budget and Finance Activities CIA and Predecessor

Organizations, CIA-RDP83-01034R000200140004-1; CIG Administrative Order (Sanitized), August 21, 1946, CIA-RDP81-00728R000100050011-7, CREST.

20. Historical Notes Budget and Finance Activities CIA and Predecessor Organizations, CIA-RDP83-01034R000200140004-1.

21. Memorandum from the Director of Central Intelligence (Vandenberg) to Secretary of State Byrnes, September 12, 1946, document 128, FRUS; Strategic Services Unit General Orders No. 16, October 19, 1946, document 130, FRUS; SSU Special Funds Chief Emmett Echols to SSU missions abroad, September 20, 1946, box 140, entry A1-210, 250/64/23/6, RG262, CREST, NARA.

22. Prepared letter for the DCI to sign to the chief disbursing officer (Treasury Department), September 26, 1946, OSS personnel file for Emerson Bigelow, box 56, 230 86/27/03, entry A1-224, RG226, NARA.

23. Lawrence Houston to Director of Central Intelligence, Hoyt Vandenberg, November 19, 1946, Treatment of Special Funds Overseas, 50dde103993247d4d83921ab, CREST.

24. Houston to Vandenberg, Treatment of Special Funds Overseas, 50dde10399 3247d4d83921ab.

25. Houston to Vandenberg, 50dde103993247d4d83921ab.

26. Houston to Vandenberg, 50dde103993247d4d83921ab.

27. Houston to Vandenberg, 50dde103993247d4d83921ab.

28. Houston to Vandenberg, 50dde103993247d4d83921ab.

29. Houston to Vandenberg, 50dde103993247d4d83921ab.

30. CIA General Counsel (Houston) to the Executive for Personnel and Administration, December 18, 1946, in Basic Administrative Authorities for CIG, January 1, 1946, CIA-RDP80R01731R001400110009-0, CREST.

8. THE PROTAGONIST, THE ENABLER, AND THE ANTAGONIST

1. Lawrence Houston to Allen Dulles, October 9, 1958, CIA-RDP80R01731R 000100160041-3, CREST; the subject header of this memo reads "E. Lyle Fisher."

2. All his friends and family called him Lyle when he was an adult, but he held on to his first initial as part of his formal signature.

3. John White, "Did You Happen To See—Lyle Fisher?," *Washington Times-Herald*, March 28, 1948.

4. The *Watchdog* (in-house GAO newspaper published by the GAO Office of Employees Association), November 1947, information obtained from an original copy, Fisher family collection.

5. Dorothy Fisher, excerpt from personal essay, 1959. Fisher family collection.

6. Roger R. Trask, *Defender of the Public Interest: The General Accounting Office, 1921–1966* (Washington, DC: US Government Printing Office, 1996), 263.

7. Mary Sparo, "Tighter War Contract Laws Urged by GAO Chief Counsel,"

Washington Post, September 10, 1947; for Warren's views see Trask, *Defender of the Public Interest*, 263.

8. Transcript of E. L. Fisher speech at the briefing conference on Government Contracts, Philadelphia, Pennsylvania, February 28, 1962, Fisher family collection.

9. Lyle was one of the first twenty-five senior officials in the federal government to receive a "supergrade" GS-18 rating; for several years, he was the only GS-18 at the GAO.

10. White, "Did You Happen to See—Lyle Fisher?"

11. 50th Anniversary Edition of the *GAO Review* (Summer 1971): 125, accessed 5 April 2024, https://www.gao.gov/assets/091095.pdf.

12. Bob Fisher is my father.

13. I found Houston's date of birth in his OSS personnel file. I can't recall seeing it anywhere else.

14. OSS personnel file for Lawrence R. Houston, box 351, entry A1-224, NARA; G. Breneman, "Lawrence R. Houston: A Biography," *Studies in Intelligence* 30, no. 1 (Spring 1986): 38; Tim Weiner, "Lawrence Houston, 82, Dies; Helped to Establish the CIA," *New York Times*, August 17, 1995.

15. OSS personnel file for Lawrence R. Houston; Kermit Roosevelt, ed., *War Report of the OSS* (New York: Walker, 1876), 128.

16. Sallie Pisani, *The CIA and the Marshall Plan* (Lawrence: University Press of Kansas, 1991), 30.

17. James Srodes, *Allen Dulles: Master of Spies* (Washington, DC: Regnery, 1999), 21; Peter Grose, *Gentleman Spy: The Life of Allen Dulles* (New York: Houghton Mifflin, 1994), 5, 36.

18. Stephen Kinzer, *The Brothers: John Foster Dulles, Allen Dulles, and Their Secret World War* (New York: Times Books, 2013), 9–12.

19. Allen Dulles, *The Craft of Intelligence* (Guilford, CT: Lyons Press, 2006), vii–viii; Grose, *Gentleman Spy*, 18–19.

20. Grose, *Gentleman Spy*, 20–23, 66; Dulles, *The Craft of Intelligence*, viii.

21. Grose, *Gentleman Spy*, 25–31; Srodes, *Dulles*, 80; Kinzer, *The Brothers*, 23.

22. Grose, *Gentleman Spy*, 37; Srodes, *Dulles*, 91.

23. Kinzer, *The Brothers*, 34–35.

24. Grose, *Gentleman Spy*, 90.

25. Grose, 112. See footnote on this page.

26. Grose, 141–142; Allen Dulles, *The Secret Surrender* (New York: Harper & Row, 1966), 12–15.

9. LEGALIZING THE WORKING FUND

1. Thomas Troy, *Donovan and the CIA* (Frederick: University Publications of America, 1981), 374, 390; George M. Elsey to Clark Clifford, March 14, 1947, document

210, Foreign Relations of the United States, 1945–1950, Emergence of the Intelligence Establishment, https://history.state.gov/historicaldocuments/frus1945-50Intel (hereafter, FRUS).

2. Comptroller General Lindsay Warren to the Director of the Budget Bureau James Webb, March 12, 1948, Historical Study of the Use of Confidential Funds, January 1, 1953, appendix B, CIA-RDP78-05246A000100010001-3, CREST, NARA.

3. CIA General Counsel (Houston) to DCI (Hillenkoetter), April 8, 1948, document 231, FRUS.

4. Houston to Hillenkoetter.

5. Houston to Hillenkoetter.

6. R. Hillenkoetter Statement at classified Hearing of the House Armed Services Committee, April 8, 1948, CIA-RDP90-00610R000100230001-1, CREST.

7. Hillenkoetter Statement, CIA-RDP90-00610R000100230001-1.

8. CIA Office of the General Counsel, *in* Proposed CIA Legislation, Memorandum for the Record (MFR), February 7, 1949, CIA-RDP59-00882R000200030086-0, CREST.

9. CIA OGC MFR, CIA-RDP59-00882R000200030086-0.

10. Mac Johnson, "Anarchy Grips Bogota, Says Eyewitnesses," *Washington Post*, April 10, 1948.

11. Arthur B. Darling, *The Central Intelligence Agency: An Instrument of Government, to 1950* (University Park: Pennsylvania State University Press, 1991), 241.

12. Darling, *The Central Intelligence Agency*, 240–241; United Press, "Marshall May Face Bogota Revolt Quiz," *Washington Post*, April 26, 1948.

13. Darling, *The Central Intelligence Agency*, 242–244; David Barrett, *The CIA and Congress: The Untold Story from Truman to Kennedy* (Lawrence: University Press of Kansas, 2005), 35.

14. Lawrence Houston to Roscoe Hillenkoetter, May 7, 1948, document 234, FRUS; Darling, *The Central Intelligence Agency*, 190. See fn. 58 at bottom of page.

15. Senate Hearing on S. 2688, 80th Cong. Rec., Senate, June 19, 1948, 9107, https://www.congress.gov/bound-congressional-record/1948/06/19/senate-section.

16. Senate Hearing on S. 2688, 9107.

17. Senate Hearing on S. 2688, 9107; Lawrence Houston to Robert Gates, March 9, 1987, CIA-RDP89G00643R001000030025-6, CREST; Also see Barrett, *The CIA and Congress*, 41, 43, Pforzeimer's notes on the CIA Act of 1949, undated, CIA-RDP01-01773R000300010006-5.pdf, CREST. I've always wanted to know what was said in that private conversation outside the Senate chamber following McMahon's floor speech. I recently found a cache of notes from Pforzheimer in the CREST system on the legislative history of the CIA Act of 1949, which sheds some light on the intense conversation that transpired. In the typed notes, Pforzheimer alludes to the confrontation, candidly stating, "The 48 Act where I blew Senator McMahon out of the water." He is clearly taking a lot of the credit here for changing McMahon's position.

18. "Minutes of Richard Bissell's meeting with the Council on Foreign Relations,

January 8, 1968," app. in Victor Marchetti and John D. Marks, *The CIA and the Cult of Intelligence* (New York: Dell, 1975), 370.

19. M.O. and S.O. refer to the OSS Morale Operations and Special Operations branches.

20. Lawrence Houston to John McCone *in* Legal Basis for Cold-War Activities, January 15, 1962, CIA-RDP73B00296R000400010028-7, CREST. Houston's ten-page legal brief on covert action discloses that the original enquiry came from Forrestal; Lawrence Houston to Roscoe Hillenkoetter, September 25, 1947, document 241, FRUS.

21. Darling, *The Central Intelligence Agency*, 257.

22. Darling, 321.

23. Policy Planning Staff Memorandum, May 4, 1948, document 269, FRUS; Draft of Policy Planning Staff's proposed NSC Directive, May 5, 1948, document 270, FRUS.

24. National Security Council Directive on Office of Special Projects [NSC 10/2], document 292, FRUS.

25. NSC 10/2, FRUS.

26. NSC 10/2, FRUS; Darling, 276. Lyman B. Kirkpatrick Jr., *The Real CIA: An Insider's View of the Strengths and Weaknesses of Our Government's Most Important Agency* (New York: Macmillan, 1968), 90; Darling, *The Central Intelligence Agency*, 273, 280; Burton Hersh, *The Old Boys: The American Elite and the Origins of the CIA* (St. Petersburg, FL: Tree Farm, 1992), 212–213.

27. Trieste was an independent city-state in 1947.

28. Along with Wisner, Kennan recommended Matthias Correa, Irving Brown, Norris Chipman (Foreign Service officer in Paris), Francis Stevens (chief of the Russian Division), and John Davies (member of Policy Planning Staff).

29. Hersh, *The Old Boys*, 177–200. See George Kennan to Robert Lovett, June 30, 1948, document 294, FRUS.

30. Kirkpatrick, *The Real CIA*, 90.

31. Darling, 275–279. NSC 10/2, document 292, FRUS.

32. Lawrence Houston to Roscoe Hillenkoetter, DCI *in* GAO Relationships for Fiscal Year 1949, June 29, 1948, CIA-RDP78-04718A000300240006-8, CREST.

33. Houston to Hillenkoetter, CIA-RDP78-04718A000300240006-8.

34. Houston to Hillenkoetter, CIA-RDP78-04718A000300240006-8.

35. Houston to Hillenkoetter, CIA-RDP78-04718A000300240006-8.

36. Memorandum on Central Intelligence Agency, January 1, 1959, CIA-RDP80-01240A000100140093-5, CREST.

37. Joseph M. Jones, *The Fifteen Weeks: An Inside Account of the Genesis of the Marshall Plan* (New York: Harbinger, 1964), 239–256; George Kennan, *George Kennan Memoirs 1925–1950* (New York: Pantheon, 1967), 325–353.

38. Richard Bissell with Jonathan E. Lewis and Frances T. Pudlo, *Reflections of a Cold Warrior: From Yalta to the Bay of Pigs* (New Haven: Yale University Press, 1996), 67–68.

39. Bissell, *Reflections of a Cold Warrior*, 68–69; Hersh, *The Old Boys*, 219–220; Hersh interviewed Bissell in 1983 and 1986.

40. Michael Warner, ed., “Finance Division to the CIA Executive, OPC, October 17, 1949,” chap. 57 in *CIA Cold War Records: The CIA under Harry Truman* (Washington, DC: Center for the Study of Intelligence, CIA, 1994), 321.

41. Warner, “Finance Division to the CIA Executive,” 321.

42. Warner, “Finance Division to the CIA Executive,” 321.

43. Warner, “Finance Division to the CIA Executive,” 321.

44. Sallie Pisani, *The CIA and the Marshall Plan* (Lawrence: University Press of Kansas, 1991), 72–73.

10. THE CENTRAL INTELLIGENCE AGENCY ACT OF 1949

1. Hillenkoetter submitted a new draft of CIA enabling legislation to Millard Tydings (D- Maryland), the chairman of the Senate Armed Services Committee, and to Sam Rayburn (D-Texas), the Speaker of the House, on February 11.

2. Roscoe Hillenkoetter to James Webb, November 29, 1948, CIA-RDP90-00610R000100170053-1, CREST, US National Archives and Records Administration, Washington, DC (NARA); Roscoe Hillenkoetter to Millard Tydings, February 11, 1949, Records of the Senate Armed Services Committee, 81st Cong., NARA; Roscoe Hillenkoetter to Samuel Rayburn, February 11, 1949, document 239, Foreign Relations of the United States, 1945–1950, Emergence of the Intelligence Establishment, https://history.state.gov/historicaldocuments/frus1945-50Intel (hereafter, FRUS); CIA calendar notes from March 5, 1949, CIA-RDP91-00682R000100090030-2, CREST.

3. C. P. Trussell, “House, 348–4, Votes a Secret Spy Bill,” *New York Times*, March 8, 1949; David Barrett, *The CIA and Congress: The Untold Story from Truman to Kennedy* (Lawrence: University Press of Kansas, 2005), 44–45.

4. W. Park Armstrong to Robert Lovett, January 11, 1949, document 238, FRUS.

5. Section 10b was the same as Section 7b of S. 2668. The language was left unchanged.

6. Armstrong to Lovett, document 238, FRUS.

7. Lawrence Houston, Memorandum for Files, Proposed CIA Legislation, February 7, 1949, CIA-RDP59-00882R000200030086-0, CREST.

8. Houston memo for files, CIA-RDP59-00882R000200030086-0.

9. Houston memo for files, CIA-RDP59-00882R000200030086-0.

10. Lawrence Houston to Allen Dulles, E. Lyle Fisher, October 9, 1958, CIA-RDP80R01731R000100160041-3, CREST.

11. 81 Cong. Rec. (1946); CIA calendar notes dated from February 25, 1949, and March 4, 1949, CIA-RDP91-00682R000100090030-2, CREST.

12. John Norris, “Spy System Legalized in Defense Bill,” *Washington Post*, March 5, 1949.

13. CIA calendar notes from March 5, 1949, CIA-RDP91-00682R000100090030-2, CREST; 81 Cong. Rec. Durham’s House floor speech, March 7, 1949, vol. 95, part 2,

1945, https://www.congress.gov/bound-congressional-record/1949/03/07/house-section; Trussell, "House, 348–4, Votes a Secret Spy Bill."

14. 81 Cong. Rec., Celler's House floor speech, March 7, 1949, vol. 95, part 2, 1945, https://www.congress.gov/bound-congressional-record/1949/03/07/house-section.

15. 81 Cong. Rec., Celler's speech, March 7, 1949, vol. 95, part 2, 1945.

16. 81 Cong. Rec., Marcantonio House floor speech, Celler's House floor speech, March 7, 1949, vol. 95, part 2,1946-1947, https://www.congress.gov/bound-congressional-record/1949/03/07/house-section; John Norris, "House Guards Debate, Passes Spy Bill, 348–4," *Washington Post*, March 8, 1949.

17. Memorandum on Central Intelligence Agency, January 1, 1959, CIA-RDP80-01240A000100140093-5, CREST.

18. Memo on CIA, CIA-RDP80-01240A000100140093-5.

19. Memo on CIA, CIA-RDP80-01240A000100140093-5. The reference for the GAO letter is B-74155.

20. Lawrence Houston, Memorandum for the Files, The Comptroller General's Views on H.R.2663, March 11, 1949, CIA-RDP57-00384R000200080080-6.

21. Pat McCarran, Chairman Senate Judiciary Committee to Millard Tydings, Chairman Armed Services Committee, March 11, 1949, Records of the Senate Armed Services Committee, 81st Cong., NARA.

22. Roscoe Hillenkoetter to Pat McCarran, March 18, 1949, Records of the Senate Armed Services Committee, 81st Cong., NARA.

23. A few days before the bill came to a vote in the Senate, James Forrestal, the former defense secretary, committed suicide. Inexplicably, he managed to open a window in his bathroom in the psychiatric ward in Bethesda Naval Hospital at 2 a.m. on May 22, and he fell thirteen floors to his death. Forrestal, who resigned on March 28, had played a major role in the formative organizational development of the CIA and in all the major decisions on NSC 10/2 and the CIA Act of 1949. I surmise that his death would have had a chilling effect on Congress that week.

24. 81 Cong. Rec. 6952, May 29, 1949; Marshall Andrews, "Senate Votes Protection for Agents of CIA," *Washington Post*, May 28, 1949; CIA OGC report, CIA-RDP59-00882R000200030086-0, CREST.

25. Roscoe Hillenkoetter to Millard Tydings, June 1, 1949, Records of the Senate Armed Services Committee, 81st Cong., NARA; "House Passes Intelligence Secrecy Bill," *Washington Post*, June 8, 1949.

26. DCI (Hillenkoetter) to the Comptroller General (Warren), August 17, 1949, CIA-RDP80-01240A000100140047-6, CREST; Memo on Central Intelligence Agency, CIA-RDP80-01240A000100140093-5.

27. Historical Notes, "Budget and Finance Activities: CIA and Predecessor Organizations," CIA-RDP83-01034R000200140004-1, CREST.

28. The Special and Administrative support staffs were originally named Covert and Overt support staffs. The names were changed four days after Hillenkoetter

ordered the reorganization "in the expectation that a more innocuous nomenclature would help to safeguard CIA's administrative contacts with outside agencies."

29. Memo on CIA, CIA-RDP80-01240A000100140093-5; The Support Services Historical Series The Office of Logistics—An Overview 1945–70, July 1, 1972, CIA-RDP93-00939R000100120001-3, CREST.

30. Arthur B. Darling, *The Central Intelligence Agency: An Instrument of Government, to 1950* (University Park: Pennsylvania State University Press, 1991), 280–281.

31. DCI to budget officer, Chief Special Support Staff, Reserve Fund, August 23, 1960, CIA-RDP80-01240A000400100017-0.

32. Michael Warner, ed., "Intelligence Memorandum 225: Estimate of Status of Atomic Warfare in the USSR," chap. 56 in *CIA Cold War Records: The CIA under Harry Truman* (Washington, DC: Center for the Study of Intelligence, CIA, 1994), 319; Robert Albright, "Grave Senate Hears Soviet A-Bomb News," *Washington Post*, September 24, 1949; Richard Rhodes, *Dark Sun: The Making of the Hydrogen Bomb* (New York: Simon & Shuster, 1995), 371–372.

11. THE MILITARY-INTELLIGENCE-INDUSTRIAL COMPLEX

1. George S. Jackson and Martin P. Claussen, "Organizational History of the Central Intelligence Agency, 1950–53," CIA History Program, HS-2 (CIA Historical Staff), 5–6 (also see footnote 1 on p. 150), https://www.cia.gov/readingroom/docs/THE%20CIA%20HISTORY%20PROGRAM%5B16307599%5D.pdf; David Barrett, *The CIA and Congress: The Untold Story from Truman to Kennedy* (Lawrence: University Press of Kansas, 2005), 120–121; Statement of Robert F. Hale, Assistant Director, National Security Division, Congressional Budget Office before the Defense and international Affairs Task Committee on the Budget U.S. House of Representatives, September 14, 1987, https://www.cbo.gov/sites/default/files/100th-congress-1987-1988/reports/87d0c97_0.pdf.

2. Notes from CIA's historical staff: Financial Operations of the Central Intelligence Agency, 1945–1952, CIA-RDP83-01034R000200140004-1, CREST.

3. "President Dwight Eisenhower's Farewell Address to the nation, January 17, 1961," YouTube, uploaded by someoddstuff, January 16, 2011, https://www.youtube.com/watch?v=CWiIYW_fBfY.

4. CIA Memorandum from David Addington. Relationship between the Central Intelligence Agency and the General Accounting Office, CIA-RDP81M00980R001500080003-5, CREST.

5. CIA OGC report, Historical Study of the Use of Confidential Funds, 7–8, January 1, 1953, CIA-RDP78-05246A000100010001-3, CREST.

6. CIA OGC Report, Historical Study of the Use of Confidential Funds, CIA-RDP78-05246A000100010001-3.

7. George Washington, First Annual Address to Congress Online by Gerhard Peters and John T. Woolley, The American Presidency Project, https://www

.presidency.ucsb.edu/documents/first-annual-address-congress-0; CIA Office of General Counsel report, Historical Study of the Use of Confidential Funds, 31, CIA-RDP78-05246A000100010001-3.

8. Annals of Congress, 1st Cong., 2nd sess., 1098–1103, 1117.

9. Henry Merritt Wriston, *Executive Agents in American Foreign Relations* (Baltimore, MD: Johns Hopkins, 1929), 157, 208–211 (see fn. 2 and 12); William Maclay, *The Journal of William Maclay United States Senator from Pennsylvania from 1789 to 1791* (New York: D. Appleton, 1890), 401 (entry for February 25, 1791). Also see *American State Papers: Foreign Relations*, 1:137–138; Annals of Congress, 13 Cong. 1st sess., 753. Act of July 1, 1790, Intercourse of the United States and Foreign Nations, Ch. 12, 2, 1–2 Stat. 128.

10. The capture of any of the four capitals offered little benefit in the form of bounty and presented a host of other problems associated with occupying an Islamic desert enclave.

11. Wriston, *Executive Agents in American Foreign Relations*, 25, 209, 249–250; Jacob Read to George Washington, February 2, 1784, Letters of Delegates to Congress, vol. 21, Library of Congress Web Archives, https://webarchive.loc.gov/all/20211105194005/https://memory.loc.gov/cgi-bin/query/r?ammem/hlaw:@field(DOCID+@lit(dg021257)); Thomas Mifflin to David Humphreys, May 17, 1784, Letters of Delegates to Congress, vol. 21, https://webarchive.loc.gov/all/20211105195054/https://memory.loc.gov/cgi-bin/query/r?ammem/hlaw:@field(DOCID+@lit(dg021477)); Expenses on Foreign Intercourse, 7 November 1792, *American State Papers: Foreign Affairs*, 1:137; Senate Executive Journal. 1st Congress, 1st sess., February 18, 1791, 74, https://memory.loc.gov/ammem/amlaw/lwej.html.

12. Under the law, the president could delegate his authority to the secretary of state.

13. Act of February 9, 1793, Ch. 4, 1–2 Stat., 299, https://maint.loc.gov/law/help/statutes-at-large/2nd-congress/session-2/c2s2ch4.pdf. Act of March 27, 1794, Ch. 12, 1-Stat. 350, https://tile.loc.gov/storage-services/service/ll/llsl//llsl-c3/llsl-c3.pdf. CIA OGC Report, Historical Study of the Use of Confidential Funds, CIA-RDP78-05246A000100010001-3.

14. Act of March 27, 1794, 3d Cong., 1st Sess., Ch. 12, 1–9 Stat., 350, https://maint.loc.gov/law/help/statutes-at-large/3rd-congress/session-1/c3s1ch12.pdf; Act of June 5, 1794, 3d Cong., 1st Sess., Ch. 46, 1–3 Stat., 376; Act of June 9, 1794, 3d Cong., 1st Sess., Ch. 64, 1–8 Stat., 395; *American State Papers: Claims*, 1:300, *American State Papers: Foreign Relations:* 2:348.

15. *American State Papers: Foreign Relations* 1:137–138.

16. *American State Papers: Foreign Relations* 2:368–381.

17. Although the missing $78,588 was the most troublesome account, other unsettled accounts on his watch also remained unresolved, such as David Humphreys's salary, which never reached him.

18. *American State Papers: Finance*, 1:752–754.

19. Wriston, *Executive Agents in American Foreign Relations*, 316, 368, 406, 526–527, 572–573.

20. The Louisiana Purchase was politically significant on several levels. As the country expanded westward, the demographics and population base of the United States changed. The addition of new states diluted the political power of the original thirteen states in the Senate, dramatically altering the geographical distribution of congressional power.

21. Annals of Cong., 7th Cong., 2nd sess., 102–103. Act of February 26, 1803, Ch. 7, 2 Stat. 2.

22. Wriston, *Executive Agents in American Foreign Relations*, 407–408; James F. Rippy, *Joel R. Poinsett: Versatile American* (Durham: Duke University Press, 1935), 37–39.

23. Samuel E. Morison, "The Henry-Crillon Affair of 1812," *Proceedings of the Massachusetts Historical Society* 49 (1947–50): 207–231.

24. *Senate Journal*, 11th Cong., 2nd sess., December 26–27, 1809, Library of Congress, https://memory.loc.gov/ammem/amlaw/lwsjlink.html#anchor11. *American State Papers: Finance* 3:123–127.

25. *Senate Journal*, December 26–27, 1809. *American State Papers: Finance* 3:123–127.

26. *American State Papers: Finance* 5: 997–998.

27. See bills H.R. 392, 20th Cong., 2nd sess., January 23, 1929, and H.R. 148, 21st Cong., 1st sess., Jan. 22, 1930.

12. THE GAO AND THE COLD WAR

1. Frederick Mosher, *The GAO: The Quest for Accountability in American Government* (Baton Rouge: Louisiana State University Press, 1984), 103.

2. Here is another important initiative where the GAO, Treasury Department, and Bureau of the Budget met to discuss a complex fiscal matter of mutual interest. In this case, the three financial controllers closely coordinated on the development a new paradigm for transforming the GAO's audit of the executive branch.

3. Roger Trask, *Defender of the Public Interest: The General Accounting Office, 1921–1966* (Washington, DC: Government Printing Office, 1996), 313; Mosher, *The GAO*, 113, 122.

4. Trask, *Defender of the Public Interest*, 322–323.

5. Mosher, *The GAO*, 113–114.

6. Trask, *Defender of the Public Interest*, 149–173; Quote taken from Mosher, *The GAO*, 125.

7. Mosher, 123–124; Trask, *Defender of the Public Interest*, 362–364.

8. Fiscal Inspector to Chief, Fiscal Division, undated, CIA-RDP80-01370R00010 0070019-4, CREST, NARA.

9. A comptroller was also appointed to the army, navy, and air force to oversee the financial operations of the armed forces.

10. Trask, *Defender of the Public Interest*, 335–336; Mosher, *The GAO*, 118–119.

11. Trask, *Defender of the Public Interest*, 376–377.

12. Mosher, *The GAO*, 151–152; Trask, *Defender of the Public Interest*, 377–381.

13. Testimony of E. L. Fisher to the House Armed Services Committee, January 10, 1956, Theodore R. McKeldin Library, University of Maryland, CIS-No: 84 H1584-A.4, 5083.

14. Here, Section 2c of the Armed Services Procurement Act of 1947 lists seventeen exceptions that allow the military to use negotiated contracts in place of formal advertised bidding. The first exception 2c (1) states contracts may be negotiated "if it is determined to be necessary in the public interest during the period of a national emergency declared by the President or the by the Congress."

15. Testimony of E. L. Fisher to the House Armed Services Committee, January 10, 1956, Theodore R. McKeldin Library, University of Maryland, CIS-No: 84 H1584-A.4, 5083.

16. Statement of Lyle Fisher at the American Management Association Meeting Hotel Astor, New York City, December 11, 1961, Fisher family records.

17. Trask, *Defender of the Public Interest*, 378.

18. Congressional testimony from Robert Keller, GAO Assistant to the comptroller general to the Armed Services Committee, April 1, 1958, 115–116, https://www.google.com/books/edition/Hearings_on_Investigation_of_National_De/LNQtAAAAMAAJ?hl=en&gbpv=1. (For complete GAO testimony, see 111–120.)

19. CIA Memorandum from David Addington, Relationship between the Central Intelligence Agency and the General Accounting Office, CIA-RDP81M00980R0015 00080003-5, CREST.

20. Addington, Relationship between the Central Intelligence Agency and The General Accounting Office, CIA-RDP81M00980R001500080003-5.

21. Organization and Functions of The Director's Office and Staff of the Psychological Strategy Board, December 20, 1951, CIA-RDP80R01731R003300410025-8, CREST.

22. Charles Norberg to L. Houston, Legislative Problems of the Psychological Strategy Board, January 15, 1952, CIA-RDP57-00384R000100190024-7, CREST.

13. 1950

1. Dean Acheson, *Present at the Creation: My Years in the State Department* (New York: W. W. Norton, 1969), 374.

2. David Barrett, *The CIA and Congress: The Untold Story from Truman to Kennedy* (Lawrence: University Press of Kansas, 2005), 84.

3. Barrett, *The CIA and Congress*, 84.

4. Arthur Darling, *The Central Intelligence Agency: An Instrument of Government, to 1950* (University Park: Pennsylvania State University Press, 1990), 301–302; Ludwell L. Montague, *General Walter Bedell Smith as Director of the Central Intelligence: October 1950–February 1953* (University Park: Pennsylvania State University Press, 1992), 9–12, 41–43.

5. National Security Council Resolution, January 13, 1948, document 336, Foreign

Relations of the United States, 1945–1950, Emergence of the Intelligence Establishment, https://history.state.gov/historicaldocuments/frus1945-50Intel. Montague, *General Walter Bedell Smith*, 41–48.

6. Montague, *General Walter Bedell Smith*, 5–9, 53–56.

7. Lyman B. Kirkpatrick, *The Real CIA: An Insider's View of the Strengths and Weaknesses of Our Government's Most Important Agency* (New York: Macmillan, 1968), 86.

8. Montague, *General Walter Bedell Smith*, 91–92, 129, 205, 209.

14. CLANDESTINE FINANCIAL ADMINISTRATION

1. Ludwell L. Montague, *General Walter Bedell Smith as Director of the Central Intelligence: October 1950–February 1953* (University Park: Pennsylvania State University Press, 1992), 39, 60–62, 67.

2. CIA's historical staff, Historical Notes Re: Budget and Finance Activities CIA and Predecessor Organizations Period: 20 September 1945–28 January 1952, CIA-RDP83-01034R000200140004-1, CREST, NARA.

3. The top administrative official at the CIA bore several different titles in the early years. Walter Ford was the first person to head administration (1946–1948). While he was serving, his title changed four times: from executive, to executive director, to executive for administration, and, finally, to CIA executive. McConnel was the first deputy director of administration.

4. George S. Jackson and Martin P. Claussen, The DCI Historical Series: "Organizational History of the Central Intelligence Agency Chapter X Conduct of the Agency Business," 34, 190 08/25/07, entry A1-21, rec. group 263.2.2, NARA, also available online at https://drive.google.com/file/d/1bDopKpGMbVuWuZtdy9ROPJ48r8ifp1jG/view; Montague, *General Walter Bedell Smith*, 85–86.

5. Montague, 85–90.

6. Allen Dulles appointed Lawrence (Red) White as the acting deputy director on July 1, 1953; he was named deputy director on May 21, 1954. White kept a personal diary of his daily work schedule at the CIA. This collection of declassified diary entries spanned his entire career and has become an important scholarly resource for CIA researchers (though there are many redactions). These notes can be found by conducting advanced searches of the CREST database.

7. James Hanrahan, "An Interview with Former CIA Executive Director Lawrence K. 'Red' White," January 7, 1998, see https://www.cia.gov/resources/csi/studies-in-intelligence/archives/vol-43-no-3/an-interview-with-former-executive-director-lawrence-k-red-white/.

8. Jackson and Claussen, "Organizational History of the Central Intelligence Agency," 45.

9. Jackson and Claussen, 41–42; Dulles-Jackson-Correa Report, January 1, 1949, CIA-RDP86B00269R000500040001-1, CREST.

10. Jackson and Claussen, 45–48 (see fn 3 on 48).

11. Montague, *General Walter Bedell Smith*, 89–90 (fn on 90).

12. Chief, Special Support Staff, Finance Division Emmett Echols to Management Officer, March 28, 1950, CIA-RDP61-00274A000100030002-2, CREST.

13. The Finance Division, Special Support Staff was formerly the Confidential Funds Division.

14. Emmett Echols to Management Officer, March 28, 1950, CIA-RDP61-00274A 000100030002-2; CIA Executive Clarence Winecoff to the DCI Roscoe Hillenkoetter, April 6, 1950, CIA-RDP61-00274A000100030002-2, CREST.

15. Lyle Shannon to the Roscoe Hillenkoetter, May 1, 1950, CIA-RDP61-00274A00 0100030002-2, CREST.

16. It was also an unpublished position under Section 7 of the CIA Act of 1949.

17. Historical Notes Re: Budget and Finance Activities Cia and Predecessor Organizations Period: 20 September 1945–28 January 1952, January 29, 1952, CIA-RDP83 –01034R000200140004-1, CREST; Clark Committee CIA Task Force Briefing on the Office of the Comptroller, CIA-RDP78-05551A000100060032-5, CREST; Jackson and Claussen, "Organizational History of the Central Intelligence Agency," 162.

18. Jackson and Claussen, "Organizational History of the Central Intelligence Agency," 160; Memorandum from the Deputy Comptroller to the Comptroller, May 7, 1952, and Organizational charts of Administration Directorate from 1946 to 1953, CIA-RDP78-03568A000400010021-3, CREST.

19. The Technical Accounting Staff was responsible for developing and installing new accounting systems and financial reporting methods and procedures for the broad range of intelligence operations carried out by the Agency, while Programs Analysis Staff developed and maintained operational methods of financial analysis and program evaluation. It prepared and distributed analytical reports and statements to appropriate Agency personnel.

20. Deputy Comptroller to the Comptroller, May 7, 1952, CIA-RDP78-03568A 000400010021-3; Jackson and Claussen, "Organizational History of the Central Intelligence Agency," 160–161; CIA Historical Staff, Historical Notes Re: Budget and Finance Activities CIA, CIA-RDP83-01034R000200140004-1.

21. Jackson and Claussen, "Organizational History of the Central Intelligence Agency," 150, 162.

22. Assistant Chief, Monetary Branch, Memorandum for the Record (MFR), April 14, 1952, CIA-RDP78-04914A000200160064-9; Office of the Comptroller: Functions and Activities, December 6, 1954, CIA-RDP78-05551A000100050001-0, CREST.

23. Office of the Comptroller, undated (~1954), CIA-RDP62-01094R00050001 0019-3, CREST; Office of the Comptroller Functions and Activities, CIA-RDP7805551A 000100050001-0.

24. Office of the Comptroller, undated, CIA-RDP62-01094R000500010019-3; Office of the Comptroller Functions and Activities, CIA-RDP78-05551A000100050001-0.

25. Jackson and Claussen, "Organizational History of the Central Intelligence Agency," 161, 181.

26. Jackson and Claussen, 156–157, 181–182; Interview with Eugene Foster Chief, Audit Staff, History of Audit Staff, 1953–1956, CIA-RDP84-00022R000400160003-1, CREST.

27. Memorandum from DD/P (Wisner) to DCI (Dulles), April 21, 1953, CIA-RDP7804718A002600370036-6, CREST. Foster Interview, CIA-RDP84-00022R000 400160003-1; Jackson and Claussen, 157. Also see internal draft of document titled, "Organization and Functions Office of the Deputy Director (Administration): Auditor-in-Chief," June 8, 1954, CIA-RDP78-04718A000900090112-1, CREST.

28. Jackson and Claussen, "Organizational History of the Central Intelligence Agency," 161.

29. Office of the Comptroller, Functions and Activities, CIA-RDP78-05551 A000100050001-0; Office of the Comptroller, undated, CIA-RDP62-01094R0005 00010019-3; CIA OGC, Historical Use of Confidential Funds, app. N, CIA-RDP78 -05246A000100010001-3, CREST.

30. CIA Budget Staff Report, CIA-RDP61-00274A000100030002-2.

31. In 1955, Allen Dulles changed the name of the Audit Office to the Audit Staff, and he changed the office head's title from "auditor in chief" to the less authoritative "chief, Audit Staff."

32. Three pages of notes from CIA's historical staff: Questions Regarding the History of the Audit Staff 1953–1956, CIA-RDP84-00022R000400160002-2, CREST.

33. CIA's historical staff: Questions Regarding the History of the Audit Staff, CIA-RDP84-00022R000400160002-2.

34. Questions and Answers Concerning GAO Audit as Discussed with the DD/S, Assistant DD/S, General Counsel, DD/S Liaison Officer (Sanitized), Comptroller and Deputy Comptroller, see note 364, CIA-RDP78-05747A000100080002-9, CREST.

35. Montague, *General Walter Bedell Smith*, 105.

36. Montague, 105–106.

37. Montague, 105–106; Jackson and Claussen, "Organizational History of the Central Intelligence Agency," 118–121.

38. Memorandum from William Jackson to Stuart Hedden: Accountability of CIA to the Public on its Expenditure of Public Funds, April 14, 1952, CIA-RD P80R01731R001300130001-7, CREST.

39. Montague, *General Walter Bedell Smith*, 106–107.

40. Lyman B. Kirkpatrick Jr., *The Real CIA: An Insider's View of the Strengths and Weaknesses of Our Government's Most Important Agency* (New York: Macmillan, 1968), 130, 140.

41. Definition from Sanction Scanner web page, https://sanctionscanner.com/kn owledge-base/front-company-826.

42. Roger Trask, *Defender of the Public Interest: The General Accounting Office, 1921–1966* (Washington, DC: Government Printing Office, 1996), 208–209.

43. Stuart Hedden, CIA Inspector General, MFR, January 2, 1952, 5033ccd499

3245e65b81466d, CREST; William Leary, Aircraft and Anti-Communist: CAT in Action 1949–1952, CIA-RDP76-00702R000100050001-2, CREST.

44. Clandestine Services History, Civil Air Transport (CAT): A Proprietary Airline 1946–1955, vol. 1, 59–60, 52371fe2993294098d51762b, CREST.

45. Clandestine Services History, Civil Air Transport (CAT): A Proprietary Airline 1946–1955, vol. 2, 1–2, 52371fe2993294098d517629, CREST.

46. Stuart Hedden, MFR, 5033ccd4993245e65b81466d. Civil Air Transport, vol. 2, 52371fe2993294098d517629.

47. Civil Air Transport, 4–5, 52371fe2993294098d517629.

48. Stuart Hedden, MFR, 5033ccd4993245e65b81466d; Sallie Pisani, *The CIA and Marshall Plan* (Lawrence: University Press of Kansas, 1991), 78.

49. Pisani, 78.

15. CIA-GAO LIAISON UNDER THE CIA ACT OF 1949

1. Lawrence Houston to Murray McConnel, November 15, 1950, CIA-RDP78-05844A000100140008-8, CREST.

2. Houston to McConnel, CIA-RDP78-05844A000100140008-8; Sheffield Edwards to Lawrence Houston, January 15, 1951, CIA-RDP84-00709R000400080098-4, CREST.

3. After updating McConnel, Houston requested top secret clearance for Lyle Fisher from Sheffield Edwards, chief of the Security Division. Fisher was "security approved for liaison purposes" for "discussions involving material classified through Top Secret."

4. Internal CIA Memorandum (names deleted), June 26, 1953, CIA-RDP57-00384R001200240037-5, CREST.

5. Internal CIA Memorandum (names deleted), CIA-RDP57-00384R00120024 0037-5, see note 384; Arthur Darling, *The Central Intelligence Agency: An Instrument of Government, to 1950* (University Park: Pennsylvania State University Press, 1990), 192.

6. Lindsay Warren to Bedell Smith, November 21, 1951, CIA-RDP90-00610R0001 00160014-5, CREST; Lawrence Houston to Allen Dulles, October 9, 1958, CIA-RDP80R01731R000100160041-3, CREST; Lawrence Houston, Memorandum for the Record (MFR), August 13, 1956, CIA-RDP59-00882R000200 180020-6, CREST.

7. Walter Pforzheimer, MFR, January 31, 1952, CIA-RDP80-01370R0003000601 24-6, CREST.

8. Pforzheimer, CIA-RDP80-01370R000300060124-6.

9. Lawrence K. White to Walter B. Smith, July 28, 1952, CIA-RDP78-04718A00 0600310004-9, CREST. The attached appendix documents the meeting.

10. This money was most likely withdrawn from the unvouchered reserve fund.

11. White to Smith, CIA-RDP78-04718A000600310004-9.

12. Memorandum from Houston to Dulles, CIA-RDP80R01731R000100160041-3.

13. White to Smith, CIA-RDP78-04718A000600310004-9.

14. US General Accounting Office, *Principles of Federal Appropriations Law,* vol. 1, chap. 2, 13–14. https://www.gao.gov/legal/appropriations-law/red-book.

15. The deleted name was most likely Edward Saunders. His name is often redacted, but sometimes it slips through the cracks. Allen Dulles was not at this meeting, but the initiative has his fingerprints all over it.

16. Houston, No-Year Appropriations for CIA, January 25, 1954, CIA-RDP59-00882R000100110037-6, CREST.

17. Houston, CIA-RDP59-00882R000100110037-6.

18. New funds amounted to only $185 million because the House Appropriations Committee allowed the CIA to carry over $150 million that would normally have expired ($185 + $150 = $335). The $150 million represented the unexpended reserve fund from 1953 ($92 million) and 1954 ($58 million).

19. Chairman of the Appropriations Committee (John Taber) to the Director, Bureau of the Budget (Rowland Hughes), April 27, 1954; Edward R. Saunders to G. A. Nease, May 11, 1954, courtesy of David Barrett, see https://irp.fas.org/budget/cia1955.pdf.

20. Lawrence Houston, MFR, March 9, 1955, CIA-RDP59-00882R000100110042-0, CREST.

16. THE ANNUAL BUDGET RITUAL

1. Dulles-Jackson-Correa Report, CIA-RDP86B00269R000500040001-1, CREST.

2. Percival Brundage, *The Bureau of the Budget* (Westport, CT: Praeger, 1970), 223–224.

3. Allen Dulles to DD/P, DD/I, DD/A, Assistant Director Communication, Director of Training, October 24, 1953, CIA-RDP80R01731R000800050013-9, CREST.

4. Chairman of the Ad Hoc Working Group (E. Saunders) to the Chairman, US Intelligence Board, June 3, 1959, CIA-RDP80–01237A000100010015-9, CREST.

5. David Barrett, *The CIA and Congress: The Untold Story from Truman to Kennedy* (Lawrence: University Press of Kansas, 2005), 26.

6. Lyman B. Kirkpatrick Jr., *The Real CIA: An Insider's View of the Strengths and Weaknesses of Our Government's Most Important Agency* (New York: Macmillan, 1968), 136.

7. "Dulles Role on Bundy Hit by McCarthy," *Washington Post*, August 5, 1953; Kirkpatrick, *The Real CIA*, 136.

8. President D. Eisenhower to Lt. Gen. J. H. Doolittle, July 26, 1954, 5076de59993247d4d82b5b74, CREST.

9. Barrett, *The CIA and Congress*, 212. White House notes are quoted from Barrett.

10. Report on the Covert Activities of the Central Intelligence Agency (Doolittle Report), submitted to Eisenhower on September 30, 1954, 5076de59993247d4d82b5b74. Includes supporting documents.

11. Doolittle Report, 5076de59993247d4d82b5b74.

12. Memorandum for Director of Central Intelligence via Deputy Director Plans, December 12, 1955, CIA-RDP88-00374R000100280010-9, CREST; Doolittle Report, part E, 5076de59993247d4d82b5b74.

13. Memo for Director of Central Intelligence, CIA-RDP88-00374R000100280010-9; Merriman Smith, "8-Man Unit Selected to Survey CIA," *Washington Post*, January 14, 1956.

14. "Spotlight on Intelligence," *Washington Post*, March 23, 1954.

15. "13 Senators Propose 'Hill' Group to Eye CIA," *Washington Post*, January 15, 1955; "Mansfield Urges Unit to Eye CIA," *Washington Post*, February 7, 1955.

16. Smith, "8-Man Unit Selected to Survey CIA."

17. Peter Grose, *Gentleman Spy: The Life of Allen Dulles* (New York: Houghton Mifflin, 1994), 445–446.

18. Grose, *Gentleman Spy*, 446; Grose cites quotes from the report.

17. SECRET PROGRAMS UNDER THE CIA ACT OF 1949

1. Sidney Gottlieb ran the MKULTRA project from 1953 to 1966.

2. Summary of Remarks by Allen Dulles at the national alumni conference of the Graduate Council of Princeton University, Hot Springs, VA, April 10, 1953, CIA-RDP80R01731R001700030015-9, CREST, NARA.

3. Summary of Remarks by Allen Dulles, CIA-RDP80R01731R001700030015-9.

4. Dulles to Wolf, April 13, 1953, doc. 0000017352_0001, www.blackvault.com.

5. Gottlieb's payment requests to the Financial Division were directed through the TSS Budget Office via a TSS budget officer. The release of funds still required signature authority from someone high up in the Comptroller's Office. The need to know stopped there.

6. Lawrence White to Edward Saunders, April 17, 1953, doc. 0000017352_0007, www.blackvault.com.

7. Allen Dulles to Walter Wolf, April 13, 1953, doc. 0000017352_0001, www.blackvault.com. The amount that Dulles obligated has been redacted from the memo, but it is cited by John Marks. Marks, *The Search for the "Manchurian Candidate": The CIA and Mind Control: The Secret History of the Behavioral Sciences* (New York: W. W. Norton, 1991), 61.

8. DD/A and DD/P are CIA's acronym convention for Deputy Director of Administration and Deputy Director of Plans.

9. Memorandum for the Record (MFR) approved by Gottlieb, Gibbons, and deFlorez (the three certifying officers), April 24, 1955, Internet Archive (website), https://archive.org/details/DOC_0000017354/page/n9; Memorandum from S. Gottlieb to E. Saunders April 27, 1953, CIA-RDP78-04913A000100030103-8, CREST.

10. Draft Proposal for Subproject 2, Internet Archive (website), https://archive.org/details/DOC_0000017415/page/n35.

11. Memorandum for Chief, Finance Division (Echols) via TSS/Budget Officer, Internet Archive (website), https://archive.org/details/DOC_0000017426/page/n17; Marks, *The Search for the Manchurian Candidate*, 100.

12. Stephen Kinzer, *Poisoner in Chief: Sidney Gottlieb and the CIA Search for Mind Control* (New York: St. Martin's Griffin, 2020), 85–86.

13. Marks, *The Search for the Manchurian Candidate*, 71.

14. Kinzer, *Poisoner in Chief*, 130–131; https://archive.org/details/mkultra-overview-of-each-project/page/n69/mode/2up.

15. Marks, *The Search for the Manchurian Candidate*, 83–84.

16. Marks, *The Search for the Manchurian Candidate*, 89–91.

17. Lawrence K. White to Chief, Technical Services Staff, November 23, 1953, CIA-RDP78-04718A000100180170-5; Eugene Foster to Lawrence K. White, April 5, 1954, CIA-RDP78-04718A000100220078-3; Lawrence K. White to Eugen Foster, April 14, 1954, CIA-RDP78-04718A000100220051-2, CREST.

18. Lawrence K. White Diary Notes dated September 12, 1957, CIA-RDP76-00183R000200110039-0, CREST.

19. John Earman, Inspector General Report, July 26, 1963, Public Intelligence (website), https://publicintelligence.net/cia-ig-MKULTRA/.

20. After beginning my research of the U-2 program, I ordered a used copy of Bissell's memoir. Richard Bissell with Jonathan E. Lewis and Frances T. Pudlo, *Reflections of a Cold Warrior: From Yalta to the Bay of Pigs* (New Haven: Yale University Press, 1996). Written inside the book is a personal note from one of the coauthors: "To General Andrew J. Goodpaster, Best Regards, Jonathan Lewis."

21. Bissell, *Reflections of a Cold Warrior*, 95.

22. Kelly Johnson was Lockheed's project manager. A central participant on the corporate side, he coordinated closely with Richard Bissell.

23. Bissell, *Reflections of a Cold Warrior*, 92.

24. David Barrett, *The CIA and Congress: The Untold Story from Truman to Kennedy* (Lawrence: University Press of Kansas, 2005), 375–376.

25. Memorandum from Lawrence Houston to Richard Bissell, July 26, 1957, CIA-RDP62B00844R000200040015-3, CREST.

26. Houston to Bissell, CIA-RDP62B00844R000200040015-3.

27. Houston to Bissell, CIA-RDP62B00844R000200040015-3.

28. Houston to Bissell, August 26, 1957, CIA-RDP62B00844R000200040015-3.

29. Bissell, *Reflections of a Cold Warrior*, 96, 99–100.

30. Richard Bissell to Allen Dulles, October 25, 1957, CIA-RDP62B00844R000200040015-3, CREST.

31. Houston to Bissell, CIA-RDP62B00844R000200040015-3.

32. Houston to Bissell, CIA-RDP62B00844R000200040015-3.

33. Jonathan E. Lewis, *Spy Capitalism: ITEK and the CIA* (New Haven: Yale University Press, 2002), 263–269.

34. Edward Saunders to Security Officer, December 31, 1958, CIA-RDP70B00783R000100140049-5, CREST.

35. Itek is not an acronym, as use of all caps in the memo suggests.

36. Saunders to Security Officer, CIA-RDP70B00783R000100140049-5.

37. Bissell was fired by Kennedy after the Bay of Pigs and left his position at the NRO in February 1962. Joseph Charyk headed the agency after that.

38. Jeffrey T. Richelson, ed., Document 2: Memorandum of Understanding, *Management of the National Reconnaissance Program* (Draft), 20 July 1961, in Top Secret in National Security Archive Electronic Briefing Book 33, National Security Archive, George Washington University (website), September 27, 2000, http://nsarchive.gwu.edu/NSAEBB/NSAEBB35/.

39. McCone did not discuss his decision with anyone beforehand. Although Saunders's health was known to be failing, senior CIA officials were not too pleased with the way he departed from the CIA. Red White expressed his own inner conflict about the decision in his diary, CIA-RDP76-00183R000400010034-4.

40. The CIA Act of 1949 is also known as Public Law 110.

41. John Bross to Executive Director, undated; Memorandum of Understanding, National Reconnaissance Office Funding, July 20, 1961, CIA-RDP72R00410R000200040005-8, CREST; Jeffrey T. Richelson, ed., Document 6: Joseph Charyk, Memorandum for NRO Program Directors/Director, NRO Staff, *Organization and Functions of the NRO*, 23 July 1962, in Top Secret in National Security Archive Electronic Briefing Book 33, National Security Archive, George Washington University (website), September 27, 2000, http://nsarchive.gwu.edu/NSAEBB/NSAEBB35/.

18. THE DULLES LETTER

1. 85 Cong. Rec. 213 (January 9, 1958) (Jackson's speech from October 10); David Barrett, *The CIA and Congress: The Untold Story from Truman to Kennedy* (Lawrence: University Press of Kansas, 2005), 263.

2. "Transcript of the President's News Conference," *Washington Post*, May 1, 1958.

3. Tim Weiner, *Legacy of Ashes: The History of the CIA* (New York: Doubleday, 2007), 148, 151–153; Wayne G. Jackson, Allen Welsh Dulles as Director of Central Intelligence February 26, 1953, to November 29, 1961, Covert Action, vol. 3, (CIA Historical Staff), 108, National Security Archive (website), https://nsarchive.gwu.edu/document/28382-document-24-wayne-g-jackson-central-intelligence-agency-allen-welsh-dulles-director, accessed 10 April 2024.

4. Weiner, *Legacy of Ashes*, 146–154. Jackson, Allen Welsh Dulles as Director, 108–113.

5. "Blame for Attack on Nixon Debated," *Washington Post*, May 16, 1958; Warren Duffee, "U.S. Says Nixon Went Despite 3 Death Threats," *Washington Post*, May 20, 1958.

6. Barrett, *The CIA and Congress*, 290–296.

7. Burton Hersh, *The Old Boys: The American Elite and the Origins of the CIA* (St. Petersburg, FL: Tree Farm, 1992), 391–393; Weiner, *Legacy of Ashes*, 153.

8. Report to the President's Board of Consultants on the Congressional Relations, CIA-RDP78-04718A002500180002-5, CREST, NARA.

9. John Scali, "The $350-Million-a-Year CIA Writes Its Own Tight-Mouthed Ticket," *Washington Post*, June 29, 1958.

10. Lawrence Houston to Allen Dulles, October 9, 1958, CIA-RDP80R01731R000100160041-3, CREST.

11. Houston to Dulles, CIA-RDP80R01731R000100160041-3.

12. Lawrence K. White, Diary Notes, October 16, 1958, CIA-RDP76-00183R000300020138-9, CREST. This reference includes the guest list for the luncheon.

19. THE END OF PUBLIC ACCOUNTABILITY

1. Joseph Campbell to Paul Kilday, Special Subcommittee CIA, Committee on Armed Services, May 29, 1959, CIA-RDP74B00415R000300110002-1, CREST, NARA.

2. Campbell to Kilday, CIA-RDP74B00415R000300110002-1.

3. Paul Kilday to Allen Dulles, June 18, 1959, CIA-RDP74B00415R000300110002-1.

4. Kilday to Dulles June 18, 1959, CIA-RDP74B00415R000300110002-1.

5. Allen Dulles to Dwight Eisenhower, June 30, 1959, CIA-RDP74B00415R000300110002-1.

6. Dulles to Eisenhower, CIA-RDP74B00415R000300110002-1.

7. Minutes of Deputies Meeting, July 24, 1959, CIA-RDP80B01676R002400060111-9, CREST.

8. The July 30, 1959, meeting with Campbell and Samuelson took place on the anniversary of the historic letter from the NIA in 1946 to the Comptroller General (Warren) that established the working fund. Reference to the meeting is found in the letter from Dulles to Warren on October 16, 1959, CIA-RDP74B00415R000300110002-1.

9. The letter from Dulles to Campbell is dated on the one-year anniversary of the retirement lunch for the former GAO general counsel on October 16, 1958.

10. Dulles to Eisenhower, CIA-RDP74B00415R000300110002-1.

11. Allen Dulles to Joseph Campbell, October 16, 1959, CIA-RDP74B00415R000300110002-1.

12. Dulles to Campbell, CIA-RDP74B00415R000300110002-1.

13. Joseph Campbell to Allen Dulles, October 21, 1959, CIA-RDP74B00415R000300110002-1.

14. Campbell to Dulles, CIA-RDP74B00415R000300110002-1.

15. Eugene Pahl, Memorandum for the File, November 16, 1959, CIA-RDP80-01240A000100140084-5, CREST.

16. Eugene Pahl, Memorandum for the File, March 22, 1960, CIA-RDP80-01240

A000100140079-1, CREST; Eugene Pahl to Lawrence White, January 11, 1961, CIA-RDP80–01240A000100140033-1, CREST.

17. Pahl memo, March 22, 1960, CIA-RDP80–01240A000100140079-1.

18. Drew Pearson, "No One Holds CIA Purse Strings," *Washington Post*, May 10, 1961.

19. Joseph Campbell to Paul Kilday, May 16, 1961, CIA-RDP74B00415R000300 110002-1.

20. Carl Vinson to Joseph Campbell, May 18, 1961, CIA-RDP74B00415R000300 110002-1.

21. Eugene Pahl, Memorandum to the Files, May 24, 1962, CIA-RDP80-0124 0A000100140060-1, CREST; Eugene Pahl, Memorandum to the Files, June 11, 1962, CIA-RDP80-01240A000100140058-4, CREST.

22. Joseph Campbell to Carl Vinson, June 21, 1962, CIA-RDP74B00415R0003 00110002-1.

23. Campbell to Vinson, CIA-RDP74B00415R000300110002-1.

24. Vinson to Campbell, July 11, 1962, CIA-RDP74B00415R000300110002-1.

20. HIDDEN COSTS

1. Dulles-Jackson-Correa Report, January 1, 1949, CIA-RDP86B00269R0005 00040001-1, CREST; George S. Jackson and Martin P. Claussen, The DCI Historical Series "Organizational History of the Central Intelligence Agency Chapter X Conduct of the Agency Business," 41–53, 7 08/25/190, entry A1-21, RG 263.2, NARA, also available online at https://drive.google.com/file/d/1bDopKpGMbVuWuZtdy9ROPJ4 8r8ifp1jG/view.

2. Lawrence Houston to Allen Dulles, October 9, 1958, CIA-RDP80R01731R000 100160041-3, CREST.

3. Allen Dulles to Dwight Eisenhower, June 30, 1959, CIA-RDP74B00415R0003 00110002-1, CREST.

4. Seymour Hersh, "Huge C.I.A. Operation Reported in U.S. against Antiwar Forces, Other Dissidents in Nixon Years," *New York Times*, December 21, 1974.

5. Gerald K. Haines, "Looking for a Rogue Elephant: The Pike Committee Investigations and the CIA," Center for the Study of Intelligence (Winter 1998–1999): 81–92.

6. *Hearing Before the Select Committee on Intelligence of U.S. House of Representatives*, 94th Cong., 1st Sess., July 31, 1975, 2.

7. U.S. Intelligence Agencies and Activities: Intelligence Costs and Fiscal Procedures—Hearings Before the Select Committee on Intelligence, Part 1, 4.

8. Intelligence Costs and Fiscal Procedures-Hearings, Part 1, 19.

9. "House Select Committee Report (HSCR), The Select Committee's Investigative Record," *Village Voice*, February 16, 1979, 72.

10. HSCR, *Village Voice*, February 16, 1979, 73.

11. For historical reasons, the House Intelligence Committee is sometimes referred to as the Nedzi–Pike Committee. This committee became the Permanent House Select Committee on Intelligence in 1977.

12. HSCR, *Village Voice*, February 16, 1979, 72.

13. Lawrence Houston preferred the term "confidential funds" to the more traditional term "unvouchered funds."

14. *Statement of Managing Director Defense Capabilities and Management (H. Hilton) before the Subcommittee on Government Efficient, Financial Management and Intergovernmental Relations, and the Subcommittee on National Security, Veterans Affairs, and International Relations, Committee on Governmental Reform,* 107 Cong., H.R., July 18, 2001.

15. Warren to John McDuffie, February 21, 1946, The Papers of Lindsay Warren, Southern Historical Collection, Wilson Library, University of North Carolina, box 12, folder 413.

16. Historical Study of the Use of Confidential Funds, p. 4, CIA-RDP78-05246A00 0100010001-3, CREST.

EPILOGUE

1. Personal Letter from L. Warren to E. L. Fisher, June 22, 1958, Fisher family collection.

2. Roger Trask, *Defender of the Public Interest: The General Accounting Office, 1921–1966* (Washington, DC: Government Printing Office, 1996), 97–98.

3. The Glen L Martin Company merged with the American-Marietta Company in 1961 to become the Martin Marietta Corporation.

4. Personal letter from Warren Burger to Dorothy Fisher, Fisher family collection.

5. Personal letter from Daggett Howard to Dorothy Fisher, July 16, 1962, Fisher family collection.

Index

Printed in the USA
CPSIA information can be obtained
at www.ICGtesting.com
CBHW031545221124
17885CB00010B/223/J

9 780700 637959